LARE

Oct. 6, 1980.

An Irreverent and Thoroughly Incomplete Social History of Almost Everything

An Irreverent and Thoroughly Incomplete Social History of Almost Everything

FRANK MUIR

A SCARBOROUGH BOOK

STEIN AND DAY/*Publishers*/New York

SECOND SCARBOROUGH BOOKS EDITION *1980*
First published in the United States of America, 1976
Copyright © 1976 by Frank Muir
All rights reserved
Printed in the United States of America
Stein and Day/*Publishers*/Scarborough House,
Briarcliff Manor, N.Y. 10510

Library of Congress Cataloging in Publication Data

Muir, Frank
  An irreverant and thoroughly incomplete social history
of almost everything.

  Includes index.
  1. English wit and humor.   2. Quotations, English.
I. Title.
PN6175.M78   1976   828'.02   75-38645
ISBN 0-8128-2208-0 (paper)

For Polly
and for Jamie and Sally

Contents

Make him [the reader] laugh and he will think you a trivial fellow,
but bore him in the right way and your reputation is assured.

W. Somerset Maugham
The Gentleman in the Parlour

Preface

Having to write a preface after labouring for five years to produce the book is an unnerving experience and something of an anti-climax; rather like an elephant who has succeeded at long last in giving birth to her calf being then required to balance a bun on her head.

But a preface has its uses. It can give readers a whiff of the author's prose style and an indication of his potential as an inducer of tedium, thus enabling them to moderate their enthusiasm, lower their sights, and so prepare themselves for the main body of the work. And a preface can also give the author a few precious moments alone with a person who has bought the book, or is having a free read of it in a bookshop, or has borrowed it from a library by mistake, in which the author can try to explain what the book is about.

There have been many descriptions of what history is, e.g. 'A vast Mississippi of falsehood' (Matthew Arnold), 'Fables that have been agreed upon' (Voltaire), 'A confused heap of facts' (Lord Chesterfield), 'Little more than the crimes, follies and misfortunes of mankind' (Gibbon), 'The biography of a few stout and earnest persons' (Ralph Waldo Emerson), 'A cyclic poem written by Time upon the memories of man' (Shelley), 'Bunk' (Henry Ford), but there are probably as many ways of looking at the past as there are writers and historians prepared to look. This book is an attempt to look at social history from the viewpoint of people who were alive at the time and were not at all happy about what was going on.

As in most histories, my book is concerned with great personages and great deeds but the concern is with their imperfections, not their glories; with the aspects of them which caused contemporaries to treat them with scorn, fury, or ridicule. The approach is that of the judge who before considering sentence asks 'Is anything known against?' Thus the Wordsworth in this book is not the Great Nature Poet but the Wordsworth with clammy hands and no sense of smell; Rousseau is not the philosopher who tried to reform education but Rousseau the despiser of intelligent women; the Age of Elegance is not represented by beaux of wit and charm but by the Whig duchess who said to the footman behind her, 'I wish to God you wouldn't keep rubbing your great greasy belly against the back of my chair.'

Embedded in the text are more than a thousand expressions of human displeasure, culled from poems, prose writings, letters, critical commentaries and reported speech. These range in power from mild disapproval to blind hate; from 'cauliflower is nothing but cabbage with a college education' (Mark Twain) to 'He was a hoary-headed and toothless baboon, who, first lifted into notice on the shoulder of Carlyle, now spits and splutters from a filthier platform of his own finding and fouling: coryphaeus or choragus of his Bulgarian tribe of autoprophagous baboons, who make the filth they feed on' (Swinburne on Ralph Waldo Emerson).

Much of the literature of disaffection is very funny to read, which is hardly surprising; hate and laughter share much the same animus. Lord Chesterfield wrote 'People hate those who make them feel their own inferiority', but people also make jokes against their superiors so as to cut them down in size. Shakespeare wrote 'We hate that which we fear', but we also make jokes of things we are afraid of – cartoonists and comedy flourish during crises – to make the bogies seem less real. Perhaps many hateful remarks are really only jokes made by somebody without a sense of humour.

An irreverent reaction is not only more fun to read than one of solemn respectfulness but it is quite likely to be a more honest and true reaction. Dr. Johnson maintained that no man is a hypocrite in his pleasures and it could be argued that no man is a hypocrite in his displeasures; in which case a great many of the quotations in the book illuminate the character of its author as much as they do the subject under attack, e.g. the child at dinner snarling 'I say it's spinach, and I say the hell with it!', Tennyson referring to a literary critic as 'A louse in the locks of literature', and Tchaikovsky writing in his journal, about Brahms, 'What a giftless bastard.' As Montaigne put it, 'What a man hates, he takes seriously.'

In no sense is this book offered as a work of scholarship – the author would not make so bold – but as a highly personal account of social history seen from a rather unusual point of view. It is hoped that when this account is added to the more orthodox view of history the reader will end up with a slightly more stereoscopic picture of the past. Each chapter cannot possibly tell the whole story, of course, so the aim has been to be representative rather than exhaustive. It was found possible to include only six chapters before the book got too heavy to be read in bed but more volumes are planned.

In the hope that a reader or two might become interested in something which he never thought would interest him – or her – and want to read more about it, I have given the derivation of each quotation. I have also given the authors' dates because many of the opinions and attitudes expressed are to a certain extent products of their time. For much the same reason I have modernized only a few of the more knobbly, impenetrable lines. For the benefit of those who want to use the book as a reference work, or to compile a speech, or to write an offensive letter to an ex-loved one, Douglas Matthews has drawn up an Index of Authors and a General Index.

As well as my commentary and the quotations, there are also comments which I call asides (beneaths?). There is little I can do to justify these discursive, sometimes almost irrelevant notes, frequently a great deal longer than the quotations which they adorn, except to plead that it is my book and there were a number of snippets of information which I found intriguing and wanted to pass on to the reader.

There is some thanking to be done. When the research began to gain momentum I was greatly helped by Margaret Murphy, who haunted the Westminster Central Library until she retired with her husband Maurice to Australia to produce television and children. Then came Mary Rolt, whom I intercepted when she left school and made a year late for art college. Mary's main base was the London Library, where her shade still sits checking punctuation. Mary was followed by Carol Menon, who waded uncomplainingly through about a hundred grim volumes which I suspected would prove unfruitful but thought should be looked at. Carol's husband, our village vicar the Rev. Nicholas Menon, also weighed in and proved to be steady as a rock on Anglo-Saxon translations, Evelyn Waugh, proof-reading and the peculiarities of my grammar. My son kept a look-out when he was at University College, London, and since, and it is he I have to thank for many of the gamier quotations. My daughter undertook the appallingly complex task of locating owners of copyright material and getting their permission to use the pieces we wanted. My wife remained understanding and un-ruffled throughout, which is no mean feat: holding a hand and soothing a fevered brow, even metaphorically, is no problem for a few days, even weeks, but five years is another matter. My secretary Penny Wreford has been indispensable. My grateful thanks to all.

Help was also forthcoming from members of the public, who heard what was afoot from a piece in *The Times* Diary and a BBC broadcast. It seems that the subject of the book has a wide appeal, for a great number of letters, with much helpful information as to possible sources of quotations, came from a variety of citizens ranging from Members of the House of Lords to an inmate of Maidstone Prison.

I am particularly grateful to those friends who encouraged me to start the book and then encouraged me to keep at it until it was finished. These begin with Denis Norden, who gutted his commonplace book to get me going and has been unfailingly helpful and encouraging throughout, J. G. Links, and Professor Asa Briggs. Other friends, upon whom I leaned for advice and help with specific chapters, which they cheerfully gave, included Dr. Bergen Evans, Father Patrick, Walter

Shewring, and the teaching staff at Ampleforth College, Sir Jack Long-land, George Benson, Michael Elliot, Edwin and Pauline Apps, Michael Meyer, the incomparable Raymond Mander and Joe Mit-chenson, Sandy Heslop, Maggie Norden, Sir Osbert Lancaster, Steve Race, John Amis, and the staffs of the London Library and the library of Royal Holloway College.

Sir Walter Raleigh began *his* preface to *The History of the World*, with the words:

> How unfit, and how unworthy a choice I have made of my self, to undertake a work of this mixture.

I know how he felt. But during those recurrent periods of self-doubt, when vital judgements had to be made as to what was included and what discarded and, indeed, whether the thing was worth proceeding with at all, I was sustained by an observation once made by the poet Edward Dahlberg:

> Every decision you make is a mistake.

FRANK MUIR

Thorpe and Monticello

Acknowledgements

I should like to thank the following writers, publishers and literary representatives for kindly giving me permission to use copyright material:

Harper and Row, Publishers, Inc. for passages by George Ade.

George G. Harrap and Co. Ltd. for some extracts from the *Ego* volumes by James Agate.

Alan Dent for a letter written to James Agate.

Kingsley Amis for a quotation from *The Green Man*, reprinted by permission of A. D. Peters and Co. Ltd.

The Estate of the late Max Beerbohm for some lines by Max Beerbohm; together with a quotation from *Zuleika Dobson* reprinted by permission of the Estate, William Heinemann Ltd., and Dodd Mead and Company, Inc.; a line from *More*, reprinted by permission of the Estate, and The Bodley Head; and a line from *Conversation with Max*, copyright © 1960 by S. N. Behrman, reprinted by permission of the Estate, Hamish Hamilton Ltd., and in the U.S.A., where it was published as *The Incomparable Max*, Random House, Inc.

A. D. Peters and Co. Ltd. for permission to reprint some lines by Hilaire Belloc and part of his poem *Heroic Poem in Praise of Wine*.

Mrs. Dorothy Cheston Bennett for an extract from the works of Arnold Bennett.

Harper and Row, Publishers, Inc., for two lines by Robert Benchley.

Professor Daniel J. Boorstin and Atheneum Publishers for a short extract from *The Image*. Copyright © 1961 by Daniel J. Boorstin, reprinted by permission of Atheneum Publishers, New York.

Mrs. Nicolete Gray, and the Society of Authors on behalf of the Laurence Binyon Estate, for a piece from the *Saturday Review*.

The Salvation Army for permission to print a temperance poem by General Evangeline Booth.

Sidgwick and Jackson for permission to reprint an extract from Rupert Brooke's poem *The Old Vicarage, Grantchester*.

A. D. Peters and Co. Ltd. for permission to reprint a piece by Ivor Brown.

Liveright Publishing Corporation for a line by John Mason Brown.

Anthony Burgess, and Deborah Rogers Ltd., for part of *The Weasels of Pop*, copyright Anthony Burgess, which originally appeared in *Punch*, Sept. 1967.

The Estate of Roy Campbell, and Curtis Brown Ltd., for a piece of the poem *Home Thoughts on Bloomsbury*.

Al Capp for permission to reprint a comment on art.

George Allen and Unwin Ltd. for an extract from *Letters From England*, by Karel Čapek.

Daily Mirror – London, for selections from the Cassandra column, written by William Connor.

Miss D. E. Collins, Eyre Methuen Ltd., and Dodd Mead and Company, for permission to quote from two poems by G. K. Chesterton to be found in *The Collected Poems of G. K. Chesterton*.

Hamish Hamilton Ltd. for a quotation from *Enemies of Promise*, by Cyril Connolly.

Derek Cooper, and Routledge and Kegan Paul Ltd., for permission to reprint two extracts from *The Bad Food Guide*, one of which involved the *Leicester Mercury* to whom my thanks also go.

The Estate of Aleister Crowley, and John Symonds and Kenneth Grant, for a passage from *The Confessions of Aleister Crowley*, copyright © 1969 by John Symonds and Kenneth Grant, reprinted by permission of Jonathan Cape Ltd., and the Hill and Wang division of Farrar, Straus and Giroux, Inc.

Martin Secker and Warburg Ltd., and E. P. Dutton and Co. Inc., for permission to quote from *Siren Land* by Norman Douglas; and Martin Secker and Warburg Ltd., with Chatto and Windus, plus Harcourt Brace Jovanovich Inc., for two pieces from *Looking Back* by Norman Douglas.

The Estate of Isadora Duncan, and Curtis Brown Ltd., for a passage from *My Life* by Isadora Duncan, copyright 1927 by Boni and Liveright Inc., renewed 1955 by Liveright Publishing Corporation, reprinted with permission from Liveright Publishing Corporation and Victor Gollancz Ltd.

Cambridge University Press for an extract from *The Nature of the Physical World* by Sir Arthur Eddington.

Christopher Fry for permission to reprint a line (on the simple four-line form sent to Mr. Fry he wrote against the heading Form of Copyright Acknowledgement: 'To my wife without whose constant encouragement I should never have filled in this form').

Hodder and Stoughton Ltd. for a quotation from *Appreciations* by Clifton Fadiman.

Macmillan London and Basingstoke for a piece from *Life of Swinburne* by Edmund Gosse.

Methuen and Co. Ltd., the Bodleian Library Oxford, and Charles

Scribner's Sons for an extract from *The Wind in the Willows* by Kenneth Grahame.

A. P. Watt and Son for a poem by Robert Graves taken from *Collected Poems, 1965.*

Mrs. Philip Guedalla for some lines by Philip Guedalla, reprinted by permission of Hodder and Stoughton Ltd.

Hamish Hamilton Ltd., and William Morris, for a brief extract from *A Life in the Theatre* by Tyrone Guthrie, copyright © 1959 by Tyrone Guthrie Hamish Hamilton, London.

Williamson Music Ltd. for part of the song *Intermission*, from 'Me and Juliet', Music by Richard Rodgers, lyrics by Oscar Hammerstein II, Copyright © 1953 by Richard Rodgers and Oscar Hammerstein II. Used by permission of Williamson Music Inc. – Administrator and Publisher throughout the Western Hemisphere, and Williamson Music Ltd. – Administrator and Publisher throughout the Eastern Hemisphere.

Liveright Publishing Corporation for a line by Percy Hammond.

The Trustees of the Hardy Estate, Macmillan London and Basingstoke, and Macmillan of Canada, for a quotation from Thomas Hardy.

William Heinemann Ltd. for permission to quote from a letter written by William Heinemann Esq.

The Estate of A. P. Herbert, and A. P. Watt and Son, for part of a poem by A. P. Herbert.

Methuen and Co. Ltd. for two brief quotes from Oliver Herford.

The Society of Authors as the literary representative of the Estate of A. E. Housman, and Jonathan Cape Ltd., and Holt, Rinehart and Winston Inc., for a quotation from *A.E.H.* by Laurence Housman; and the Society of Authors, together with the Cambridge University Press, and Holt, Rinehart and Winston Inc., for a quotation from the prefaces to *Juvenal* and *Manilius*, both edited by A. E. Housman.

Edward Arnold (Publishers) Ltd. for a quotation from Sir Robert Hutchison.

Mrs. Laura Huxley, Chatto and Windus Ltd., and Harper and Row, Publishers, Inc. for a passage from *Do What You Will* by Aldous Huxley.

Michael Meyer, and MacGibbon and Kee, for quotations from *Henrick Ibsen: Vol. 3. The Top of a Cold Mountain*, by Michael Meyer.

Mrs. Dorinda Maxse, holder of the literary copyright of Henry Arthur Jones, for permission to quote from *My Dear Wells* by Henry Arthur Jones.

Eyre and Spottiswoode (Publishers) Ltd. for a piece from *An Anthology of Invective and Abuse* by Hugh Kingsmill.

Mrs. George Bambridge, Macmillan of London and Basingstoke, and

Doubleday, for permission to quote a line by Rudyard Kipling; and Mrs. George Bambridge for permission to quote part of a poem from *The Definitive Edition of Rudyard Kipling's Verse*, published by Hodder and Stoughton Ltd.

Faber and Faber Ltd. for permission to reprint part of 'A Study of Reading Habits' from *Whitsun Weddings* by Philip Larkin.

Laurence Pollinger Ltd., the Estate of the late Mrs. Frieda Lawrence, and the Viking Press Inc., for extracts from *The Collected Letters of D. H. Lawrence*, and for the poem *Nottingham's New University* by D. H. Lawrence. This was published in the U.S.A. in *The Complete Poems of D. H. Lawrence* edited by Vivian de Sola Pinto and F. Warren Roberts. Copyright © 1964, 1971 by Angelo Ravagli and C. M. Weekley, Executors of the Estate of Frieda Lawrence Ravagli. All rights reserved. Reprinted by permission of the Viking Press Inc.

Methuen and Co. Ltd., for an extract from *The Demon of Progress in the Arts* by Wyndham Lewis.

Faber and Faber Ltd., and Doubleday, for permission to reprint a comment made by Don Marquis.

The Estate of W. Somerset Maugham, William Heinemann Ltd., and Doubleday, for some lines by W. Somerset Maugham.

Alfred A. Knopf Inc. for permission to quote items from *Prejudices* by H. L. Mencken.

Grove Press Inc., and Calder and Boyars Ltd., for a piece from *Tropic of Cancer* by Henry Miller, copyright © 1961 by Grove Press Inc.; and another from *Tropic of Capricorn* by Henry Miller, copyright © 1961 by Grove Press Inc.

William Heinemann Ltd., and Simon and Schuster Inc., for permission to quote a line from *Robert Morley: Responsible Gentleman* by Robert Morley and Sewell Stokes.

Oxford University Press for permission to use an extract from *The Uses of the Past* by Herbert J. Muller.

Little, Brown and Company for permission to reprint two poems, 'The Caraway Seed' and 'Further Reflections on Parsley', both from *Verses from 1929 On* by Ogden Nash, copyright 1942 by Ogden Nash. And to J. M. Dent and Sons Ltd. who included the poems in a volume entitled *Good Intentions* by Ogden Nash.

David Higham Associates Ltd. for permission to quote from *The Old School*, edited by Graham Greene.

Hugh Noyes for permission to quote from an early piece (source as yet untraced) by Alfred Noyes.

Mrs. Sonia Brownell Orwell, and Secker and Warburg, for permission to reprint a line from 'Why I Write', by George Orwell, from the volume *England Your England*.

The Viking Press Inc. for permission to reprint 'Bohemia' from *The Portable Dorothy Parker*, copyright 1928, copyright © renewed 1956 by Dorothy Parker. And to Gerald Duckworth and Co. Ltd. who published the poem in *The Collected Dorothy Parker*.

Frederick Warne and Co. Ltd. for a line from *The Tale of the Flopsy Bunnies* by Beatrix Potter.

Laurence Pollinger Ltd. on behalf of the Estate of the late John Cowper Powys for permission to use a piece from *Autobiography* by John Cowper Powys, published by Macdonald and Co (Publishers) Ltd. and Colgate University Press.

Jack Loudan for permission to quote from his biography of Amanda McKittrick Ros *O Rare Amanda*.

Mrs. Harton for permission to reprint the letter which her late husband, the Rev. F. P. Harton, wrote to Penelope Chetwode.

The Literary Estate of Amanda McKittrick Ros, and Chatto and Windus, for permission to include an extract from the Introduction to *Delina Delaney* by Amanda McKittrick Ros.

George Allen and Unwin Ltd. for permission to use a paragraph from *Sceptical Essays* by Bertrand Russell, and George Allen and Unwin Ltd, and Little, Brown and Company in association with The Atlantic Monthly Press, for permission to use a paragraph from *The Autobiography of Bertrand Russell*.

The Atlantic Monthly for permission to reprint two quotations from *Poetry Considered* by Carl Sandberg.

Oxford University Press for permission to quote from *The Oxford Companion to Music*, edited by Percy A. Scholes.

New Statesman for permission to quote two poems by Stanley J. Sharpless.

The Society of Authors on behalf of the Bernard Shaw Estate for permission to use a number of brief extracts from Bernard Shaw's work.

David Higham Associates Ltd. for permission to reprint some lines written by Edith Sitwell and Osbert Sitwell.

Harold Matson Co. Inc. for permission to use a quote from H. Allen Smith.

Harcourt Brace Jovanovich for permission to quote excerpts from *Afterthoughts* by Logan Pearsall Smith, and to Constable and Company, who have published the pieces as *All Trivia*.

Lawrence Gowing of the University of Leeds for permission to quote a line by Adrian Stokes.

The Society of Authors as agents for the Strachey Trust for permission to reprint an extract from *The Leslie Stephen Lecture for 1925: Pope* by Lytton Strachey; and for a paragraph from a letter written by Lytton Strachey printed in *Lytton Strachey* by Michael Holroyd.

Gerald Duckworth and Co. Ltd. for a comment written by Alfred Sutro in *A Seat in the Stalls*.

Putnam and Co. Ltd. for a passage from *Star on the Door* by Maggie Teyte.

The Estate of Angela Thirkell for permission to quote a line from *Pomfret Towers* by Angela Thirkell, copyright © the Estate of Angela Thirkell (Hamish Hamilton Ltd. London 1938).

Mrs. James Thurber and Hamish Hamilton Ltd. for permission to reprint a cartoon caption by James Thurber, copyright © 1945 James Thurber, copyright © 1973 Helen W. Thurber and Rosemary Thurber Sauers. From *The Thurber Carnival*, published by Harper and Row. Originally printed in *The New Yorker*. Reprinted in England in *Vintage Thurber* © 1963 Hamish Hamilton, London.

Princeton University Press, and Routledge & Kegan Paul Ltd, for permission to present a line abstracted from *The Collected Works of Paul Valéry*, edited by Jackson Matthews, Bollingen Series XLV.

The Washington Post for permission to reprint a piece from Paul Hume's column of musical criticism.

A. D. Peters and Co. Ltd. for permission to quote from *Decline and Fall* by Evelyn Waugh.

Associated Book Publishers Ltd. for permission to use a brief piece from *The Dinner Knell* by Thomas Earle Welby.

The Estate of H. G. Wells for kindly allowing me to use several extracts from the writings of H. G. Wells.

Constable and Company Ltd. for permission to use a few words by Edith Wharton.

Liveright Publishing Corporation for permission to use some lines by Alexander Woolcott.

Field and Stream for permission to reprint Ed Zern's review of *Lady Chatterley's Lover*, which appeared in his column 'Exit Laughing' in the issue of November 1959.

Great efforts have been made to trace and acknowledge copyright holders but it is, in some cases, a complex and formidable task. If I have left anybody off then I can only apologize and hope that the book goes rapidly into another edition so that I can make amends.

F. M.

MUSIC

Music

Music is unique among the fine arts in that it calls for a response not only from the head and the heart but also, frequently, from one or more of the feet. It can be enjoyed gregariously or in solitude and has been described by Sydney Smith as 'the only cheap and unpunished rapture upon earth'.

But not everybody enjoys it. Questing minds throughout the ages have been bothered by it. A learned judge put the question:

> What is the use of music?
> Mr. Justice Eve (1856–1940)

A learned philosopher had an answer:

> Music is essentially useless, as life is.
> George Santayana (1863–1952)
> *Little Essays*

Another writer with a philosophical turn of mind had a shot at defining it:

> Music is but a fart that's sent
> From the guts of an instrument.
>
> Anon.
> *Wit and Drollery*, 1645

An earnest young chaplain of the same period also dismissed music as being fundamentally trivial:

> It is but *wanton'd Air*, and the *Titillation* of the spirited *Element*.
> Owen Felltham (1602?–1668)
> *Resolves*

The Ancients were, as usual, suspicious of something as pleasant as music. A Greek historian warned:

> Music was invented to deceive and delude mankind.
> Ephorus (b. fourth century B.C.)
> Preface to the *History*

And a distinguished Roman physician wrote:

> Much musike marreth mennes maners.
> Galen (*c.* A.D. 129–199)

1

A zealous reformer thought that there ought to be a law against it:

Musick is almost as dangerous as Gunpowder; and it may be requires looking after no less than the *Press* or the *Mint*. 'Tis possible a publick Regulation might not be amiss.

Jeremy Collier (1650–1726)
A Short View of the Immorality and Profaneness of the English Stage,&c.

A saintly poet made a little proverb out of one of music's short-comings:

Music helps not the toothache.

George Herbert (1593–1633)
Jacula Prudentum

And Dr. Johnson could find little merit in it:

It is a method of employing the mind, without the labour of thinking at all, and with some applause from a man's self.

Samuel Johnson (1709–1784)
Quoted by James Boswell: *The Journal of a Tour to the Hebrides*

A modern composer echoed Turner's pronouncement on painting when he was asked by a batch of American newspapermen to comment on music:

It's a rum go!

Ralph Vaughan Williams (1872–1958)

William Cobbett, the vigorous journalist and radical politician, listed some well-known appreciators of music – Salome, dancer and provoker of decapitation; Nero, instrumentalist and ogre; cannibal tribes, dancers and anthropophagi – and drew a conclusion:

A *great* fondness for music is a mark of great weakness, great vacuity of mind: not of hardness of heart; not of vice; not of downright folly; but of a want of capacity, or inclination, for sober thought.

William Cobbett (1762–1835)
Advice to Young Men, and (incidentally) to Young Women, in the Middle and Higher Ranks of Life

Cobbett also warned the young against the pernicious effects of paper money and tea.

Many visitors from abroad complained of the lack of good music in English life. There seemed to be plenty of the other sort:

These people have no ear, either for rhythm or music, and their un-natural passion for pianoforte playing and singing is thus all the more repulsive. There is nothing on earth more terrible than English music, except English painting.

Heinrich Heine (1797–1856)
Lutezia

A German explorer believed that it was more than mere ineptitude:

The ancient Greek philosophers were not at all happy with some of the music which the populace was playing and singing, and decided that there was Good Music and Bad Music. The Greeks had a word for each mode (roughly, 'flavour') into which their music was divided, and Plato in *The Republic* and Aristotle in his *Politics* passed moral judgement on them. Mixolydian and Hypolydian were reckoned to be fairly harmless, being rather gloomy and depressing: music for mourning. Hypodorian scraped by, being tender and gentle. Dorian was Good Music, being military and masterful. The villain was music in the Lydian mode; this was Bad Music, soft, sensual and capable of doing all manner of damage.

Cicero recorded that the Spartans kept their music clean and decent by limiting the number of strings on the lyre, which meant that musicians could not play the subtler, dangerous modes. When a famous musician visited Sparta and it was seen that he was corrupting the fighting men with the charm of his beautiful music his lyre was inspected; it was found that he had added a number of new strings to it to make it more versatile. The lyre was confiscated. Plato approved of this kind of state intervention:

Musical innovation is full of danger to the State, for when modes of music change, the laws of the State always change with them.

Plato (428–347 B.C.)
The Republic

The musician with too many strings to his lyre was Timotheus (447–357 B.C.), who should have known better than to try out his important innovation at Sparta; which was about as sensible as trying out a new ballet at the Aldershot Garrison Theatre.

By Elizabethan times, singing a soft love-song to a lute had become so popular and fashionable that a classical scholar (and keen musician) felt he had to warn students against its enfeebling effect:

Lutinge and singinge take awaye a manlye stomake ... these Instruments make a mannes wit so softe and smoothe so tender and quasie, that they be lesse able to brooke stronge and tough studie.

Roger Ascham (1515–1568)
The Scholemaster

The Puritans came out strongly against soft, gentle music. It not only depraved the young, it seems, but was the cause of profligacy in lady poets:

> I say of Musick as *Plato, Aristotle, Galen,* and many others haue said of it; that it is very il for yung heds, for a certaine kinde of nice, smoothe sweetnes in alluring the auditorie to nicenes, effeminacie, pusillanimitie, and lothsomnes of life ... and made apt to all wantonnes and sinne. And therefore Writers affirme *Sappho* to haue been expert in musick, and therefore whorish.
>
> Philip Stubbes (*fl.* 1583–1591)
> *The Anatomie of Abuses*

They were still treating it as one of life's little evils at the beginning of the eighteenth century:

> This Sort of Musick warms the Passions, and unlocks the Fancy, and makes it open to Pleasure like a Flower to the Sun ... when the Music is soft, exquisite and airy, 'tis dangerous and ensnaring.
>
> Jeremy Collier (1650–1726)
> *A Short View of the Immorality and Profaneness of the English Stage*

At the opposite end of the scale to sensual, worldly music in the Lydian mode was Church music, traditionally sombre:

> ... at conventicle, where worthy men,
> Misled by custom, strain celestial themes
> Through the prest nostril.
>
> William Cowper (1731–1800)
> *The Task*

Early Puritan and Noncomformist congregations developed a special nasal whine for use when singing hymns, or indeed praying.

The mode of hymn music was so majestic and glum that a leading evangelist of the nineteenth century was moved to ask:

> Why should the devil have all the good tunes?
>
> The Rev. Rowland Hill (1744–1833)
> *Sermons*

No connection with the Rowland Hill who invented the penny post. The Rev. Rowland Hill was an eccentric but hypnotic preacher. With the poet Cowper he wrote a number of tuneful hymns. He also wrote *Cowpock Inoculation Vindicated.*

But Voltaire thought that hymn music was what it was because the Almighty knew what He liked:

> The Most High has a decided taste for vocal music, provided it be lugubrious and gloomy enough.
>
> Voltaire (1694–1788)
> *Philosophical Dictionary*

Besides those many people who objected to certain sorts of music for a reason, because it was corrupting, or emasculating, or sinful, or dreary, there were also a great number of people – including many eminent personages – who detested every sort of music.

The majority of human beings are born with a capacity for enjoying some kind of music, but a small proportion are born with no appreciation of music at all. They have what is known among musicians as a 'tin ear'.

Some 'tin ears', like Shakespeare's Bottom, were blissfully unaware that they were musically subnormal:

> BOTTOM: I have a reasonable good ear in music. Let's have the tongs and the bones.
>
> William Shakespeare (1564–1616)
> *A Midsummer-Night's Dream:* Act IV, sc. i

Others, like Charles Lamb, were fully aware and unrepentant:

> I am constitutionally susceptible of noises. A carpenter's hammer, in a warm summer noon, will fret me into more than midsummer madness. But those unconnected, unset sounds are nothing to the measured malice of music.
>
> Charles Lamb (1775–1834)
> *Essays of Elia:* 'A Chapter on Ears'

Dr. Johnson was a more complicated case. It was as if he admired music and wanted to like it but could not. He would occasionally issue pronouncements like 'had I learnt to fiddle I should have done nothing else' (Boswell: *Journal of a Tour to the Hebrides*) and 'it is the only sensual pleasure without vice' (Hawkins: *Johnsoniana*), but he also admitted sadly:

> All animated nature loves music – except myself!
>
> Samuel Johnson (1709–1784)
> Quoted in *Dr. Burney's Memoirs*
>
> Burney was a good witness, being an eminent musician. He was the father of the novelist Fanny Burney.

Instrumental virtuosity gave him no pleasure:

> Dr. Johnson was observed by a musical friend of his to be extremely inattentive at a concert, whilst a celebrated solo player was running up the divisions and subdivisions of notes upon his violin. His friend, to induce him to take greater notice of what was going on, told him how extremely difficult it was. 'Difficult do you call it, Sir?' replied the Doctor; 'I wish it were impossible.'
>
> Quoted by William Seward (1747–1799)
> Supplement to *Seward's Anecdotes*

Another musician and author – like Dr. Burney he had written a history of music – was in no doubt about Johnson's ear:

> To the delights of music, he was equally insensible: neither voice nor instrument, nor the harmony of concordant sounds, had power over his affections, or even to engage his attention. Of music in

5

general, he has been heard to say, 'it excites in my mind no ideas, and hinders me from contemplating my own.'

Quoted by Sir John Hawkins (1719–1789)
Life of Samuel Johnson

Perhaps the real truth about where Johnson stood in regard to music was revealed by Boswell:

We had the musick of the bagpipe every day, at Armidale, Dunvegan, and Col. Dr. Johnson appeared fond of it, and used often to stand for some time with his ear close to the great drone.

James Boswell (1740–1795)
Journal of a Tour to the Hebrides

A number of other literary men revealed eccentric tastes in music-substitutes. For example, a seventeenth-century French man of letters, tutor to the duc d'Orléans:

La Motte de Vayer could not endure music, but delighted in thunder.

Quoted by William Cooke:
Memoirs of Samuel Foote, Esq., 1805

An American essayist and lover of the simple, outdoor life revealed that the only music he really enjoyed was wind whistling through the telegraph-wires:

As I went under the new telegraph-wire, I heard it vibrating like a harp high overhead. It was as the sound of a far-off glorious life, a supernal life, which came down to us, and vibrated the lattice-work of this life of ours.

H. D. Thoreau (1817–1862)
Journal

The celebrated and formidable headmaster of Rugby School managed to convey the impression that his substitute was superior to the real thing:

Flowers are my music.

Dr Thomas Arnold (1795–1842)
Quoted by Arthur Stanley: *Life of Dr. Arnold*

The poet Alexander Pope not only had a tin ear but nursed a suspicion that everybody else had too:

Pope was so very insensible to the charms of music that he once asked Dr. Arbuthnot, whether the rapture which the company expressed upon hearing the compositions and performance of Handel did not proceed wholly from affectation.

Quoted by Joseph Warton: *Works of Alexander Pope*, 1797

Sir Isaac Newton's approach to music was scientific:

Newton, hearing Handel play upon the harpsichord, could find nothing worthy to remark but the elasticity of his fingers.

Ibid.

And it was all a great mystery to the American poet Emerson:

> Because I have no ear for music, at the Concert of the Quintette Club, it looked to me as if the performers were crazy, and all the audience were make-believe crazy, in order to soothe the lunatics and keep them amused.
>
> Ralph Waldo Emerson (1803–1882)
> *Journals*

Perhaps America's most distinguished tin ear was General Ulysses S. Grant, eighteenth President of the United States:

> I know only two tunes; one of them is 'Yankee Doodle', and the other isn't.
>
> Ulysses S. Grant (1822–1885)

> In a sense 'Yankee Doodle' isn't, either. The American song 'Yankee Doodle' is sung to a very old, traditional English air, known during the early eighteenth century as 'Kitty Fisher's Locket'. As Kitty Fisher was a famous whore the song was not suitable for polite company.

Perhaps an even greater agony than that suffered by people who had to listen to music when they disliked it was suffered by those who had to listen to bad music when they loved good music.

A very great deal of this kind of pain has been inflicted, through the centuries, by makers of home-made music:

> Hell is full of musical amateurs. Music is the brandy of the damned.
>
> George Bernard Shaw (1856–1950)
> *Man and Superman*

> Before he began his work in the theatre Shaw was, from 1888 to 1894, a music critic for the *Star* – at two guineas a week – and then the *World*. He wrote under the pseudonym 'Corno di Bassetto'.

The word 'music' came from the Greek word *mousike*, which included all the muses; in the ancient world all poetry was sung.

The ability to sing sweetly or to play an instrument agreeably was approved of as being a suitably genteel accomplishment in ancient Rome; although singers could be rather boring:

> All singers have this fault: if asked to sing among friends they are never so inclined; if unasked, they never leave off.
>
> Horace (65–8 B.C.)
> *Satires*: I.3

Up to the time of the Stuarts singing and playing continued to be an aristocratic, even kingly, form of diversion and with the rise of the middle class during the seventeenth century increasing numbers of ordinary citizens took it up. Samuel Pepys was a keen amateur musician who enjoyed playing, alone or with friends, and going to concerts at his nobler friends' houses. On one occasion a lady he knew – also an amateur musician – gave him a little concert on her harpsichord:

7

I took leave and went to hear Mrs. Turner's daughter (at whose house Sir J. Mennes lies) play on the Harpsicon; but Lord, it was enough to make any man sick to hear her; yet I was forced to commend her highly.

Samuel Pepys (1633–1703)
Diary, 1 May 1663

By the eighteenth century polite society had become decidedly less musical. Lord Chesterfield wrote sternly to his son:

I insist upon your neither piping nor fiddling yourself. It puts a gentleman in a very frivolous, contemptible light; brings him into a great deal of bad company; and takes up a great deal of time, which might be much better employed.

Lord Chesterfield (1694–1773)
Letters to his Son

But the middle and lower classes continued to pipe, fiddle and sing away happily, and during the nineteenth century it became a useful social asset for a young man or woman to pick his way through a nocturne on the parlour piano or warble a ballad; songs of unfulfilled love, preferably involving a death or two, were much esteemed:

I am saddest when I sing; so are those that hear me; they are sadder even than I am.

Artemus Ward (1834–1867)
Lecture

Music was such an important part of home entertainment that most parents who could afford to insisted on their children taking lessons:

The music teacher came twice each week to bridge the awful gap between Dorothy and Chopin.

George Ade (1866–1944)

Even when a child displayed no musical gifts at all it was rarely let off the hook; some kind of aptitude was wished upon it:

My mother used to say that my elder sister had a beautiful contralto voice. This was arrived at not through her ability to reach the low notes—which she could not do—but because she could not reach the high ones.

Samuel Butler (1835–1902)
Note-Books

Another kind of distress caused by amateur singers came about because in order to improve they had to practise:

A vile beastly rottenheaded foolbegotten brazenthroated pernicious piggish screaming, tearing, roaring, perplexing, splitmecrackle crashmecriggle insane ass of a woman is practising howling below-stairs with a brute of a singingmaster so horribly, that my head is nearly off.

Edward Lear (1812–1888)
Letter to Lady Strachey, 24 Jan. 1859

8

The mysterious fate of a girl in a poem by Owen Meredith would have made sense if it had been established that she was an amateur folk-singer who had been practising too loudly.

> She sat with her guitar on her knee,
>   But she was not singing a note,
> For someone had drawn (ah, who could it be?)
>   A knife across her throat.
>> Owen Meredith (Lord Lytton) (1831–1891)
>> *Going Back Again*

Amateur sopranos fell, it seems, into two main groups. Those whose range was too limited:

> She was a singer who had to take any note above A with her eyebrows.
>> Montague Glass (1877–1934)

And those who had a good range but no particular style:

> She was a town-and-country soprano of the kind often used for augmenting grief at a funeral.
>> George Ade (1866–1944)

Everybody in their lives must have sat in an agony of ennui through at least one amateur recital where the singer, eyebrows soaring, has been a little flat on the high notes and a little sharp on all the others. There can be few of us saintly enough never to have echoed Coleridge's thought:

> Swans sing before they die — 'twere no bad thing
> Should certain persons die before they sing.
>> Samuel Taylor Coleridge (1772–1834)
>> *Epigram on a Volunteer Singer*

Another contributing factor to the misery of sensitive Victorians condemned, evening after evening, to listen to ungifted amateurs wading through drawing-room ballads, was the quality of the lyrics:

> Why 'words for music' are almost invariably trash now, though the words of Elizabethan songs are better than any music, is a gloomy and difficult question.
>> Walter Savage Landor (1775–1864)
>> *Essays*

In fact, the suspicion that when words were to be accompanied by music they were not selected with quite as much care had occurred to a writer some two thousand years previously:

> For music any words are good enough.
>> Aristophanes (*c.* 448–*c.* 380 B.C.)
>> *The Birds*

9

And the point was reiterated during the opera boom of the eighteenth century:

> Nothing is capable of being well set to music that is not nonsense.
>
> Joseph Addison (1672–1719)
> *Spectator*, No. 18

During Victorian times the sales of sheet-music ballads were so enormous that composers rooted through the works of the limpest of minor lyric poets in the hope of finding something which could be set to music:

> The farmer's daughter hath soft brown hair
> (Butter and eggs and a pound of cheese);
> And I met a ballad, I can't say where,
> Which wholly consisted of lines like these.
>
> C. S. Calverley (1831–1884)
> *Ballad*

Amateur singers usually limited their ambition to the parlour, the pub and the village hall; few had enough confidence to venture upon the public concert platform. A notable exception was Margaret Truman, daughter of the then President of the United States, Harry S. Truman. On 5 December 1950, Miss Truman gave a public recital in Washington. The *Washington Post* reported:

> Miss Truman is a unique American phenomenon with a pleasant voice of little size and fair quality ... yet Miss Truman cannot sing very well. She is flat a good deal of the time ... she communicates almost nothing of the music she presents ... There are few moments during her recital when one can relax and feel confident that she will make her goal, which is the end of the song.
>
> Paul Hume
> Music critic of the *Washington Post*

> President Truman read this review the following morning and immediately wrote to Paul Hume. In his letter can be detected a note of fatherly displeasure:
> 'I have just read your lousy review buried in the back pages. You sound like a frustrated old man who never made a success, an eight-ulcer man on a four-ulcer job, and all four ulcers working. I have never met you, but if I do you'll need a new nose and plenty of beefsteak and perhaps a supporter below. Westbrook Pegler, a guttersnipe, is a gentleman compared to you. You can take that as more of an insult than as a reflection on your ancestry.'

Perhaps the people who suffered most from listening to music were, paradoxically, the people who were born with finely tuned listening equipment and a deep sensitivity towards music. Any performance which fell short of perfection caused them something near physical pain.

Such a person was the Rev. F. P. Harton, vicar of Baulking.

One of his parishioners was the writer Penelope Chetwode, wife of the poet John Betjeman. It seems that the regular parish organist was taken ill and Mrs. Betjeman gallantly undertook to play the harmonium in the church until the lady recovered. All seemed to be going well. Then, one morning, a letter arrived from the vicar:

Baulking Vicarage

My dear Penelope,

I have been thinking over the question of the playing of the harmonium on Sunday evenings here and have reached the conclusion that I must now take it over myself.

I am very grateful to you for doing it for so long and hate to have to ask you to give it up, but, to put it plainly, your playing has got worse and worse and the disaccord between the harmonium and the congregation is becoming destructive of devotion. People are not very sensitive here, but even some of them have begun to complain, and they are not usually given to doing that. I do not like writing this, but I think you will understand that it is my business to see that divine worship is as perfect as it can be made. Perhaps the crankiness of the instrument has something to do with the trouble. I think it does require a careful and experienced player to deal with it.

Thank you ever so much for stepping so generously into the breach when Sibyl was ill; it was the greatest possible help to me and your results were noticeably better then than now.

Yours ever,

F. P. Harton.

Music is defined in the *Oxford Dictionary* as 'that one of the fine arts which is concerned with the combination of sounds with a view to beauty of form and the expression of emotion'. This is a civilized concept, but the sounds, the raw material of music, were made, and still are, by all primitive people.

The three basic ways of producing sounds at will were to blow down some sort of tube, to pluck a string which had been stretched tight, and to shake, scrape or hit something hollow. Nobody knows what urged our forefathers to produce these noises; various authorities have suggested that it was in order to reproduce human speech, or as a help to hunting or as a mating-call, but it seems fairly certain that primitive man believed that the sounds which he could produce by these means had magical properties.

Man quickly learned that he could make a nicely mysterious noise by blowing down a large shell, or a horn which had dropped off a cow, but that blowing down a reed which had had a notch cut in it near the top produced a much pleasanter sound; too quiet to use as an alarm or as a frightener but a noise worth making for its own sake. It is widely believed that some kind of simple reed flute was the world's first music-making instrument.

The ancient civilizations progressed from blowing down reeds to producing various musical sounds from the hollow shin-bones of animals. And from there to playing upon flutes made from wooden sticks which had been carefully bored and provided with finger-holes to enable a range of notes to be played.

The flute was an important instrument to the Greeks and Romans, who believed that it produced sounds which had a magical quality of wide and wonderful application:

> Spartans played upon the flute to alarm the enemy.
>
> Plutarch (c. A.D. 45–after 120)

> The sound of the flute will cure epilepsy, and a sciatic gout.
>
> Theophrastus (c. 370–288/5 B.C.)

> Pain is relieved by causing a vibration in the fibres of the afflicted part.
>
> Coelius Antipater (after 121 B.C.)

> Specific for the bite of a viper.
>
> Aulus Gellius (c. A.D. 130–c. 180)

Various designs of flute produced noises of differing character. A Greek philosopher warned against the flute's powers of arousement:

> The flute is not an instrument which has a good moral effect; it is too exciting.
>
> Aristotle (384–322 B.C.)
> *Politics*

While the Roman poet Ovid warned against the soporific effect:

> The music of the zither, flute, and the lyre enervates the mind.
>
> Ovid (43 B.C.–A.D. 18)
> *Remedorium Amoris*
>
> Ovid was advising lovers how to summon up the necessary resolve to break with outworn mistresses.

Playing the flute became a recognized profession in the ancient world:

> A misspent life.
>
> Antisthenes (c. 445–c. 360 B.C.)
> Antisthenes was the founder of Cynicism.

It seemed to have been a relatively short life:

> To Flute-players, nature gave brains there's no doubt,
> But alas! 'tis in vain, for they soon blow them out.
>
> Old Greek proverb
> Quoted by Athenaeus (fl. c. A.D. 200)
> *The Learned Banquet*

Playing the early flutes with their narrow bores must have been fairly strenuous and, when a volume of sound was called for, positively painful. Contemporary pictures and carvings frequently showed the flute

12

being held in the fist like a hammer, with the flautist's cheeks blown out like balloons. It became customary for a while for the players to wear a kind of cheek-truss, a harness which took some of the strain off the cheeks and left a hole for the player to blow through.

But tragedies occurred to the incautious:

> Harmonides, a young Flute-player, and scholar of Timotheus, at his first public performance, in order to *elevate* and *surprise*, began his solo with so violent a blast, that *he breathed his last breath into his flute*, and died upon the spot.
>
> Lucian (b. *c.* A.D. 120)
> Quoted by Dr. Charles Burney (1726–1814)
> *A General History of Music*

Flute-playing nowadays, according to a modern writer, is less dramatic:

> FLUTE, n. A variously perforated hollow stick intended for the punishment of sin, the minister of retribution being commonly a young man with straw-colored eyes and lean hair.
>
> Ambrose Bierce (1842–1914?)
> *The Enlarged Devil's Dictionary*

The world's first keyboard instrument was the organ. The idea of putting a number of variously sized flutes in a frame and directing air from a bellows to them via a keyboard was put into practice as long ago as the third century B.C. by a well-known Egyptian inventor (and barber), Ctesibius. Ctesibius's organ, remarkably like every other pipe organ since, with twenty keys, two banks of pipes and a system of stops, was called by the Greeks a *Hydraulikon*, or water-organ.

The mental picture of a water-organ squirting jets of water out of its pipes in time with the music is unhappily false; the function of the water was only to keep the air in the air-reservoir at a constant pressure, much the same principle as the gasometer.

The Romans called it a *Hydraulus* and it was played at public events, by Nero amongst others, to provide incidental music to gladiatorial combats, circuses and horse-races. The sheer force of the noise it produced made it unattractive to sensitive Romans:

> The organ is an instrument composed of divers pipes, formed into a kind of tower, which, by means of bellows, is made to produce a loud sound.
>
> Cassiodorus (*c.* 490–*c.* 583)

> It does seem to have produced an exceedingly loud noise. Contemporary accounts record that the sound of a *hydraulus* could be heard sixty miles away and that many of the organists had to wear ear-plugs. Perhaps because of the volume of sound it produced, or perhaps because of its association with pagan nastiness, the early Church would have nothing to do with it. The Church changed its mind and began to install organs in churches and monasteries in about the eighth century.

13

A popular instrument in the Roman army, according to Procopius, was the bagpipe – also, of course, played upon by Nero. The Roman army seems to have introduced the thing into England. A fifteenth-century Welsh bard had the pleasure of hearing the bagpipe played at a Saxon wedding:

> Each roared with throat at widest stretch
> For Will the Piper – low born wretch!
> Will forward steps, as best he can,
> Unlike a free, ennobled man;
> A pliant bag 'tween arm and chest,
> While limping on, he tightly prest,
> He stares – he strives the bag to sound;
> He swells his maw – and ogles round;
> He twists and turns himself about –
> With fetid breath his cheeks swell out ...
> The churl did blow a grating shriek,
> The bag did swell and harshly squeak,
> As does a goose from nightmare crying,
> Or dog, crushed by a chest when dying;
> This whistling-box's changeless note
> Is forced from turgid veins and throat;
> Its sound is like a crane's harsh moan,
> Or like a gosling's latest groan;
> Just such a noise a wounded goat
> Sends from her hoarse and gurgling throat.
>
> Lewis Glyn Cothi (1447–1486)
> *The Saxons of Flint*

The bagpipe was played in most countries, particularly in rural areas. Perhaps it reached its height of popularity when Mme. Pompadour played the French bellows version, the *musette*.

But not everybody was affected by bagpipe music as pleasantly as were Dr. Johnson and the Pompadour:

> ... Others, when the bag-pipe sings i' the nose,
> Cannot contain their urine.
>
> William Shakespeare (1564–1616)
> *The Merchant of Venice:* Act IV, sc. i

According to ancient myth, the notion that music could be produced by twanging a taut string was discovered by the Egyptian minor god Thoth, a kind of private secretary to Osiris, when he tripped over a dead tortoise whose cartilages, 'constricted by desiccation, were rendered sonorous'. Early lyres were made from tortoise shells, with three strings of twisted gut stretched across them.

Plutarch's more romantic version was that Apollo was moved to invent the lyre after enjoying the twang of Diana the Huntress's bowstring. The invention was also associated with many other gods, includ-

14

ing Hermes (the Roman version of Thoth), Amphion, Linus and Orpheus.

The lyre was the Greek national musical instrument, played as the accompaniment to poetry and as a solo instrument: it was a gentler, more social instrument than the flute. The Greek lyre developed into a graceful instrument; from the sound-box projected two curved, bow-like arms connected by a cross-brace; the strings were connected from the brace to the sound-box and the player dampened the strings with his left hand as he stroked them with his plectrum: a huge wooden or ivory baton the size and shape of a large banana.

Players of early stringed instruments had a nerve-racking time trying to keep their strings in tune long enough to get through a piece, according to contemporary reports; the strings sagged when it was hot weather and snapped in the cold. There is no evidence that the insides of cats were ever used to make strings. The usual method in the ancient world was to take a length of lamb's intestine, roll it into a fine thread and dry it in a moderate sun:

Is it not strange that sheep's guts should hale souls out of men's bodies?
William Shakespeare (1564–1616)
Much Ado About Nothing: Act II, sc. iii

The Greek philosophers' concern with the damage which lyre music could wreak when it was played solely for pleasure was proved to be true when the instrument was taken up enthusiastically by Nero, who played it solely for his own satisfaction. Nero even gave a public recital on his lyre, a breach of decorum which infuriated Roman society:

Perhaps it was because Nero played the fiddle, they burned Rome.
Oliver Herford (1863–1935)

Nero could not have 'fiddled' because the fiddle is played with a bow, which was unknown. Some modern authorities think that it is just possible that there was a fiddle-like technique used at some period in playing the lyre, the huge plectrum being dragged across the strings lengthways instead of being used as a pick.

In the ninth century a strange and spectacular development occurred in music: the arrival of the bow. Strange, because nobody is quite sure where the idea of scraping a stringed instrument with a tight length of horsehair came from, although it was possibly Arabia, and spectacular, because within a few years the whole of Europe was playing 'fiddles' – the colloquial name for any violin-like instrument played with a bow.

The earliest European fiddles were bowed lutes. The lute – which had an almond-shape body, double strings and frets (raised bars across the finger-board) – was the medieval equivalent of the Grecian lyre. Lutes were difficult to keep in tune – it was said that a lutanist aged eighty must

15

have spent at least sixty of those years tuning his instrument – and keen players were recommended to take their lutes to bed with them to keep them in good condition (Mace: *Musick's Monument*, 1676).

A good lutanist produced a warm, silvery tone. There were others:

> He lumbryth on a lewde lewte roty bulle joyse,
> Rumbill downe, tumbil downe, hey go now now.
> He fumblyth in his fyngering an ugly good noise,
> It semyth the sobbyng of an old sow.
>
> John Skelton (1460–1529)

During the fifteenth century a move was made to start playing the Spanish guitar with a bow. This was a bit awkward to play in the normal guitar position so it became the practice to play the instrument downwards, gripping it between the knees or the legs, according to its size. From this developed the family of instruments known as viols. Viols were light and delicate, with thin strings, making them eminently suitable for playing in a room.

Shortly after viols became popular violins were introduced. In spite of their superficial resemblance to viols, music historians insist, hand on heart, that there is no connection at all between the two instruments, pointing out that violins have no frets, are built on different principles, have only four strings and are played against the chest or under the chin.

Until the middle of the sixteenth century, when the violin with its stronger tone and its greater capability for virtuoso performance began to supersede the viol, the two instruments were both popular, but in different spheres. The viol was the more gentlemanly instrument, used for making private music. The violin became the instrument used for public music; for dancing, feasts, marriages, revels of any sort. It was the professional fiddler's instrument; a bit common:

> We call viols those with which gentlemen, merchants, and other virtuous people pass their time ... The other type is called violin; it is commonly used for dancing ... I have not illustrated the said violin because you can think of it as resembling the viol, added to which there are few persons who use it save those who make a living from it through their labour.
>
> Jambe de Fer, 1556
> Quoted by D. Boyden: *The History of Violin Playing from its Origins to 1761*

Judging from his name ('iron leg') M. de Fer might well have played the viola da gamba.

A certain amount of class distinction entered into music during the Middle Ages. The Roman name for a professional musician was *Joculator*; this became 'juggler' in English and was the word used to describe the practitioners at the bottom end of the entertainment world, the conjurers, acrobats, bear-leaders and actors as well as the fiddlers. These wandering troupes were unpopular with the Church and the state, being masterless men and rarely very law-abiding:

> He was a fiddler, and consequently a rogue.
> Jonathan Swift (1667–1745)
> Letter to Stella, 25 July 1711
> Even today the slang word among musicians for a violinist is a 'gipsy'

The next grade up from jugglers were the respectable and skilled professional musicians: town bandsmen ('Waits'), harpists and lutanists who accompanied singers of poetry, and players at court and in private houses. They became known as *Ménestriers* – because they 'ministered' to a need for music – which became, in English, minstrels.

Good minstrels were well paid and became part of the household of a great noble. A notable example was Taillefeu, William the Conqueror's personal bard. Taillefeu was so close to the Conqueror that he asked permission to strike the first blow at the Battle of Hastings. According to the story, he advanced up the beach singing tales of Charlemagne and Roland and juggling with his sword, and added to his personal glory by becoming the first man to be killed at the Battle of Hastings.

At the top end of the social scale were the Troubadours. Their equivalent in Germany were the Minnesingers, so called not because they were small in stature but because the German word *Minne* meant love. These aristocrats wrote and composed, but did not necessarily perform, passionate songs mainly in praise of idealistic love. Troubadours only flourished for two hundred years. By the end of the thirteenth century the form had declined; in Germany the Minnesingers were replaced by Mastersingers, artists and craftsmen who kept the old Minnesinger tradition going under strict guild control.

During most of the medieval period the only keyboard instrument available was the organ, but in the early fifteenth century the clavichord came into use, the first instrument to do with strings what the organ did with flutes.

The principle of the clavichord had been worked out by Pythagoras in the sixth century B.C. On pressing a key a tongue of brass at the other end of the key rose up and struck a string. The piece of brass, known as 'the tangent', not only produced a note but measured off the right amount of string to give that note, and stayed put until the key was released. Originally clavichords had only one string and only simple melodies could be played, but more strings were added, giving a chromatic scale and allowing harmonies.

The clavichord sound was sweet and beautiful, and if the key was wobbled with the finger a pleasing vibrato could be achieved which was given the delightful name of the 'bebung'. But the clavichord had a limitation which restricted its use to private pleasure and the training of organists and singers: from a few feet away it was inaudible.

By the beginning of the sixteenth century a somewhat louder instrument had emerged which was to be the dominant keyboard instrument for three hundred years: the harpsichord. Or rather, the harpsichord family, which included the virginal – a smaller, oblong version which may have been so called because it was played upon by virgin young ladies but had nothing to do with the virgin Queen Elizabeth because it preceded her – and the spinet, a graceful, leg-of-mutton shaped instrument.

When the key of a harpsichord was pressed, a 'jack' with a quill projecting from its side rose up, plucked the string, and dropped back again. The sound it produced was a brilliant, staccato twang:

A scratch with a sound at the end of it.
A performance on a bird-cage with a toasting-fork.
Quoted by Percy A. Scholes (1877–1958)
The Oxford Companion to Music

Many masterly composers wrote for, and played, the harpsichord including William Byrd, John Bull, Purcell, Scarlatti, Handel and Bach, but the instrument, like the clavichord, had limitations. One snag was that it needed considerable maintenance; the strings were thin and needed constant tuning – often during a performance – and the quills which did the plucking were forever wearing out at the wrong moment. But the harpsichord's main weakness was that hitting the keys harder or more gently, or wobbling the fingers, made small noticeable difference; the player had little or no command over the force and emphasis of the sound which he was producing.

The seventeenth century, with the Western world steadily moving away from medievalism, proved to be a period of remarkable musical innovation.

One of the results of the Italian Renaissance, and the passionate pursuit of all things Greek and Roman which it produced among the Italian aristocratic intelligentsia, was the development of a new kind of musical presentation. A small group of men in Florence wanted to put on plays as they imagined the ancient Greeks had done, with the lines sung. This was virtually impossible when the music was in a complicated form, such as the madrigal, where the words were difficult to distinguish and the audience could not follow what was going on. So they devised a simple kind of exposition where the singer delivered the lines in a more or less natural inflexion, accompanied only by chords from the orchestra. These recitative passages overcame the problem of moving the plot along and the singers could then indulge in bouts of flowery vocal display which came to be called 'arias'.

18

And so in 1600, after a few exploratory attempts had been received with enthusiasm, the group of Florentine dilettanti presented Peri's *Eurydice*, generally accepted as the world's first opera.

A brief description of opera was given in an American radio programme in the 1940s:

> Opera is when a guy gets stabbed in the back and instead of bleeding he sings.
> Ed. Gardner (1905–1963)
> *Duffy's Tavern*

Having invented opera, Italy proceeded to dominate it for three hundred years. Italian, and Italian-trained, singers and composers were exported to most other nations, and the whole terminology of opera was, and still is, Italian.

English-speaking countries tended to be less than entirely won over by it.

> Going to the Opera, like getting drunk, is a sin that carries its own punishment with it, and that a very severe one.
> Hannah More (1745–1833)
> Letter to her sister, 1775

Much of the antipathy towards opera was on the grounds that it was all a bit silly; not the stuff to appeal to intelligent men:

> An opera, like a *pillory*, may be said
> To *nail our ears down*, and *expose our head*.
> Edward Young (1683–1765)
> *Satires*

That it was foreign:

> An exotic and irrational entertainment.
> Samuel Johnson (1709–1784)

And artistically suspect:

> The most rococo and degraded of all art forms.
> William Morris (1834–1896)

Another aristocratic innovation of the seventeenth century was ballet, which has proved to be even more of a minority interest than opera:

> I don't understand anything about the ballet. All I know is that during the intervals the ballerinas stink like horses.
> Anton Chekhov (1860–1904)

But those who did understand it and like it tended to like it very much. They have been described:

> The regular and insatiable supporters of ballet are people too sluggish of intellect to listen to a play on the one hand, and too devoid of imagination to listen to fine music without accompanying action, on the other.
> Alan Dent (b. 1905)
> Drama critic of the *News Chronicle*, 1952

19

Arnold Haskell, the writer and lecturer on ballet, coined a word to describe the more besotted supporters. He adapted a Russian word and called them – Balletomanes:

BALLETOMANE: Someone who wants new ballets and free tickets.
Sol Hurok (b. 1888–1974)

Dancing as a spectacle was brought to a high level of skill and beauty by the ancient Greeks. It played an important part in Greek drama, religion and social life, and contemporary carvings illustrated elaborate and graceful displays, including mime. But even in those days there were those who disapproved:

I see no pleasure in gazing at an effeminate fellow, with lascivious postures and ridiculous grimaces ... and this to the noise of a foolish harp, all which with their frequent rehearsals and continued din of stamping and jumping, are truly ridiculous and unbecoming a man of your parts and education. You give me no hopes of your conversion, as long as you are disposed to commend such vile and cursed filthy exercises.

Crato, in a dialogue with the satirist Lucian
Lucian (b. c. A.D. 120)

Dancing continued to be popular during the Middle Ages, both in hovel and castle. One of the upper-class medieval forms of diversion was to ride forth at night, masked and carrying torches, to call on a neighbouring castle. There a little entertainment of dancing was put on, after which the guests mingled with the hosts, masks were removed and there was much conviviality.

During the Renaissance this ancient frolic was transformed by Lorenzo de Medici, and others, into a more rational entertainment with a theme and songs. It also became very spectacular, with a mixture of music, dance and text.

These 'masques', as they were called, were introduced into France by Maria de' Medici and might possibly have developed into a species of French opera had it not been for Louis XIV, who was more interested in dancing than singing – his nickname of the 'Sun King' originated from the 'sun' costume which he wore when he danced in the *Ballet de la Nuit* at court when he was fifteen (it lasted thirteen hours). Under Louis' patronage, the literary and dramatic elements of the masque were subdued and the spectacle and dancing strengthened. The result was the birth of ballet.

Under the King's patronage a ballet school was founded in Paris and France dominated the world of ballet for the next two hundred years: as the terminology of opera is Italian so that of ballet is French.

Woodwind instruments were somewhat loud and shrill at that time, good in the open air but unsuitable for chamber music. Due to Louis XIV's taste for music – and his taste was as good as a command – a subtler, more precise instrument was devised for his orchestra. And so, about the year 1650, appeared the orchestral oboe, or 'French hoboy':

> Hard to pronounce and play, the OBOE –
> (With cultured folk it rhymes with 'doughboy'
> Though many an intellectual hobo
> Insists that we should call it oboe).
> However, be that as it may,
> Whene'er the oboe sounds its A
> All of the others start their tuning
> And there is fiddling and bassooning.
> Its plaintive note presaging gloom,
> Brings anguish to the concert room,
> Even the player holds his breath
> And scares the audience to death
> For fear he may get off the key,
> Which happens not infrequently.
> This makes the saying understood:
> It's an ill wood wind no one blows good.'
>
> Laurence McKinney (b. 1891)

In the late seventeenth century J. C. Denner of Nuremberg gave the world the clarinet:

> CLARIONET, n. An instrument of torture operated by a person with cotton in his ears. There are two instruments worse than a clarionet – two clarionets.
>
> Ambrose Bierce (1842–1914?)
> *The Devil's Dictionary*

England in the seventeenth century abounded with amateur musicians, but there was little patronage available for professionals; the quality and quantity of English music was nowhere near that of other European countries. The main patrons were courts, each with a chapel, banqueting hall and, frequently, theatre. The English court of the seventeenth century, when there was one, had neither the extravagant taste for music of Louis XIV nor his money to pay for it, and there was only one court; there were a great number of courts scattered over Italy, and Germany had over three hundred, with their little orchestras and their resident composers.

The English Puritans, contrary to expectancy, enjoyed music as much as their more free-living compatriots – Oliver Cromwell had a huge orchestra for his daughter's wedding celebrations; it is recorded that he danced until five in the morning – but they strongly disapproved of music in their services apart from congregational hymn and psalm-singing, and Calvinists disapproved even of those. So the Puritans banished organs from churches. The organs were promptly bought up cheap by inn and tavern keepers and musical evenings at the local pub became a feature of English life. A French visitor (R.C.) did not approve:

> That nothing may be wanting to the height of luxury and impiety of this abomination, they have translated the organs out of the Churches to set them up in taverns, chaunting their dithyrambics and bestial bacchanalias to the tune of those instruments which were wont to assist them in the celebration of God's praises.
>
> Anon. French traveller
> Trans. John Evelyn, 1659

It is an interesting thought that the Puritans' action led to a tradition of musical entertainment in public houses which culminated in the Music Halls of the nineteenth century – and Marie Lloyd.

One contribution which England did make to seventeenth-century music, and a big one, was the invention of the public concert. There was plenty of music which the public could hear, but it was mixed with other things; there was music played before, after or during plays; on state occasions; at fairs and festivals, etc. The first man in the world to invite the public to listen to a concert of music for itself alone, on payment of an entrance fee, was a violinist named John Banister.

Banister had been leader of Charles II's royal band but had been dismissed for making rude remarks about some French musicians whom the King had hired. For an entrance fee of a shilling the concertgoer sat at one of the small tables which were strewn about 'ale-house fashion' and ordered refreshment. At the far end of the room was a platform, with curtains, on which Mr. Banister and a group of musicians gave what he called 'a Parley of Instruments'.

When Banister died in 1697 a very different sort of musician became the world's second musical impresario: Thomas Britton, the Musical Small-coal Man. Britton was a humble charcoal seller ('small-coal' was charcoal; ordinary coal was then known as 'sea-coal', because it arrived from ports such as Newcastle by ship) who humped his charcoal round London in a sack on his back. He was an archetypal English semi-eccentric, slightly mad, kindly, passionately devoted to a number of pursuits; besides his love of music he had a scholarly knowledge of the occult sciences and chemistry; he was so skilful and discriminating as a bibliographer and book-collector that he was asked to help form the Harleian Library.

Britton's concerts ran for thirty-six years and were hugely popular; musicians like Handel and Dr. Pepusch – who arranged the music for *The Beggar's Opera* – were happy to give their services. Admission seems to have been free, but a dish of coffee could be had for a penny.

The concerts were given in what had been the hay-loft above Britton's coal shop, a converted stable in Jerusalem Passage, and the audience, which included distinguished foreign visitors and such leaders of society as the Duchess of Queensberry, had to climb up a steep ladder set against the outside wall. It was a small loft:

> Any Body that is willing to take a hearty Sweat, may have the Pleasure of hearing many notable Performances in the charming Science of Musick.
>
> Ned Ward (1667–1731)
>
> On winter Saturdays, when the Earl of Oxford, the Duke of Devonshire and the Earls of Winchilsea, Pembroke and Sunderland set out on their book-buying sprees, they would be joined by Britton in his blue smock with his reeking sack of charcoal on his back; a striking example of the democratic effect of a shared obsession. In 1714, when Britton was an old man, a friend, as a jape, introduced him to a famous ventriloquist, Mr. Honeyman, 'The Talking Smith', without mentioning that Mr. Honeyman was a ventriloquist. The ensuing demonstration so frightened Britton that he died of shock.

The eighteenth century started strongly with the invention of the piano. The organ sprang fully armed, as it were, from the loins of Ctesibius in the third century B.C., but the world had to wait another two thousand years for a keyboard stringed instrument which could be played softly or loudly according to the player's touch.

What held up the development was a design problem. The requirement was simple and had been known for centuries; a little hammer at the end of the key which, when the key was pressed, would be flung against the string, producing a soft or a loud note according to how strongly it had been flung. The trouble was that a simple little hammer on a hinge did not do the job. If the touch on the key was light the hammer failed to reach the string, and if the key was thumped the hammer hit the string, bounced back and hit it again.

The problem was solved by a Florentine instrument maker, Bartolommeo Cristoforo, who produced in 1709 his *gravicembalo con piano e forte* (harpsichord with soft and loud). This had an ingenious and complicated mechanism sitting on the end of each key which, in its later version, had a double action and an escapement. The double action gave a faster acceleration which meant that the lightest touch would produce a note, and the escapement allowed the hammer to fall back and be checked however hard the key was hit, so there was no bouncing.

Nobody took much notice of the piano for the first half of the century; composers were still writing for the harpsichord.

The first piano was heard in England about 1760. The early pianos were the shape of what we now call grand pianos, but round about 1760 a German refugee from the Seven Years War, Herr Zumpe, settled in England and began making Square pianos (really oblong) which were small and simple and became extremely popular, establishing a lead in piano-making which England held for a century. Examples of

English Square pianos are fairly common nowadays in antique shops; frequently converted into drinks cabinets or Hi-Fi cabinets and passed off as spinets, which they are not.

Music in eighteenth-century England prospered. Concert halls were built in many large towns, and various music societies and clubs were founded to further particular kinds of music and the work of particular composers. John Gay initiated a new form of musical entertainment, ballad opera, with the production in 1728 of *The Beggar's Opera*, a satirical play interspersed with well-known ballads which had been given new lyrics.

But, with the exception of ballad opera, which only lasted as a form for twenty-five years, Britain's best music and musicians were foreign. Like art, music was only socially acceptable if it was imported.

A clerical playwright saw the invasion by foreign music as another instance of national decline, linking it with widespread illiteracy, the South-Sea Bubble gambling fever and the breakdown of the class system:

> In days of old, when Englishmen were men,
> Their music, like themselves, was grave and plain;
> The manly trumpet, and the simple reed,
> Alike with citizen and swain agreed ...
> But now, since Britons are become polite,
> Since few can read, and fewer still can write;
> Since South-Sea schemes have so enrich'd the land,
> That footmen 'gainst their lords for boroughs stand;
> Since masquerades and op'ras made their entry,
> And Heydegger reign'd guardian of our gentry;
> A hundred various instruments combine,
> And foreign songsters in the concert join:
> The Gallic horn, whose winding tube in vain
> Pretends to emulate the trumpet's strain;
> The shrill-toned fiddle and the warbling flute,
> The grave bassoon, deep base, and tinkling lute,
> All league, melodious nonsense to dispense,
> And give us sound, and show, instead of sense.
>
> James Miller (1706–1744)

John Heidegger, a Swiss, was the impresario who ran the Opera House in the Haymarket. He instituted masquerades: masked fancy-dress balls which became so licentious that they had to be banned by the authorites. They continued, under the new name of 'ridottos'. Heidegger's other claim to immortality was being the ugliest man in London. He was quite cheerful about this and once made a wager with Lord Chesterfield that his lordship could not produce someone uglier. His Lordship rustled up a hideous old woman who was faintly uglier, but Heidegger put her bonnet on and was acclaimed the winner.

Italian opera arrived in England at the beginning of the century. It was sung in Italian, except by non-Italian members of the cast who sang their bits in their own language, and quickly became the most fashionable form of entertainment in London. The tin ears of England found it hard going:

> He [Sir Isaac Newton] said he never was at more than one Opera.
> The first Act he heard with pleasure, the 2nd stretch'd his patience,
> at the 3rd he ran away.
>
> The Rev. William Stukeley (1687–1765)
> *Diary*, 18 April 1720

Joseph Addison made an early attempt to stem the tide by writing an opera in English. *Rosamund*, with music by Thomas Clayton, was produced at Drury Lane in 1707:

> The loss of Rosamund in the second act of this drama is not compen-
> sated by a single interesting event in the third, which drags and lan-
> guishes for want of her so much, that neither the flat and forced
> humour of Sir Trusty and Grideline, nor the elegant compliments
> made to the Duke of Marlborough and Blenheim, ever kept the
> audience awake in the performance.
>
> Dr. Charles Burney (1726–1814)
> *A General History of Music*

Rosamund lasted for three performances.

Some years later Garrick also had a patriotic go:

> Garrick has produced a detestable English opera, which is crowded
> by all true lovers of their country. To mark the opposition to Italian
> operas, it is sung by some cast singers, two Italians, and a French
> girl, and the chapel boys; and to regale us with sense, it is Shake-
> speare's Midsummer-Night's Dream, which is forty times more non-
> sensical than the worst translation of any Italian opera-books.
>
> Horace Walpole (1717–1797)
> Letter to Richard Bentley, 23 Feb. 1755

Addison's and Garrick's efforts to produce an understandable opera were not admired by a modern sage:

> Opera in English is, in the main, just about as sensible as baseball
> in Italian.
>
> H. L. Mencken (1880–1956)

The eighteenth century was the Golden Age of Italian opera. Some-body worked out that something like twenty thousand operas must have been written during the period in various parts of Europe. Nearly all of them were based on classical history and Greek mythology, and a great number of them were entitled *Orpheus and Eurydice*.

During the seventeenth century, and until Gluck reformed it at the latter part of the eighteenth century, opera coagulated into a kind of costumed concert. Leading singers were grossly pampered and overpaid, particularly those sopranos and altos who were castrated men, which almost all the highly successful ones were (the last *castrato* sang in London in 1844). Costumes were odd and traditional and little attempt was made at acting, or telling a dramatic story; opera had become a show-case for singers; the recitative was mumbled through and treated as a little rest between the flashy arias. It was quite normal for an audience to play a game, during the boring bits of plot:

> Draughts are an admirable invention – just the thing to fill up the gaps whilst the long recitatives are being sung.
>
> Charles de Brosses (1709–1777)
> *Lettres familières écrites d'Italie en 1739 et 1740*

The rules governing the number of arias and who sang them were rigid. An Italian writer who submitted a libretto to an opera company in the middle of the eighteenth century was reminded of his responsibilities:

> You must begin by pleasing the actors and actresses; you must satisfy the musical composer; you must consult the scene-painter ...
> The three principal personages of the drama ought to sing five airs each; two in the first act, two in the second, and one in the third. The second actress and the second soprano can have only three; and the inferior characters must be satisfied with a single air each, or two at the most ... He must observe the same precaution in distributing the bravura airs, the airs of action, the inferior airs, and the minuets and rondeaus. He must above all things avoid giving impassioned airs, bravura airs, or rondeaus, to inferior actors. Those poor devils must be satisfied with what they get, and every opportunity of distinguishing themselves is denied them.
>
> Carlo Goldoni
> Quoted by George Hogarth (1783–1870)
> *Memoirs of the Musical Drama*, 1838

The standard of singing seems to have been very high. At any rate, the soloists, vain and rapacious as many of them were, were fawned upon by society. All over Europe it was believed that only Italians could sing well:

> A German singer! I should as soon expect to get pleasure from the neighing of my horse.
>
> Frederick the Great, King of Prussia (1712–1786)
> The Italian language was peculiarly suitable for singing, having no awkward diphthongs and virtually no final consonants.

Singer-worship extended into social circles and leading soloists gave private, and extremely well-paid, concerts in the homes of rich and noble admirers; a song-recital became an accepted element of assemblies and parties.

Further down the social scale, where hiring a currently fashionable *castrato* was out of the question, the hostess had to make do with a lady from the local opera company:

26

Nor cold, nor stern, my soul! yet I detest
  Those scented rooms, where, to a gaudy throng,
Heaves the proud harlot her distended breast
  In intricacies of laborious song.
Samuel Taylor Coleridge (1772–1834)

England's great composer, George Frederick Handel, was a German who left the service of the Elector of Hanover to settle in England. A few years later the Elector followed him as George I.

Besides composing, Handel gave concerts. In 1733 he stood in for a theatre company which had been banned and gave a series of five concerts in the Sheldonian Theatre, Oxford:

> The players being denied coming to Oxford by the Vice-Chancellor, and that very rightly, tho' they might as well have been here as Handell and his lowsy crew, a great number of foreign fidlers.
>
> Thomas Hearne (1678–1735)
Diary, 6 July 1733

Handel joined in the rough and tumble of the opera craze, writing a great many and going into management. After some financial troubles he turned to composing oratorios, a form which he introduced into Britain. Oratorio began in Italy about the same time as opera, which in Italy it closely resembled. It has been described as 'religious recreation' and consists of a work on a religious theme sung by a choir and soloists with a full orchestra. On the Continent it was usually presented in a theatre in full costume but, probably due to the Bishop of London's refusal to let his choir perform a religious work in fancy dress, Handel staged his oratorios in concert halls, without scenery and with the cast in their everyday (best) clothes. This 'English' or 'Concert' form of oratorio became immensely popular in England – when written by Handel – although a clergyman, later, begged to differ:

> Nothing can be more disgusting than an Oratorio. How absurd, to see five hundred people fiddling like madmen about the Israelites in the Red Sea!
>
> Rev. Sydney Smith (1771–1845)
Letter to Lady Holland, 1 Oct. 1823

Perhaps Handel's greatest admirer was George III, who encouraged massive concerts to commemorate Handel; these were held in Westminster Abbey towards the end of the century and the King rewrote an account of one of them – Dr. Burney had not done sufficient justice to Mr. Fischer's oboe playing – thus becoming perhaps our only kingly music critic.

One of the few reliefs from the stifling dullness of court life at Windsor Castle was the concerts, held almost every evening in the concert room at nine p.m. The King also had a band playing on the terrace on Sundays; a pernicious thing to do considering his neighbours, according to a pious physician and divine:

> The music on the terrace on Sundays, is pregnant with evil from Windsor to London; it infects all the neighbourhood ten miles round Windsor, and oh! what an irreligious example to the youths of Eton!

Sir James Stonhouse (1716–1795)
Letter to Sarah More, 17 Oct. 1791

When the organ was rediscovered in the Middle Ages it resumed its career in a crude form; in the early models the organist played by punching slides with his clenched fists. After some centuries of development it arrived back at roughly the stage it was in when the Romans left it. There seemed to be little more that anyone could do to it apart from small refinements. However, in 1751 a certain J. A. Maresch, who was attached to the orchestra of the Russian Empress Elizabeth, invented a totally new form of multiple horn operation. His invention – a kind of human organ – was tremendously successful in Russia, the nobles buying and selling them among themselves like football teams; but they did not catch on in other parts of the world, perhaps because they needed a large supply of musical serfs.

Sir Robert Ker Porter, an Englishman who failed as a history painter, emigrated to Russia and married a Russian princess, gave an eye-witness account:

> This instrument consists of 40 persons, whose life is spent blowing one note. The sounds produced are precisely similar to those of an immense organ; ... the effect produces much sublimity, when the *performers are unseen*: but when they are visible, it is impossible to silence reflections which jar with their harmony. To see human nature *reduced to such a use*, calls up thoughts very inimical to admiration of strains so awakened.

Sir Robert Ker Porter (1777–1842)
Travels

> There must have been a bit more to it than forty serfs peaceably blowing forty one-note Russian horns; a sight no more harrowing than watching a brass band. Was it, perhaps, a keyboard instrument which Ker Porter saw? When the organist pressed a key did a hammer descend on the skull of the appropriate serf? Or a spike ascend? Was J. A. Maresch's invention inspired by the organ devised by the Abbot of Baigne for Louis XI? According to Bouchet's *Annales d'Aquitaine*: 'Out of a number of hogs, of several ages, which he mustered up, and placed under a tent or pavilion, covered with velvet (before which he had a sound-board of wood, all painted, with a number of keys) he made an organ, and as he played upon the said keys with little spikes, which pricked the hogs, he made 'em cry in such time and consort as highly delighted the king and all his company.'

French ballet made rapid strides forward during the eighteenth century, and individual star dancers, especially ballerinas, scored great personal triumphs in Britain.

Women did not dance in public until 1681, when Mlle. Lafontaine led a small ensemble on stage in the ballet *Le Triomphe de l'Amour*, but very soon ballet had become so popular that operatic composers and librettists, particularly in France, had somehow to find plenty of occasions when their cast could logically break into a mixed dance.

At that time ballet was still very much under the influence of its French court traditions; scenes from Greek mythology or glorious history were represented by ladies and gentlemen lumbering about the stage in high heels, cumbersome costumes, leather masks and high wigs. Then, in the middle of the eighteenth century, a brilliant director of dancing was appointed to the Paris Opéra, Jean Noverre – Garrick called him 'the Shakespeare of the Dance' – who set out to make some reforms. He stated his intentions:

> To break hideous masks, to burn ridiculous perukes, to suppress clumsy panniers, to do away with still more inconvenient hip-pads, to substitute taste for routine, to indicate a dress more noble, more accurate, and more picturesque.
>
> Jean Noverre (1727–1810)
> *Lettre sur la danse et sur les ballets*

Noverre also developed miming. This meant that dancing could be more than just a set of animated pictures; it could tell a story. Noverre's new kind of Dramatic Ballet was able to involve the emotions of the audience with relevant, rather than merely classical or symbolic, situations.

There were grumbles:

> Our dancers ennoble what is coarse, but they degrade what is heroic.
>
> Joseph Joubert (1754–1824)
> *Pensées*, No. 283

Some star dancers added their own personal reforms. Mlle. Sallé pleased London audiences by dancing *Pygmalion*, a good old classical piece, in a simple robe of muslin. And the great Camargo not only introduced the *entrechat à quatre* (a movement in which the dancer rises in the air and criss-crosses her feet twice before touching down) but wore skirts which came half way up her shins. This athletic dancing, performed in dangerously short skirts, obliged Mlle. Camargo for modesty's sake to pioneer a garment which did not come into general use for another hundred years: ladies' drawers. Mlle. Camargo's drawers seemed to have been a cross between knickerbockers and tights; they had the charming name of *caleçon de précaution*.

The marketing managers of modern record-clubs have slapped various labels on to nineteenth-century music to divide it up into convenient parcels, e.g. The Romantic Age, The Age of Opulence, The Revolutionary Age, but a case could be made for leaving the century intact and calling it The Age of the Piano.

Advances were made in the technology of other musical instruments – wood-wind instruments were given improved valves and better fingering; the valve trumpet was invented and trumpet-players no longer had to sit amid a pile of assorted U-tubes, then necessary in order to change pitch – but the improvement in piano design and manufacture was dramatic.

Early in the century the Upright, or Cottage, piano superseded the Square piano, metal frames permitted stronger, tighter stringing, composers – including Mozart and Beethoven – began writing specifically for the piano and virtuoso soloists, like Chopin and Liszt, extended the range of playing techniques.

But perhaps the most extraordinary impact of the piano was in the home. To Victorians a piano in the parlour, played or unplayed, became a symbol of the household's respectability and solvency; the music-stand proudly supported copies of Badarzewska's *Maiden's Prayer* and Brinley Richards's *Warblings at Dawn* (with *Warblings at Eve* standing by for an encore); by the middle of the century the piano had become the most widely owned instrument in the world.

Unhappily there were more parlour pianos than there were tolerably talented pianists. By the end of the century George Bernard Shaw was moved to ask:

> Is the piano a musical instrument?
>
> George Bernard Shaw (1856–1950)
> *Fortnightly Review*: 'The Religion of the Pianoforte'

A new irritation had been added to urban life:

> Some new neighbours, that came a month or two ago, brought with them an accumulation of all the things to be guarded against in a London neighbourhood, viz., a pianoforte, a lap-dog, and a parrot.
>
> Jane Welsh Carlyle (1801–1866)
> Letter to Mrs. Carlyle, 6 May 1839

And to social life:

> PIANO, n. A parlor utensil for subduing the impenitent visitor. It is operated by depressing the keys of the machine and the spirits of the audience.
>
> Ambrose Bierce (1842–1914?)
> *The Devil's Dictionary*

All over the continent of Europe there was the same enthusiasm for the piano, as travellers noted in their journals:

> If the Devil some good night should take his hammer and smite in shivers all and every piano of our European world, so that in broad

30

Europe there was not one piano left soundable, would the harm be great? Would not, on the contrary, the relief be considerable? For once that you hear any real music from a piano, do you not five hundred times hear mere artistic somersaults, distracted jangling, and the hapless pretence of music? Let him that has lodged wall neighbour to an operatic artist of a stringed music say.

Thomas Carlyle (1795–1881)
Journal, Ghent, 4 a.m.

The piano was equally ubiquitous in the U.S.A. Although in the Deep South it seems to have been relegated to the position of first reserve to America's national instrument:

> Den come again, Susanna,
>   By de gas-light ob de moon;
> We'll tum de old piano
> When de banjo's out ob tune.
>
> Stephen Collins Foster (1826–1864)
> *Ring de Banjo*

Every hotel which had pretensions had a piano:

There is always a piano in an hotel drawing-room, on which, of course, some one of the forlorn ladies is generally employed. I do not suppose that these pianos are in fact, as a rule, louder and harsher, more violent and less musical, than other instruments of the kind. They seem to be so, but that, I take it, arises from the exceptional mental depression of those who have to listen to them.

Anthony Trollope (1815–1882)
North America

Even the saloons out West were enlivened by piano music. Due either to a high standard of musical appreciation among the drinkers or a low standard of musicianship among the pianists there seems to have been a high rate of mortality amongst saloon piano players.

Oscar Wilde saw a notice above a saloon piano in Leadville, Colorado:

> Please do not shoot the pianist.
> He is doing his best.
>
> Quoted by Oscar Wilde (1856–1900)
> *Impressions of America, Leadville*

The nineteenth century was also the Age of the Public Concert. The first important composer to earn his living from public and subscription concerts and copies of his compositions was Beethoven.

Before the days of paid concerts and copyright a composer had to find himself a job with a princeling, or a bishop, or a noble, and play the organ, rehearse the choir and compose the sort of music which pleased his patron. He was paid with a wage and his keep.

Unless a patron particularly asked to hear a composition again he did not expect to hear a piece of music more than once, consequently composers had to work swiftly and many had enormous outputs, e.g. Bach, 295 cantatas as well as other works; Handel, 22 oratorios, 47 operas, etc. They developed techniques of conserving their ideas, of laying down a steady ground-bass and leaving plenty of room for the instrumentalists to extemporize; they borrowed from each other and repeated ideas from their earlier works. Handel wrote his *Messiah* in twenty-two days; an early, rather sensual love-song of his called *No, I won't Trust You, Blind Love, Cruel Love* turned up in *Messiah* as *For Unto Us a Child is Born*.

Until the nineteenth century composers had virtually no profits from the sale of copies of their work. During the great opera-writing boom of the eighteenth century the usual fee for the score was about £100. Once the music had been published it was pirated by anybody who wanted to play it; the only people who made money out of sheet music were the publishers and, because most musicians preferred to play from manuscript copies, the copyists. It was not unusual for a popular opera to make more money for the copyist than the composer.

So little importance was attached to the ownership of scores that the manuscript of Bach's *St. Matthew Passion* only came to light when it was bought as wrapping-paper from the estate of a deceased cheesemonger.

By the second half of the eighteenth century the patronage system was beginning to break up. Political and financial conditions were changing and many household composers were finding the going hard. When the Archduke Ferdinand contemplated taking the young Salzburg musician Wolfgang Amadeus Mozart into his household as court musician he first wrote to ask his mother's advice. The Empress's reply gives an indication of the prestige accorded musicians in many parts of eighteenth-century Europe:

> You ask my opinion about taking the young Salzburg musician into your service. I do not know where you can place him, since I feel that you do not require a composer, or other useless people. But if it would give you pleasure, I have no wish to prevent you. What I say here is only meant to persuade you not to load yourself down with people who are useless, and to urge you not to give such people the right to represent themselves as being in your service. It gives one's service a bad name when such types run about like beggars; besides, he has a large family.
>
> Empress Maria Theresa (1717–1780)
> Letter to the Archduke Ferdinand, 1771

A bit hard on Mozart, who was a bachelor of sixteen at the time, his family consisting of his father, mother, and sister Maria Anna. Perhaps the incident marked the end of the grand era of patronage; after writing 41 symphonies, 20 operas and operettas, 27 piano concertos, 27 string quartets and 7 violin sonatas, Mozart, the greatest writer of 'pure' music ever, died in poverty and was buried in a common, unmarked grave.

The rapid and massive increase in concert-going which took place during the early years of the nineteenth century produced some strange results. The general level of public musical appreciation turned out to be much lower than that of aristocratic patronage and the soloists whom the public was most eager to pay to see were those who exhibited stunning virtuosity on their instrument, like Paganini on his violin; or Liszt, hair falling over his eyes, thumping his piano to pieces. The Cult of the Virtuoso became established.

It became fashionable to argue the merits of respective composers:

> Some cry up Haydn, some Mozart,
> Just as the whim bites. For my part,
> I do not care a farthing candle
> For either of them, nor for Handel.
>
> Charles Lamb (1775–1834)
> Letter to Mrs. William Hazlitt, 24 May 1830

The nobility arranged outdoor concerts to divert their guests at country house-parties, hiring brass bands of various ethnic descriptions, such as German bands and Russian bands:

> Duke of Sussex said that the execution of the Russian band was perfect, which I denied, as their hanging was omitted.
>
> Joseph Jekyll (d. 1837)
> Letter to Lady G. Sloane Stanley, 15 Aug. 1831

It became the custom to brighten up 'at homes' and dinner-parties with a recital of music. How far this reflected a hunger for music in middle-class society can be gauged from a word of advice in a Victorian etiquette book (fourteenth edition, 1887):

> When music is given at afternoon "at homes", it is usual to listen to the performance, or at least to appear to do so; and if conversation is carried on, it should be done in a low tone, so as not to disturb or annoy the performers.
>
> 'A Member of the Aristocracy'
> *Manners and Rules of Good Society*

Some concert sopranos had spectacular careers during the century, commanding enormous fees and meeting with public adulation on the scale of twentieth-century Beatlemania. Almost everybody loved Jenny Lind, 'the Swedish Nightingale':

> Then we went to Jenny Lind's concert, for which a gentleman here gave us tickets, and at the end of the first act we agreed to come away. It struck me as atrociously stupid. I was thinking of something else the whole time she was jugulating away, and O! I was so glad to get to the end and have a cigar.
>
> William Makepeace Thackeray (1811–1863)
> Letter to Mrs. Brookfield, 1850

33

'The Swedish Nightingale' was then jugulating away at her best. A few months later she went on a tour of the U.S.A. under contract to Phineas P. Barnum, from which she returned with a profit in excess of £20,000. This she spent on founding art scholarships and on extending hospitals in Liverpool and London.

Another change in music which came about at the turn of the eighteenth century and the beginning of the nineteenth, parallel with the emancipation of musicians from the courts of patronage, was the change in the sort of music being written. The 'learned style', represented at its best by Bach, was music for the chamber: fugue and cantata, and intricate polyphony which appealed to the mind. This had been transformed by Haydn and Mozart into the 'gallant style', symphonies and string quartets; graceful and elegant music for the senses – and the concert hall. The tremendous genius of Beethoven embraced these forms and went on to demonstrate new potentials; he developed the jaunty *scherzo*, or 'musical joke', he instigated stormy, dramatic opening movements, and poetic, introspective *adagios*; it was powerful music, written when Napoleon was changing the map of Europe and revolutions, artistic, social and political, were quietly or noisily happening in most countries.

This stir-up strengthened the growth of the spirit of Romanticism; of music which reflected the Romantic concern with the individual, with nationalism, with history, literature and beauty, with music's content rather than its shape.

Music had become so much a part of public life that newspapers and journals began to give systematic reports of concerts, the first in England being the *Morning Post*. The first English newspaper to employ a trained musician as its music critic was *The Times*. British music critics soon developed a reputation for being obstinately reactionary and treating all attempts at musical innovation to 'vigorous and unblenching criticism'.

The first wave of Romantic composers was briskly dealt with:

> Berlioz, musically speaking, is a lunatic; a classical composer only in Paris, the great city of quacks. His music is simply and undisguisedly nonsense.
>
> *Dramatic and Musical Review*, 7 Jan. 1843

Chopin, the 'poet of the piano', wrote such extraordinary piano music, sometimes fierce, sometimes delicate and melancholy, that only calling attention to a Delilah-like influence in his private life could explain how he came to write such stuff:

> The entire works of Chopin present a motley surface of ranting hyperbole and excruciating cacophony ... There is an excuse at present for Chopin's delinquencies; he is entrammeled in the enthralling

bonds of that arch-enchantress, George Sand, celebrated equally for
the number and excellence of her romances and her lovers.

Musical World, 28 Oct. 1841

It was widely believed that there was a discernible connection between
a composer's genius and what he got up to in the boudoir. H. L. Mencken
wrote: 'The music critic Huneker could never quite make up his mind
about a new symphony until he had seen the composer's mistress.'

Liszt was a leader of the writers of progressive music, 'The Music
of the Future' as they termed it:

Turn your eyes to any one composition that bears the name of Liszt,
if you are unlucky enough to have such a thing on your pianoforte,
and answer frankly, if it contains one bar of genuine music. Composition indeed! – decomposition is the proper word for such hateful
fungi, which choke up and poison the fertile plains of harmony,
threatening the world with drought.

Musical World, 30 June 1855

Besides his compositions, Liszt also played. He was probably the most
astonishing and successful solo pianist the world had ever seen:

Liszt is a mere commonplace person, with his hair on end – a snob
out of Bedlam. He writes the ugliest music extant.

Dramatic and Musical Review, 7 Jan. 1843

'Snob' is used in its early sense of a vulgar, ostentatious person.

Mendelssohn wrote music of great charm and beauty, but it was not
robust enough, according to a man of letters:

Are you overrun in London with 'Champagne Charlie is my Name'?
A brutal Thing; nearly worthless – the Tune, I mean – but yet not
quite – else it would not become so great a Bore. No: I can see,
to my Sorrow, that it has some Go – which Mendelssohn had
not.

Edward FitzGerald (1809–1883)
Letter to W. F. Pollock, 11 Nov. 1867

Brahms, honest and sincere, continued the Romanticism of Beethoven, using the classic symphony as his form:

I played over the music of that scoundrel Brahms. What a giftless
bastard!

Tchaikovsky (1840–1893)
Diary, 9 Oct. 1886

Another prolific French composer was Saint-Saëns. Although he disliked 'modernistic' music he was attacked by the critics for being
'coarsely realistic' in his *Danse Macabre*, and for making his *Déluge* sound
too much like a deluge:

It is one's duty to hate with all possible fervor the empty and ugly in art; and I hate Saint-Saëns the composer with a hate that is perfect.

J. F. Runciman: Saturday Review, 12 Dec. 1896

Russian music percolated into the rest of Europe and the U.S.A. in the latter half of the century, to be greeted by shock waves of xenophobia. Critics seemed to have been almost as alarmed by the composers' names as by their music:

Rimsky-Korsakov—what a name! It suggests fierce whiskers stained with vodka!

Musical Courier, 27 Oct. 1897

There was an apprehensive feeling that scratching a Russian composer would reveal a Tartar yahoo:

The Finale of the Fourth Symphony of Tchaikovsky pained me by its vulgarity ... Nothing can redeem the lack of nobleness, the barbarous side, by which, according to ethnographs and diplomats, even the most polished Russian at times betrays himself.

Musical Review, 26 Feb. 1880

Tchaikovsky's Fifth Symphony was judged to be unstable, ending inevitably in a Russian pogrom:

The Tchaikovsky Fifth Symphony was in part a disappointment ... The second movement showed the eccentric Russian at his best, but the Valse was a farce, a piece of musical padding, commonplace to a degree, while in the last movement, the composer's Calmuck blood got the better of him, and slaughter, dire and bloody, swept across the storm-driven score.

Musical Courier, 13 March 1889

While the Violin Concerto disintegrated into a vulgar Russian peasant brawl:

The violin is no longer played; it is pulled, torn, drubbed. The *Adagio* is again on its best behaviour, to pacify and to win us. But it soon breaks off to make way for a finale that transfers us to a brutal and wretched jollity of a Russian holiday. We see plainly the savage vulgar faces, we hear curses, we smell vodka. Friedrich Vischer once observed, speaking of obscene pictures, that they stink to the eye. Tchaikovsky's Violin Concerto gives us for the first time the hideous notion that there can be music that stinks to the ear.

Neue Freie Presse, Vienna, 5 Dec. 1881

Western critics found Prokofiev baffling; he seemed to pile dissonance upon dissonance, and there were not enough tunes:

The music of *The Love for Three Oranges*, I fear, is too much for this generation ... Mr. Prokofiev might well have loaded up a shotgun with several thousand notes of various lengths and discharged them against the side of a blank wall.

Edward Moore: Chicago Tribune, 31 Dec. 1921

A composer who began with the extreme Romanticism of Liszt and Wagner and came out the other end was the Hungarian-born Béla Bartók. His use of dissonance and wild rhythms made him an easy target for leaden humour:

> If the reader were so rash as to purchase any of Béla Bartók's compositions, he would find that they each and all consist of unmeaning bunches of notes, apparently representing the composer promenading the keyboard in his boots. Some can be played better with the elbows, others with the flat of the hand. None require fingers to perform nor ears to listen to.
>
> *Musical Quarterly*, July 1915

Bartók's music was described by the *Cincinnati Enquirer* as 'tonal chaos arising from the diabolical employment of unrelated keys simultaneously' and by the London *Sunday Times* as 'ugliness and incoherence'.

But Bartók's Fourth Quartet invoked a clearly defined series of images in the mind of the drama critic, Alan Dent:

> The opening *Allegro* took me straight back to childhood and gave me in turn the rusty windlass of a well, the interlinking noises of a goods train that is being shunted, then the belly-rumblings of a little boy acutely ill after a raid on an orchard, and finally the singular alarmed noise of poultry being worried to death by a Scotch terrier.
>
> The second movement gave me continuously and throughout its short length the noise of a November wind in telegraph poles on a lonely country road.
>
> The third movement began with a dog howling at midnight, proceeded to imitate the regurgitations of the less-refined or lower-middle-class type of water-closet cistern, modulating thence into the mass snoring of a Naval dormitory around the dawn — and concluded inconsequently with the cello reproducing the screech of an ungreased wheelbarrow.
>
> The fourth movement took me straight back to the noises I made myself, on wet days indoors, at the age of six, by stretching and plucking a piece of elastic.
>
> And the fifth movement reminded me immediately and persistently and vividly of something I have never thought of since the only time I heard it: the noise of a Zulu village in the Glasgow Exhibition — a hubbub all the more singular, because it had a background of skirling Highland bagpipes. *Both* noises emerged in this final movement of this Fourth Quartet of Béla Bartók.
>
> Alan Dent (b. 1905)
> Letter to James Agate, 26 Nov. 1945

Opera during the nineteenth century continued to be almost entirely imported from Italy. It was exotic, expensive entertainment, a minority interest of the fashionable and the cognoscenti. For those who were neither it was not an agreeable way of spending an evening:

> I have sat through an Italian Opera, till, for sheer pain, and inexplicable anguish, I have rushed out into the noisiest places of the crowded streets, to solace myself with sounds, which I was not obliged to follow, and get rid of the distracting torment of endless, fruitless, barren attention!
>
> Charles Lamb (1775–1834)
Essays of Elia: 'A Chapter on Ears'

A literary man who went to an opera almost by accident did not have a happy time:

> I actually went, one idle night before Jane came, to Covent Garden; found it a very mystery of stupidity and abomination; and so tiresome that I came away long before the end, and declare that the dullest sermon I ever heard was cheery in comparison.
>
> Thomas Carlyle (1795–1881)
Letter to his sister, Mrs. Aitken, 6 July 1834

Members of the aristocracy and polite society who went to the opera, even though they loathed it, because it was *à la mode*, were used to suffering for the cause – thus fashion doth make heroes of us all – but it was a bit hard on their less modishly inclined guests. The Rev. Sydney Smith pulled all stops out to avoid being taken to see Rossini's *Semiramis*, including pulling rank:

> My Dear Lady Holland,
>
> I have not the heart, when an amiable lady says, 'Come to *Semiramis* in my box', to decline; but I get bolder at a distance. *Semiramis* would be to me pure misery. I love music very little – I hate acting; I have the worst opinion of Semiramis herself, and the whole thing (I cannot help it) seems so childish and foolish that I cannot abide it. Moreover it would be rather out of etiquette for a Canon of St. Paul's to go to an opera, and where etiquette prevents me from doing things disagreeable to myself, I am a perfect martinet. All these things considered, I am sure you will not be a Semiramis to me, but let me off.
>
> Rev. Sydney Smith (1771–1845)
Letter to Lady Holland, 6 Nov. 1842

The exotic world of opera continued to be ruled by the leading singers, usually female, who seemed to grow increasingly imperious, rich and enormous as the century progressed. Costumes and scenery became more costly and magnificent, until by the last quarter of the century operatic productions were almost as top-heavy as prima donnas.

Leading singers demanded showy arias, full of vocal gymnastics. After a well-received display the singer would do it again as an encore. If there was any applause left after that it was quite normal for the singer to render a popular ballad of the day, irrespective of the damage it was doing to any dramatic content the opera might have had up to that point:

> How wonderful opera would be if there were no singers.
>> Gioacchino Antonio Rossini (1792–1868)

But, as a distinguished operatic singer remarked later:

> Nobody really sings in an opera—they just make loud noises.
>> Amelita Galli-Curci (1889–1963)

Operatic singers have been treated with caution ever since in the theatre. The possession of a superb voice is one thing, but:

> God in His Almighty Wisdom and Fairness has not always given the greatest voices to the persons with the greatest intellect or the best education, or to the most beautiful of His creatures.
>> Tyrone Guthrie (1900–1971)
>> *A Life in the Theatre*

The one composer whose operas were avoided by aria-and-encore-hungry prima donnas was Wagner, who would have none of it. To Wagner the play was the thing; the singers were there to sing the words—he wrote his own librettos—which helped to expound the opera's dramatic story. Even the music was used, almost like a chorus of singers, as part of dramatic exposition:

> Wagner has done undeniably good work in humbling the singers.
>> Max Beerbohm (1872–1956)

Wagner's operas broke through the established operatic conventions; the stories, the ultimate in Romantic German nationalism, and the force of his music, using a huge orchestra and entirely new devices of musical expression, created a form of musical art which he called 'Music Drama'. His critics nearly foamed at the mouth.

He was accused of being a contagious ailment:

> Is Wagner a human being at all? Is he not rather a disease? He contaminates everything he touches—he has made music sick. I postulate this viewpoint: Wagner's art is diseased.
>> Friedrich Nietzsche (1844–1900)
>> *Der Fall Wagner*

> Nietzsche really did hate Wagner. After being a great admirer he suddenly turned into a bitter enemy of everything that Wagner stood for and wrote copiously against him.

Of being a sadist:

> With Wagner amorous excitement assumes the form of mad delirium. The lovers in his pieces behave like tom-cats gone mad, rolling in contortions and convulsions over a root of valerian. They reflect a state of mind in the poet which is well-known to the ... expert. It is a form of Sadism. It is the love of those degenerates who, in sexual transport become like wild beasts. Wagner suffered from 'erotic mad-

ness', which leads coarse nature to murder and lust, and inspires higher degenerates' with works like *Die Walküre, Siegfried,* and *Tristan und Isolde.*

Max Nordau (1849–1923)
Degeneration

Of being a Communist:

Being a Communist, Herr Wagner is desirous of forcing the arts into fellowship with his political and social principles ... This man, this Wagner, this author of *Tannhäuser,* of *Lohengrin,* and so many other hideous things—and above all, the overture to *Der Fliegende Holländer,* the most hideous and detestable of the whole—this preacher of the 'Future', was born to feed spiders with flies.

Musical World, 30 June 1855

Of giving pleasure to royalty:

This revelling in the destruction of all tonal essence, raging satanic fury in the orchestra, this demoniacal, lewd caterwauling, scandal-mongering, gun-toting music, with an orchestral accompaniment slapping you in the face ... Hence, the secret fascination that makes it the darling of feeble-minded royalty, the plaything of the camarilla, of the court flunkeys covered with reptilian slime, and of the blasé hysterical female court parasites who need this galvanic stimulation by massive instrumental treatment to throw their pleasure-weary frog-legs into violent convulsion ... the diabolical din of this pig-headed man, stuffed with brass and sawdust, inflated, in an insanely destructive self-aggrandizement, by Mephistopheles' mephitic and most venomous hellish miasma, into Beelzebub's Court Composer and General Director of Hell's Music—Wagner!

J. L. Klein (1810–1876)
Geschichte des Dramas, Vol. III

Of failing to give pleasure to royalty:

The latest bore—but it is colossal—is *Tannhäuser.* I think I could compose something like it tomorrow, inspired by my cat scampering over the keys of the piano. Princess Metternich exerted herself hugely in pretending to understand it.

Prosper Mérimée (1803–1870)
Lettres à une inconnue, 21 March 1861

Of being barmy:

Wagner is evidently mad.
Hector Berlioz (1803–1869)
Letter, 5 March 1861

Of being barmy and, unkindest cut of all, impotent:

Wagner is a madman, a madman from pride. His music of the future is a monstrosity. Sterile by nature like all monsters, Wagner is impotent to reproduce himself.

H. Prévost
Étude sur Richard Wagner

The operas came as a bit of a shock to ordinary members of the opera-going public. John Ruskin, the art critic, went to a performance of *The Mastersingers*:

> Of all the *bête*, clumsy, blundering, boggling, baboon-blooded stuff I ever saw on a human stage, that thing last night beat—as far as the story and acting went—and of all the affected, sapless, soulless, beginningless, endless, topless, bottomless, topsiturviest, tuneless, scrannelpipiest—tongs and boniest—doggrel of sounds I ever endured the deadliness of, that eternity of nothing was the deadliest, as far as its sound went. I never was so relieved, so far as I can remember, in my life, by the stopping of any sound—not excepting railroad whistles—as I was by the cessation of the cobbler's bellowing.

John Ruskin (1819–1900)
Letter to Mrs. Burne-Jones, 30 June 1882

Ruskin was fastidious in his musical taste; he was whatever is the opposite of a tin ear—perhaps a golden ear. He wrote to a friend, John Brown, on 6 Feb. 1881: 'Beethoven always sounds to me like the upsetting of a bag of nails, with here and there an also dropped hammer.'

Not surprisingly perhaps, Wagner was not to the taste of Rossini:

> One can't judge Wagner's opera *Lohengrin* after a first hearing, and I certainly don't intend hearing it a second time.

Gioacchino Antonio Rossini (1792–1868)

And again:

> Wagner has beautiful moments but awful quarter hours.

Gioacchino Antonio Rossini (1792–1868)
Quoted by Major H. W. L. Hime: *Wagnerism, a Protest*

The year before he died Wagner wrote a different kind of opera, a solemn 'Sacred Music Drama', *Parsifal*:

> The kind of opera that starts at six o'clock and after it has been going three hours, you look at your watch and it says 6.20.

David Randolph (b. 1914)

Wagner probably had more abuse and invective heaped upon him, and from a greater height, than any other composer in the history of music. Perhaps he drew a little comfort from the comment of an American writer:

> Wagner's music is better than it sounds.

Bill Nye (1850–1896)

The story of the progress of dancing during the nineteenth century started, literally, with a bang. Two bangs, in fact, as both duellists managed to discharge their pistols.

The rumpus was about the introduction into England from Germany in 1812 of the waltz. Before this, there was little personal contact between dancing partners; a holding of finger-tips, a hand resting upon an arm. But in the waltz there was a delicious propinquity, exciting music, and exhilarating steps which whirled the interlocked couple round the room. Guardians of public morality immediately pronounced the waltz to be 'will-corrupting', 'disgusting', 'immodest'; an 'outright romp in which the couples not only embrace throughout the dance but, flushed and palpitating, whirl about in the posture of copulation'.

General Thornton of the First Regiment of Guards was one of the waltz's most enthusiastic supporters, so when an author, Theodore Hook, spoke out against it the General called him out.

A report from *The Times*:

> Monday morning a duel took place between General Thornton and Mr. Theodore Hook. After exchanging one shot each, the affair was amicably settled. It originated in a silly dispute on the subject of the dance called the *Waltz*, the General having praised it in high terms, and the Author having bitterly reprobated it as leading to the most licentious consequences.
>
> *The Times*, 22 July 1812

> There is something fishy about this much-quoted episode; it has the ring of a jape which went a little wrong. Hook was no moralist, he was an exuberant young man-about-town aged twenty-three, a friend of the Prince of Wales, and already famous for his practical jokes, such as the 'Berners Street hoax' in which he sent out four thousand letters and caused the house of a woman he was quarrelling with to be besieged by an army of people from chimney-sweeps and carters to the Lord Mayor and the Duke of Gloucester. It seems likely that Hook's comments about the waltz were satirically intended. If it was a jape it misfired slightly because the General had to resign his commission as a result of the duel.

Lord Byron happily kept the pudding stirred by writing a supposedl‹ anti-waltz poem. He published it anonymously, under a significan pseudonym:

> Hot from the hands promiscuously applied,
> Round the slight waist, or down the glowing side ...
> The breast thus publicly resigned to man
> In private may resist him — if it can.
> 'Horace Hornem, Esq.' (Lord Byron, 1788–1824)
> *Waltz*

The nineteenth century proved to be the Golden Era of French ba let. About 1820 the ballerina Taglioni popularized toe-dancing, whic called for special built-up shoes and did away for ever with the hig heels which were customary. It also diminished the importance of ma dancers, whose insteps were not designed by nature for tiptoe wor

Skirts became a little shorter, modesty being preserved – an prurience increased – by M. Maillot's invention of pink tights.

42

Clothing became freer. The Romantic leanings were towards wispy draperies, informal hair-styles and ballerinas who looked remote, sylph-like, and not long for this world. All these factors led to ballet moving on from its preoccupation with legs and feet and acquiring a whole new vocabulary of gymnastic, virtuoso movements:

> The French, whether men or women, have no idea of dancing but that of moving with agility, and of distorting their limbs in every poss-ible way, till they really alter the structure of the human form ... The French Opera-dancers think it graceful to stand on one leg or on the points of their toes, or with one leg stretched out behind them, as if they were going to be shod, or to raise one foot at right angles with their bodies, and twirl themselves round like a *te-totum*, to see how long they can spin, and then stop short all of a sudden; or to skim along the ground, flat-footed, like a spider running along a cob-web, or to pop up and down like a pea on a tobacco-pipe, or to stick in their backs till another part projects out behind *comme des volails*, and to strut about like peacocks with infirm, vain-glorious steps, or to turn out their toes till their feet resemble apes, or to raise one foot above their heads, and turn swiftly round upon the other, till the petticoats of the female dancers (for I have been thinking of them) rise above their garters, and display a pair of spindle-shanks, like the wooden ones of a wax-doll, just as shapeless and as tempting.
>
> William Hazlitt (1778–1830)
> *Notes of a Journey through France and Italy*

So much for virtually the whole repertoire of ballet dance steps.

As opera throughout the world was dominated by Italian prima donnas so ballet was ruled, throughout the century, by French-trained ballerinas, who commanded enormous fees and had armies of admirers.

The first major French ballet company visited New York in 1827. They had a spot of bother with their tights, glimpses of which during pirouettes caused gentlemen to breathe heavily and ladies to stalk out of the theatre, but they changed these for Turkish pantaloons and were an enormous success; their leading dancer, Céline Celesti, was soon reported to be getting $50,000 a year.

Another great star was Fanny Elssler, whose sensual style of dancing in the 1840s, skirt hitched up to expose thigh, attracted so many senators that a session of Congress had to be abandoned because they could not raise a quorum. The poet Emerson said of her dancing, to his fellow Transcendentalist Margaret Fuller, 'Margaret, this is poetry,' to which she replied, 'Waldo, this is religion.'

Others were less enthusiastic about the French import:

> The pirouette ... is a movement, in which a woman ... poising herself on one limb, extends the other ... at right angles, and ... spins around some eight or ten times, leaving her drapery, 'transparent' and short as it is at the best, to be carried up ... as far as it will go ... Is there

a father or a mother, a husband or wife, a brother or sister in Christendom ... who would view it with anything but horror?

North American Review, 1833

Ballet had been danced mainly to existing music, but as the nineteenth century progressed French composers began to write specifically
for the dance. And as music moved through the eras of Romanticism,
Impressionism and Realism, so did ballet. By the last quarter of the
century it had got itself into something of a state. Productions had
become lavish and expensive and the current trend of Realism was less
suitable for expression through dancing than Impressionism or
Romanticism; *Round the Town* and *The Press* were not quite the same
thing as *Giselle* and *Coppélia*.

A new lease of life came to ballet from Russia, with a little help
from America.

Russia was introduced to ballet in 1734, when it was imported from
France as part of the Francophile feeling which had overcome most
European rulers at that period. Up to the turn of the century it had
remained essentially French in style:

The ballet ... is simply a lewd performance.

Count Leo Tolstoy (1828–1910)
What Is Art?

But in America a dancer, Isadora Duncan, was propounding and
demonstrating a new theory of what the dance should be. Miss Duncan
did not believe in a vocabulary of steps and movements; she clad herself
in flowing draperies, as depicted on Greek vases, and moved about the
stage in a kind of free-flow, expressing herself to the music:

In less inspired moments she followed the music as a bear might
pursue a mouse.

Adrian Stokes (b. 1902)
Tonight the Ballet

Isadora Duncan's art met with a mixed reception in American cities –
the city of Boston, Mass., was deeply shocked at finding that she danced
on the public stage with her feet stark naked – but it is widely believed
that her utterly unformal approach to dancing provided the inspiration
which the dancer and choreographer Fokine, and the impresario Diagh-
ilev, needed to generate a refreshing new approach to ballet, which
superseded the French style, and with its restoration to prominence
of the male dancer, its use of commissioned work from contemporary
composers and its imaginative, unconventional choreography, laid the
foundations of modern ballet.

If Isadora Duncan was really the spot of oil which released the hinge
and allowed ballet to swing forward into the twentieth century, the
achievement would have given her little satisfaction:

I am the enemy of ballet which I look upon as false, absurd and outside the domain of art ... I thank God that a cruel destiny did not inflict on me the career of a ballet dancer.

Isadora Duncan (1878–1927)
My Life

The development of serious music in the twentieth century has been more by consolidation and experimentation than by revolution. During the two previous centuries musical styles went in one era and out of the other, but twentieth-century music has been largely a matter of refining existing forms; it lends itself less easily to convenient labels.

Concert halls continued to be well attended although, particularly during the early years of the century, an unknown proportion of audiences were only there to fulfil their social duty:

Even before the music begins there is that bored look on people's faces. A polite form of self-imposed torture, the concert.

Henry Miller (b. 1891)
Tropic of Cancer

Recitals remained a genteel and praiseworthy form of entertainment, eminently suited to such needs as raising money for charity:

Pianoforte recital by F. M. at Frinton Hall last night in aid of Tendring Parish funds. Hall centrally heated, but draughty. Uncomfortable chairs. Rush-bottomed chair (cost about 3s.) for pianist. Old Broadwood baby grand. Pedal creaked. Rotten tone. Ladies of Frinton and Tendring parishes in evening dress. Two parsons, who felt they must speechify afterwards. Pianist a man about 40, agreeably slight curt smile. Ferocious look when he was playing often. Beethoven, Rameau, Chopin, Scarlatti, Debussy, Liszt, etc. Piano impossible. Intense, almost tragic sadness of provincial musical affairs, second-rate or tenth-rate under bad conditions. A gentle snobbishness (artistically) among the women. One man (friend of pianist) called out 2 or 3 times after a piece, amid the applause, 'Core, core', very loudly and staccato. And he had his encore. Audience determined to appreciate high-class music, and applauding the noisiest and most showy. Crass inertia and stupidity of sundry women around me, determined to understand and to enjoy nothing.

Arnold Bennett (1867–1931)
Journal, 21 Feb. 1912

A snobbishness began to develop amongst concert goers that the only worthwhile music was to be found at 'Op concerts', so called because the music played was distinguished enough to have been given an Opus Number and its composer was safely out of the way:

The public doesn't want new music; the main thing it demands of a composer is that he be dead.

Arthur Honegger (1892–1955)

There was a growing interest in old musical instruments and compositions; sackbuts and shawms, viols and harpsichords were con structed and played. And there was renewed enthusiasm for attending evenings of fugues and cantatas:

> Of the audience at a chamber-music concert, an Oxford don once remarked, 'They look like the sort of people who go to the English Church abroad.'
>
> Quoted by W. H. Auden 1907–1974)
> *A Certain World*

At a White House youth concert on 6 August 1962 President Kennedy had the satisfaction of announcing that more people in the U.S.A. went to symphony concerts than went to baseball games (he went on to say that he thought that, nevertheless, both baseball and the country would endure). But many more people did not go to symphony concerts than went; usually because they found the music baffling:

> Classical music is the kind that we keep hoping will turn into a tune.
>
> Kin Hubbard (1868–1930)

But also because a feeling had grown that 'classical' music was for 'them', not 'us', that it was an upper-class intellectual pleasure which was a thumping bore for everybody else. When the Mikado detailed the list of humiliating punishments he had devised to fit the people he disliked, he reserved a dismal fate for a humble entertainer:

> The music-hall singer attends a series
> Of masses and fugues and 'ops'
> By Bach, interwoven
> With Spohr and Beethoven,
> At Classical Monday Pops.
>
> W. S. Gilbert (1836–1911)
> *The Mikado*

The tendency to think of all 'serious' music as difficult, dull and pretentious, even when it was light and witty, increased during the twentieth century owing to the spectacular success of another kind of music – 'popular' music – which appealed to non-musical people and required no training or knowledge of music from its listeners. It could be enjoyed by anybody who liked humming a catchy tune, or dancing, or tapping their feet to a strong rhythmic beat.

The element of hummability in popular music emerged early in the nineteenth century when favourite music-hall songs – like 'Champagne Charlie', which Edward FitzGerald found so compulsive – began to be whistled and sung by everybody but the genteel:

> One never realises the vulgarity of human beings so acutely as when listening to the mindless bawling of popular songs.
>
> John Sullivan
> *But for the Grace of God*

46

The combination of dancing and modern popular music could be said to have begun with the 'cake-walk', a dance which was brought to the public's attention during the second half of the nineteenth century, mainly by touring Minstrel shows. It originated as a plantation frolic among the negro slaves of the Mississippi valley and was called the 'cake-walk' because the dancers, dressed in such finery as they could muster, strutted up and down the floor like grand ladies and gentlemen and the one who produced the showiest walk was presented with a cake.

The syncopated accompaniment to cake-walks was usually played on a banjo, but from it developed a new style of music, usually written for the piano which was then in its heyday, which came to be called 'ragtime'. Ragtime music went through many forms, but it was originally a formal, almost neo-classical style of composition, to be played as written.

At the turn of the century the cake-walk, with the freedom for self-expression which it allowed dancers, and ragtime, with its syncopated rhythm, had become the rage among the young people of the U.S.A.:

A wave of vulgar, filthy and suggestive music has inundated the land. Nothing but ragtime prevails, and the cake-walk with its obscene posturings, its lewd gestures ... Our children, our young men and women, are continually exposed to its contiguity, to the monotonous attrition of this vulgarizing music. It is artistically and morally depressing and should be suppressed by press and pulpit.

Musical Courier, 13 Sept. 1899

The third and most important element which went to make up popular music was the emergence of a revolutionary new musical idiom – Jazz:

JAZZ: Music invented by demons for the torture of imbeciles.

Henry van Dyke (1852–1933)

Jazz (or 'jass' as it was sometimes written – originally a West African negro word for sexual activity and excitement) began as the home-made music of plantation workers in the New Orleans area and came in two varieties: sad and cheerful. It detailed the woes of human existence in the music of the 'blues', and it celebrated life with up-beat entertainment music – raucous, rhythmic and inventive. Both were present on occasions like a New Orleans funeral when the accompanying band would play the blues on the way to interment and celebratory jazz marches on the way back.

One particular feature of jazz which was a radical departure from almost all 'serious' music was the part played by improvisation. Jazz music, in its early form, was made by the instrumentalists, not by a composer. The players, many of whom had an excellent ear and sense of rhythm but were musically illiterate, began with a simple melody line or chord sequence and from there took off into virtuoso flights of extempore invention, each to his own talent. This was known in the trade as 'putting in the dirt'.

During the early years of the century jazz became fortuitously identified with brothels; a circumstance which, together with the origin of the word 'jazz', made it even more odious to those who did not like it. In 1897 an area of New Orleans – 'Storyville' – was set aside as an officially approved red-light district and given over entirely to brothels and bars. As every self-respecting madam had to have a 'professor' playing piano in her house parlour, and most of the bars had bands, and the minds of Storyville's customers were on other things than music, Storyville not only provided a huge number of early jazz musicians with steady employment but with working conditions which encouraged them to experiment freely and develop their own stylistic techniques.

The respectable sector of New Orleans was not at all happy about this cuckoo which the city had inadvertently reared:

> Why is the jass music, and, therefore, the jass band? As well ask why is the dime novel or the grease-dripping doughnut. All are manifestations of a low streak in man's tastes that has not yet come out in civilization's wash. Indeed, one might go farther, and say that jass music is the indecent story syncopated and counterpointed ... In the matter of jass, New Orleans is particularly interested, since it has been widely suggested that this particular form of musical vice had its birth in this city – that it came, in fact, from doubtful surroundings in our slums. We do not recognize the honor of parenthood, but with a story in circulation it behooves us to be last to accept the atrocity in polite society, and where it has crept in we should make it a point of civic honour to suppress it. Its musical value is nil, and its possibilities of harm are great.
>
> *Times-Picayune*, New Orleans, 17 June 1917

Later in the year 1917 the United States Navy Department shut down Storyville (the number of prostitutes in New Orleans immediately increased). The jazz musicians drifted up-river to Chicago and from there dispersed to other parts of the country. White musicians took an increasing interest. In a few years the taste for jazz music had spread across the continent of America and into Europe:

> The latest type of popular music, jazz music, affects me as deliberately evil. It does not seem to me to be vulgar by inadvertence; it is propaganda for vulgarity. Its popularity testifies to a widespread *nostalgie de la boue*. If our sociologists were also musicians they would find considerable social significance in the popularity of jazz.
>
> John Sullivan
> *But for the Grace of God*

Ragtime/jazz became big business. Successful composers became millionaires and virtuoso instrumentalists became national heroes.

Watered-down, commercialized jazz was promoted by massive corporations through sheet-music, gramophone records, chains of dance-halls and the new invention of talking-pictures:

> It was the first time, I suddenly realised, that I had ever clearly *seen* a jazz-band. The spectacle was positively frightening ...
>
> Oh, those mammy-songs, those love-longings, those loud hilarities! How was it possible that human emotions intrinsically decent could be so ignobly parodied? I felt like a man who, having asked for wine, is offered a brimming bowl of hog-wash. And not even fresh hog-wash. Rancid hog-wash, decaying hog-wash. For there was a horrible tang of putrefaction in all that music. Those yearnings for Mammy of Mine and My Baby, for Dixie and the Land where Skies are Blue and Dreams come True, for Granny and Tennessee and You—they were all a necrophily. The Mammy after whom the black young Hebrews and the blond young muffin-faces so retchingly yearned was an ancient Gorgonzola; the Baby of their tremulously gargled desire was a leg of mutton after a month in warm storage; Granny had been dead for weeks; and as for Dixie and Tennessee and Dream Land—they were odoriferous with the least artificial of manures.
>
> Aldous Huxley (1894–1963)
> *Do What You Will*

All the elements of popular music prospered in the period between the wars. Hollywood musicals spread the songs of composers like Irving Berlin, Jerome Kern and Cole Porter round the world for everybody to hum in the bath; dancers went through a succession of styles from the charleston and the tango to Latin-American specialities; jazz music proved to be so flexible and its permutations so numerous that its devotees gently withdrew genuine New Orleans-style jazz from popular music and established it as an art form in itself. It now has its own place in music, with a committed following. The offshoots went through a number of phases and names, culminating, in the 1930s, with 'swing':

> A degenerated and demoralizing musical system is given a disgusting christening as 'swing' and turned loose to gnaw away the moral fiber of young people ... Jam sessions, jitterbugs and cannibalistic rhythmic orgies are wooing our youth along the primrose path to Hell!
> The Most Reverend Francis J. L. Beckman, Archbishop of Dubuque
> Lecture, 25 Oct. 1938

After the Second World War popular music was beamed almost entirely towards the young, who for the first time had considerable spending power. Manipulated by commercial promoters, subject to the caprices of fashion, Croesus-like in its wealth, this music went through a number of labelled phases, Skiffle, Rhythm and Blues, Soul, Rock and Roll, plain Rock, and, together with a new attitude towards clothes, colours and graphic design, became part of young people's culture: Pop.

With Pop arrived a new phenomenon, a non-musician with considerable influence over young people's musical taste: the disc jockey:

> There have to be these adults, *jeunes premiers manqués,* failed film-extras, tanned and teethed, voltaic with manic enthusiasm, spurting their vacuous encomia (the simulated orgasms of the impotent), knowledgeable in the brief pathetic chronicles of the shag-haired twangers, bright and kidding and empty-eyed, their mean little slogans like potato crisps ('Don't be LATE for your DATE with the GREAT!'), their English either con-man's synthetic Received Standard or matey Provincial-swallowed-up-in-American, their poverty-stricken hyperbolic laudations the ultimate shame of all language (when such mean and cheap janglings are 'great', what term do we reserve for *Tristan* and the Choral Symphony?). Do they merit vitriol, even a drop of it? Yes, because they corrupt the young, persuading them that the mature world, which produced Beethoven and Schweitzer, sets an even higher value on the transient anodynes of youth than does youth itself. For this they stink to heaven ... they are the Hollow Men. They are electronic lice.
>
> Anthony Burgess (b. 1917)
> *Punch:* 'The Weasels of Pop', 20 Sept. 1967

By the 1970s, popular music bore little resemblance to the form it had at the beginning of the century. The song element was much less potent, dancing had dwindled to a little light weaving and trudging in discos and the mass marketing of pop records – to increasingly younger buyers – became more and more a matter of skilfully manipulating temporary trends and fads:

> I think popular music in this country is one of the few things in the twentieth century that have made giant strides in reverse.
>
> Bing Crosby (b. 1904)
> *This Week* magazine

The story of music in England raises some interesting points. There was a heady period during the late 1960s when London was acknowledged to be the centre of the musical world. This was partly due to the high level of musicianship to be found in London but, alas, chiefly due to the favourable rate of exchange of the pound and the lower union rates of pay, which made it more economical for international orchestras to record here. The reality is that apart from producing instrumentalists and orchestras of the highest quality Britain has contributed little to music at international level. Why should we produce more interpretive talent than creative talent? Why did the Continent produce all the really great composers? Something in the soil? Was it the lack of much real patronage in Britain which resulted in the lack of great composers, or did the combination of conditions which produced com-

50

posers of genius in other lands also breed patrons to encourage and appreciate them?

On advice, no attempt will be made to pontificate upon these problems:

> If a literary man puts together two words about music, one of them will be wrong.

Aaron Copland (b. 1900)
Quoted in *Tempo*, Summer 1969

EDUCATION

Education

There is an English proverbial saying that your schooldays are the happiest days of your life. It is not known what man, or what sort of man, first uttered the sentiment but there has been at least one helpful suggestion:

> Show me the man who has enjoyed his schooldays and I will show you a bully and a bore.
>
> Robert Morley (b. 1908)
> *Robert Morley: Responsible Gentleman*

The popular and successful actor-dramatist spent some years at Wellington College.

Whoever spoke so glowingly of the happiness of school life was no doubt an adult. Children are normally less enthusiastic:

> ... the whining school-boy, with his satchel
> And shining morning face, creeping like snail
> Unwillingly to school.
>
> William Shakespeare (1564–1616)
> *As You Like It:* Act II, sc. vii

Particularly on a warm, sunny day:

> But to go to school in a summer morn,
> Oh, it drives all joy away!
> Under a cruel eye outworn,
> The little ones spend the day—
> In sighing and dismay.
>
> William Blake (1757–1827)
> *The Schoolboy*

It would have been cold comfort to those children to realize that they were enjoying their happiest days; that later days were going to be even more miserable. Mercifully, children don't usually philosophize to that extent about the unavoidable: school is just something which has to be endured, like chicken-pox and parents. It was up to adults to argue about education. To define it:

> EDUCATION, n. That which discloses to the wise and disguises from the foolish their lack of understanding.
>
> Ambrose Bierce (1842–1914?)
> *The Devil's Dictionary*

55

To estimate its effect on society:

> Soap and education are not as sudden as a massacre, but they are more deadly in the long run.
>
> Mark Twain (1835–1910)
> *The Facts Concerning My Recent Resignation*

Its value in turning out leaders of men:

> The world's great men have not commonly been great scholars, nor its great scholars great men.
>
> Oliver Wendell Holmes (1809–1894)
> *The Autocrat of the Breakfast-Table*

And military geniuses:

> The Battle of Yorktown was lost on the playing fields of Eton.
>
> H. Allen Smith (b. 1906)

Its relevance to commerce:

> I respect no study, and deem no study good, which results in money-making.
>
> Seneca (*c.* 5 B.C.–A.D. 65)
> *Epistolae ad Lucilium*

The importance of academic qualifications:

> A Master of Art
> Is not worth a fart.
>
> Andrew Boorde (1490?–1549)
> *The Jests of Scoggin*

The rewarding life which students live:

> They are thin and pale, their feet are cold, their heads are hot, the night is without sleep, the day a fear of interruption, — pallor, squalor, hunger, and egotism.
>
> Ralph Waldo Emerson (1803–1882)
> *Representative Men:* 'Montaigne'

The respect in which a student is held:

> A mere scholar, a mere ass.
>
> Robert Burton (1577–1640)
> *Anatomy of Melancholy*

The placid, sedentary nature of study within a university:

> Superfluity of lecturing causes ischial bursitis.
>
> Sir William Osler (1849–1919)

Ischial bursitis = roughly, a numb bum.

The importance of giving a child the best possible education, however expensive:

> You can't expect a boy to be depraved until he has been to a good school.
>
> Saki (H. H. Munro) (1870–1916)
> *A Baker's Dozen*

56

To educationists it all seemed, at times, to be of dubious value:

Education is the process of casting false pearls before real swine.
Irwin Edman (1896–1954)

And to some laymen, too:

We are faced with the paradoxical fact that education has become one of the chief obstacles to intelligence and freedom of thought.
Bertrand Russell (1872–1970)
Sceptical Essays

Many people did not find education a rivetingly interesting topic:

It is tiresome to hear education discussed, tiresome to educate, and tiresome to be educated.
William Lamb, second Viscount Melbourne (1779–1848)

Lord Melbourne spoke from experience. He was political tutor to the young Queen Victoria.

An early comment on teaching as a career came from a philosopher and statesman who was tutor to Nero:

It is when the gods hate a man with uncommon abhorrence that they drive him into the profession of a school-master.
Seneca (*c*. 5 B.C.–A.D. 65)
Epistolae ad Lucilium

Seneca was given poison by his pupil Nero, recovered but was eventually forced by him to commit suicide.

The teaching profession has been sniped at for a number of reasons. It has been said that to become a schoolmaster is in itself a confession of failure:

He who can, does. He who cannot, teaches.
George Bernard Shaw (1856–1950)
Maxims for Revolutionists

That it was a career that people drifted into rather than chose:

'I expect you'll be becoming a schoolmaster, sir. That's what most of the gentlemen does, sir, that gets sent down for indecent behaviour.'
Evelyn Waugh (1903–1966)
Decline and Fall

That teaching tended to give the teacher a false sense of values:

The vanity of teaching often tempteth a man to forget he is a blockhead.
George Savile, first Marquess of Halifax (1633–1695)
Maxims

That it was an unhealthy existence:

> Every schoolmaster, after the age of forty-nine, is inclined to flatulence, is apt to swallow frequently and to puff.
>
> Harold Nicolson (1886–1968)
> *The Old School:* Ed. Graham Greene

That teachers were slightly apart from, and lesser than, ordinary mortals:

> Why are we never quite at our ease in the presence of a schoolmaster? — because we are conscious that he is not quite at his ease in ours. He is awkward, and out of place, in the society of his equals. He comes like Gulliver from among his little people, and he cannot fit the stature of his understanding to yours. He cannot meet you on the square. He wants a point given him, like an indifferent whist-player. He is so used to teaching, that he wants to be teaching *you* ... The jests of a schoolmaster are coarse, or thin. They do not *tell* out of school. He is under the restraint of a formal and didactic hypocrisy in company, as a clergyman is under a moral one. He can no more let his intellect loose in society, than the other can his inclinations. — He is forlorn among his co-evals; his juniors cannot be his friends.
>
> Charles Lamb (1775–1834)
> *Essays of Elia:* 'The Old and the New Schoolmaster'

That university professors and lecturers became so in order to defect from the complications of ordinary life:

> Perhaps there is something innate that in the first place disposes a man to become a University teacher or specialist. He is, I suspect, more often than not by nature and instinctively afraid of the insecure uproar of things. Visit him in college and you will see that he does not so much live there as lurk.
>
> H. G. Wells (1866–1946)
> *The World of William Clissold*

And that teachers lower down the scale were hardly worth bothering about:

> The truth is that the average schoolmaster, on all the lower levels, is and always must be ... next door to an idiot, for how can one imagine an intelligent man engaging in so puerile an avocation?
>
> H. L. Mencken (1880–1956)
> *New York Evening Mail*, 23 Jan. 1918

A line drawn on a graph to show the effectiveness of education through the centuries would come out rather like the profile of a hip-bath. It would start fairly high with primitive man, zoom to its peak with ancient Greece, wobble a little with Rome, plunge down steeply with the Dark Ages, revive a little with the Middle Ages, descend again during the seventeenth and eighteenth centuries and begin a firm upward sweep at the middle of the nineteenth century.

58

Education to primitive man was a family matter: the conversion of a child at puberty into an adult. For a boy it usually entailed being knocked about a bit and having snippets cut off his body to demonstrate what a harsh world it was, and being taught the customs and killing skills which the tribe had accumulated. For girls it meant being led off and taught to distinguish between edible and non-edible herbs, how to brew beer, bind wounds and generally make themselves useful to the men.

Schools came into being when the Chinese invention of writing penetrated into Egypt. Society, based on the keeping of records, became more complex and the necessary techniques of painting on paper or scratching on wax or chipping into stone were too complicated and new to be learnt from parents or tribal wise man.

Greek civilization took education to its heights. They studied literature and music, gymnastics, philosophy, and laid down the rules of mathematics and astronomy – the last two essential for fixing feast-days. They believed that education should aim at a healthy mind in a healthy body, although Sparta concentrated more on the healthy body and Athens on the healthy mind. They had itinerant teachers for remote regions, 'sophists'; elementary schools for the young, advanced education for older boys; Athens even had a kind of university. The New Education which emerged in Greece and the principles of education laid down by Plato and Aristotle were the beginnings of modern schooling.

A hint of the way education was going to go under the Romans was the manner of the death of Archimedes, the great mathematician and inventor. Roman invasion troops had little respect for geometry:

> Syracusa being taken, nothing greved Marcellus more than the losse of Archimedes, who beinge in his studie when the citie was taken, busily seeking out by him selfe the demonstracion of some Geometricall proposition which he hadde drawen in figure, and so earnestly occupied therein, as he neither sawe nor hearde any noyse of enemies that ranne uppe and downe the citie, and much lesse knewe it was taken: He wondered when he sawe a souldier by him, that bad him go with him to Marcellus. Notwithstandynge, he spoke to the souldier, and had him tary untill he had done his conclusion, and brought it to demonstracion: but the souldier being angry with his aunswer, drew out his sword and killed him.
>
> Plutarch (A.D. c. 50–125)
> *Lives*

Roman education, at least to begin with, was not, as it had been in Greece, the responsibility of the civic authorities:

> My foolish parents taught me to read and write.
> Martial (A.D. c. 40–104)
> *Epigrams:* Bk. ix, epig. 73

59

But as Rome conquered more of the known world it set up schools in all its newly acquired territories: grammar schools where the children of conquered nations had to learn Latin, an unenviable task which gave the conquerors a distinct advantage:

> The Romans would never have had time to conquer the world if they had been obliged to learn Latin first of all.
>
> Heinrich Heine (1797–1856)
> *Das Buch le Grand*

Another subject widely taught in Roman schools was the art of rhetoric, which Romans firmly believed was the highest accomplishment of a civilized man. Rhetoric had nothing to do with the creative processes or science or the pursuit of truth, it was verbal eloquence: the ability to persuade a man, or a group of men, that such-and-such was so whether it was so or not. Its study entailed practising suitable stances and gestures, voice-control and the techniques of oratory:

> The Romans taught their children nothing that was to be learned sitting.
>
> Montaigne (1533–1592)
> *Essays*

Montaigne was, he said, quoting Seneca.

When the barbarians overran the Roman Empire in the fifth century general education came to a full stop; the network of civic schools teaching Latin grammar and rhetoric was closed down and it was to be over a thousand years before the state again became responsible for educating its citizens.

There wasn't much of a cultural glimmer during the Dark Ages of the sixth and seventh centuries. The monasteries survived, but the monks were in them for inward contemplation not for intellectual pursuits. When St. Benedict founded his order in the monastery on Monte Cassino he laid down in his Rule that the monks should spend two hours a day reading holy books but no monk was to be allowed a pen or book of his own.

It was more the secular clergy who kept a thread of learning going, even though with some reluctance. The Church had to have small schools in which to train young clergy in the workings of the Church, but when the tuition began to extend to teaching a little grammar there were repercussions; Greek and Roman literature told of pagan heroes and gods:

> We are almost ashamed to refer to the fact that a report has come to us that your brotherhood is teaching grammar to certain people ... If it should be clearly proved hereafter that the report we have heard is false and that you are not devoting yourself to the vanities of worldly learning, we shall render thanks to God for keeping your

heart from defilement by the blasphemous praises of infamous men.

Pope Gregory the Great (c. 540–604)
Letter to Desiderius, Bishop of Vienne: *Epistles*, XI, 54

The Pope's wish to keep education confined to the clergy, and potential clergy, and to restrain this too study of Christian literature might have worked on the Continent, but when he sent Augustine to convert England, Augustine ran into a snag: the people of England did not speak Latin. So Augustine not only had to build churches in England, he also had to build grammar schools so that the people could understand what was going on in the churches.

This was the beginning of the Church's thousand-year monopoly of general education in Europe. Prodded into action by enlightened monarchs like Charlemagne and King Alfred the Great the Church built a network of bishop's schools and grammar schools across Europe. It has been estimated that by the Middle Ages England had four hundred Church grammar schools, teaching boys from various backgrounds, for a population of two and a half million – a far better figure than that reached in Victorian times.

The result of this domination of education by the Church was that clergymen were virtually the only people able to read and write – the words 'cleric' and 'clerk' were originally the same word – and so government and political administration was firmly in the hands of ecclesiastics.

After Charlemagne's death a different set of barbarians made life darker once again for Europe, but when they were finally overcome the Continent moved into a much more settled phase: what is now called the Middle Ages. One of the social changes at this time was the development of towns: self-contained, fortified miniature states. Town life was gregarious. It stimulated civic pride, resulting in new interest in local education and eventually in towns endowing their own schools. A widespread interest in study and learning grew and the towns provided a convenient point of focus for students to congregate round a particularly popular teacher. Three of the earliest towns to have these teaching groups were Bologna, where the speciality was law; Paris – theology; and Oxford – the liberal arts.

As most of the students came from other towns and were 'foreigners' without any civic recognition or rights they formed themselves into a kind of guild for mutual protection, electing their own authorities and dividing themselves into four groups according to nationality. As these establishments of students and teachers were made up of four 'nations' they came to be called 'universities'.

By the beginning of the thirteenth century Oxford was established as a university. In 1209 Cambridge achieved the same status. According to a contemporary chronicler this happened because of a striking display of student unity and student–master concord at the University of Oxford:

> About this time a certain clerk who was studying in Arts at Oxford slew by chance a certain woman, and, finding that she was dead, sought safety in flight. But the mayor and many others, coming to the place and finding the dead woman, began to seek the slayer in his hostel which he had hired with three other clerks his fellows; and, not finding the guilty man, they took his three fellow clerks aforesaid, who knew nothing whatsoever of the homicide, and cast them into prison; and, after a few days, at the king's bidding but in contempt of all ecclesiastical liberties, these clerks were led out from the city and hanged. Whereupon some three thousand clerks, both masters and scholars, departed from Oxford, so that not one of the whole University was left; of which scholars some pursued their study of the liberal Arts at Cambridge, and others at Reading, leaving Oxford utterly empty.
>
> Roger de Wendover (d. 1236)
Flores Historiarum

The mayor's action, if it ever happened, was an indication of the violent antipathy which frequently blew up between 'town' and 'gown'. Oxford University returned to normal strength twenty years later when there was another general-post and a large contingent of disgruntled students migrated from Paris.

Probably the most popular and influential figure in university education was Peter Abelard (1079–1142), who taught in Paris. He instituted a method of resolving theological questions by argument, by questioning everything; an innovation hardly likely to have commended itself to the Church authorities and for which he later suffered. His philosophy – 'constant questioning is the first key to wisdom. For through doubt we are led to enquiry, and by enquiry we discern the truth' – became the accepted method of dealing with burning issues for over two hundred years.

The medieval university teachers of philosophy and theology, known as the Schoolmen, went on from Abelard to subject all the scriptural writings and early commentaries to such minute scrutiny, argument and nit-picking that when a new spirit came into education one of the Schoolmen, Duns Scotus, gave his name to a new word in the English language:

> DUNCE. A dolt; a stupid person. The word is taken from *Duns* Scotus (c. 1265–1308), so called from his birthplace, Dunse, in Scotland, the learned schoolman. His followers were called Dunsers or Scotists. Tyndal says, when they saw that their hair-splitting divinity was giving way to modern theology, 'the old barking curs raged in every pulpit' against the classics and new notions, so that the name indicated an opponent to progress, to learning, and hence a dunce.
>
> Brewer's Dictionary of Phrase and Fable

It was not the custom for medieval noblemen to send their children to school. The girls were sometimes sent to a nunnery for a spell to inculcate good manners and a bit of Latin or put out to a relation; the boys were sent as servants and pages to other nobles where they were taught how to serve at table, carve, put his Lordship to bed, and other knightly skills, as well as how to play an instrument, talk, dance and control accounts. The plum situation was with a chancellor, who could not only read and write and converse in Latin and French but also fix the lad up with a place at court. One chancellor whom kind-hearted fathers must have avoided was William of Longchamp, Richard the Lionheart's odious chancellor and Bishop of Ely:

> All the sons of the nobles acted as his servants, with downcast looks, nor dared they to look upward towards the heavens unless it so happened that they were addressing him; and if they attended to anything else they were pricked with a goad, which their lord held in his hand.
>
> Roger de Hoveden (d. 1201?)
> *Cronica*

Noblemen also hired schoolmasters to give their children private tuition at home. This does not seem to have been wholly successful:

> Lorde God, howe many good and clene wittes of children, be nowe a dayes perisshed by ignorant schole maisters.
>
> Sir Thomas Elyot (1490?–1546)
> *The Boke Named the Governour*
>
> This book, a treatise on how the ruling class should be educated, was the first book on education to be written in English and not Latin. Elyot believed that future rulers should be given strenuous physical exercises as well as Plato and lessons in courtly manners.

One of the reasons for the low standard of teaching was that it was poorly paid. The English governing class was more interested in the schooling of its horses than its offspring:

> It is pitie, that commonlie more care is had, yea and that emonges verie wise men, to finde out rather a cunnyng man for their horse than a cunnyng man for their children. They say nay in worde, but they do so in deede. For, to the one they will gladlie give a stipend of 200 Crounes by year, and loth to offer to the other 200 shillings.
>
> Roger Ascham (1515–1568)
> *The Scholemaster*

Schoolmastering was not much of a job in the schools either:

> Always damned to thirst and hunger, to be choked with dust in their unswept schools (schools, shall I term them, or rather elaboratories, nay, bridewells, and houses of correction?), to wear out themselves

in fret and drudgery; to be deafened with the noise of gaping boys; and in short, to be stifled with heat and stench.

Erasmus (1466?–1536)
In Praise of Folly

'Bridewells' and 'houses of correction' were no doubt references to the tremendous beatings which pupils had to endure. Roger Ascham pointed out the folly of this traditional and pointless brutality in *The Scholemaster.* He wrote, in reference to his friend Sir Richard Sackville, 'a fond schoolmaster, before he was fullie fourtene years old, drove him with fear of beating from all love of learning'. The origin of the book was a remark made by Sir William Cecil at a dinner party: 'I have strange news brought me this morning, that divers scholars of Eton be run away from the school by fear of beating.'

The renaissance of learning crept across Europe in two waves, and under the leadership of humanists like Erasmus, Sir Thomas More and John Colet education in England began to change direction.

Although the humanists were against severe corporal punishment the word 'humanist' did not mean somebody concerned with individual human beings, or with being 'humane'; it simply meant—in those days—somebody devoted to the culture and moral philosophy of ancient Greece and Rome through the study of classical literature. The humanists were tireless in ferreting out old manuscripts, copying them and later, with the discovery of printing, publishing them.

The effect on education was considerable. To the old medieval seven liberal Arts—the Quadrivium: arithmetic, geometry, astronomy and music; and the Trivium: grammar, rhetoric and logic—was added the study of classical literature, ancient history and Greek. Great store was set on elegance of style in writing prose and poetry and the Schoolmen's logical bickering over theological points was replaced by a more philosophical approach. Corrupted medieval Latin was changed back to pure Ciceronian Latin.

One formidable result of the humanist influence was that for the next three hundred years the main concern of education was to produce gentlemen and scholars able to talk and write fluent Latin and Greek, two alien and dead languages.

The Reformation hastened another change. Village schools and many grammar schools were the property and responsibility of monasteries. In addition there were a number of schools and university colleges endowed by towns, guilds and rich men wishing to make a noticeably handsome gift to the Church. These 'public schools', like Eton, were founded and endowed for the specific purpose of providing poor boys with good education. But after the dissolution of the monasteries and the parcelling off of their properties so many schools closed down through lack of funds that the poor boys were ruthlessly elbowed out of the public schools and universities by the rich:

They were created by their founders at the first, onelie for pore men's sons, whose parents were not able to bring them up unto learning: but now they have the least benefit of them, by reason the rich do so incroch upon them. In some grammar schooles likewise, which send scholers to these universities, it is lamentable to see what briberie is used; for yet the scholer can be preferred, such briberye is made, that pore men's children are commonly shut out, and the richer sort received.

Statute 31 Elizabeth, cap. 6, 1589

Like many an Act passed to correct abuses it did not have the slightest effect.

By the end of the sixteenth century education in England had settled into a torpor from which it was not to be aroused for another two and a half centuries. Local schools taught reading, writing and arithmetic. Grammar schools added Latin. Universities, staffed entirely by more or less learned clergymen, taught theology and the classics; their concern was partly to provide an educated professional class but mainly to produce a stream of clergymen able to continue the work of the Church or, failing that, to teach.

Teaching had established itself as an underpaid, uncomfortable, underestimated profession:

The teacher's life is painfull and therefore would be pityed: it wrastles with unthankfulnesse above all measure ... Our calling creepes low and hath pain for companion.

Richard Mulcaster (1530?–1611)
Positions

Pain was also an ever-present companion to schoolboys:

I knew one [schoolmaster], who in Winter would ordinarily in a cold morning, whip his Boyes over for no other purpose than to get him-selfe a heat.

Henry Peacham (1576?–1643?)
The Compleat Gentleman

A tradition grew in university colleges of occasionally electing scholarly semi-lunatics to high office. An early eccentric was Dr. Ralph Kettell, third President of Trinity College. A contemporary wrote, 'Dr. Kettell's braine is like a Hasty-pudding, where there is Memorie, Judgemente and Phancy all stirred together – all just so jumbled together.' John Aubrey remembered him well:

He was irreconcilable to long haire; called them hairy Scalpes, and as for Perriwigges (which were then very rarely worne) he beleeved them to be the Scalpes of men cute off after they were hang'd, and so tanned and dressed for use. When he observed the Scolars haire longer than ordinary (especially if they were Scolars of the Howse) he would bring a paire of Cizers in his Muffe (which he commonly wore) and woe be to them that sate on the outside of the Table. I remember he cutt Mr. Radford's haire with the knife that chipps the bread on the Buttery Hatch ... When he scolded at the idle young boies of his colledge, he used these names, viz. Turds, Tarrarags (these were the worst sort, rude Rakills) Rascal-Jacks, Blindcinques, Scobberlotchers.

John Aubrey (1626–1697)
Brief Lives

Even Puritans occasionally behaved in an un-Puritan fashion:

Of Dr. Thomas Goodwin, when ffelow of Catherine Hall. – He was somewhat whimsycall, in a frolic pist once in old Mr. Lothian's pocket (this I suppose was before his trouble of conscience and conversion made him serious) ... He prayed with his hatt on and sitting.

Thomas Woodcock (*fl.* 1695)
Papers

Later, Dr. Thomas Goodwin, fortunately in serious mood, was one of those who stood at the bedside of the dying Oliver Cromwell.

One of the most vigorous university administrators was John Fell, D.D., Dean of Christ Church, Oxford. He was a fervent royalist and after the Restoration threw himself into restoring the college buildings and bringing the religion, education and discipline of the college up to scratch:

I do not love thee, Doctor Fell,
The reason why I cannot tell;
But this I know, and know full well,
I do not love thee, Doctor Fell.

Tom Brown (1663–1704)

It is ironic that the powerful and zealous Dr. Fell, who was also Vice-chancellor of Oxford University, Bishop of Oxford and chaplain to Charles II, should be chiefly remembered through Tom Brown's curiously durable little verse. The legend is that Dr. Fell offered to mitigate some punishment if Brown could give an extempore translation of Martial's epigram 'Non amo te, Sabidi ...' This Brown proceeded to do as 'I do not love thee, Dr. Fell ...' What is more likely is that Brown was parodying a version translated by Thomas Forde, in *Virtus Rediviva*, as 'I love thee not, Nel, but why I can't tell'. What is even more likely is that the Fell–Brown confrontation never took place at all. Brown no doubt had little love for the Doctor – he failed to get his degree and left to become one of Grub Street's most prolific and licentious hacks – but it does not ring true that the learned Dr. Fell would choose that particular epigram for translation, or that Brown would provoke matters with such a cheeky reply. But that is the story.

One Cambridge intellectual and theologian spoke out strongly against learned colleagues who cashed in on their learning:

I hate and scorn that Kestrell kind
Of bastard scholars that subordinate
The precious choice inducements of the mind
To wealth or worldly good. Adulterate
And cursèd brood! Your wit and will are born
Of th'earth and circling thither do return.

66

Profit and honour be those measures scant
Of your slight studies and endeavours vain,
And when you once have got what you did want
You leave your learning to enjoy your gain.
Your brains grow low, your bellies swell up high,
Foul sluggish fat ditts up your dullèd eye.

Henry More (1614–1687)
Minor Poems: 'Cupid's Conflicts'

One feels that Dr. More would not have approved of dons taking up high posts in industry, or going into television.

Educational theory took wing in the seventeenth century with the publication of Francis Bacon's *The Advancement of Learning*. Bacon rejected the old, other-worldly philosophies of Aristotle in favour of a more secular, practical education which used the new discoveries of science to advance knowledge, trained the intellect to think usefully and was more concerned with things than with mere words in a language.

Another theorist was John Locke, who didn't really approve of schools at all; he believed that young gentlemen should be brought up as individuals. One of his objections to schools was the interminable floggings which were considered indispensable to education:

> Beating is the worst, and therefore, the last means to be used in the correction of children ... Children learn to dance and fence without whipping; nay, arithmetic, drawing, etc., they apply themselves well enough to without beating: which would make one suspect that there is something strange, unnatural and disagreeable to that age, in the things required in grammar schools or in the methods used there, that children cannot be brought to, without the severity of the lash, and hardly with that too.

John Locke (1632–1704)
Thoughts Concerning Education

The lash was probably necessary because of the way the classics were taught, requiring the child to learn great stretches by heart and be able to repeat them parrot-fashion. One advantage of this method was that it required little skill from the teacher.

John Milton agreed with Bacon that the value of classical writings was in the information they provided; that children should be taught what the ancients had to say about morals, laws and natural history rather than be forced to learn the words and grammar and compose verses in them:

> First we do amiss to spend seven or eight years meerly in scraping together so much miserable Latine and Greek, as might be learnt otherwise easily and delightfully in one year. And that which casts our proficiency therein so much behind, is our time lost partly in too oft idle vacancies given both to Schools and Universities, partly in a preposterous exaction, forcing the empty wits of Children to compose Theams, Verses and Orations, which are the acts of ripest

67

judgment and the final work of a head fill'd by long reading and observing, with elegant maxims, and copious invention. These are not matters to be wrung from poor striplings, like blood out of the Nose.

John Milton (1608–1674)
A Tractate of Education

Milton referred to his old college, Christ's College, Cambridge, as 'a stony-hearted step-mother'.

These speculative ideas had great influence on educational theory and practically none whatever on educational practice during the century.

It was the same all over Europe. Proficiency in the Greek and Latin languages and the ability to quote from them marked a fine scholar:

Brimful of learning, see that pedant stride,
Bristling with horrid Greek, and puff'd with pride!
A thousand authors he in vain has read,
And with their maxims stuff'd his empty head;
And thinks that without Aristotle's rule,
Reason is blind, and common sense a fool!

Nicolas Boileau-Despréaux (1636–1711)

It was the sort of learning which was useless to many ordinary young men:

I remember twenty yeares since he [Sir Henry Blount] inveighed much against sending youths to the Universities ... because they learnt there to be debaucht, and that the learning that they learned there they were to unlearne againe, as a man that is buttond or laced too hard, must unbutton before he can be at his ease.

John Aubrey (1626–1697)
Brief Lives

The effect of the state of education was, according to Dean Swift, a dull and disagreeable society:

Few are qualified to shine in company, but it is in most men's power to be agreeable. The reason, therefore, why conversation runs so low at present is not the defect of understanding but pride, vanity, ill-nature, affectation, singularity, positiveness, or some other vice, the effect of bad education.

Dean Swift (1667–1745)
Thoughts on Various Subjects

An antiquarian blamed the decay of university life on the young bloods who flooded into Oxford at the Restoration. He gave the exact date at which the decay set in:

Their aime is not to live as students ought to do, viz. temperat, abstemious, and plaine and grave in apparell; but to live like gents, to keep dogs and horses, to turne their studies and coleholes into places to receive bottles, to swash it in apparell, to weare long periwigs, etc., and the theologists to ride abroad in grey coats with swords by their sides. The masters have lost their respect by being themselves scandalous and keeping company with undergraduates. Fresh nights, caroling in public halls, Christmas sports, vanished, 1661.

Anthony Wood (1632–1695)

> Wood was an unusually peevish, bad-tempered, dull man. It is a large claim, but he was possibly the most dislikeable man Oxford has so far produced.

Fifty years later further decay of learning, according to another antiquarian, coincided with the cancellation of his pancakes:

It hath been an old custom in Oxford for the scholars of all houses, on Shrove Tuesday, to go to dinner at ten clock, (at which time the little béll, called *pan-cake bell*, rings, or at least should ring, at St. Maries), ... and it was always followed in Edmund hall, as long as I have been in Oxford, till yesterday, when they went to dinner at twelve, and to supper at six, nor were there any fritters at dinner, as there used always to be. When laudable old customs alter, 'tis a sign learning dwindles.

Thomas Hearne (1678–1735)
Diary, 27 Feb. 1723

> Old scholars don't seem to have changed much down the centuries. In 1972 a Cambridge lecturer was heard to remark, after a particularly exasperating college committee-meeting, 'It is extraordinary that an all-male society should produce so many old women.'

Matters were vastly different in the American colonies. The Pilgrim Fathers who landed in Massachusetts Bay in 1620, fearful that their successors might grow up unlettered and therefore easy prey for Satan, got education off to a flying start. Within sixteen years of the founding of the Massachusetts Bay colony some eight pioneer townships had built themselves a little grammar school, and the colony had founded a college.

Perhaps a typical early colonial grammar school was the 'Free School' built in 1645 at Roxbury, then a small town outside Boston (the term Free School did not mean that tuition was provided for nothing – all but the poorest parents had to pay – but that the school provided a liberal education). The school would be for boys only but Indians were accepted. The normal practice of endowment was for the township to provide a slice of land and to build the structure of the school, also to guarantee the master's wages, but most of the income would come from the pupils – who would also be expected to contribute firewood – and from random donations made by pious townsmen of something useful and productive, like a cow or a slave.

According to a letter written about 1681 by the schoolmaster of Roxbury grammar school to the civic fathers, these schools – even in the

69

most advanced and prosperous part of the colony – were not exactly abodes of ease and luxury:

> Of inconveniences I shall instance in no other than that of the school-house, the confused and shattered and nastie posture that it is in, not fitting for to reside in; the glass broken, and thereupon very raw and cold, the floor very much broken and torn up to kindle fires, the hearth spoiled, the seats, some burnt and others out of kilter, so that one had as well nigh as goods keep school in a hog stie as in it.

> Quoted by Charles K. Dillaway
> *The Free Schoole of Roxburie*

The first university was begun in 1636 when the colony voted £400 and a piece of land towards establishing 'a schoale or colledge' for higher education. No name had been decided upon but in 1638 a young assistant pastor with a bit of money died and left half his possessions, £700 and 320 books, to the new project. In gratitude to the benevolence of the late John Harvard the community decided to name their college after him. Harvard University represents perhaps the most spectacular investment in posterity ever made by a minor cleric.

Unhampered by the English view that education was no concern of the government the Puritans of the Massachusetts colony, no doubt helped by their uncompromising zeal, led the way in colonial education, passing in 1647 an extraordinary act which demanded that all towns of fifty households in size must provide and pay an elementary schoolmaster and all towns of over a hundred families must build and maintain a grammar school capable of preparing boys for a university. Towns which failed to comply with the act were to be fined.

By the end of the seventeenth century the record of progress was impressive: most townships provided some form of community-financed education, Virginia had built the colonies' second university, College of William and Mary, and Harvard had produced the first Indian graduate – Caleb Cheeshahteaumuk, B.A.

Education in England during the eighteenth century progressed, if it could be called progress, from a state of stagnation to one of confusion and decadence.

During the Commonwealth, Parliament had set up a number of schools for the children of dissenters but had failed to endow them with enough money to keep them going in a healthy condition. James II passed a Bill permitting Catholics to build their own schools, which enabled dissenting communities to found a few more of their own, but the beginning of the eighteenth century saw general education at what was probably its lowest point ever. The Age of Enlightenment – a new interest in science, a sceptical look at anything which still smacked of medievalism – was increasingly secular in thought; the Established

Church lacked the vigour to cope with that and the increasingly virile Evangelical movement and still do something about its ailing schools. Most poor people got no education at all. Those who did were taught by wretchedly paid clerics, or by a cobbler or carpenter eking out his earnings by making use of a spare bit of his workshop:

> It is here not at all uncommon to see on doors in one continued succession, *'children educated here'*; *'shoes mended here'*; *'foreign spirituous liquors sold here'*; and *'Funerals furnished here'*.
>
> Carl Philipp Moritz (1756–1793)
> *Travels of a German in England*

To combat this state of affairs a religio-charitable organization was set up, the Society for Promoting Christian Knowledge, which embarked upon a vast scheme for building charity-schools to 'inculcate a love of industry and a fear of God in the poor'. They built over 2000 little schools throughout England and Wales in forty years, which thoroughly alarmed employers who could see their supply of cheap labour drying up.

The widespread reaction among the privileged at the unprivileged being taught to read and write was satirized in an ironic essay:

> It is manifest that in a free nation where slaves are not allowed, the surest wealth consists in a multitude of laborious poor.... To make society happy and people easy under the meanest circumstances, it is requisite that great numbers of them should be ignorant as well as poor ... A man who has had some education, may follow husbandry by choice ... but he won't make a good hireling and serve a farmer for a pitiful reward, at least he is not so fit for it as a day labourer that has always been employed about the plough and dungcart, and remembers not that ever he has lived otherwise.
>
> Bernard Mandeville (1670?–1733)
> *Essay on Charity and Charity Schools*

A few years later a philosophical writer expressed the view that 'ill-judged and improper education' – whatever that was – actually did the poor a disservice; it deprived them of a blessing in disguise:

> Ignorance is the opiate of the poor, a cordial, administered by the gracious hand of providence.
>
> Soame Jenyns (1704–1787)
> *Free Enquiry into the Nature and Origin of Evil*

> Dr. Johnson, who knew what it was to be poor, wrote 'this author and Pope perhaps never saw the miseries which they imagine thus easily to be born'.

The poor on their part also viewed education with a certain amount of suspicion, for much the same reason that some of the rich distrusted it, because it blurred social barriers: the mother of Stephen Duck, the Thresher Poet who almost became Poet Laureate, removed him from school at the age of fourteen because she was afraid that he might become 'too fine a gentleman for the family that produced him'. But

71

most of the antagonism came from farmers and manufacturers who were afraid – quite rightly, as it turned out – that educating drudges would make them unwilling to remain drudges:

> The charity school is another universal nursery of idleness: nor is it easy to conceive or invent anything more destructive to the interests and very foundation principles of a nation entirely dependent on its trade and manufactures than the giving of an education to the children of the lowest class of her people that will make them contemn those drudgeries for which they were born.
>
> Anon. 1763
> *Considerations of the Fatal Effects to a*
> *Trading Nation of the Excess of Public Charity*

Disillusion with the higher, classical education which their own sons had to endure increased among the squirearchy and the middle classes:

> Too servile a submission to the books and opinions of the ancients has spoiled many an ingenious man, and plagued the world with abundance of pedants and coxcombs.
>
> James Puckle (1677?–1724)

It is extraordinary how many boys did survive the servile submission to Greek and Latin. One such was the ingenious Mr. Puckle who wrote a very successful book called *The Club* and also invented a six-shooter revolver 'that discharges soe often and soe many bullets, and can be so quickly loaden as renders it next to impossible to carry any ship by boarding'. Mr. Puckle sought capital to advance his patent, but the public decided that the device was only capable of doing damage to shareholders.

Learning was little respected for its own sake:

> Gray says, very justly, that learning never should be encouraged, it only draws out fools from their obscurity; and you know, I have always thought a running-footman as meritorious a being as a learned man. Why is there more merit in having travelled one's eyes over so many reams of papers than in having carried one's legs over so many acres of ground?
>
> Horace Walpole (1717–1797)
> Letter to Richard Bentley, 6 May 1755

The Bentley written to was not the great scholar, which is probably just as well, but his son, the amateur artist who designed some of the Gothic features in Walpole's house, Strawberry Hill.

The teachers, it was pointed out later in the century, had little to say of any use to a society which was steadily coming to the boil:

> The tigers of wrath are wiser than the horses of instruction.
>
> William Blake (1757–1827)
> *Proverbs of Hell*

Blake had a profound contempt for the classical education offered by the universities, mixed with a contempt for the Anglican Church which controlled them. In fact he detested all organized religions. In his poem 'Jerusalem', originally in the preface to his long poem *Milton*, occurs the famous reference to the 'dark satanic mills'. Blake's long poems were allegorical almost to the point of opacity and there is good reason to believe that by the 'dark satanic mills' he meant the universities, or the churches, or both together. 'Jerusalem' is the official hymn of the Women's Institute.

A learned man's capacity for literary work gave him some chance of employment outside the Church, but it was highly competitive work; publishers paid erratically and patronage was uncertain:

Mark what ills the scholar's life assail,
Toil, envy, want, the patron, and the jail.
Samuel Johnson (1709–1784)
The Vanity of Human Wishes

But off went the well-to-do young men to their public schools to be, as they knew full well:

Lash'd into Latin by the tingling rod.
John Gay (1688–1732)
The Birth of the Squire

Flogging in public schools – which has been given as the reason for so many eighteenth- and nineteenth-century English gentlemen enjoying a little corporal punishment later in life, 'le vice Anglais' – continued to be the classics master's teaching-aid throughout the century. Although Dr. Johnson noticed, without much satisfaction, a slight weakening in the tradition:

There is now less flogging in our great schools than formerly, but then less is learned there; so that what the boys get at one end they lose at the other.
Samuel Johnson (1709–1784)
Boswell's *Life*

The tradition had recovered its strength by the time Charles Lamb attended Christ's Hospital, the Blue Coat School, in the 1780s. Lamb seems to have enjoyed his schooldays, but the picture he painted of the discipline at Christ's Hospital was fairly hair-raising. On his first day there, aged seven, he met a boy in fetters – the punishment for running away. The second time a boy ran away he was put into a dungeon with straw and a blanket, and fed on bread and water. For a third attempt the boy was flogged and expelled:

The scourging was, after the old Roman fashion, long and stately. The lictor accompanied the criminal quite round the hall. We were generally too faint with attending to the previous disgusting circumstances, to make accurate report with our eyes of the degree of corporal suffering inflicted. Report, of course, gave out the back knotty and livid ...
    J.B. had a heavy hand. I have known him double his knotty fist at a poor trembling child (the maternal milk hardly dry upon its lips) with a 'Sirrah, do you presume to set your wits at me?' – Nothing was more common than to see him make a headlong entry into the

73

schoolroom, from his inner recess, or library, and, with turbulent eye, singling out a lad, roar out, 'Od's my life, Sirrah' (his favourite adjuration), 'I have a great mind to whip you,'—then, with as sudden a retractive impulse, fling back into his lair—and, after a cooling lapse of some minutes (during which all but the culprit had totally forgotten the context) drive headlong out again, piecing out his imperfect sense, as if it had been some Devil's Litany, with the expletory yell— *'and I WILL too.'* ...

Perhaps we cannot dismiss him better than with the pious ejaculation of C. [Coleridge]—when he heard that his old master was on his death-bed—'Poor J.B.!—may all his faults be forgiven; and may he be wafted to bliss by little cherub boys, all head and wings, with no *bottoms* to reproach his sublunary infirmities.'

Charles Lamb (1775–1834)
Christ's Hospital Five and Thirty Years Ago

The food was badly prepared and meagre. Coleridge, undernourished, went down with severe attacks of jaundice and rheumatic fever. The heavy-handed 'J.B.' was John Boyer—or Bowyer—a notorious flogger but also, as was so often the case, a good classics scholar.

The 'great schools' were uncomfortable, freezing cold in winter and noisy; it was usual for the large halls to have a number of classes going on at the same time. At night the boys were put into dormitories, often several to a bed, and locked in, unsupervised, for the night:

Public schools are the nurseries of all vice and immorality.

Henry Fielding (1707–1754)
Joseph Andrews

To tough, extravert boys it was probably not too awful a life; home life at that time could be equally brutal, and enterprising lads found time and opportunities to pursue their own interests. Like the boy Hanger, who was at Eton in the 1760s:

From the moment I came into the *fifth form*, I studied everything but my book ... At that early period I had a most decided preference for female society, and passed as much time in the company of women as I have ever done since.

A carpenter's wife was the first object of my early affections; nor can I well express the nature of my obligations to her. Frequently have I risked breaking my neck in getting over the roof of my boarding house at night, to pass a few hours with some favourite grizette of Windsor. During the latter part of my time at Eton, to *perfect my education*, I became attached to, and was very much enamoured of, the daughter of a vendor of cabbages.

George Hanger, fourth Baron Coleraine (1751?–1824)
The Life, Adventures, and Opinions of Col. George Hanger

The boy Hanger fulfilled in later life the expectancies aroused by his school career. He served as a major in the American War of Independence, returned to England wounded, was imprisoned in the King's Bench prison for debt, inherited his title from a brother, refused to use it and became a coal-merchant. He was a crony of the Prince Regent.

The great schools must have been a terrifying prospect to the parents of a gentle, shy boy:

> Placing him at a public school is forcing an owl upon day.
> Samuel Johnson (1709–1784)
> Boswell's *Life*

Towards the end of the century the poet William Cowper was so upset by the general decadence of public schools, their opportunities for boys to go astray in various directions, and the almost total lack of religious instruction, that he wrote a powerful poem warning parents what lay ahead of their lad when they packed him off to school:

> There shall he learn, ere sixteen winters old
> That authors are more useful, pawned or sold;
> That pedantry is all that schools impart,
> But taverns teach the knowledge of the heart;
> There waiter Dick, with Bacchanalian lays,
> Shall win his heart and have his drunken praise,
> His counsellor and bosom-friend shall prove,
> And some street-pacing harlot his first love.
> William Cowper (1731–1800)
> *Tirocinium or A Review of Schools*

Lads like the boy Hanger might well have looked forward to leaving school and going to a university, secure in the knowledge that the physical, bawdy life they had enjoyed at school would be even more enjoyable in the easy-going world of Oxford or Cambridge:

> To Eaton sent, o'er every Form you leapt,
> No studious Eves, no toilsome Mattins kept,
> Thence Christ's Quadrangle took you for its own;
> Had Alma Mater e'er so true a Son!
> Half seven Years spent in Billiards, Cards and Tippling,
> And growing every day a lovelier stripling;
> With half a College Education got,
> Half Clown, half Prig, half Pedant and half Sot.
> James Miller (1706–1744)
> *On Politeness*

For Thomas Gray, frail and nervous, going up from Eton to Cambridge was another matter. After a pleasant time at Eton beavering away at Latin and Greek with his friends Richard West and Horace Walpole he found Peterhouse, Cambridge, where mathematics and philosophy were taught, repugnant. He called it 'a country flowing with syllogisms and ale' and he was totally out of key with the whoring, drinking and riding to hounds which most of his fellow-students preferred to working. He wrote to West, who was at Oxford:

> Surely it was of this place, now Cambridge but formerly known by the name of Babylon, that the prophet spoke when he said, 'the wild beasts of the desert shall dwell there, and their houses shall be full

75

of doleful creatures, and owls shall build there, and satyrs shall dance there.'

Thomas Gray (1716–1771)
Letter to Richard West, Dec. 1736

West replied, 'Oxford, I can assure you, has her owls that match yours.'

Six years later Gray returned to live for a while at Pembroke College, Cambridge, describing something of what he felt about the place in a poem:

> Hail, horrors, hail! ye ever gloomy bowers,
> Ye gothic fanes, and antiquated towers
> Where rushy Camus' slowly winding flood
> Perpetual draws his humid train of mud.

Thomas Gray (1716–1771)
Hymn to Ignorance

Although individual colleges varied, Oxford had always been the centre of resistance to change, pro High Church and pro the Divine Right of Kings, while Cambridge had been the centre of reformation and dissension. As Macaulay wrote of the fiery period in the brief reign of the Catholic queen, Mary, 'Cambridge had the honour of educating those celebrated Protestant bishops whom Oxford had the honour of burning.' Oxford was Jacobite and Cambridge was the heart of intellectual puritanism. During the Civil Wars Oxford became a royalist headquarters and Cambridge was occupied by Parliamentarians. Educationally, Oxford stuck to theology and the classics, Cambridge led in mathematics, rather old-fashioned philosophy and science.

When the last Stuart departed, the close link between Oxford and the monarchy was broken and Cambridge came in for a crack of the whip. In 1714 George I, under advice from the Whig Lord Townshend, presented the extremely important library amassed by the Bishop of Ely to Cambridge, at the same time dispatching a garrison of troops to Oxford:

> The king, observing with judicious eyes,
> The state of both his universities,
> To one he sends a regiment: For why?
> That learned body wanted loyalty.
> To th'other books he gave, as well discerning
> How much that loyal body wanted learning.

Anon.

The epigram has been attributed to both Joseph Trapp (1679–1747) and Thomas Warton (1688?–1745). Warton succeeded Trapp as professor of poetry at Oxford. Both were High Church Tories. Trapp might have a slight edge, having been quoted as the author in Nichols's *Literary Anecdotes*.

The epigram was answered by another from a staunch Cambridge

Whig, a brilliant but eccentric physician who went about bearing a spy-glass and a muff:

> The King to Oxford sent a troop of horse,
> For Tories own no argument but force:
> With equal skill to Cambridge books he sent,
> For Whigs admit no force but argument.
>
> Sir William Browne (1692–1774)

Higher education based upon a thorough knowledge of Greek and Latin was irrelevant enough to the rising middle classes of England about to make their careers as bankers, merchants and farm-managers, but it was even more irrelevant to American Indians.

By 1744 the American colonies had three degree-awarding colleges, Harvard, William and Mary, and Yale. These were based on English university colleges, teaching young gentlemen Greek and Latin grammar, rhetoric, mathematics and philosophy. In June 1744, after the commissioners of Maryland and Virginia had negotiated a treaty with the Indians of the Six Nations at Lancaster, Pennsylvania, they cordially invited them to send some of their sons to William and Mary College to enjoy the benefits of a classical education.

The Indians considered the invitation. This was their reply:

> We know that you highly esteem the kind of Learning taught in those Colleges, and that the Maintenance of our young Men, while with you, would be very expensive to you. We are convinc'd, therefore, that you mean to do us Good by your Proposal; and we thank you heartily. But you, who are wise, must know that different Nations have different Conceptions of things; and you will therefore not take it amiss, if our Ideas of this kind of Education happen not to be the same with yours. We have had some Experience of it. Several of our young People were formerly brought up at the Colleges of the Northern Provinces; they were instructed in all your Sciences; but, when they came back to us, they were bad Runners, ignorant of every means of living in the Woods, unable to bear either Cold or Hunger, knew neither how to build a Cabin, take a Deer, or kill an Enemy, spoke our Language imperfectly, were therefore neither fit for Hunters, Warriors, nor Counsellors, they were totally good for nothing. We are, however, not the less oblig'd by your kind Offer, tho' we decline accepting it; and, to show our grateful Sense of it, if the Gentlemen of Virginia will send us a Dozen of their Sons, we will take Care of their Education, instruct them in all we know, and make Men of them.
>
> Quoted in *Biography and History of the Indians of North America*
> Ed. Samuel G. Drake. Boston. Second edition, 1834

> Nevertheless one cannot help feeling that this splendid retort was more likely to have been penned by one of their educated though effete graduates from the Northern Provinces rather than by a fleet-of-foot, cold warrior.

William Cooke recorded in *Memoirs of Samuel Foote Esq.* that the story of the Indians and William and Mary College was a great favourite with Benjamin Franklin, who told it frequently at dinner parties during the years he was in London. This is understandable because the story illustrated one of Franklin's preoccupations, the need for a system of schools which gave some sort of practical training to colonial boys.

The trouble was that education, which had been given such a promising start by the strongly Calvinistic New England colony, was beginning to fall apart by the middle of the eighteenth century. This was for three reasons; frontier towns were too far away to be bothered with regulations from some central colonial authority, all the various sects and denominations wanted to start their own schools teaching their own brand of religion, and the English-style of classical secondary education based on the intellectual requirements of clergymen was totally unsuited to rearing manufacturers, farmers and frontiersmen.

The result was the rise during the century of a number of private 'academies' – the old British word, borrowed from Milton, for dissenters' schools. These establishments, founded by Benjamin Franklin amongst others, broke away from state control to become either privately owned by the headmaster, or controlled by a church or a group of citizens who differed as to religion but agreed as to the need for education in their neighbourhood. By the time of the War of Independence these academies were at least trying to offer middle class children a form of education which would fit them for their task of becoming leading citizens. Not always, it seems, with much success:

> They (academies) commit their pupils to the theatre of the world, with just taste enough of learning to be alienated from industrious pursuits, and not enough to do service in the ranks of science.
>
> Thomas Jefferson (1743–1826)
> *Writings*

But it was a start. As in England, very few poor children were lucky enough to get any education at all.

A large proportion of the student population of Britain's universities did not bother to take degrees; they were only there, as it were, for the ride. Taking a degree at Oxford did not appear to have been too severe an ordeal in 1770:

> I was examined in Hebrew and History: 'What is the Hebrew for the Place of a Skull?' said the Examiner. 'Golgotha,' I replied. 'Who founded University College?' I answered 'King Alfred'. 'Very well, sir,' said the Examiner, 'then you are competent for your degree.'
>
> Lord Eldon (1751–1838)
> Quoted in Woodforde's *Diary of a Country Parson*

Nor, it seems, did becoming a professor require much in the way of qualifications:

> What do you think of being Greek Professor at one of our Universities? It is a very pretty sinecure, and requires very little knowledge (much less than, I hope, you have already) of that language.
>
> Lord Chesterfield (1694–1773)
Letters, 15 Jan. 1748

There must have been earnest scholars quietly working away in college garrets and sober, conscientious tutors. But there were many of the other kind:

> Dr. J - - k - - n was Fellow of Magdalen in Oxford, and went frequently to Abington, a market-town 5 miles off; was a good customer to the landlady at the Red-Lion, and brought others that spent their money freely. But, as time went on, he was pretty deep in her debt, and she by dunning him made the debt a matter of talk. In this state of resentment, on his part, for the publication of his slackness of pay, he went to Abington one day, resolved to pay the debt. The landlady was gone out to a lying-in visit, in her best clothes, and had left her common apparel in a chamber adjoining to the dining-room. J——n saw them, dressed himself in them, and then opened a sash-window and stood shewing his bare backside at the window to all the town, who took it and reported it to be the landlady's.
>
> From a Common-Place Book is kept by Charles Phelps, Vicar of South Lynn, 1757

Adam Smith, the first man to make a study of political economy, went to school in Scotland. At that time education was flourishing in Scotland – they had four universities to England's two – but Smith won an exhibition to Balliol College, Oxford, turning up on horseback in June 1740. Thirty-six years later he wrote his famous description of an English university:

> A sanctuary in which exploded systems and obsolete prejudices find shelter and protection after they have been hunted out of every corner of the world.
>
> Adam Smith (1723–1790)
Wealth of Nations

A critical description of eighteenth-century Oxford University, educationally moribund, a comfortable club for sleepy clergymen, came from Edward Gibbon, the historian:

> To the university of Oxford I acknowledge no obligation; and she will as cheerfully renounce me for a son, as I am willing to disclaim her for a mother. I spent fourteen months at Magdalen College; they proved the fourteen months the most idle and unprofitable of my whole life: the reader will pronounce between the school and the scholar; but I cannot affect to believe that nature had disqualified me for all literary pursuits ... The fellows or monks of my time were decent easy men, who supinely enjoyed the gifts of their founder;

their days were filled by a series of uniform employments; the chapel and the hall, the coffee-house and the common room, till they retired, weary and well satisfied, to a long slumber. From the toil of reading, or thinking, or writing, they had absolved their conscience; and the first shoots of learning and ingenuity withered on the ground, without yielding any fruits to the owners or the public. As a gentleman commoner, I was admitted to the society of the fellows, and fondly expected that some questions of literature would be the amusing and instructive topics of their discourse. Their conversation stagnated in a round of college business, Tory politics, personal anecdotes, and private scandal: their dull and deep potations excused the brisk intemperance of youth; and their constitutional toasts were not expressive of the most lively loyalty for the house of Hanover.

Edward Gibbon (1737–1794)
Memoirs of my Life

At St. John's College, Cambridge, William Wordsworth, happy at being neglected by his teachers, quietly got on with reading what he wanted to read. He thought the services in chapel a 'mockery' and the dons quaint old 'humorists':

Men unscoured, grotesque
In character, tricked out like aged trees.

William Wordsworth (1770–1850)
The Prelude

The end of the eighteenth century brought profound changes to the educational systems of most European countries. The French revolutionaries abolished universities in France, Napoleon set up a French university rather like an army, entirely under his control, and French education became the concern of the state. Prussia too took education under state control and organized it extremely efficiently. Nothing at all happened to English education.

The trouble with education in England was that nobody bothered much about it; it didn't seem to be important. Workers learnt their jobs by being told what to do and gradually getting better at it. Most firms were still small and were managed by their owners. Being able to read the Bible was all that most poor people ever managed to achieve and as late as 1841 a third of the men and a half of the women who signed the parish register at their wedding made a mark because they could not write.

One or two abortive efforts were made on behalf of the working classes. A string of Mechanics Institutes were built in manufacturing towns to provide classes to teach industrial workers the scientific basis of their labours. These failed because the workers couldn't understand what the teachers were talking about: the Institutes were then used as lecture halls where little improving talks were given.

The ruling class sent its boys to a 'good school' and then up to a university for a year or so of congenial company and a little tuition in the classics because it was the normal thing to do, not because there was any particular advantage any more in being able to speak a dead language:

> Don't quote Latin; say what you have to say, and then sit down.
> Arthur Wellesley, Duke of Wellington (1769–1852)
> His advice to a new member of Parliament

The beginning of the nineteenth century was a jittery period politically. The Napoleonic wars were alarming England, there was a strong whiff of revolution – or, almost as unwelcome, reform – in the air which caused the forces of reaction to close ranks. Those in command called the times 'seditious'; those who were commanded called them 'oppressive'. The last thing the nation's leaders wanted at that time was an educated rank-and-file:

> Attending a Cabinet when there was a tendency to Mutiny in the Fleet, Sir Thomas Troubridge, who was afterwards lost, I think, in the London in his way to the Cape or the East Indies, and who was a most excellent Officer, was asked his opinion what was best to be done. He said let me hang a hundred Lawyers, and we shall hear no more of the business. I asked what he could mean – what were these People that he called Lawyers. He replied, Fellows that can read and write. They are the Fellows, that I call Lawyers, and make the whole of the Mischief.
> Lord Eldon (1751–1838)
> *Lord Eldon's Anecdote Book*

> Lord Eldon, after having so brilliantly passed his degree examination, had risen in law to become Lord Chancellor. Sir Thomas Troubridge was Lord of the Admiralty.

In the new democratic republic of the United States it was a different story; an educated rank-and-file was precisely what the authorities *did* want.

Reformers, like Horace Mann, took the view that if a single nation was to be created out of a mixed bag of religious sectarians and European immigrants, the way to start was to make sure that every boy and girl went free to an elementary school and there absorbed a common language and culture.

This was a vastly unpopular idea to a great many citizens who were comfortably entrenched in their old colonial traditions. The schools would have to be paid for by local taxation, and many rich people objected to being made to pay for the education of other people's children. Even more violent opposition came from the various religious bodies. The reformers saw that a system of state-controlled Common Schools could not possibly give religious instruction in all the denominational points of view, e.g. Roman Catholic, Quaker, Baptist, Con-

81

gregationalist, Calvinist, and so must give no religious instruction at all. State schools were to be secular.

The debate was fierce during the whole of the first half of the century but steady progress was made, state after state passing the necessary legislation, and a network of free Common Schools began to grow, teaching not only the three R's but also English grammar, geography, history, and sometimes book-keeping and music. By 1860 most states had public schools and over half the nation's boys and girls were getting some formal education.

The next move was to provide state secondary education. Private education in academies and universities controlled by religious bodies was richly endowed and firmly defended but gradually an alternative free secondary education became available in public high schools. And the ultimate aim of a complete universal education provided free by the state became a reality when the first state universities were established. By the time of the Civil War twenty states had their own universities.

An odd and very American phenomenon was the success of the lyceum movement in the pre-Civil War period. Lyceums were small local associations who rented a hall and listened to a hired lecturer talking on some improving topic; a kind of adult Further Education. Lyceums were originally formed, in 1826, as an American version of the British system of Mechanics' Institutes but, perhaps because ambition flourished more strongly in the republic, or there were more working-class men anxious to move up into the lower-middle class, they rapidly outstripped their British counterpart. Within a few years the lyceum movement had spread across the nation. It enjoyed some thirty-five fruitful years until the Civil War, after which education gave way to entertainment and the lecturers on Science and Morality were replaced by Swiss bell-ringers and humorists such as Artemus Ward and Petroleum Nasby.

In their heyday lyceums were a valuable source of extra money for authors and essayists, some – like Ralph Waldo Emerson, 'the lyceum is my pulpit' – earning almost their entire income from lecture tours. Most of Emerson's essays began life as lyceum lectures, being passed over to the printer for publication when they became too familiar to the circuit.

Other star lyceum lecturers were Horace Greeley, Horace Mann – who used the platform to campaign for free Common Schools – William Makepeace Thackeray and Oliver Wendell Holmes, although Professor Holmes was not too happy in his work:

> A lecturer is a literary strumpet, subject for a greater than whore's fee to prostitute himself.
>
> Oliver Wendell Holmes (1809–1894)
> Remark made to Herman Melville

Perhaps the beginning of educational reform in Britain can be dated from the day in 1833 when an almost empty House of Commons passed a resolution granting the educational charities a sum of £20,000 to help them build new primary schools. This was the first time in history that the state had involved itself in education.

The reforms which began to take effect in grammar-school and public-school education were wide and lasting, reflecting the vast changes in social and economic life brought about by industrial wealth and the rise of the British Empire. But the state was not involved.

The aristocratic upper class continued to send its sons to Eton, Harrow or one of the ancient endowed schools, and then up to a university. It was an education in the classics; unproductive knowledge which was worn, as a mandarin wore long finger-nails, as a symbol of status.

The upper middle class, many of them rich industrialists and entrepreneurs, wanted their sons to have the same education as the upper class so that, impelled by the wealth behind them, they could rise to any heights of the social ladder. This demand led to the foundation of a number of new public schools, e.g. Cheltenham College (1841), Marlborough College (1843), run as profit-making concerns and usually called 'college' in imitation of the ancient Winchester College (1382) and Eton College (1440).

The most influential of these new public schools was Rugby which, under Thomas Arnold, became the model for the great Victorian public school tradition. Arnold laid down the aims of a public school in order of priority: 'What we must look for here is, 1st, religious and moral principles: 2ndly, gentlemanly conduct: 3rdly, intellectual ability.'

He was the product of an English public school and university ...
He had little education and highly developed muscles – that is to say, he was no scholar, but essentially a gentleman.
Henry Seton Merriman (1862–1903)
The Sowers

The new public schools stressed the School Spirit and encouraged inter-school and inter-House rivalry. They also adopted traditions from the older schools; like the system of fagging:

When Lord Holland was a schoolboy, he was forced, as a fag, to toast bread *with his fingers* for the breakfast of another boy. Lord H's mother sent him a toasting-fork. His fagger broke it over his head, and still compelled him to prepare the toast in the old way. In consequence of this process his fingers suffered so much that they always retained a withered appearance.

Samuel Rogers (1763–1855)
Recollections of the Table-Talk of Samuel Rogers

And appointing senior boys as monitors to supervise the behaviour of the juniors:

The oppressions of these young brutes are heart-sickening to call to recollection. I have been called out of my bed, and *waked for the purpose*, in the coldest winter nights – and this not once, but night after night – in my shirt, to receive the discipline of a leathern thong, with eleven other sufferers, because it pleased my callow overseer.

Charles Lamb (1775–1834)
Christ's Hospital Five and Thirty Years Ago

These practices were approved of as being character-forming:

Torture in a public school is as much licensed as the knout in Russia.

William Makepeace Thackeray (1811–1863)
Vanity Fair

The public schools attached great importance to organized games and sport. It was felt that hurtling about a muddy field and kicking or hitting a ball produced a healthier boy and therefore a manlier man:

There is a manliness in the athletic exercises of public schools which is as seductive to the imagination as it is utterly unimportant in itself. Of what importance is it in after-life whether a boy can play well or ill at cricket, or row a boat with the skill and precision of a waterman? If our young lords and esquires were hereafter to wrestle together in public, or the gentlemen of the Bar to exhibit Olympic games in Hilary Term, the glory attached to these exercises at public schools would be rational and important. But of what use is the body of an athlete when we have good laws over our heads, or when a pistol, a postchaise, or a porter can be hired for a few shillings? A gentleman does nothing but ride or walk; and yet such a ridiculous stress is laid upon the manliness of the exercises customary at public schools – exercises in which the greatest blockheads commonly excel the most – which often render habits of idleness inveterate, and often lead to foolish expense and dissipation at a more advanced period of life.

Sydney Smith (1771–1845)

Inter-school competitions and matches were inaugurated. Fierce rivalries developed. Some schools were more concerned with the progress of their First Elevens and Fifteens than with their academic standards. Their claim to distinction as a public school lay:

With the flannelled fools at the wicket or the muddied oafs at the goals.

Rudyard Kipling (1865–1936)
The Islanders

Compulsory games were fine for athletic boys gifted with good muscular coordination, but they were periods of extended humiliation for aesthetic lads whose hands and feet were not entirely under control:

Oh! those interminable hours when I stood fielding, never being allowed to bowl a single 'over' and finally when my innings came round, always out for nothing! I well remember—but this was in the Big School, after I had missed a catch at 'long-leg'—saying to myself in bitter degradation and complete misery:
'O Lord take away my life, for I am not worthy to live!'
It is that cricket-field that in all the sharp and bitter moments of life as they come to me now, gives me a sense of wholesome proportion: 'At least I am not playing cricket!' I can say to myself and, on the strength of that, become like the much-enduring Ulysses.

John Cowper Powys (1872–1963)
Autobiography

The new public schools continued to teach the classics, but they added a few more useful subjects to the curriculum, such as Modern History:

The very ink with which all history is written is merely fluid prejudice.

Mark Twain (1835–1910)
Following the Equator

Or, expressed more epigrammatically:

History is bunk.
Henry Ford (1863–1947)

Henry Ford, the great pioneer of motor-car construction, came out with his remark during a court case in June 1919.

The increasing demand for books about history brought a new creature into existence, the professional historian:

HISTORIAN: An unsuccessful novelist.
H. L. Mencken (1880–1956)

History repeats itself; historians repeat each other.
Philip Guedalla (1889–1944)

Guedalla was a successful biographer and non-repetitive historian.

It has been said that though God cannot alter the past, historians can; it is perhaps because they can be useful to Him in this respect that He tolerates their existence.

Samuel Butler (1835–1902)
Erewhon Revisited

Another subject which came to be taught regularly in public schools was Modern Languages:

Life is too short to learn German.

Thomas Love Peacock (1785–1866)

It is good to be on your guard against an Englishman who speaks French perfectly; he is very likely to be a card-sharper or an attaché in the diplomatic service.

W. Somerset Maugham (1874–1966)

Mathematics was more widely taught:

Mathematics may be defined as the subject in which we never know what we are talking about, nor whether what we are saying is true.

Bertrand Russell (1872–1969)
Mysticism and Logic

That arithmetic is the basest of all mental activities is proved by the fact that it is the only one that can be accomplished by a machine.

Arthur Schopenhauer (1788–1860)

The first machine capable of doing sums was patented by Blaise Pascal, the French theologian and mathematician, in 1647.

The lower middle classes could not afford to send their boys away to a public boarding-school, and didn't want to anyway. They were not looking for a classical education which would lead to university but a useful education which would help their sons to get on. To meet this widespread need a number of fee-paying day schools, at grammar-school level, were opened, mainly by civic authorities and philanthropists. Some of these, like the City of London School and Liverpool College, soon achieved public-school status.

One innovation introduced by these schools was the study of the English language and English literature, first taught by the Rev. Edwin Abbott at the City of London School in 1866. Earlier, many parents would not have approved:

My children shall be carefully warned against literature. To fence, to swim, to speak French, are the most they shall learn.

Walter Savage Landor (1774–1865)
Letter to Robert Southey, 1825

English Literature was not a subject for study at Oxford University until 1895.

A curious black-spot in education, which argued strongly for some kind of government control, was the existence of a number of very cheap and extremely dubious private boarding-schools. For some reason they were centred in Yorkshire. These establishments, which operated what amounted to a kind of advanced baby-farming, had been in existence for at least a hundred years before Charles Dickens exposed them in *Nicholas Nickleby*:

Of the monstrous neglect of education in England, and the disregard of it by the State as a means of forming good or bad citizens, and miserable or happy men, [private] schools long afforded a notable example. Although any man who had proved his unfitness for any other occupation in life, was free, without examination or qualification, to open a school anywhere; although preparation for the functions he undertook, was required in the surgeon who assisted to bring a boy into the world, or might one day assist, perhaps, to send him out of it; in the chemist, the attorney, the butcher, the baker, the candlestick maker; the whole round of crafts and trades, the schoolmaster excepted; and although schoolmasters, as a race, were the blockheads and impostors that might naturally be expected to spring from such a state of things, and to flourish in it; these Yorkshire schoolmasters were the lowest and most rotten round in the whole ladder. Traders in the avarice, indifference, or imbecility of parents, and the helplessness of children; ignorant, sordid, brutal men, to whom few considerate persons would have entrusted the board and lodging of a horse or a dog; they formed the worthy cornerstone of a structure, which, for absurdity and a magnificent high-minded laissez-aller neglect, has rarely been exceeded in the world.

We hear sometimes of an action for damages against the unqualified medical practitioner, who has deformed a broken limb in pretending to heal it. But, what of the hundreds of thousands of minds that have been deformed for ever by the incapable pettifoggers who have pretended to form them!

Charles Dickens (1812–1870)
Preface: *Nicholas Nickleby*

The monopoly of university education in England which Oxford and Cambridge had enjoyed for centuries was given a jolt in 1828 when University College, London, was opened. This was a private-enterprise project, totally middle class in its aim to provide education in practical subjects not taught at Oxford or Cambridge:

A humbug joint-stock subscription school for Cockney boys, without the power of granting degrees or affording honours or distinctions, got up in the bubble season.

John Bull, 7 May 1827

University College did not propose to give religious instruction. This earned it various epithets, such as 'the God-less institution of Gower Street' and 'the radical infidel College', and stirred non-radical churchgoers to promote a rival, Christian college, which was opened in the Strand as King's College in 1831. Both colleges were desperately short of money, but in 1836 they were incorporated and given a charter as the 'University of London'.

One of the subjects which University College taught was Science, for which it was able to award the new degree of B.Sc. The study of physics, chemistry, metallurgy and such was vital to a country whose wealth came from manufacturing, but the importance of science was seldom acknowledged by poets:

Knowledge is not happiness, and science
But an exchange of ignorance for that
Which is another kind of ignorance.

Lord Byron (1788–1824)
Manfred

Its sudden new importance to mankind struck a chill:

Alas! can we ring the bells backward? Can we unlearn the arts that pretend to civilize, and then burn the world? There is a march of science; but who shall beat the drums for its retreat?

Charles Lamb (1775–1834)

It was only in 1840 that a name was given to a man of science. William Whewell, Master of Trinity College, Cambridge, wrote, 'We need very much to describe a cultivator of science in general. I should incline to call him a scientist.'

The development of thinking in scientific terms, of rational cause and effect based on verifiable data, gained ground during the century. Taken to its extreme it made it difficult for one distinguished mathematician and astrophysicist to walk through a doorway:

I am standing on the threshold about to enter a room. It is a complicated business. In the first place I must shove against an atmosphere pressing with a force of fourteen pounds on every square inch of my body. I must make sure of landing on a plank travelling at twenty miles a second round the sun—a fraction of a second too early or too late, the plank would be miles away. I must do this whilst hanging from a round planet head outward into space, and with a wind of aether blowing at no one knows how many miles a second through every interstice of my body. The plank has no solidity of substance. To step on it is like stepping on a swarm of flies. Shall I not slip through? No, if I make the venture one of the flies hits me and gives a boost up again; I fall again and am knocked upwards by another fly; and so on. I may hope that the net result will be that I remain about steady; but if unfortunately I should slip through the floor or be boosted too violently up to the ceiling, the occurrence would be, not a violation of the laws of Nature, but a rare coincidence. These are some of the minor difficulties. I ought really to look at the problem four-dimensionally as concerning the intersection of my world-line with that of the plank. Then again it is necessary to determine in which direction the entropy of the world is increasing in order to make sure that my passage over the threshold is an entrance, not an exit.

Verily, it is easier for a camel to pass through the eye of a needle than for a scientific man to pass through a door.

Sir Arthur Eddington (1882–1944)
The Nature of the Physical World

Following close behind London came a widespread programme of university building: the 'red-brick' universities of the provinces.

First in the field was Durham. Durham University was built in 1833 by the Cathedral chapter, mainly to divert the reformers' attention from the embarrassingly enormous fortune which the See had acquired through its coalfields. The 'golden canons', reputed to have enjoyed £10,000 a year, divided up most of the professorships amongst themselves.

The first of the many civic universities grew from Owens College, Manchester. This was followed by others at Newcastle, Leeds, Bristol, Sheffield, Birmingham and Liverpool; they were usually founded by the city and endowed by local industrialists to provide a higher education in subjects relevant to the needs of local industry.

D. H. Lawrence was moved to verse when he realized that a new university, Nottingham, had been endowed by the founder of Boots the Cash Chemists:

In Nottingham, that dismal town
where I went to school and college,
they've built a new university
for a new dispensation of knowledge.

Built it most grand and cakeily
out of the noble loot
derived from shrewd cash-chemistry
by good Sir Jesse Boot.

Little I thought, when I was a lad
and turned in modest penny
over on Boot's Cash Chemist's counter,
that Jesse, by turning many

millions of similar honest pence
over, would make a pile
that would rise at last and blossom out
in grand and cakey style

into a university
where smart men would dispense
doses of smart cash-chemistry
in language of common-sense!

That future Nottingham lads would be
cash-chemically B.Sc.
that Nottingham lights would rise and say:
— By Boots I am M.A.

From this I learn, though I knew it before
that culture has her roots
in the deep dung of cash, and lore
is a last offshoot of Boots.

D. H. Lawrence (1885–1930)
Nottingham's New University

The education of middle-class girls was haphazard. A few went to girls' boarding-schools where they were miserable and badly instructed. Most stayed at home and were taught genteel accomplishments and a little reading and writing by governesses, who were untrained and frequently ladylike but semi-illiterate. In 1846 a Benevolent Association was founded to train girls into becoming efficient governesses, but the standard of teaching at girls' schools was so bad that none of the applicants could pass the entrance examination. The next step was to start from scratch and set up special training classes. Two of the early pupils were to become the great pioneers of feminine education, Miss Buss and Miss Beale.

Miss Buss was appointed headmistress of the North London Collegiate School in 1850, and Miss Beale became Head of Cheltenham College for Young Ladies in 1858 (narrowly missing being appointed to a Diocesan Penitentiary at Highgate). Miss Beale avoided the word 'mistress', with its unfortunate overtones, and labelled her staff House Ladies and Class Teachers. This had the effect of demoting them socially: a 'teacher' was an instructor in elementary schools with no social status while a 'school-master' – a word insisted on by Dr. Arnold – was usually a clergyman and was accepted as a 'gentleman'.

The girls were brought up in the strictest propriety. They were chaperoned when they had to attend examinations in public halls and unceasing vigilance was maintained by the Heads. Stirrings of the flesh were not countenanced at North London Collegiate and Cheltenham:

> Miss Buss and Miss Beale
> Cupid's darts do not feel.
> Oh, how different from us
> Are Miss Beale and Miss Buss.
>
> Anon. pupil

The new girls' boarding-schools were modelled on the boys' schools, with the addition of a few feminine items like needlework and dancing.

Just as much emphasis was put on team-spirit, sport and the Honour of the House; even well into this century:

> The use of physical force not being favoured in girls' schools, I got away with my observations about the House with a whole skin, but that was about all that did come undamaged through this expensive potting shed of the English Rose.
>
> E. Arnot Robertson (1903–1963)
> *The Old School*, Ed. Graham Greene: 'Sherborne'

Educational reforms finally reached the teeming millions of illiterates, the working classes labouring in the fields and in the factory towns. Money was available from pious philanthropists and although there were misgivings – some employers were worried that a knowledge of arithmetic would only result in the lower classes querying their wages – it was generally agreed that something should be done. The poor, too, wanted something to be done, which was a change of attitude perhaps due to their experience of trying to understand what was going on during the Reform Bill and Chartist agitations of the 1830s and 1840s. The man who probably did more than anybody else to lay the foundations of a good elementary-school system was a civil servant, Dr. J. P. Kay, who was the chairman of a committee appointed by the Privy Council to watch what was happening to the grant which the government had made to help the charities. Dr. Kay, inspired by continental practices, instituted a teacher-training scheme, a system of apprenticeship for teachers.

Oxford and Cambridge, serene behind their crumbling stone and ancient brick, were touched but lightly by the mood of reform.

In 1848 Cambridge instituted a Moral Sciences Tripos, which was criticized as encouraging a 'shabby superficiality of knowledge'. The tripos included, to the displeasure of many, a course in the new science of Political Economy:

> The dismal science.
> Thomas Carlyle (1795–1881)
> *Latter-Day Pamphlets*

Turning the pursuit of wealth into a subject for study at an ancient university appalled John Ruskin, the art critic:

> The Science of Political Economy *is* a Lie,—wholly and to the very root (as hitherto taught). It is also the damnedest, that is to say, the most Utterly and to the Lowest Pit condemned of God and His Angels, that the Devil, or Betrayer of Men, has yet invented, except his (the Devil's) theory of Sanctification. To this 'science' and to this alone (the Professed and organized pursuit of Money) is owing *All* the Evil of modern days. I say All. The Monastic theory is at an end. It is now the Money theory which corrupts the church, corrupts the household life, destroys honour, beauty, and life throughout the universe. It is *the* Death incarnate of Modernism, and the so-called science of its pursuit is the most cretinous, speechless, paralysing plague that has yet touched the brains of mankind.
> John Ruskin (1819–1900)
> Letter to John Brown, 1862

> Ruskin, who believed that there were more important and beautiful things in life, inherited a fortune and managed to give almost all of it away during his lifetime.

Examinations began to loom large among the various dreads facing students. The ancient method of establishing how much learning had filtered through students' natural defences was by means of disputations: two-man debates at the end of which a winner was declared.

During the eighteenth century these disputations were gradually re-placed by oral examinations and then by written papers:

Examinations are formidable even to the best prepared; for the greatest fool may ask more than the wisest man can answer.

Charles Colton (1780?–1832)
Lacon

Colton, Eton and King's College, Cambridge, did so well at his exams that his college provided him with a parish. He proved to be more inter-ested in fishing and gambling than preaching. The result of his gambling was a string of debts from which he fled to America and then to France. After winning and losing an art gallery at the gaming tables of the Palais Royal he became ill and finished up by disproving in practice a theory he had expressed in *Lacon* that nobody commits suicide from bodily anguish.

One small reform instituted by Oxford and Cambridge was a series of written examination papers for grammar-school boys to take, thus—tentatively–paving the way for entrance to the universities being granted on the basis of merit rather than on social standing.

There was a belief at that time that good examination results not only demonstrated a candidate's academic proficiency but were in some mysterious way an indication of high moral principles and reli-ability of character. Beginning in 1855 with the Home and Indian Civil Service, examinations became the official method by which the Civil Service selected its staff:

When one sees some of the human specimens which the mills of the Civil Service Commission grind out for our governance, when one finds oneself at the mercy of boors who occupy responsible posts only because they had a mathematical or historical kink, or a mere knack (because it is a knack, up to a point) of passing examinations—why, then one cannot help thinking that there is something to be said for Lord Palmerston's point of view.

Norman Douglas (1868–1952)
Looking Back

Lord Palmerston's point of view was that appointment to government posts should be by patronage. This enjoyable and often lucrative privilege of appointing relations or the friends of old friends to well-paid and un-demanding positions–which, when it worked, meant that the job was filled by somebody known to be able and loyal–was the real power enjoyed by powerful men. To the English ruling class the most hated doc-trine of the French Revolution was 'the career open to the talents'.

Apart from an increased interest in athletics and games, and in politi-cal debating, Oxford sailed sedately on, little changed, into the twen-tieth century:

It is not an exciting place, and its education operates as a narcotic rather than as a stimulant. Most of its students devote their lives to a single profession, and we may observe among them a kind of sacred torpidity.

Walter Bagehot (1826–1877)
Biographical Studies: 'Mr. Gladstone'

Bagehot took his degree at University College, London.

Oxford continued to be regarded as England's pinnacle of learning; the standard against which others could be measured:

> The clever men at Oxford
> Know all that there is to be knowed,
> But they none of them know one half as much
> As intelligent Mr. Toad.

Kenneth Grahame (1859–1932)
The Wind in the Willows

Socially, it was accepted as the finishing-school for upper-class young men:

> I was a modest, good-humoured boy. It was Oxford that has made me insufferable.

Max Beerbohm (1872–1956)
Going Back to School

The two universities continued to differ slightly. Cambridge retained its traditional dominance in mathematics and the sciences; Oxford remained the centre of Anglican theology, although Cambridge as well as Oxford required its senior members to affirm their belief in orthodox Church of England doctrine.

A famous travel guide was not enthusiastic about foreign tourists including Cambridge in their itinerary:

> Oxford is on the whole more attractive than Cambridge to the ordinary visitor; and the traveller is therefore recommended to visit Cambridge first, or to omit it altogether if he cannot visit both.

Baedeker's Great Britain, 1887

Perhaps Herr Baedeker had been over-charged by the townspeople:

> For Cambridge people rarely smile
> Being urban, squat, and packed with guile.

Rupert Brooke (1887–1915)
The Old Vicarage, Grantchester

Like Oxford, Cambridge moved into yet another century with almost all its traditions and privileges intact:

> Trinity is like a dead body in a high state of putrefaction. The only interest of it is in the worms that come out of it.

Lytton Strachey (1880–1932)
Letter to a friend, 1903
Quoted by Michael Holroyd: Lytton Strachey

The government came to grips with the increasing need to organize elementary education by passing, in 1870, the Elementary Education Bill. This Bill urged the religious schools to keep going but filled in the gaps with new state elementary schools, some of the money being diverted from the rates. Illiteracy dropped rapidly. According to some people this resulted in dissident elements becoming more fluent in questioning the opinions of their betters:

> Modern education has devoted itself to the teaching of impudence, and then we complain we can no more manage our mobs.
>
> John Ruskin (1819–1900)

Acts and Codes fluttered down from the authorities in a steady shower as the machinery of state education got up steam and started to roll forward. In 1876 attendance was compulsory for children up to the age of ten, and up to thirteen for those who could not get a grip on the three R's. By the 1880s the children had to take five subjects:

> Pressing people to learn things they do not want to know is as unwholesome and disastrous as feeding them on sawdust.
>
> George Bernard Shaw (1856–1950)

In 1889 the government, worried by the better standard of goods manufactured in Germany and the U.S.A., passed the Technical Instruction Act, providing for technical schools to be set up and financed by a sum of money locked up in the rates, 'Whisky Money': this was a fund originally set up to compensate licensees whose public houses were closed down.

The 1890 Education Act abolished fees – all but utterly destitute parents had previously paid a few coppers a week, 'school pence' – and every child was entitled to free elementary education.

By the turn of the century many local education authorities provided evening classes for those who had missed schooling when they were young or who wanted to better themselves:

> 'Whom are you?' said he, for he had been to night school.
>
> George Ade (1866–1944)
> *Bang! Bang!:* 'The Steel Box'

There was a strong feeling among the lightly educated that a thorough education brought with it almost mystical powers:

> That's what education means – to be able to do what you've never done before!
>
> Quoted by George Herbert Palmer (1842–1933)
> *Life of Alice Freeman Palmer*
>
> Palmer was the formidably well-educated professor of philosophy at Harvard University. The remark was made by his cook when the equally formidable Mrs. Palmer, president of Wellesley College, walked into the kitchen and, without any previous experience, baked a loaf of bread.

Teaching at last became a respectable profession by the end of the nineteenth century, with its own union to keep an eye on pay scales and professional associations to examine ways of improving teaching methods. Many teachers made extra money by supplying the growing need for new text-books; these they could make 'required reading' in their own schools:

> There is nothing on earth intended for innocent people so horrible as a school. To begin with, it is a prison. But it is in some respects more cruel than a prison. In a prison, for instance, you are not forced to read books written by the warders and the governor.
>
> George Bernard Shaw (1856–1950)
> *Parents and Children*

One important part of the 1902 Education Act was the encouragement of state secondary schools, mainly fee-paying day grammar schools, which fed bright boys to the civic universities and thence into careers in management and the minor professions:

> Higher education and great numbers — that is a contradiction in terms.
>
> Friedrich Nietzsche (1844–1900)

In 1944 the Education Act did away with fees and made a complete state education available free to every child. Successive governments then struggled, desperately or regretfully according to their political inclinations, to make education egalitarian, with equal opportunities for everybody within a standardized system of state schools:

> True education makes for inequality; the inequality of individuality, the inequality of success; the glorious inequality of talent, of genius; for inequality, not mediocrity, individual superiority, not standardization, is the measure of the progress of the world.
>
> Felix E. Schelling (1858–1945)
> *Pedagogically Speaking*

The authorities split children into two streams by means of an exam, the 'Eleven-Plus'. Those who passed went to a grammar school and those who failed went to a new sort of school, tactfully named Secondary Modern. This was an unhappy arrangement because nobody took any interest in going to a school, however tactfully named, which was for children who had failed to pass an exam. The authorities then sought to make things 'fairer' by suppressing grammar schools and lumping all the children together into an even newer sort of school, vast establishments called Comprehensive Schools. This move produced howls of rage from parents who saw nothing 'unfair' about a bright child being able to go to a grammar school and be seen to go to a grammar school, which was, it was pointed out, the oldest kind of school in the tradition of English education.

There was also a suggestion that public schools should be abolished, on the grounds that they were an anachronism, perpetuators of class distinction, and they had a monopoly on the production of senior civil servants. The suggestion aroused a great wave of pro-public-school feeling, even amongst those who had never been to one:

> The cult of the public schools, and the curious sentiment now attached to them, are fruits of the complicated, emotionalism of the mid-Victorian epoch.

Hugh Kingsmill (1889–1949)
Anthology of Invective and Abuse

The class distinctions inherent in a system in which British schooling was split into three levels were put into verse by an entrant in a *New Statesman* competition (to be sung to the tune of Masefield's *Cargoes*):

> Crocodile from Grey Towers, Ancient Seat of Learning,
> Trailing down the avenue, pair by snooty pair,
> With a cargo of snobbery,
> Hauteur, prejudice,
> Exaggerated accents and upper-class stare.
>
> Arnold-haunted small-fry from the local Grammar,
> Standing in a huddle, waiting for the bus,
> With a cargo of sniggers,
> Spectacles, horseplay,
> Brashness and Angst stemming from Eleven-plus.
>
> Hordes of little bastards from the Secondary Modern,
> Gadarening home to the Children's Hour and News,
> With a cargo of comics,
> Candy floss, ice cream,
> Hollywood values and low I.Q.s

Stanley J. Sharpless
New Statesman and Nation, 1956

The grand era of the public schools was those years when the sun of the British Empire was at its zenith and the schools, still very much under the influence of the great Dr. Arnold's precepts, were sending forth a steady flow of superbly fit chaps, light on imagination but strong on team-spirit and integrity, to be administrators at home and abroad.

But later on in the century some of the schools were beginning to fray at the edges a little. Perhaps they reflected not only the national weakening of religious spirit but also the decline in self-confidence which crept in during the last quarter of the nineteenth century. A writer recalled life at Uppingham in 1881:

> A mildewy scriptural odour pervaded the institution—it reeked of Jeroboam and Jesus; the masters struck me as supercilious humbugs; the food was so vile that for the first day or two after returning from holidays I could not get it down. The only good which ever came out of the place was cheese from the neighbouring Stilton,

and that, of course, they never gave us. And the charges ... On my mother's death I found, among her papers, these Uppingham accounts: God, how they swindled her! I daresay all that is changed now.

Norman Douglas (1868–1952)
Looking Back

About the same time boys at Clifton College, Bristol, might have been gazing wistfully out of the classroom windows at the trees and sky and the birds as the voice of their Second Master, Mr. Brown, droned on, probably unaware that Mr. Brown's thoughts were outside too:

> I'm here at Clifton, grinding at the mill
> My feet for thrice nine barren years have trod;
> But there are rocks and waves at Scarlett still,
> And gorse runs riot in Glen Chass—thank God!

T. E. Brown (1830–1897)
Collected Poems: 'Clifton'

Besides being a schoolmaster Brown was also a poet. He is best known for his narrative poems written—with a hanging garden of apostrophes—in the Manx dialect. He also wrote 'A garden is a lovesome thing, God wot!'

The public school which has probably deflected the wind of change more successfully than most is Eton, the most famous school in the world. Eton shares its peculiar status with Harrow and together they form the two 'top' schools, to which aristocratic boys go by custom and humbler but rich boys go if they can get in.

A playwright of sensibility (Educ: Glasgow Academy and Dumfries Academy) tried to put into words the particular charisma which Eton and Harrow had and imparted to their sons:

> I went with N. to the Lord's match. 15,000 tall hats—one cad hat (mine) ... The Ladies comparatively drab fearing rain but the gents superb, colossal, sleek, lovely. All with such a pleased smile. Why? Because they know they had the Eton something or the Harrow something ... I felt I was nearer to grasping what the something is than ever before. It is a sleek happiness that comes of a shininess which only Eton (or Harrow) can impart. This makes you 'play the game' as the damned can't do it; it gives you manners because you know in your heart that nothing really matters so long as you shine with that sleek happiness. The nearest thing to it must be boot polish.

J. M. Barrie (1860–1937)
Letter to Lady Cynthia Asquith, 10 July 1920

For the best part of a century most states in America have enjoyed an educational system which did away with the 'elementary schools for the poor, secondary schools for the rich' European tradition in favour of a complete system of education, supposedly free to everybody.

Ideally, in the great American 'ladder' system of schooling, a boy or girl can begin at the lowest grade and work his or her way up the ladder until he or she graduates from university. Or falls off.

There are, accordingly, a great number of degree-awarding institutions in America – some 1300 were counted in 1960 – including liberal arts colleges, business schools, technical and professional schools and about 130 universities. Students are able to choose from an enormous range of courses and tend to be increasingly involved with contemporary social and political issues. A seventeenth century Master of Trinity or the first President of Harvard would be greatly surprised by the tribulations facing the president of a modern university in the U.S.A.

> I find the three major administrative problems on a campus are sex for the students, athletics for the alumni, and parking for the faculty.
>
> Clark Kerr (b. 1911)
> President of the University of California
> *Time*, 17 Nov. 1958

One feature of British education which has never caught on in America, or indeed any other country, is the boarding-school, to which our little ones are packed off at the age of eight.

It seems that only we know what is good for children:

> Suddenly, just as they have reached an age when their intelligence and sensitiveness, which have after this fashion been encouraged, can respond to the stimuli of their surroundings, they are whisked off to places of dreary internment, where the most extraordinary tribal values and standards prevail: and though these, as it were, labour camps are varied according to their years, they remain in one or another of them (unless they have the good fortune to be expelled with ignominy) until such time as their characters have been formed in the same hard, dense and unpleasant mould as that of those who teach them.
>
> Osbert Sitwell (1892–1969)

In his *Who's Who* entry Sir Osbert wrote 'Educ: educated during the holidays from Eton.'

LITERATURE

Literature

Ever since the written word became available in a portable form, literature has inspired, informed and beguiled all manner of men from commoners to kings. Not all kings, of course:

> I see no point in reading.
>
> Louis XIV (1638–1715)
> Quoted by Louis, Duc de Saint-Simon, *Mémoires*

Nor all commoners:

> Get stewed: books are a load of crap.
>
> Philip Larkin (b. 1922)
> *A Study of Reading Habits*

To many people literature seemed to be a time-wasting form of self-indulgence:

> Never read a book, Johnnie, and you will be a rich man.
>
> Sir Timothy Shelley (1753–1844)
>
> A word of advice from the poet Shelley's father to his younger son.

An expensive pleasure:

> How long most people would look at the best book before they would give the price of a large turbot for it!
>
> John Ruskin (1819–1900)
> *Sesame and Lilies*

Books have been criticized for being too commonplace:

> Literature is the orchestration of platitudes.
>
> Thornton Wilder (b. 1897)
> Quoted in *Time*, 12 Jan. 1953

Too confusing:

> I hate books, for they only teach people to talk about what they do not understand.
>
> Jean-Jacques Rousseau (1712–1778)
> *Émile*

And too big:

> A great book, a great evil.
>
> Callimachus (*c.* 305–*c.* 240 B.C.)
> Fragments
>
> Callimachus, who worked in the Ptolemy's library at Alexandria, preferred short poems; perhaps because they were easier to shift about.

The craft of writing, frequently regarded by non-writers as an undemanding, amiable way of earning a living, has been otherwise described by professional writers:

> The most seductive, the most deceiving, the most dangerous of professions.
>
> John Morley (1838–1923)
> *Edmund Burke: an Historical Study*

> Writing a book is a horrible, exhausting struggle, like a long bout of some painful illness.
>
> George Orwell (1903–1950)
> *England Your England:* 'Why I Write'

Many successful authors have pointed out that the rewards of authorship are out of proportion to its agonies:

> The only reward to be expected for the cultivation of literature is contempt if one fails and hatred if one succeeds.
>
> Voltaire (1694–1778)
> Letter to Mlle. Quinault

> The life of writing men has always been ... a bitter business. It is notoriously accompanied, for those who write well, by poverty and contempt; or by fatuity and wealth for those who write ill.
>
> Hilaire Belloc (1870–1953)

The Bible pointed out that anybody who became an author made himself vulnerable to attack:

> Behold, my desire is, that the Almighty would answer me, and that mine adversary had written a book.
>
> Job xxxi. 35

It has been suggested that the wrong people take to writing:

> The reason why so few good books are written is that so few people who write know anything.
>
> Walter Bagehot (1826–1877)

And that people take to writing for the wrong reason:

> A man starts upon a sudden, takes Pen, Ink, and Paper, and without ever having had a thought of it before, resolves within himself he will write a Book; he has no Talent at Writing, but he wants fifty Guineas.
>
> Jean de la Bruyère (1646–1696)
> He would be lucky nowadays to make the present-day equivalent of fifty guineas for a first novel.

It seems that the Ancient World, too, was plagued by hopeful would-be writers:

> All dare to write, who can or cannot read.
>
> Horace (65–8 B.C.)
> *Epistles,* II

> An incurable itch for scribbling takes possession of many, and grows inveterate in their insane breasts.
>
> Juvenal (A.D. 60–140)

Dabbling in light verse became fashionable in ancient Rome and society became infested with ungifted amateurs. The trouble with Roman scribblers was that they were not content with passing their verses round in manuscript but had to read them out aloud to their victim:

> That no man willingly meets you, that, wherever you arrive, there is flight and vast solitude around you, Ligurinus, do you want to know what is the matter? You are too much of a poet. This is a fault passing dangerous ... You read to me while I am standing, and read to me while I am sitting; while I am running you read to me, and read to me while I am using a jakes.
>
> Martial (c. A.D. 40–104)
> *Epigrams:* Bk. III, epig. 44

> Jakes = Elizabethan word for the lavatory. Actually a euphemism, as all names for the thing are, including 'lavatory' which is the plumber's word for a wash-basin, 'toilet' which was a lady's dressing-table, and 'loo' which came from the old Edinburgh custom of emptying the chamber-pot out of a tenement window with the cry of warning to pedestrians passing beneath – 'Guardy-loo!' 'Jakes' derives from 'Jack's place', a reference to the inventor of the appliance, Sir John Harington (1561–1612). Sir John wrote a satirical account of his invention entitled *Metamorphosis of Ajax* – a pun on 'a jakes'. The invention required running water to operate it, which was not available to most citizens beneath the rank of queen, so the convenience hung fire until the late eighteenth century. But Sir John did install one for his godmother, Queen Elizabeth, in Hampton Court Palace.

From the early days of literature it was noted that writers, as a breed, were a bit odd.

> I have never yet known a poet who did not think himself super-excellent.
>
> Cicero (106–43 B.C.)
> *Tusculanae Disputationes*

It was suspected that witty writers were almost certainly immoral:

> Diseur de bons mots, mauvais caractère.
> Blaise Pascal (1623–1662)
> *Pensées*

They aged rapidly:

> Poets are almost always bald when they get to be about forty.
> John Masefield (1878–1967)

Their work was more important to them than their women-folk:

> If a writer has to rob his mother, he will not hesitate; the 'Ode on a Grecian Urn' is worth any number of old ladies.
>
> William Faulkner (b. 1897)

The oddest creature of all, according to many male writers, was a female writer:

> Perhaps the saddest lot that can befall mortal man is to be the husband of a lady poet.
>
> George Jean Nathan (1882–1958)

A favourite myth was that the creative impulse depended for its potency on a whiff of lunacy:

> All poets are mad.
> Robert Burton (1577–1640)
> *Anatomy of Melancholy*

Poets began to be accepted as reputable citizens in the nineteenth century, about the same time as painters, hitherto respectable, were at great pains to make themselves disreputable. But in the early days of Queen Victoria's reign a Whig man of letters was still able to state:

> Perhaps no person can be a poet, or can even enjoy poetry, without a certain unsoundness of mind.
>
> Thomas Babington Macaulay (1800–1859)
> *Milton*

> The image of a poet as an unstable figure lurching about waving a quill pen, his eye in a fine frenzy rolling, does not quite match up to the known behaviour of, say, Thomas Gray or T. S. Eliot.

Another widely held fallacy was that authors talked and looked like the characters in their books. In reality, of course, it was because many of them were unable to charm or outwit people when talking face to face that they became writers in the first place. Visitors to literary luncheons should not be too hopeful:

> A Transition from an Author's Books to his Conversation, is too often like an Entrance into a large City, after a distant Prospect. Remotely, we see nothing but Spires of Temples, and Turrets of Palaces, and imagine it the Residence of Splendour, Grandeur, and Magnificence; but, when we have passed the Gates, we find it perplexed with narrow Passages, disgraced with despicable Cottages, embarrassed with Obstructions, and clouded with Smoke.
>
> Samuel Johnson (1709–1784)
> *The Rambler:* No. 14, 5 May 1750

Authors had a reputation for being jealous of each other's fame and losing no opportunity of putting the boot in:

> Envy's a sharper spur than pay,
> No author ever spared a brother,
> Wits are game-cocks to one another.
>
> John Gay (1685–1732)
> *Fables:* 'The Elephant and the Bookseller'

Plato was accused by Athenaeus of envy, by Theopompus of lying, by the Suidas of avarice, by Aulus Gellius of robbery, by Aristophanes of impiety and by Porphyry of incontinence. Later writers could benefit from a cautionary word from Dr. Johnson:

> The best advice to authors would be, that they should keep out of the way of one another.
>
> Samuel Johnson (1709–1784)
> *Lives of the Poets:* 'Rowe'

Johnson would have enjoyed himself at meetings of the Society of Authors: he wrote, 'the reciprocal civility of authors is one of the most risible scenes in the farce of life'.

An American man of letters held out hope for authors in the afterlife:

> There is probably no hell for authors in the next world – they suffer so much from critics and publishers in this.
>
> Christian Nestell Bovee (1820–1904)
> *Summaries of Thought:* 'Authors'

Until recent years – and sometimes even today – authors looked upon publishers as thieving, conniving skinflints:

> Now Barabbas was a publisher.
>
> Thomas Campbell (1777–1844)

Often wrongly attributed to Lord Byron. Campbell was a poet ('The Pleasures of Hope', 'Ye Mariners of England', 'Lord Ullin's Daughter', etc.) and one of the men who agitated for the founding of London University. According to *Notes and Queries* there was a famous incident when Napoleon personally ordered the execution of Johann Palm, a German publisher who had been printing subversive pamphlets. Later, at an authors' dinner, Campbell gave the toast, 'To Napoleon!' Consternation reigned. Campbell then went on, 'I agree with you that Napoleon is a tyrant, a monster, the sworn foe of our nation. But, gentlemen – he once shot a publisher!'

> A Petty Sneaking Knave I knew –
> O Mr. Cromek, how do ye do?
>
> William Blake (1757–1827)

Robert Cromek, whom the *D.N.B.* describes as a 'shifty speculator' was a publisher of illustrated books who contrived to do many artists – including Blake – out of their rightful earnings.

Nowadays, it would seem, publishing attracts a different sort of person:

> As repressed sadists are supposed to become policemen or butchers so those with irrational fear of life become publishers.
>
> Cyril Connolly (1903–1974)
> *Enemies of Promise*

An author's relationship with his publisher should be one of trust and contentment. But, alas, it not always is:

> It is with publishers as with wives: one always wants somebody else's.
>
> Norman Douglas (1868–1952)

The chronic suffering which an author can endure from having the wrong publisher is as nothing to the acute pangs of agony which a bad review can inflict. It is not surprising that writers have expressed a few cogent thoughts on critics:

> A critic is a legless man who teaches running.
>
> Channing Pollock (1880–1946)
> *The Green Book*

> Criticism is the art wherewith a critic tries to guess himself into a share of the artist's fame.
>
> George Jean Nathan (1882–1958)
> *The House of Satan*

> A critic is a man who knows the way but can't drive the car.
>
> Kenneth Tynan (b. 1927)

Besides aphorisms, there is also a large body of fine abusive verse and prose directed at the heads of literary critics:

> Hot, envious, noisy, proud, the scribbling fry
> Burn, hiss and bounce, waste paper, stink, and die.
>
> Edward Young (1683–1765)
> *Love of Fame*

Young's best-known work was *The Complaint; or Night Thoughts on Life, Death, and Immortality*, an exercise in religious gloom which did much to make fashionable a new, sepulchral school of writing.

> As for you, little envious Prigs, snarling, bastard, puny Criticks, you'll soon have railed your last: Go hang yourselves.
>
> François Rabelais (1490?–1553)
> *Gargantua and Pantagruel*

> Critics! appall'd I venture on the name,
> Those cut-throat bandits in the path of fame,
> Bloody dissectors, worse than ten Monroes:
> He hacks to teach, they mangle to expose.
>
> Robert Burns (1759–1796)
> *The Poet's Progress*

Burns was usually well reviewed, but he clearly did not like critics. The name-calling he indulged in when addressing one critic included: thou

106

eunuch of language ... thou pimp, of gender ... murderous accoucheur of infant learning ... thou pickle-herring in the puppet show of nonsense ... scavenger ... arch-heretic ... butcher. Monroe was a famous anatomist at Edinburgh University.

Writers harped on the parasitic nature of criticism; neatly expressed in Alfred, Lord Tennyson's description of the critic Churton Collins:

A louse in the locks of literature.
Alfred, Lord Tennyson (1809–1894)
Quoted by Edmund Gosse

And again:

Critics are like horse-flies which prevent the horse from ploughing.
Anton Pavlovitch
Quoted by Anton Chekhov: *Fragments of Recollections*

Or:

The critic's symbol should be the tumble-bug; he deposits his egg in somebody else's dung, otherwise he could not hatch it.
Mark Twain (1835–1910)
Mark Twain's Notebook

It seemed to authors that those who could write well did, and those who couldn't turned beastly:

They who write ill, and they who ne'er durst write,
Turn critics out of mere revenge and spite.
John Dryden (1631–1700)
Conquest of Granada

Dryden's prefaces to his plays and poems, mostly written in self-justification, marked the beginning of the modern school of descriptive criticism and earned him Dr. Johnson's commendation, 'the father of English criticism'.

Becoming a critic seemed a cheap and easy way of achieving power:

Criticism is a study by which men grow important and formidable at very small expense.
Samuel Johnson (1709–1784)
The Idler, No. 60

And compared to creative writing it was undemanding work:

Criticism occupies the lowest place in the literary hierarchy: as regards form, almost always; and as regards moral value, incontestably. It comes after rhyming-games and acrostics, which at least require a certain inventiveness.
Gustave Flaubert (1821–1880)
Letters

Until the late seventeenth century the literary critic addressed his comments to the author, admonishing him for poor work or giving him full marks. Since John Dryden the critic has addressed himself to the

107

reader. And in the last two hundred years the dictionary definition of a critic has undergone a significant change. Dr. Johnson's dictionary gave as the primary definition of a critic:

'A man skilled in the art of judging of literature.'

The secondary definition was:

'A censurer; a man apt to find fault.'

The present *Oxford English Dictionary* reverses the priorities. A critic nowadays is primarily:

'One who pronounces judgement on any thing or person; *esp.* one who passes severe or unfavourable judgement; a censurer, fault-finder, caviller.'

Only secondarily is he now:

'One skilful in the judging of literary or artistic works.'

So it seems that since the time of Dr. Johnson a critic's function has changed from that of discrimination to that of condemnation.

Even though criticism, i.e. censuring, fault-finding and cavilling, is no longer written for the author's benefit it is difficult for him to avoid seeing it. If it is sufficiently wounding there will be friends anxious to show it to him. And however magnanimously he reacts to the critic's words in public, his private emotions are another matter. It was to hearten authors during those dark moments that an anonymous fellow-sufferer wrote:

> When you hark to the voice of the Knocker,
> As you list to his hammer fall,
> Remember the fact that the knocking act
> Requires no brains at all.
>
> Anon.
> *The Quarrelsome Trio*

The first kind of literature produced by man was poetry. Next came drama, i.e. dramatic poetry, and then lagging many centuries behind, prose.

> BOSWELL: Then, Sir, what is poetry?
> JOHNSON: Why, Sir, it is much easier to say what it is not.
> Samuel Johnson (1709–1784)
> Boswell's *Life*, 11 April 1776

Indeed it is, but many writers have had a go at providing a definition:

> Poetry is devil's wine.
> St. Augustine (354–430)
> *Contra Academicos*

108

Poetry is a kind of ingenious nonsense.

Isaac Barrow (1630–1677)

Barrow, a compulsive versifier in Latin, was a distinguished mathematician and theologian. His pupil, Sir Isaac Newton, quoted the remark to Joseph Spence, who put it into his *Anecdotes*.

Poetry is a comforting piece of fiction set to more or less lascivious music.

H. L. Mencken (1880–1956)
Prejudices: Series III

Poetry is the achievement of the synthesis of hyacinths and biscuits.

Carl Sandburg (1878–1967)
Atlantic Monthly: 'Poetry Considered', March 1923

Poetry is that stuff in books which doesn't quite reach to the margins.

Anon. schoolchild

Poetry has a special shape of its own, which prose has not, because it began as a song.

Once early man had mastered the trick of standing upright he became a hunter and a warrior, and it was instinctive to celebrate a kill or to bemoan a defeat by stamping about in a rhythmic fashion and indulging in a good deal of grunting and howling. When language came into being this bellowing fined down into the ritual chanting of tribal songs.

As man became more civilized he invented various gods to explain to himself why the sun made things grow, why water ran downhill, and so on, and he made up songs about them. He also sang reassuring songs about the splendid and cruel exploits of his tribal heroes. He probably told stories as well, but songs, with their special shape, were easier to remember.

When writing was first developed it was used to make civic records, royal inventories and similar documents, not to record stories, but eventually the songs and myth-poems sung by wandering poets were put down on papyrus by scribes. The greatest of these wandering poets was Homer (or, as was said in reply to the accusation that he never existed, another Greek poet of the same name). Homer lived some time between the tenth and seventh centuries B.C. but his mighty epics, the *Iliad* and the *Odyssey*, were probably not written down until the sixth century, and then only as an aid to singers' memories.

It was many centuries later that the Greeks began recording prose — mainly works of biography and history which leant heavily on myth.

When Rome became the leading power in the known world it discovered the pleasures of Greek poetry. During the second century B.C. a prominent Roman statesman, Scipio Aemilianus, encouraged the translation of Greek works into Latin and became one of literature's first patrons:

109

PATRON: n.s. One who countenances, supports or protects. Commonly a wretch who supports with insolence, and is paid with flattery.

Samuel Johnson (1709–1784)
Dictionary

Libraries had existed as store-houses for royal archives as long as there had been books. The first Greek to collect books systematically was Aristotle. His method of arrangement was taken as the model for the Ptolemies' enormous libraries, consisting of hundreds of thousands of papyrus and vellum rolls, which were built at Alexandria and other cities.

The Romans were slow to start. They began, perhaps typically, by impounding and importing Greek libraries as war-loot. By the time of Cicero libraries had become a fashionable extravagance and rich Romans had taken to adding them to their villas as a symbol of wealth.

Edward Gibbon, in *The Decline and Fall of the Roman Empire*, noted that one fashionable Roman, Gordian, had amassed 60,000 books and 22 concubines. Stoics, who foreswore property, did not approve of hoarding either commodity:

> Since you cannot read all the books which you may possess, it is enough to possess only as many books as you can read.

Seneca (54? B.C.–A.D. 39)
Ad Lucilium

> Sound enough logic when applied to concubines but not very good in relation to books. Reference books, for instance.

The Latin language had great beauty and precision and, before decadence set in, poets and prose-writers developed it into a unique literary medium. But almost everything they wrote owed something to Greek techniques and forms:

> Roman literature is Greek literature written in Latin.

Heinrich von Treitschke (1834–1896)

Greek and Roman poetry did not rhyme. When the notion of making the last words of lines rhyme with each other came into use (according to Isaac D'Israeli the practice crept in either from China or Wales) classically minded poets were upset. It was something else to worry about:

> The troublesome and modern bondage of Rhyming.

John Milton (1608–1674)
Preface to *Paradise Lost*

And it cheapened the product:

> Till barbarous nations, and more barbarous times,
> Debased the majesty of verse to rhymes.

John Dryden (1631–1700)
To the Earl of Roscommon

The last great works of literature written before the barbarians put a stop to that sort of thing were the theological books of the Christian Fathers. These ceased at the end of the fourth century and no more outstanding books were written for about seven hundred years.

Christianity, always a bookish religion, set up libraries in monasteries, thus preserving a great deal of the world's theologically acceptable literature from destruction.

But monastic libraries were surprisingly small; most with only a few dozen works. They were hardly 'lending' libraries:

> The lending of books, as well the smaller without pictures as the larger with pictures, is forbidden under the penalty of excommunication.
>
> Ingulf, Abbot of Croyland (d. 1109)
> *The Croyland History*

During the Dark Ages and the Middle Ages people went back to chanting their tall stories of heroics and villainy. Minstrels again became welcome – and rich – visitors to castles, and their songs reflected the themes of Chivalry: the heroism of the absentee knight, the unattainability of his good lady left behind, the pure thoughts of the lusty young pages growing up around her. The songs became fictional chronicles of the times, and those accounts of elegant adultery were the main literature of the people for three hundred years.

Mediaeval 'estoires' of derring-do did not impress one Elizabethan:

> In our forefathers' time . . . few books were read in our tongue, saving certain books of Chivalry . . . as one for example, *Morte Arthure* the whole pleasure of which book standeth in two special points, in open manslaughter and bold bawdry.
>
> Roger Ascham (1515–1568)
> *Toxophilus*

Books started to look like books in the third century when the practice of writing on rolls of parchment was dropped in favour of folding the parchment into convenient leaves, stitching the leaves together and making a sandwich of it with flat wooden covers. But each book had to be copied out by hand, usually by a professional scribe or by a monk in a monastery's scriptorium. It was slow, laborious work – although the monk was usually exempted from potato-lifting and other manual duties – and the going rate was twenty years to transcribe a hundred bibles. This output was adequate during the ages when for many hundreds of years hardly any layman from Emperors downwards could read and write; Charlemagne could read, but even he had to dictate his letters. But by the fifteenth century there was a growing number of literate middle-class citizens – professional men, merchants, administrators, students – who made up a vast potential book-buying public with hardly any books to buy.

111

Then occurred a technological development which transformed literature, giving it new purposes, a new readership and a new face:

The greatest misfortune that ever befell man was the invention of printing.

Benjamin Disraeli (1804–1881)
Lothair

In 1440 – or thereabouts – Gutenberg stumbled upon the concept of printing from movable type rather than from a wooden block. The other great advance, which had not occurred to the Chinese, was printing on both sides of the paper. The beginnings of printing were wilfully shrouded in mystery; Gutenberg in Mainz, Laurens Costar in Haarlem, and many other 'ingenious mechanics', worked away in cellars in great secrecy.

The object of their labours was not to free literature from the bondage of scribes but to make a lot of money by reproducing manuscripts cheaply and quickly by machinery. At the beginning they passed off their work as manuscripts and the type-face they used was a facsimile of the scribes' lettering.

Incunabula, that is to say those books produced in the nursery days of printing before the year 1501, were immediately and hugely successful. Even grocers took to selling them; and importing them when the home supply dried up. By the year 1500 the price of printed books had dropped by four-fifths.

England's first printer, William Caxton, was typical of the kind of man who took up The Mystery. He was a reasonably prosperous cloth mercer who became interested in translating books. As he lived thirty years in the Low Countries he wrote French well – rather better than he wrote English – but he knew little or no Latin. He learned printing probably at Cologne and he translated and printed his first book, the first book to be printed in the English language, *The Recuyell of the Histories of Troy*, in 1474. He was welcomed back to England in 1476, and in 1477 he issued the first book to be printed in England, *The Dictes and Sayings of the Philosophers*.

The early printers were not scholars but small businessmen and entrepreneurs, and the majority of early books were not works of scholarship but books of popular appeal, mainly translated from the French. Once the manuscript faking had been dropped the printers issued a steady stream of old 'Romances', treatises on hawking, hunting and the playing of chess, books of anecdotes such as *Merry Tales of the Madmen of Gotham* and *Scogan's Jestes* ('Jest' did not originally mean a joke but came from the old word 'geste', a deed). The effect of this flood of simple reading matter was to attract a new public of simple, non-academic readers.

The sixteenth century also saw the beginning of a new breed of non-academic, non-religious writers; and more authors meant even more books, which meant more authors ...

Between 1440 and 1500 about 40,000 books were published. The figure for the sixteenth century rose to half a million:

> The multitude of books is a great evil. There is no measure or limit to this fever of writing; everyone must be an author; some out of vanity to acquire celebrity; others for the sake of lucre and gain.
>
> Martin Luther (1483–1546)
> *Table-Talk*

At that stage, men of power had not spotted that a merchant poring over his manual of hawking, or a villager spelling out his almanac with its recipes and signs of the zodiac and predictions, could just as easily have been drinking in a brisk call to revolution.

In the reign of Henry VIII books lost their innocence and became 'organs of the passions of mankind'. Printing became the medium of protest, and pamphlets urging church reform circulated widely. The authorities began to take notice; Cardinal Wolsey wrote to the Pope:

> This new invention of printing has produced various effects of which your Holiness cannot be ignorant. If it has restored books and learning, it has also been the occasion of those sects and schisms which appear daily. Men begin to call in question the present faith and tenets of the Church; the laity read the Scriptures and pray in their vulgar tongue ... The mysteries of religion must be kept in the hands of the priests.
>
> Cardinal Wolsey (1475?–1530)
> Letter to Pope Clement VII

> The Catholic Church believed that the Bible should be in Latin and that its meanings needed interpretation by a priest. The Protestant reformers believed that the Bible should be read by everybody in their own language and that its messages needed no clerical interpretation.

Cardinal Wolsey closed down the press under his control at St. Albans and many monasteries followed his example, but the tracts continued to pour forth. The presses had gone underground.

By 1524 there was a flourishing book-running trade smuggling pro-Luther pamphlets into Norfolk and Colchester from Holland. A considerable thorn in the side of the Catholic Church was Tyndale's translation of the New Testament into English – with many Protestant notes – copies of which were smuggled into England from the Continent. When copies were found they were ceremonially burnt. The Bishop of Durham, in an excess of zeal, paid an agent to travel to Antwerp and buy up all the copies he could find there. The agent, Augustine Packington, was outmanoeuvred into buying all Tyndale's unsold copies, thus providing Tyndale not only with the capital he needed to print another edition but with enough over to commission eleven wood-blocks to illustrate his new translation of the Book of

Exodus. The printed word had proved to be a slippery thing to control.

The world's first publishers were possibly Egyptian undertakers; it was the custom in ancient Egypt for the undertaker to insert into each burial place a Book of the Dead, which contained magical formulae and useful information for the afterlife. In ancient Rome the job of publishing was much like it is today. A publisher chose a poem, or oration, or philosophical work, paid the author a fee for reproduction rights, paid a batch of scribes to make copies of the work, and sold his copies from suitable premises. His errors of judgement were on display outside on the pavement: jars of 'remaindered' parchment rolls at marked-down prices. In medieval times almost all manuscripts were copied and issued by the Church and the universities, and were mainly ecclesiastical in content. With the invention of printing, book-publishing became once again the province of laymen.

For something like three hundred years after William Caxton the book trade remained a kind of one-man cottage-industry operation, the printer being his own publisher, his own bookseller (he sold his wares from the front of his printing shop) and sometimes his own author.

In an effort to bring this motley, unorganized, rapidly growing and potentially dangerous industry to heel, and to stop the flood of seditious and heretical literature, the Stationers' Company was given a monopoly on all books published in England. This edict of 1534 meant that a printer could be prosecuted if he issued a book which had not been licensed by the Stationers' Company, which was a guild and therefore answerable to authority.

Stationers were so called because they remained stationary instead of moving about; they sold parchment and ink and books from stalls, or 'stations', rather than carrying them round the streets in packs on their backs as did their humbler colleagues, the pedlars and chapmen:

> If I were to paint Sloth ... by Saint John the Evangelist I swear, I would draw it like a stationer that I know, with his thumb under his girdle, who if a man comes to his stall and ask him for a book, never stirs his head, or looks upon him, but stands stone still, and speaks not a word: only with his little finger points backwards to his boy, who must be his interpreter, and so all the day, gaping like a dumb image, he sits without motion.
>
> Thomas Nashe (1567–1601)
> *Pierce Penilesse*

This censorship by licensing lasted for nearly two hundred years and was bitterly resented by authors and printer-publishers, partly because the books they wanted to sell were just the books which the Stationers'

114

Company was there to suppress – in which case they usually went ahead and printed anyway, on a hit-and-run basis – and partly because the licensing officer frequently abused his powers:

> He prayseth no booke, but what sells well, and that must be his owne Coppy too or els he will have some flirt at it: No matter, though there be no cause; For, he knowes he shall not be questioned for what he sayes; or if he be, his impudence is enough to outface it … If he gett any written Coppy into his powre … it shall be contrived and named alsoe, according to his owne pleasure: which is the reason, so many good Bookes come forth imperfect, and with foolish titles. Nay, he oftentymes giues bookes such names as in his opinion will make them saleable, when there is little or nothing in the whole volume suitable to such a Tytle.
>
> George Wither (1588–1667)
> *The Schollers Purgatory, discouered In the Stationers Commonwealth*

George Wither was, briefly, a rather good lyric poet. He then turned Puritan, wrote a good deal of propaganda, was in and out of prison, and tried to pull a fast one on the Stationers' Company, without success. This last exploit earned Wither some satirical attention from Ben Jonson in his masque *Time Vindicated*. In 1642 Wither managed to raise a troop of horse for the parliamentary cause and was given Farnham Castle to defend. Not relishing the prospect he withdrew his troops and was promptly captured by the royalists. He would have been executed, but the poet Sir John Denham pleaded with the King for clemency on the grounds that 'so long as Wither lives I will not be accounted the worst poet in England'.

The sixteenth century was a difficult time for poor scholars trying to earn a crust with their pen. Printer-publisher-booksellers did not normally expect to share their profits with the author and noble patronage was hard to come by; the upper classes still tended to look upon literary composition more as a modish intellectual amusement than as an addition to national culture worthy of their encouragement:

> Giue an Ape but a nut, and he wil looke your head for it; or a Dog a bone, and hele wag his tayle: but giue me one of my young Masters a booke, and he will put of his hat and blush, and so go his waie.
>
> Thomas Nashe (1567–1601)
> *Pierce Penilesse*

Thomas Nashe was a controversialist with a gift for witty, bitter abuse, a dangerous accomplishment at a period when Queen Elizabeth's ministers dealt briskly with any author thought to be trying to rock the ship of state, and he remained desperately poor all his life. One safe outlet for his gift was the pamphlet war he conducted against the rather dull, humourless classical poet Gabriel Harvey. At that time the English language was what anybody wanted to make of it. John Lyly was writing in an involved, flowery style which came to be called euphuism after the title of one of his books, *Euphues*. Poets like Sir

115

Thomas Wyatt and the Earl of Surrey were developing a delicate Italia-nate style. Thomas Nashe wrote powerful, eccentric prose which he called 'swelling and boisterous', and when he ran short of words to de-scribe the unfortunate Dr. Harvey he invented new ones:

> There is a Doctor and his Fart that haue kept a foule stinking stirre in Paules Churchyard; I crie him mercy, I slaundered him, he is scarce a Doctor till he hath done his Acts: this dodipoule, this didopper, this professed poetical braggart hath raild vpon me, without wit or art, in certaine foure penniworth of Letters and three farthing-worth of Sonnets; nor do I mean to present him and *Shakerley* to the Queens foole-taker for coatch-horses: for two that draw more equallie in one Oratoriall yoke of vaine-glorie, there is not vnder heauen . . . Why thou arrant butter whore, thou cotqueane & scrattop of scoldes, wilt thou neuer leaue afflicting a dead Carcasse, continually read the rethorick lecture of Ramme Allie? a wispe, a wispe, rippe, rippe, you kitchin-stuffe wrangler!
>
> Thomas Nashe (1567–1601)
> *Strange Newes of the Intercepting Certaine Letters*

In 1602 England got its first almost-public library when Sir Thomas Bodley opened the great Bodleian Library at Oxford. Sir Thomas had a little problem with his librarian. For some reason, librarians managed to win a reputation during the century of being uncultured fellows:

> Unlearned men of books assume the care,
> As eunuchs are the guardians of the fair.
> Edward Young (1683–1765)
> *Love of Fame*

By the year 1739 the unlearnedness of librarians had become enough of a stock joke to earn a place in Joe Miller's joke book:

> A Nobleman having chose a very illiterate Person for his Library Keeper, one said it was like *a Seraglio kept by an Eunuch.*
> John Mottley (1692–1750)
> *Joe Miller's Jests or, the Wits Vade-Mecum*, Para. 90

> Sir Thomas Bodley's problem was that his chosen librarian was far from being illiterate and had no intention of being a eunuch. Dr. James was a formidable scholar and he wanted to get married. Sir Thomas, who was all in favour of the eunuch principle being applied to librarians, urged Dr. James to remain celibate and overcome his 'unseasonable and un-reasonable motions', warning him that 'marriage is too full of domestic impeachments'. Dr. James married. Furthermore, by threatening to with-hold his labour he managed to get his salary increased from £5. 13s. 4d. a quarter to £40 p.a.

Written English settled down a little in the seventeenth century, helped by the publication of the Authorized Version of the Bible, which was written in a prose style which managed to be at the same time rich, simple, noble and timeless. A little credit might perhaps go to King James I, our most literary monarch – which is not saying very much; when John Stow the great antiquarian, nearly eighty and poverty-stricken, asked the King for help he was granted letters patent under the great seal 'to gather the benevolence of well-disposed people within this realm of England: to ask, gather, and take the alms of all our loving subjects.' In other words, he was given a licence to beg.

The King wrote a little, which was not uncommon among monarchs. What was most unusual was that he had his work printed and published. Authorship did not become socially acceptable until much later in the century. One of the first times it was mentioned as a recognised trade was in a pamphlet primly disapproving of the King getting himself mixed up in it:

> Since writing of books has grown into a trade, it is as discreditable for a king to become an author as it would be for him to be a practitioner in a profession.
>
> Anon. (c. 1615)

Authors wrote for a variety of reasons in those days. The King wrote because he had things to say about Scots poetry and kingship and the brutish habit of smoking. Academics wrote new translations, and commentaries on the classical authors; in an effort to return to the pure Latin of Cicero the ancient authors were subjected to more scholarly criticism:

> Seneca writes as a Boare does pisse, *scilicet* by jirkes.
>
> Dr Ralph Kettell (1563–1643)
President of Trinity College, Oxford
Quoted by John Aubrey: Brief Lives

scilicet = that is to say.
  Fair comment on Seneca's frequently uneven and sibilant lines, e.g.:
    'Quis candidatus laboret:
    Quis alienis:
    Quis suis varibus pugnet:
    Quis consulatum.'

Robert Burton had a good reason for writing *The Anatomy of Melancholy*, but it rebounded:

> He composed his book with a view of relieving his own melancholy, but increased it to such a degree, that nothing could make him laugh.
>
> James Granger (1723–1776)
Biographical History of England

Nobody as yet wrote for the money which would come from the sale of copies of their book. The most that booksellers would do for their authors, and then reluctantly, was give them a pound or two in exchange for total copyright.

John Milton wrote the great epic poem *Paradise Lost* not because he felt a burning need to 'justify God's ways to man' but because he wanted to write a great epic poem. He originally toyed with the notion of basing a poem on the King Arthur legend but eventually decided that there was more scope and majesty in the story of the Fall of Man. And so, in 1667, his great cathedral of blank verse was published:

> **Paradise Lost is one of the books which the reader admires and lays down, and forgets to take up again. Its perusal is a duty rather than a pleasure.**
>
> Samuel Johnson (1709–1784)
> *Lives of the Poets:* 'Milton'

> **Read not Milton, for he is dry.**
> C. S. Calverley (1831–1884)
> *Of Reading*

> **Our language sunk under him.**
> Joseph Addison (1672–1719)
> Quoted by Samuel Johnson, *Lives of the Poets:* 'Milton'

> It was a good thing that Milton did not write it for the money. He sold the copyright to a bookseller, Simmons, for £5 plus another £5 after three editions of 1500 copies had been sold. His widow sold what was left of the copyright for £8.

Although authors made little or no money out of their work during the seventeenth century, shrewd bookseller-publishers made fortunes.

Perhaps the first professional publisher in the modern sense of the word was Jacob Tonson, who made a huge fortune from buying and exploiting copyrights, beginning with his purchase of a half-share in *Paradise Lost*. He published much of Addison and Pope's work, made a lot of money from investments in the South Sea and Mississippi schemes and retired to the country, from where he sent little presents of home-brewed cider to his friends the Dukes of Grafton and Newcastle.

One of Tonson's authors was John Dryden, the playwright and poet, who penned a fragment of description of his publisher under Tonson's portrait:

> **With leering Looks, Bull-fac'd, and freckl'd fair,**
> **With two left Legs, and *Judas*-colour'd Hair,**
> **And frowzy Pores that taint the ambient Air.**
> John Dryden (1631–1700)
> Printed later in *Faction Displayed*

> Dryden thought that Tonson was a little too sharp in his dealings.

The Restoration restored, amongst other things, a looser censorship of the written word and a relish for the coarse and improper: excellent conditions for the production of vigorous satire.

The most vigorous satirist of the day was Dryden, the leading man of letters. A fair specimen of late seventeenth-century satire at its most powerful was Dryden's attack on the dramatist Shadwell, a stout person addicted to opium, who became one of the more forgettable Poet Laureates. In the poem *Absalom and Achitophel,* a piece of aggression against the anti-Catholic plotter, the Earl of Shaftesbury, Shadwell was cast as *Og*:

> Now stop your noses, Readers, all and some,
> For here's a Tun of Midnight work to come,
> *Og*, from a Treason Tavern rowling home.
> Round as a Globe, and Liquored ev'ry chink,
> Goodly and Great he Sayls behind his Link;
> With all this bulk there's nothing lost in *Og*,
> For ev'ry inch that is not Fool is Rogue:
> A Monstrous mass of foul corrupted matter,
> As all the Devils had spew'd to make the batter.
> When wine has given him courage to Blaspheme
> He curses God, but God before Curst him;
> And if man cou'd have reason, none has more
> That made his Paunch so rich and him so poor.
> With wealth he was not trusted, for Heav'n knew
> What 'twas of old to pamper up a *Jew*;
> To what would he on Quail and Pheasant swell,
> That ev'n on Tripe and Carrion cou'd rebell?
> But though Heav'n made him poor (with rev'rence speaking)
> He never was a poet of God's making;
> The Midwife laid her hand on his Thick Skull
> With this prophetick blessing – Be thou Dull.

John Dryden (1631–1700)
Absalom and Achitophel

Those were eventful times for authors. The Earl of Rochester, suspecting that Dryden had a hand in an *Essay on Satire* which attacked Rochester, hired a posse of ruffians who thumped the poet with cudgels as he emerged from Will's Coffee House on the evening of 18 December 1679.

In the same year that *Paradise Lost* was published (1667) *The History of the Royal Society of London for the Improving of Natural Knowledge,* by Thomas Sprat, was published and the polite world of letters became acutely aware of Science. Sprat wrote:

> **Poetry is the parent of superstition.**

Thomas Sprat (1635–1713)
History of the Royal Society

By the beginning of the eighteenth century most of the superstition inherited from medieval days had departed from poetry in favour of a recapturing of the formal, witty, polished verse perfected by Virgil, Horace and Ovid in the first century A.D., Rome's Augustan Age.

The most remarkable figure of England's Augustan Age of literature was Alexander Pope. He was a tiny man, just four feet six inches tall, and very frail – when young he had nearly been killed by a cow – and he had to be strapped into a canvas corset to keep him upright. His legs were so thin that he wore three pairs of stockings to give them some appearance of substance.

Pope was secretive and devious, both in promoting his career and in day-to-day affairs:

> He hardly drank tea without a stratagem.
>
> Samuel Johnson (1709–1784)
> *Lives of the Poets:* 'Pope'

A little sensitive about his modest background, his father had been a well-to-do linen draper, Pope put it about that he was connected with the Earls of Downe. This did not fool one genuine aristocrat, who wrote about Pope and his friend Swift:

> It is pleasant to consider, that, had it not been for the good nature of these very mortals they contemn, these two superior beings were entitled by their birth and hereditary fortune, to be only a couple of link-boys.
>
> Lady Mary Wortley Montagu (1689–1762)
> Letter to the Countess of Bute, 1752

Lady Mary Wortley Montagu was remarkable in her own right. She was highly intelligent and articulate, the eldest daughter of the Earl of Kingston. As her family did not bother much with an education for her she taught herself Latin whilst still a child and eloped, for love, at the age of twenty-three. She went to Constantinople with her husband but he turned out to be a bore so she left him. She introduced inoculation into England, wrote verse, and travelled abroad, growing more eccentric and careless of her clothes as she grew older – to the horror of a fastidious Englishman who glimpsed her:

> Her dress, her avarice, and her impudence must amaze any one that never heard her name. She wears a foul mob, that does not cover her greasy black locks, that hang loose, never combed or curled; an old mazarine blue wrapper, that gapes open and discovers a canvass petticoat. Her face swelled violently on one side with the remains of a ——, partly covered with a plaister, and partly with white paint, which for cheapness she has bought so coarse, that you would not use it to wash a chimney.
>
> Horace Walpole (1717–1797)
> Letter to the Hon. H. S. Conway, Florence, 25 Sept. 1740

Lady Mary was friendly with Pope at one time and she and her husband took a villa near his at Twickenham, but something went wrong and Pope quarrelled violently with her. Many reasons have been put forward for Pope's change of face, the most likely being that when he told her of the deep passion he had for her she burst into a peal of laughter. A second possibility was that he flew into a rage when she borrowed some bed sheets from him and returned them unwashed. A

120

third was that she did not share his gamy sense of humour and passed a disparaging remark about an epitaph Pope had written concerning two rural lovers who had been struck by lightning:

Here lye two poor Lovers, who had the mishap
Tho very chaste people, to die of a Clap.

Alexander Pope (1688–1744)
Letter to Lady Mary Montagu, 1 Sept. 1718

Edith Sitwell later sided with Pope and described Lady Mary as:

A dilapidated macaw with a hard, piercing laugh, mirthless and joyless, with a few unimaginative phrases, with a parrot's powers of observation, and a parrot's hard and poisonous bite.

Edith Sitwell (1887–1964)
Alexander Pope

Malicious quarrels conducted in verse seem to have given Pope much satisfaction:

The verses, when they were written, resembled nothing so much as spoonfuls of boiling oil, ladled out by a fiendish monkey at an upstairs window upon such of the passers-by whom the wretch had a grudge against.

Lytton Strachey (1880–1932)
The Leslie Stephen Lecture for 1925: *Pope*

He ladled his boiling oil over Lady Mary in a number of poems. In a typical section he described the home life of Lady Mary and her husband Edward, poetically styled Avidien:

Avidien or his wife (no matter which,
For him you'll call a dog, and her a bitch)
Sell their presented partridges and fruits,
And humbly live on rabbits and on roots.
One half-pint bottle serves them both to dine,
And is at once their vinegar and wine.
But on some lucky day (as when they found
A lost bank-bill, or heard their son was drown'd)
At such a feast, old vinegar to spare,
Is what two souls so generous cannot bear.

Alexander Pope (1688–1744)
Imitations of Horace

The reference to the son drowning was only an artistic insult; he died in his sixties at Padua after swallowing a fish-bone. Lady Mary eventually returned to England, allegedly expiring with the words, 'It has all been most interesting.'

One of Lady Mary's lifelong friends was Lord Hervey. This would have been enough to earn him a ladleful of boiling oil, but he also wrote some sharp anti-Pope pamphlets, in one of which he hinted that Pope's father was a common hatter. Hervey's unfortunate appearance made him vulnerable to attack from 'the wicked wasp of Twickenham';

because of epilepsy he existed on a diet of asses' milk and biscuits and he coloured his chalk-white face with rouge. He was bisexual but he had eight children by his wife and shared a mistress, Miss Vane, with the Prince of Wales.

The attack came in what is widely accepted as Pope's masterpiece, *An Epistle to Dr. Arbuthnot*. What was perhaps characteristic of Pope was that he wrote the poem partly to explain what a sweetly reasonable man he really was. Lord Hervey appeared in the poem as *Sporus*:

> Let Sporus tremble – 'What? that Thing of silk,
> '*Sporus*, that mere white Curd of Ass's milk?
> 'Satire or Shame alas! can *Sporus* feel?
> 'Who breaks a Butterfly upon a Wheel?'
> Yet let me flap this Bug with gilded wings,
> This painted Child of Dirt that stinks and stings;
> Whose Buzz the Witty and the Fair annoys,
> Yet Wit ne'er tastes, and Beauty ne'er enjoys,
> So well-bred Spaniels civilly delight
> In mumbling of the Game they dare not bite.
> Eternal Smiles his emptiness betray,
> As shallow streams run dimpling all the way.
> Whether in florid Impotence he speaks,
> And, as the Prompter breathes, the Puppet squeaks
> Or at the ear of *Eve*, familiar Toad,
> Half Froth, half Venom, spits himself abroad,
> In Puns, or Politicks, or Tales, or Lyes,
> Or Spite, or Smut, or Rymes, or Blasphemies.
> Did ever Smock-face act so vile a Part?
> A trifling Head, and a corrupted Heart!
> *Eve*'s Tempter thus the Rabbins have exprest,
> A Cherub's face, a Reptile all the rest;
> Beauty that shocks you, Parts that none will trust,
> Wit that can creep, and Pride that licks the dust.
>
> Alexander Pope (1688–1744)
> *Epistle to Dr. Arbuthnot*

In an early issue of the first edition of the poem Lord Hervey was called *Paris*. This almost certainly referred to the homosexual Roman pantomimic dancer *Paris* whom Nero put to death, not to the Greek hero. It would seem that Pope started with the name *Paris* and then decided that *Sporus* – the name of Nero's castrated slave 'wife' – had an even nastier connotation.

Although Pope made and kept some good friends, like Swift and John Gay and Dr. Arbuthnot, he was morbidly sensitive to antagonism and swung into action whenever he suspected a friend or a foe of belittling him or his work. It did not matter whether the belittler was a powerful man or a Grub Street hack, he was for it.

One of Pope's more extraordinary vendettas was against Colley Cibber, the actor-manager, dramatist and Poet Laureate.

Dr. Johnson wrote that though 'Pope attacked Cibber with acrimony, the provocation is not easily discoverable'. Pope might have been enraged at Cibber having been made Poet Laureate on the strength of a few dismal odes, but Pope was a Roman Catholic and was therefore debarred from any official office, or honours, or, indeed, from living in London.

Cibber thought the antipathy began when he ad-libbed some fairly harmless remarks about Pope during a performance of *The Rehearsal*. Pope went back-stage afterwards in something of a state, 'his lips pale and his voice trembling, to call me to account for the insult; and accordingly fell upon me with all the foul language that a Wit out of his senses could be capable of, choaked with the foam of his passion'.

Pope then went home and continued to fall upon Cibber in print:

> Cibber! write all thy Verses upon Glasses,
> The only way to save 'em from our Arses.
> Alexander Pope (1688–1744)

Pope's *The Dunciad*, an attack on all the writers both great and small who had annoyed him, had as its chief butt Lewis Theobald, a poverty-stricken scholar and editor who had printed forty-four pages of mistakes which he had found in Pope's edition of Shakespeare. In a new issue of *The Dunciad* Pope demoted Theobald and made Cibber the chief butt. What particularly infuriated Pope was the common practice at that time of writers imitating other writers:

> Now wits gain praise by copying other wits
> As one Hog lives on what another shits.
> Alexander Pope (1688–1744)
> *The Dunciad*

A colourful metaphor but zoologically inaccurate. Pope was right though, in resenting imitation – the rest of his century was to be plagued with soggy, flat-footed imitations of his own work.

None of these attacks troubled the easy-going Cibber. For some reason the line which got under his skin and stung him into counter-attacking was a reference to him in the *Epistle*:

> Has not C–*lly* still his Lord, and Whore?
> Alexander Pope (1688–1744)
> *Epistle to Dr. Arbuthnot*

Cibber's revenge was to publish a letter describing what happened one evening when the line about having a Lord and a Whore fitted Pope:

He may remember then, (or if he will not, I will) when Button's coffee-house was in vogue, and so long ago as when he had not translated above two or three books of Homer; there was a late young nobleman (as much his *Lord* as mine) who had a good deal of wicked humour. This noble wag ... one evening slily seduced the celebrated Mr. Pope as a wit, and myself as a laughter, to a certain house of

123

carnal recreation, near the Haymarket; where his lordship's frolic proposed was, to *slip his little Homer*, as he called him, at a girl of the game ... in which he so far succeeded, that the smirking damsel, who served us with tea, happened to have charms sufficient to tempt the little-tiny manhood of Mr. Pope into the next room with her: at which, you may imagine, his lordship was in as much joy, at what might happen within, as our small friend could probably be in possession of it: but I ... observing he had staid as long as without hazard of his health he might, ... threw open the door upon him, where I found this little hasty hero, like a terrible *Tom-Tit*, pertly perching upon the mount of love! But such was my surprize that I fairly laid hold of his heels, and actually drew him down safe from his danger.

Colley Cibber (1671–1757)
A Letter from Mr. Cibber to Mr. Pope, Inquiring into the
Motives that Might Induce Him in His Satyrical Works,
to be so Frequently Fond of Mr. Cibber's Name

Soon after the pamphlet was published a newspaper printed an artist's impression of the dramatic scene in the house of carnal recreation. Cibber followed this with a second *Letter* in which he probed for the poet's nerve with a more lyrical description of what happened:

'When crawling in thy dangerous deed of darkness, I gently, with a finger and a thumb, picked off thy small round body by thy long legs, like a spider making love in a cobweb.'

Pope never denied that the incident took place.

Pope must have been one of the first authors to make a rich living from the sale of his books rather than from government pensions and handouts from patrons. But he was the leading poet of his day. At the other end of the scale came the Grub Street hacks, who were often, rather unfairly, the objects of his satire.

Grub Street was renamed Milton Street in 1830 – not after John Milton the poet but, it seems, the builder who owned the lease – only to disappear without trace in the 1970s beneath the concrete of the Barbican building scheme. The street was originally the centre of London's bow-and-arrow-making trade, but it declined into an unsavoury haunt of bowling-alleys and dicing-houses. In the middle of the seventeenth century it became a hide-out for dissenters with their printing-presses – Oliver Cromwell lived there at one period – and by the end of the seventeenth century it had sunk to its lowest as the lodging-house centre for impoverished dictionary compilers, and writers of 'small histories' and 'temporary poems'. Grub Street, more a concept of instant, scurrilous, hit-and-run publishing than a geographical location, had a system whereby booksellers provided subsistence-level bed and board for hack writers in exchange for their output. This sometimes worked, but the booksellers were a tough, rough, competitive lot and they were in and out of the sponging-houses almost as frequently as their employees.

One of the best-known writers of 'temporary poems' gave a description of what life was like as a Grub Street man-of-letters:

Without formal petition
Thus stands my condition:
I am closely blocked up in a garret,
Where I scribble and smoke,
And sadly invoke
The powerful assistance of claret.
Four children and a wife,
'Tis hard on my life,
Beside myself and a muse,
To be all clothed and fed,
Now the times are so dead,
By my scribbling of doggerel and news.
And what shall I do,
I'm a wretch if I know,
So hard is the fate of a poet;
I must either turn rogue,
Or, what's as bad, pedagogue,
And so drudge like a thing that has no wit.
My levee's all duns,
Attended by bums,
And my landlady too she's a teaser,
At least four times a day
She warns me away,
And what can a man do to please her?
Here's the victualler and vintner,
The cook and the printer,
With their myrmidons hovering about, sir:
The tailor and draper,
With the cur that sells paper,
That, in short, I dare not stir out, sir,
But my books sure may go,
My master Ovid's did so,
And tell how doleful the case is;
If it don't move your pity,
To make short of my ditty,
'Twill serve you to wipe your arses.

Tom Brown (1663–1704)
The Poet's Condition

The biggest difficulty facing a would-be professional author at the opening of the eighteenth century was his lack of legal right to royalties on the sale of his books. Under the Romans, and well into the medieval period, the copyright in a manuscript belonged to whoever owned the piece of material it was written upon; it was a simple matter of owning a lump of tangible property. When printing came to England the government made haste to censor it by giving the Stationers' Company a monopoly on publishing, thus making the Stationers' Company the holder of all copyrights.

Pressure built up during the latter part of the seventeenth century against the Stationers' Company monopoly, and strong pleas were made to successive governments to end it. The campaign eventually succeeded and in 1709 an Act, Statute 8 Anne, *c.* 19, was passed, the first in the world to give an author a right to his own property.

The booksellers who were behind the Act had no thought of bringing prosperity to the trade of author; it was a monopoly-breaking move for the benefit of the bookselling trade and authors were merely the excuse for it. By the wording of the act an author owned the copyright of his work, but the action of having it published gave the bookseller fourteen years exclusive rights in the work, after which the rights were supposed to revert to the author. In effect this meant that once the booksellers had paid the author a few guineas for the copyright, they could exploit the property, or barter it among themselves, for a period of fourteen years without necessarily paying anything more to the author:

> What Authors lose, their Booksellers have won,
> So Pimps grow rich, while Gallants are undone.
>
> Alexander Pope (1688–1744)

Booksellers numbered several colourful characters in their midst, including a Stephen Fletcher who won himself a paragraph in a contemporary diary:

> He was a very proud, confident, ill-natured, impudent, ignorant fellow, peevish and froward to his wife (whom he used to beat), a great sot, and a whoring prostituted wretch, and of no credit, though he always made a great stir and bustle.
>
> Thomas Hearne (1678–1735)
> Diary, 16 Sept. 1727

froward = perverse.
Hearne, an antiquarian, was inclined to be a bit peevish and froward himself. He was dealt with by Pope as Wormius in *The Dunciad*.

Oliver Goldsmith was one author who regretted that the Act had been passed. He wrote of it as:

> That fatal revolution whereby writing is converted to a mechanic trade; and booksellers, instead of the great, become the patrons and paymasters of men of genius.
>
> Oliver Goldsmith (1728–1744)
> *The Distresses of a Hired Writer*

Goldsmith had some squalid experiences as a bookseller's hack writer.

Having dealings with many booksellers in the early eighteenth century was a weary and tedious business for authors:

> Happy is the Man who has no other Acquaintance with Booksellers, than what is Contracted by Reading the News in their Shops, and perhaps now and then buying a Book of them; but he that is so

> unfortunate as to have business with them about Translating, Printing or Publishing any Thing to the World has a Miserable Time of it, and ought to be endowed with the Patience of *Job*.
>
> Bernard de Mandeville (1670–1733)
The Virgin Unmask'd

Undoubtedly the most colourful and unscrupulous bookseller-publisher of the eighteenth century, if not of all time, was the Unspeakable Curll: Edmund Curll (1675–1747). He was Grub Street personified, publishing everything likely to make him a swift guinea from hardcore pornography to Erdewicke's *Survey of Staffordshire*. He was utterly without principles and was renowned in his own day for such dishonest practices as including famous names on the title page although little or nothing of the text had been written by them, pirating other booksellers' works, giving lascivious titles to books with humdrum contents and stealing well-known people's correspondence and whipping out a volume of their letters.

Horace Walpole was understandably nervous at making his correspondence from abroad too interesting:

> And then one should have that odious Curl get at one's letters, and publish them like Whitfield's Journal, or for a supplement to the Traveller's Pocket-companion.
>
> Horace Walpole (1717–1797)
˙Letter to Richard West, Bologna, 1739

Daniel Defoe was shocked by some ripe bawdy books published by Curll, and wrote (anonymously) in a paper which he edited:

> There is indeed but one bookseller eminent among us for this abomination, and from him the crime takes the just denomination of *Curlicism*. The fellow is a contemptible wretch a thousand ways: he is odious in person, scandalous in his fame; he is marked by Nature, for he has a bawdy countenance, and a debauched mien; his tongue is an echo of all the beastly language his shop is filled with, and filthiness drivels in the very tone of his voice.
>
> Daniel Defoe (1661?–1731)
Weekly Journal, 5 April 1718

Curll replied with a pamphlet. His argument nobly defending the good name of pornography was one only too familiar to some modern Sunday newspaper editors:

> With relation to the publishing these books, I am farther to assure your old man [Defoe], that they cannot by the laws of nature and nations be termed *bawdy* books, since they treat only of matters of the greatest importance to society, conduce to the mutual happiness of the nuptial state, and are directly calculated for antidotes against debauchery and unnatural lewdness.
>
> Edmund Curll (1675–1747)
Curlicism Display'd

Seven years later Curll published two more of his antidotes to debauchery and unnatural lewdness, entitled *The Nun in her Smock* and *The Treatise of Flogging*. The antidotal value of these works was not obvious and Curll was prosecuted. He spent a few months in prison while his case dragged on. Eventually he got off with a fine but was convicted on another charge, a political affront, and was sentenced to an hour in the Charing Cross pillory – which could have been very painful, even lethal. But Curll had leaflets spread through the crowd saying that he was there for affirming his devotion to the late Queen Anne. The mob cheered him and carried him off to the nearest tavern.

A few physical indignities came his way. He was forced to go on his knees at the bar of the House of Lords, begging their lordships' pardon for various libels, seditions and piracies. He was tossed in a blanket by the boys of Westminster School for printing inaccurate Latin. He was poisoned by Alexander Pope in the Swan Tavern, Fleet Street, for a bit of double-dealing concerning Lady Mary Wortley Montagu: Pope slipped an emetic into Curll's drink, reported as being ground glass, and Curll had a rather unpleasant few hours. But on the whole Curll got away with it. He never made much money, but he published a great many books, some of considerable value to scholarship.

It could not have been his physical charms which carried him through:

> Curll was in person very tall and thin, an ungainly, awkward, white-faced man. His eyes were a light grey, large, projecting, goggle, and purblind. He was splay-footed and baker-kneed ... he was a debauchee.
>
> Thomas Amory (1691?–1788)
Life of John Buncle, Esq.

baker-kneed = knock-kneed.

A literary innovation of the early eighteenth century, which Curll's inventive machinations helped to establish as a profitable line for booksellers, was Instant Biography. When a person of note died a 'True and Authentic Account' of his life would be cobbled together by a hack from such snippets of gossip as could be garnered in a few hours and rushed through the press – frequently with a 'True and Authentic' account of what might be in the will as an appendix – before the wreaths had withered on the grave:

> Biography is one of the new terrors of death.
>
> Dr. John Arbuthnot (1667–1735)
Quoted by Robert Carruthers: *Life of Pope*

It was a competitive business and the rewards went to the first man to get his book out. Vigilance was called for:

> Our Grubstreet *biographers* watch for the death of a great man, like so many undertakers, on purpose to make a penny of him.
>
> Joseph Addison (1672–1719)
Freeholder, No. 35

The word 'biographer' was comparatively new then, only going back as far as 1661. Dr. Johnson used Addison's comment in his dictionary to illustrate the use of the word. 'Biography' was first used in print by Dryden in the preface to his translation of Plutarch's *Lives* (1683).

A lady later on in the century regretted that biographers did not take pains to stress the virtues of their subject:

This new-fashioned biography seems to value itself upon perpetuating every thing that is injurious and detracting.

> Hannah More (1745–1833)
> Letter to a sister, April 1786

But fairness, a modern biographer pointed out, was not a factor that came into it much:

Biography, like big game hunting, is one of the recognised forms of sport, and it is unfair as only sport can be.

> Philip Guedalla (1899–1944)
> *Supers and Supermen*

Although writing had now become a recognized profession it was still not regarded by the upper echelon of society as a very honourable way of earning a living (if the existence led by the authors who were dependent on Curll, and all the would-be Curlls, could be called living).

The Elizabethan attitude still lingered on that writing poetry, playing a musical instrument and treading a measure were social accomplishments which the nobility enjoyed practising at home, in private. A member of the aristocracy would no more have thought of accepting money for a book than he would of playing music for a fee or dancing for profit:

A person of quality should never turn author ... one of the most distinguished prerogatives of mankind, writing, when duly executed does honour to human nature. If done for the purpose of making money it is contemptible.

> Lady Mary Wortley Montagu (1689–1762)
> Letter to Lady Bute, 23 July 1753

This lofty attitude towards literature lingered on here and there for another century:

To practise art in order to earn money, flatter the public, spin facetious or dismal yarns for reputation or cash — that is the most ignoble of professions.

> Gustave Flaubert (1821–1880)
> Letter to his mother, Rome, 8 April 1851

Flaubert had a little money of his own.

Besides the aristocrats who would not have taken the booksellers' money even if they had been offered it, there were other authors who, almost by tradition, had never asked for money for their work. These included many technical and religious writers, travellers, and political or social satirists:

> I never got a farthing by anything I writ, except one about eight years ago.

Jonathan Swift (1667–1745)
Letter to Wm. Pulteney Esq., Dublin, 12 May 1735

The one exception was *Gulliver's Travels*, for which his friend Pope – and who better – negotiated a copyright fee of £200.

Dr. Johnson was quite clear where he stood on the question of whether an author should require money for his services:

> No man but a blockhead ever wrote, except for money.

Samuel Johnson (1709–1784)
Boswell's *Life*, 5 April 1776

An author in the eighteenth century had two alternatives to trying to screw his rights out of the booksellers. One was to find a patron. This he did, and had done for centuries, by asking permission to dedicate his volume to an important personage. If the personage found the volume pleasing he was expected to toss a bag of gold to the author, find him a sinecure job in government or, if the author was a clergyman, get him a richer parish. The traditional way to a personage's favours was through his vanity, and sixteenth and seventeenth-century personages, from the King downwards, were bombarded with volumes prefixed with dedications so servile and flattering that only an idiot or somebody ill with ego could believe them.

A fair example of the cringing dedication was one prefixed to an assize sermon and dedicated to the Lord Chief Justice:

> For the greatest Obscurities of the Law, Its most sullen difficulties scatter before Your Lordship's Eye, as the Clouds before the Sun. The most intricate Knotty Cases, you Untye with that Ease and Dexterity, as that they seem of themselves to open. It is not in You to cut or force, It consists not with that sweetness of Temper, by which You so charm all You have to deal with, as that You seem most deservedly to inherit that Glorious Title of the Great Vespasian, of being the Darling of Mankind. For the very Curse of the Law You manage with that Tenderness and Indulgent Affection, as even that the Condemn'd go away Satisfied, if not pleas'd. That I might not therefore appear the only stubborn Thing in Nature, I submit and subscribe my Self, My Lord, Your Honors most humble and obedient Servant, Ab. Campion.

Prefixed to an assize sermon, 13 March 1693/4
Ab. Campion, D. D., Rector of Monks Risborough
Quoted in *Notes and Queries*, 22 Aug. 1896

The alternative to writing a servile dedication to a potential patron was to publish by subscription, a practice which grew up in the latter half of the seventeenth century. The snag with this method was that it could only be used by well-known, 'star' writers. In a sense it was a kind of patronage by a syndicate; a writer would announce that he had a new book on the stocks and a large number of people would be asked to order, and pay for, copies in advance. In return they would have their names in a List of Subscribers in the front of the book. *Paradise Lost* was the first book to be published by subscription, making the publisher Tonson a good profit but making Milton nothing at all because he had already parted with the copyright. But John Dryden, according to Pope who was obsessed with knowing this kind of information, made £1200 by publishing his translation of Virgil by subscription – a huge sum in those days – and Pope himself cleared over £5000 with his translation of Homer, making him financially independent for life.

Samuel Johnson's great dictionary was not financed by subscription but by a syndicate of seven booksellers led by Robert Dodsley. Dodsley managed to persuade Johnson to dedicate his Plan of the dictionary to the aristocratic and literate statesman Lord Chesterfield, whose name would lend distinction to the enterprise. Johnson loathed the implications of the patronage system but agreed – to win himself a bit more time to finish writing the Plan – and produced a superbly uncringing dedication.

Dodsley's hopes were dashed. Chesterfield accepted the Plan, had a few words with Johnson and sent him ten pounds, an amount which Johnson felt was too derisory to bother about, and did nothing more. Seven years later, when the colossal work was almost complete after immense difficulties and hardship, Chesterfield got wind of it and wrote two essays in *The World* complimentary to Johnson and the dictionary. It was altogether a shabby episode; not only was Chesterfield associating himself with a work which he had done little to help upon its way but one of the essays contained a cheap joke about a pair of would-be lovers who missed their assignation because they were unable to produce the kind of correct spelling which the dictionary taught.

Johnson's famous letter of reproach to Lord Chesterfield, which followed, was not full of Johnsonian sound and fury but was instead beautifully judged in style so as to condemn Chesterfield in his own cool, exact language; the supreme example of a creative man's contempt for privileged insincerity:

My Lord,
   I have been lately informed by the proprietor of the *World*, that two papers, in which my *Dictionary* is recommended to the public, were written by your lordship. To be so distinguished is an honour, which, being very little accustomed to favours from the great, I know not well how to receive, or in what terms to acknowledge.

When, upon some slight encouragement, I first visited your lordship, I was overpowered, like the rest of mankind, by the enchantment of your address, and could not forbear to wish that I might boast myself *le vainqueur du vainqueur de la terre* – that I might obtain that regard for which I saw the world contending; but I found my attendance so little encouraged, that neither pride nor modesty would suffer me to continue it. When I had once addressed your lordship in public, I had exhausted all the art of pleasing which a retired and uncourtly scholar can possess. I had done all that I could; and no man is well pleased to have his all neglected, be it ever so little.

Seven years, my lord, have now passed since I waited in your outward rooms, or was repulsed from your door; during which time I have been pushing on my work through difficulties, of which it is useless to complain, and have brought it at last to the verge of publication, without one act of assistance, one word of encouragement, or one smile of favour. Such treatment I did not expect, for I never had a patron before.

The shepherd in Virgil grew at last acquainted with Love, and found him a native of the rocks.

Is not a patron, my lord, one who looks with unconcern on a man struggling for life in the water, and when he has reached ground encumbers him with help? The notice which you have been pleased to take of my labours, had it been early, had been kind; but it has been delayed till I am indifferent, and cannot enjoy it; till I am solitary, and cannot impart it; till I am known, and do not want it. I hope it is no very cynical asperity not to confess obligations where no benefit has been received, or to be unwilling that the public should consider me as owing that to a patron which Providence has enabled me to do for myself.

Having carried on my work thus far with so little obligation to any favourer of learning, I shall not be disappointed though I should conclude it, if less be possible, with less: for I have been long wakened from that dream of hope, in which I once boasted myself with so much exultation, my Lord – Your lordship's most humble, most obedient servant,

Sam Johnson.

Samuel Johnson (1709–1784)
Letter to Lord Chesterfield, 7 Feb. 1775

The letter did not even dent Lord Chesterfield's bullet-proof urbanity. He left the letter lying on his hall table where visitors could read it, and even read it aloud to Dodsley, the bookseller, remarking 'this man has great powers'. But literary patronage was never the same again.

Philip Dormer Stanhope, fourth Earl of Chesterfield, statesman and diplomatist, essayist and wit, is chiefly remembered today because he gave his name to an overcoat and a large, overstuffed sofa, and he wrote a remarkable volume of letters.

Letters written by the late Right Honourable Philip Dormer Stanhope, Earl of Chesterfield, to his son, Philip Stanhope, Esq.; late Envoy Extraordinary at the court of Dresden: together with several other pieces on various subjects was a collection of the letters which Lord Chesterfield wrote to his natural son with the object of instructing the lad in the ways of the world. They were not designed to be improving sermons but to be a survival-kit in a cynical and privileged society:

> I borrowed here a volume of Lord Chesterfield's Letters, which I had heard very strongly commended. And what did I learn? — That he was a man of much wit, middling sense, and some learning; but as absolutely void of virtue, as a Jew, Turk, or Heathen, that ever lived ... truth he sets at absolute defiance. He continually guards him [his son] against it. Half his letters inculcate deep dissimulation, as the most necessary of all accomplishments. Add to this, his studiously instilling into the young man all the principles of debauchery, when himself was between seventy and eighty years old ... if he is rewarded according to his desert, his name will stink to all generations.
>
> John Wesley (1703–1791)
> Diary, 11 Oct. 1775

> They teach the morals of a whore, and the manners of a dancing master.
>
> Samuel Johnson (1709–1784)
> Boswell's *Life*

The letters failed in their objective. When the son died at the age of thirty-six Chesterfield learnt that he had married in secret; a course of action not recommended in the letters. And he had chosen a rather plain girl of lowly birth. The idea of the letters might have come from Chesterfield's grandfather, the great George Savile, Marquess of Halifax, who wrote *Advice to a Daughter* to his daughter, Chesterfield's mother. *Advice to a Daughter*, published in 1688, was hugely popular for a century, both in England and on the Continent. It was no more successful than Chesterfield's *Letters* in its objective: Halifax's daughter turned out an intolerable shrew and, according to Horace Walpole, her husband wrote in her copy of her father's *Advice*, 'Wasted effort!'

Another eighteenth-century innovation, and another source of free manuscripts to booksellers, was the rise of literary Ladies of Quality. One of the more forceful of these was Mrs. Elizabeth Montagu, a powerful figure in London society.

Mrs. Montagu was extremely rich, a happy circumstance which she did nothing to hide. She built a mansion in Portman Square, one room of which she herself covered with feathers from almost every known bird. It was in that room that she later gave a breakfast party for seven hundred guests. Her best-known literary work was an essay (of 288 pages) defending Shakespeare against the opinions of Voltaire.

Assemblies and dinner-parties were dreadfully dull affairs in those days for ladies with any kind of intellectual powers, consisting mainly of trivial gossip and card-games. Mrs. Montagu, armed with her wealth, was able to break through the ennui-inducing conventions and institute 'conversation parties' where card-playing was forbidden and ladies were encouraged to discuss literary matters.

133

Admiral Edward Boscawen, a bluff sea-dog known as 'the old Dread-nought' or 'Wry-necked Dick', was so peeved at his wife's enthusiasm for these relaxed, intellectual evenings that he gave the literary ladies the contemptuous name of 'blue-stockings':

A blue-stocking is the scourge of her husband, children, friends, serv-ants, and every one.

Jean-Jacques Rousseau (1712–1778)
Correspondence

It seems that the first 'blue-stocking' was in fact a man. He wore in-formal blue worsted stockings to one of the literary meetings as a brave gesture of revolt against the formal black silk stockings required by con-vention. He was a minor poet, a writer of leaden heroic couplets, named Benjamin Stillingfleet.

Many of the ladies who made up the Blue-Stocking Clubs wrote as well as discussed. As they grew older they tended to develop middle-age word-spread and to adopt a lofty moral tone. This was particularly true of Hannah More:

Mrs. Hannah More ... has written a great deal of poetry which I have never read.

William Hazlitt (1778–1830)
Lectures on the English Poets

She was born with a birch rod in her hand, and worst of all was a shameless flatterer and insatiable of flattery. Her acceptance of a pension in compensation for a husband is a vile blot, never to be expunged, in her character.

Caroline Bowles (1786–1854)
Letter to Robert Southey, 21 Dec. 1834

Miss More was engaged to a Mr. Turner whose ardour cooled. He con-trived to postpone the wedding for some six years and then persuaded Miss More to accept £200 a year instead.

Every blue-stocking will remain a spinster as long as there are sens-ible men on earth.

Jean-Jacques Rousseau (1712–1778)
Correspondence

Rousseau was, like Admiral Boscawen and Martin Luther, one of that large body of men which did not admire intelligence in women. One of his highly intelligent lady friends was Louise Florence Pétronille Tardieu d'Esclavelles, Marquise d'Epinay. In his *Confessions* he wrote, 'she was very thin, very pale, and had a bosom which resembled the back of her hand'. He remained a bachelor, embracing whenever necessary his servant girl, Thérèse Levasseur, comfortingly stupid but well rounded. The resultant five children he put into a Foundling Hospital.

Boswell, on his way back from Corsica, was asked to escort Mlle. Levas-seur to England where Rousseau was taking refuge. This was like asking a rabbit to escort a lettuce. On the second night of the journey the twenty-six-year-old, gauche Boswell was given his first lesson in skilful love-making by the older, experienced and enthusiastic Mlle. Levasseur. There were thirteen lessons during the brief journey. Boswell found her conversa-tion boring.

Perhaps the biggest change in literature which occurred during the eighteenth century was the spectacular rise of the novel.

For some time, middle-class wives and daughters had been freed by new manufacturing processes from their traditional labours of brewing beer, moulding soap, weaving and so on, and they had acquired a certain amount of leisure. They began to read more books, particularly those undemanding, exciting romantic adventures known nowadays to the book trade and to pushers of hospital library-trolleys as 'light love'.

Moralists were dismayed at the corruption inherent in susceptible ladies reading books not wholly written to improve morals:

> Novels are receipts to make a whore.
> Matthew Green (1696–1737)
> *The Spleen*

Matthew Green's recipe for overcoming boredom was a journey into the countryside and a deep draught of inward contemplation.

One of the earliest of the Light Love/Heavy Adventure writers was the splendidly named Mrs. Aphra Behn (1640–1689). Mrs. Behn, daughter of a barber, spent a while spying for Charles II in Antwerp rather unsuccessfully – she did manage to warn the government that the Dutch were about to send a fleet up the Medway but nobody took any notice of her – and she also introduced milk punch into England; but her fame rests on a number of plays abounding with 'coarse' dialogue, and some novels, very popular in her day, with such promising titles as *The Amours of Philander and Sylvia, The Fair Jilt, The Lucky Mistake, The History of the Nun or the Fair Vow-Breaker* and *Oroonoko*. This last was said to have given Rousseau the germ of his philosophy of the Noble Savage. Mrs. Behn was the first woman in history to earn her living as an author and her remains were appropriately entombed in the cloisters of Westminster Abbey.

Mrs. Behn's stirring tales of adventure and love were a hangover from the old medieval 'estoires'. The modern novel could be said to have begun with Daniel Defoe. Defoe gave his heroes ordinary proper names – Robinson Crusoe, Moll Flanders, Duncan Campbell, etc. – set them in recognizable surroundings and gave them, and the reader, a sense of time. *Robinson Crusoe* was the first great novel having as its hero an ordinary, contemporary human being: a merchant who behaved according to the Protestant ethic even when marooned on a desert island, marshalling his resources prudently, working hard and reaping what he had sown, secure in the knowledge that God was on the side of him who showed a credit balance.

The next development, a big leap forward, was the publication of Samuel Richardson's *Pamela*, the first novel to examine a simple human

135

relationship in great (very great) detail, and with considerable psychological insight:

> In *Pamela* Richardson produced an essay in vulgarity – of sentiment and morality alike – which has never been surpassed.
>
> W. E. Henley (1849–1903)
Athenaeum

> *Pamela* told the story of a poor servant girl's struggles to retain her virginity, despite her employer's lustful machinations, in order that she could subsequently yield it to him for the best possible price: marriage. This ethically dubious plot was considered highly moral in the eighteenth century.

Richardson, like Defoe, was not a scholar; he had a small printing establishment. The great success of his books in England and on the Continent surprised him, but he learnt to relish the pleasures of fame:

> That fellow Richardson ... could not be contented to sail quietly down the stream of reputation, without longing to taste the froth from every stroke of the oar.
>
> Samuel Johnson (1709–1784)
Quoted by Hester Lynch Piozzi, *Anecdotes of the Late Samuel Johnson*

A third great former of the novel, Henry Fielding, came from a good family and had a classical education. He began as a playwright, but he was too much of a reforming crusader for the government to stomach and the Licensing Act (1737) was passed, clamping a political censorship on the theatre. Fielding turned to writing novels. Whereas Defoe and Richardson were strong on incident and short on plot, Fielding with *Tom Jones* established the use of a huge, complicated plot which served to produce a great number of comic situations and memorable minor characters:

> Richardson had picked the kernel of life – while Fielding was contented with the husk.
>
> Ibid.

Fielding reacted strongly against the prevailing notion that virtue was a kind of cast-iron chastity belt which only required the right key, i.e. social and financial advancement, to open it. The hero of *Tom Jones* was something of an anti-hero; he leapt into a number of beds in the cause of self-preservation, or for the fun of it, but he was fundamentally good-hearted; his faults were the human failings of an ordinary healthy male animal. Fielding had a warm and generous attitude towards human affairs which was not expected of a moralist:

> Fellows like Fielding ... who pretend that if you are a gay drunkard, lecher, squanderer of your goods, and fumbler in placket holes you will eventually find a benevolent uncle, concealed father, or benefactor who will shower on you bags of ten thousands of guineas, estates,

and the hands of adorable mistresses – these fellows are dangers to the body politic.

Ford Madox Ford (1873–1939)
The English Novel from the Earliest Days to the Death of Conrad

The fourth major novelist was Laurence Sterne: *Tristram Shandy* and *A Sentimental Journey*. Sterne had an eccentric style, totally unlike those of the other three; his work was comic and cheerfully erotic:

A bawdy blockhead.

Oliver Goldsmith (1728–1774)
Citizen of the World, Letter 74

Sterne probably had less immediate influence on the novel than had the other three because of his technical virtuosity; *Tristram Shandy*, with its range of comedy styles, its odd construction and its typographical tricks, was more a parody of the novel than a novel:

Nothing odd will do long. *Tristram Shandy* did not last.

Samuel Johnson (1709–1784).
Boswell's *Life*

The only 'public' libraries were for the use of clergy, scholars and university students; anybody wanting a little light reading matter had either to buy a book or borrow one from a friend. But the need for beguiling literature was growing, probably stimulated even further by the success of the Richardson and Fielding novels. The answer to meeting the needs of this new kind of readership was the formation, and immediate prosperity, of commercially run subscription, or 'circulating' libraries, which lent books over a short period for a fee. The first of these seems to have been established at Edinburgh in 1725 by Allan Ramsay. The first in London was opened at 132, Strand, in 1740 by a Mr. Batho. It was said that within seventy years every large village and town throughout the country had a circulating library:

Slop-shops in literature.

Mrs. Elizabeth Griffith (1720?–1793)
Preface to *The History of Lady Barton*

The success of many of these libraries had little to do with a passion for literature; or for that matter, with men. The libraries at fashionable watering-places and in large towns were elegant establishments which also sold trinkets, held the little lotteries which were popular at the time, and acted as a female equivalent of the male coffee-shop. It was the first place where a newly arrived visitor would go to find out who was in town, and to catch up on the gossip and scandal:

A circulating library in a town is an evergreen tree of diabolical knowledge.

Richard Brinsley Sheridan (1751–1816)
The Rivals: Act I, sc. 11

Dr. Johnson reflected soberly on the unfulfilled ambitions of those scholarly authors whose works lay on the shelves, dusty and unrequested:

> No Place affords a more striking Conviction of the Vanity of human Hopes, than a Publick Library.
>
> Samuel Johnson (1709–1784)
> *The Rambler*, No. 106, 23 Mar. 1751

But the libraries were not there to circulate scholarly works; they were there to meet the needs of an entirely different kind of reader:

> Behold her now! She on her sofa looks
> O'er half a shelf of circulating books:
> This she admired, but she forgets the name,
> And reads again another, or the same.
> She likes to read of strange and bold escapes,
> Of plans and plottings, murders and mishaps,
> Love in all hearts, and lovers in all shapes.
> She sighs for pity, and her sorrows flow
> From the dark eyelash on the page below;
> And is so glad when, all the misery past,
> The dear adventurous lovers meet at last —
> Meet and are happy; and she thinks it hard,
> When thus an author might a pair reward —
> When they, the troubles all dispersed, might wed —
> He makes them part, and die of grief instead.
>
> George Crabbe (1754–1832)
> *Posthumous Tales*, xv

The middle part of the eighteenth century has been called the Age of Prose, mainly because most of the poetry published was written by ungifted amateurs in imitation of Pope.

A notable exception was Thomas Gray's *Elegy Written in a Country Church Yard*. This was a little wobbly in its nature notes – e.g. ploughmen of that period normally plodded homeward at midday – but Gray was at least attempting to describe what the countryside was really like rather than writing about Strephons and Chloes lolling about in mythical glades:

> Sir, he was dull in company, dull in his closet, dull everywhere. He was dull in a new way, and that made many people think him GREAT. He was a mechanical poet.
>
> Samuel Johnson (1709–1784)
> Boswell's *Life*

The Age of Prose was dominated by the towering figure of Dr. Johnson, lexicographer, essayist, critic, editor, Parliamentary reporter (he invented the speeches because he was not allowed in), scholar, and formidable conversationalist:

> Here lies Sam Johnson: – Reader, have a care,
> Tread lightly, lest you wake a sleeping bear:

Religious, moral, generous, and humane
He was; but self-sufficient, proud, and vain,
Fond of, and overbearing in, dispute,
A Christian and a scholar – but a brute.

Soame Jenyns (1704–1787)
Suggested epitaph

Johnson revelled in argument, but he not only refused to suffer fools gladly, he refused to suffer them at all. Dinner parties became strewn with the walking-wounded he had cut down in mid-sentence:

> Johnson made the most brutal speeches to living persons; for though' he was good-natured at bottom, he was ill-natured at top. He loved to dispute to show his superiority. If his opponents were weak, he told them they were fools; if they vanquished him, he was scurrilous.

Horace Walpole (1717–1797)
Letters

An example of Johnson's overbearing manner and tactlessness – or intellectual honesty – was the sharp quarrel he had with Boswell's father, Lord Auchinleck, over politics and the Church. He happened to be Lord Auchinleck's house guest at the time:

> My father's opinion of Dr. Johnson may be conjectured from the name he afterwards gave him, which was URSA MAJOR. But it is not true, as has been reported, that it was in consequence of my saying that he was a *constellation* of genius and literature. It was a sly abrupt expression to one of his brethren on the bench of the Court of Session, in which Dr. Johnson was then standing; but it was not said in his hearing.

James Boswell (1740–1795)
The Journal of a Tour to the Hebrides: Sat. 6 Nov.

> Boswell was clearly under the impression that it was his father who had given Johnson his famous nickname of the Great Bear. But there was an earlier reference, made by the poet Thomas Gray. According to Sir Samuel Egerton Brydges (in his *Autobiography*, published in 1834), Gray was strolling with his friend Bonstetten about the year 1769 (four years before Johnson and Boswell set out for their tour of the Hebrides). Gray was walking along – 'when he exclaimed with bitterness, "Look, look, Bonstetten! the great bear! There goes *Ursa Major!*" This was Johnson. Gray could not abide him.'

Most of Johnson's essays were written for *The Rambler* and *The Idler*, both of which ran for two years. The essays, although full of commonsense observation, were expressed in Johnson's most majestic prose style:

Casts of manure a wagon-load around
To raise a simple daisy from the ground;
Uplifts the club of Hercules, for what?
To crush a butterfly or brain a gnat!

John Wolcot, 'Peter Pindar' (1738–1819)

Wolcot was a prolific and fairly successful professional satirist in the knock-about vein. He got a steady mileage out of George III but seemed to carry no real hatred for his victims. At the age of sixty-two he launched a fist attack upon a rival satirist, William Gifford, in Wright's bookshop in Piccadilly. He lost the fight on a technical knockout; not only was he thrown out into the mud but he had attacked the wrong man – he thought he was pummelling John Gifford. At the age of sixty-nine he was prosecuted (unsuccessfully) on a charge of raping his landlady.

The enviable position Johnson won for himself in the world of letters was duly envied by less successful colleagues:

> Pomposo, – insolent and loud,
> Vain idol of a scribbling crowd,
> Whose very name inspires an awe,
> Whose every word is sense and law ...
> Who, cursing flattery, is the tool
> Of every fawning, flattering fool –
> Who wit with jealous eyes surveys,
> And sickens at another's praise;
> Who, proudly seized of learning's throne,
> Now damns all learning but his own.
>
> Charles Churchill (1731–1764)
> *The Ghost*

There was a good deal of real antipathy here. Johnson thought of Churchill as 'a shallow fellow', and profoundly disapproved of Churchill's aggressively Whig politics and his licentious behaviour. Churchill was a founder-member of the Hellfire Club at Medmenham Abbey which, it was said, was dedicated to holding 'unimaginable orgies' – an imagination-challenging phrase. Churchill had an impressive list of seductions to his discredit, but he behaved with unusual generosity to his victims when all passion had been spent.

Johnson's stature has not diminished over the last two hundred years because he happened to have been hero-worshipped by the odd little Scot, James Boswell, who kept detailed notes of everything Johnson said and did after their first meeting in 1763.

The first book Boswell published about Johnson was the account of the tour he made with Johnson to Scotland and the Hebrides, published in 1785 as *The Journal of a Tour to the Hebrides with Samuel Johnson, Ll.D.*:

> Have you got Boswell's most absurd enormous book? – the best thing in it is a bon mot of lord Pembroke. The more one learns of Johnson, the more preposterous assemblage he appears of strong sense, of the lowest bigotry and prejudices, of pride, brutality, fretfulness, and vanity – and Boswell is the ape of most of his faults, without a grain of his sense. It is the story of a mountebank and his zany.
>
> Horace Walpole (1717–1797)
> Letter to the Hon. H. S. Conway, 6 Oct. 1785

mountebank = a quack who mounted a bank, or a bench, at fairgrounds in order to harangue potential customers.
zany = a mountebank's comic assistant.

140

When Johnson died in 1784, Boswell gathered together all the notes he had made during the years he was in close contact with him and, in 1791, produced *The Life of Samuel Johnson, Ll.D.*, the 'ana of anas', generally agreed to be the greatest biography in the English language.

It has been a source of perplexity, dismay and grief ever since to many men of letters that the *Life*, a masterpiece, was written by a man who could be reasonably described as a drunken, lecherous, snobbish buffoon:

> Many of the greatest men that ever lived have written biography. Boswell was one of the smallest men that ever lived, and he has beaten them all ... Servile and impertinent, shallow and pedantic, a bigot and a sot, bloated with family pride, and eternally blustering about the dignity of a born gentleman, yet stooping to be a tale-bearer, an eavesdropper, a common butt in the taverns of London ... Everything which another man would have hidden, everything the publication of which would have made another man hang himself, was matter of exaltation to his weak and diseased mind ...
>
> There is not in all his books a single remark of his own on literature, politics, religion, or society, which is not either commonplace or absurd ... He had, indeed, a quick observation and a retentive memory. These qualities, if he had been a man of sense and virtue, would scarcely of themselves have sufficed to make him conspicuous; but because he was a dunce, a parasite, and a coxcomb, they have made him immortal.
>
> Thomas Babington Macaulay (1800–1859)
> *Edinburgh Review*, Sept. 1831

The eighteenth century has collected labels like an old suitcase, e.g. the Age of Prose, the Age of Transition, the Age of Reason, the Age of Enlightenment. All these labels could happily be stuck upon the works of three writers, Rousseau, Voltaire and Edward Gibbon.

Voltaire's contempt for established authority, both religious and civil, and Rousseau's dismissal of the social order in favour of a simple return to nature caused alarm to many God-fearing, orderly citizens:

> JOHNSON: Rousseau, Sir, is a very bad man. I would sooner sign a sentence for his transportation, than that of any felon who has gone from the Old Bailey these many years. Yes, I would like to have him work in the plantations.
> BOSWELL: Sir, do you think him as bad a man as Voltaire?
> JOHNSON: Why, Sir, it is difficult to settle the proportion of iniquity between them.
>
> Samuel Johnson (1709–1784)
> Boswell's *Life*

> Rousseau's opening statement in *Du contrat social*, 'Man was born free and everywhere he is in chains', was bitterly resented and denied by the socially complacent.

Edward Gibbon's *Decline and Fall of the Roman Empire,* published in six volumes between 1776 and 1788, was much in key with the French writers' preoccupation with Enlightenment and Reason, and their dismissal of historical and religious myth. The *Decline and Fall,* sceptical, lucid and thoroughly researched, treated history as–in Gibbon's own words–'little more than the crimes, follies, and misfortunes of mankind'. Despite opposition from churchmen the book was immediately successful and made Gibbon famous. He was elected a member of Johnson's literary club:

> An ugly, affected, disgusting fellow ... poisons the literary club to me ... I class him among infidel wasps and venomous insects.
>
> James Boswell (1740–1795)
> *Letters to Temple*

Boswell's usual reaction to anybody whom he thought stood between him and his sun.

Gibbon, on bended knee, presented a copy of Vol. 2 to H.R.H. the Duke of Gloucester. The royal reaction indicated the measure of the Hanover dynasty's interest in literature:

> Another damned, thick, square book! Always scribble, scribble, scribble! Eh! Mr. Gibbon?
>
> William Henry, Duke of Gloucester (1743–1805)
> Quoted by Henry Best: *Personal and Literary Memorials*

The sceptics turned out to be right. The eighteenth century ended not with a whimper but with a bang. The French Revolution, the American War of Independence, the acceleration of the Industrial Revolution, exploded the comfortable Augustan age concept of a permanent society designed by the Great-Architect-in-the-Sky, with a place for everybody and everybody keeping to his place. The world was on the change.

The Age of Prose, which began at the death of Pope, was brought to an end by the arrival on the literary scene of William Wordsworth.

If the key word for the beginning of the century was 'sense', the key word for the century's end was 'sensibility'. In the seventeenth century Descartes had written 'I think, therefore I am'. During the eighteenth century Rousseau made out a case for saying 'I feel, therefore I am', and Laurence Sterne had introduced a new word into the language, 'sentimental'.

As a young man Wordsworth, like most intelligent liberal-minded young men of his day, thought that the French Revolution was going to point the way to a fine, clean, new world. He went to France, had an affair with a girl which ended in the birth of a daughter, and had plans to join the revolutionaries. The Reign of Terror disillusioned him and he resolved to remain in England and devote himself to writing poetry.

His first major collection of poems was *Lyrical Ballads*. This was published in 1798 and is generally accepted as marking the beginning of the Romantic Revival. In the preface Wordsworth clearly stated that his aim was to wean public taste away from the rigid, classic diction in which poetry had been set, like concrete, for a hundred and fifty years, and replace it with poetry written in the language of simple, ordinary speech. His friend Samuel Taylor Coleridge contributed three pieces to the volume. Wordsworth did not think much of one of these, *The Rime of the Ancient Mariner*. Coleridge's side of it was to write of the supernatural in a realistic way:

> Let simple Wordsworth chime his childish verse,
> And brother Coleridge lull the babe at nurse.
>
> Lord Byron (1788–1824)
> *English Bards and Scottish Reviewers*

The public was by no means ready for Wordsworth's simple verse. It was also a little bewildered to find *Tintern Abbey*, with lines like 'For I have learned, to look on nature, not as in the hour of thoughtless youth, but hearing oftentimes the still, sad music of humanity' a few pages away from 'And often after sunset, Sir, when it is light and fair, I take my little porringer, and eat my supper there':

> Two voices are there: one is of the deep;
> It learns the storm-cloud's thunderous melody ...
> And one is of an old half-witted sheep
> Which bleats articulate monotony ...
> And, Wordsworth, both are thine.
>
> James Kenneth Stephen (1859–1892)
> *Lapsus Calami: A Sonnet*

Wordsworth moved permanently to the Lake District in 1799 and in a few years the last traces of his youthful radicalism had evaporated and he had become staunchly patriotic. The early part of the nineteenth century was a difficult time for writers who were at all critical of the administration. Repressive measures were taken by George III's ministers at the first whiff of radical thinking; between 1812 and 1822 there were 270 government prosecutions of writers and their publishers for alleged libel. Wordsworth approved:

> What a beastly and pitiful wretch that Wordsworth ... I can compare him with no one but Simonides, that flatterer of the Sycilian tyrants.
>
> Percy Bysshe Shelley (1792–1822)
> *Letters*

> The Sicilian poet Simonides (fifth century B.C.) is credited with being the world's first hack-writer of eulogies. He turned them out to order for the tyrants who ruled Sicily.

Although nature had not gone wholly unobserved during the Augustan age – poets like Thomas Gray, and James Thomson in his *Seasons*, had begun to describe the countryside in naturalistic terms; and landowners glanced from their windows at their own acres of nature arranged for their pleasure by landscape gardeners like Capability Brown – Wordsworth's Lake District poetry was something different again. He was not concerned with describing a pretty hollyhock, but he was very concerned with the effect that seeing a pretty hollyhock had on his soul. In Wordsworth's poetry nature was not a painted backdrop, or a colour photograph, but an experience. He had a great number of experiences in the Lake District:

> Wordsworth went to the lakes, but he never was a lake poet. He found in stones the sermons he had already hidden there.
>
> Oscar Wilde (1854–1900)
> *The Decay of Lying*

Classicists found little pleasure in Wordsworth's nature poetry:
> Dank, limber verses, stuft with lakeside sedges,
> And propt with rotten stakes from rotten hedges.
> Walter Savage Landor (1775–1864)

And William Blake nearly died from the effects of a preface:

> What appears to have disturbed his mind, on the other hand, is the preface to the Excursion. He told me six months ago that it caused him a bowel complaint which nearly killed him.
>
> Henry Crabb Robinson (1775–1867)
> Letter to Dorothy Wordsworth, Feb. 1826

As the years went by Wordsworth grew into a Celebrity. Visitors would trail for miles to his cottage and leap into the air in the hope of seeing over the hedge and catching a glimpse of the Great Poet examining a flower. He lived with his wife, but his intimate was really his sister Dorothy who, after a slight leaning towards Coleridge, became almost morbidly devoted to her brother, and vice versa.

Wordsworth was a sturdy, clumsy figure with a large nose and burning eyes; he had no sense of smell:

> The languid way in which he gives you a handful of numb unresponsive fingers is very significant.
>
> Thomas Carlyle (1795–1881)

In 1842 Wordsworth accepted a Civil List pension and in 1843 he succeeded Southey as Poet Laureate:

> Just for a handful of silver he left us,
> Just for a riband to stick in his coat.
> Robert Browning (1812–1889)
> *The Lost Leader*

144

The young rebel had matured, seen the error of his ways, and ended up a distinguished and pompous member of the Establishment:

> In his youth, Wordsworth sympathized with the French Revolution, went to France, wrote good poetry, and had a natural daughter. At this period, he was a 'bad' man.
> Then he became 'good', abandoned his daughter, adopted correct principles, and wrote bad poetry. Bertrand Russell (1872–1970)

> The older Wordsworth did not take kindly to being crossed, or even challenged. The young John Keats, at a party, was about to agree enthusiastically with something which Wordsworth was saying when Mrs. Wordsworth leaned over and whispered 'Mr. Wordsworth is never interrupted'.

Sir Walter Scott made a huge contribution to the Romantic Revival. Part of romanticism was a harking back to medieval tales, and the retelling of history in emotional terms. Scott was temperamentally right for this kind of work and he was deeply interested in Scottish antiquity. He began by writing long narrative poems like *Marmion*, which was set in the sixteenth century:

> In short, what I felt in Marmion I feel still more in the Lady of the Lake – viz. – that a man accustomed to case words in metre, and familiar with descriptive Poets and Tourists, himself a Picturesque Tourist, must be troubled with a mental strangury, if he could not lift up his leg six times in six different corners, and each time p––– a canto.
> Samuel Taylor Coleridge (1772–1834)
> Letter to William Wordsworth, 1810

Scott, like Wordsworth, was intensely patriotic and occasionally issued a loyal piece, like *The Field of Waterloo*, a poem which he published in 1815 to raise money for the soldiers' widows. It was not his *métier*:

> The corpse of many a hero slain
> Pressed Waterloo's ensanguined plain;
> But none by salvo or by shot
> Fell half so flat as Walter Scott!
> Thomas, first Baron Erskine (1750–1823)

> Epigrams like the above circulated widely and their authorship is usually uncertain. The above has been attributed to William Beckford because it was written in Beckford's hand in his copy of Scott's poem, but Beckford was always jotting things down in his books and the epigram is much more in line with Erskine's sense of humour than with Beckford's. Erskine, a witty, vain, free-spending lawyer, dragged himself up from an impoverished childhood to become the highest-paid lawyer of his day, and Lord Chancellor. At the age of fifteen he had been struck by lightning.

Realizing that Lord Byron wrote better narrative poetry than he did, Scott – a thorough professional – turned to writing novels. He was a prodigious spender and wrote to renew the money he spent. In a short burst of rewarding energy he served up an astonishing number of long historical novels:

> Sir Walter Scott (when all's said and done) is an inspired butler.
>> William Hazlitt (1778–1830)
>> *Mrs. Siddons*

Scott virtually invented the historical novel. And through his novels he invented the tourist's idea of Scotland. He also developed the public's taste for stories of medieval romance, a form which was to be further explored by Tennyson, the Pre-Raphaelites and others:

> Then comes Sir Walter Scott with his enchantments . . . sets the world in love with dreams and phantoms; with decayed and swinish forms of religion; with decayed and degraded systems of government; with the silliness and emptiness, sham grandeurs, sham gauds, and sham chivalries of a brainless and worthless long-vanished society. He did measureless harm; more real and lasting harm, perhaps, than any other individual that ever wrote.
>> Mark Twain (1835–1910)

Scott was offered the Poet Laureateship but declined it. It was accepted by Robert Southey, another professional. Southey was a voluminous writer of verse, histories, biographies, and prose of every sort. He worked for a while as a critic for the *Quarterly Review*, changed his politics, as did Wordsworth, from pro to anti the French Revolution and at one time contemplated emigrating with Coleridge and another friend to found an ideal settlement where all were equal – a pantisocracy – on the banks of the river Susquehanna. He worked so hard that he eventually died from softening of the brain.

His patriotic works as Poet Laureate included an unfortunate poem describing the late King George III appearing, successfully, before a heavenly tribunal. As the late King had, according to his critics, lost America, suspended the Habeas Corpus Act and gone mad, the poem was taken to be a challenge to liberal thinking. The challenge was taken up by Lord Byron, who described what he thought of Southey in a poem which had the same name as Southey's, *The Vision of Judgement*:

> He had written praises of a regicide;
>> He had written praises of all kings whatever;
> He had written for republics far and wide,
>> And then against them bitterer than ever;
> For pantisocracy he once had cried
>> Aloud, a scheme less moral than 'twas clever;
> Then grew a hearty anti-jacobin –
>> Had turn'd his coat – and would have turn'd his skin.
>
> He had sung against all battles, and again
>> In their high praise and glory; he had call'd

Reviewing 'the ungentle craft', and then
  Become as base a critic as e'er crawled —
Fed, paid, and pampered by the very men
  By whom his muse and morals had been maul'd:
He had written much blank verse, and blanker prose,
And more of both than anybody knows.

Lord Byron (1788–1824)
The Vision of Judgement

Little of Southey's work is read now. It does not seem to have been particularly easy reading then:

Beneath these poppies buried deep,
The bones of Bob the bard lie hid;
Peace to his manes; and may he sleep
As soundly as his readers did!

Death, weary of so dull a writer,
Put to his books a *finis* thus.
Oh! May the earth on him lie lighter
Than did his quartos upon us!

Thomas Moore (1779–1852)
Epitaph on a Well-Known Poet

This is a twist on a mock epitaph for Sir John Vanbrugh, who built Blenheim Palace and other substantial pieces of masonry, which went:

Lie heavy on him, earth! for he
Laid many heavy loads on thee.
(Dr Abel Evans, 1679–1737)

Both verses were parodies of an epigram by Martial; a tender epitaph for a young slave girl Erōtion on whom Martial begged the earth to press lightly, 'for she pressed light on thee'.

To many people the phrase 'the Romantic Poets' immediately conjures up the names of Byron, Keats and Shelley. If Wordsworth had died young it is probable that his image, too, would have been suffused with the glamour attached to original talent cut off in early flower. Equally, had Byron, Keats and Shelley lived to be eighty they might, like Wordsworth, have ended up as dignified and honoured citizens, upholding the status quo and writing bad poetry, if writing anything at all. This is particularly true of Byron:

Byron! — he would be all forgotten today if he had lived to be a florid old gentleman with iron-grey whiskers, writing very long, very able letters to *The Times* about the Repeal of the Corn Laws.

Max Beerbohm (1872–1956)
Zuleika Dobson

But they died romantically young: Byron at the age of thirty-six, Keats at twenty-five, Shelley at twenty-nine. And abroad at that. Byron died of fever in Greece, Shelley was drowned off Leghorn, and Keats succumbed to tuberculosis in Rome.

Of the three only Keats could really be said to be much of a 'romantic' man in the modern sense of the word. He was frail, athletic, kind, humorous – the poor son of a stable groom. He had one hopeless love, for Fanny Brawne, and this was unfulfilled.

Neither Byron nor Shelley was all that aristocratic. Byron inherited his title, and encumbered estates, from a distant relation, a great-uncle. Shelley's grandfather made the family's fortune by two runaway marriages, both to heiresses, and then obtained a baronetcy for political considerations.

Byron's limp was not a light, charming disability of one foot but an ugly, painful teetering on tip-toes – both his Achilles tendons were deformed – and his right foot was wrongly shaped and bent inwards. His mother gave him a difficult childhood – she referred to him as 'limping brat' – and at the age of nine he was seduced by his nurse May Gray, who also taught him the Bible. Subsequently he had a great number of mistresses, but his women seemed to make him more hag-ridden than happy. He was bisexual.

Shelley, tall and stooping, shy, the anarchist of the three, made all his women unhappy. He was obsessed with the struggle – any old struggle – against tyranny, and a permanent suspicion that he was the victim of persecution made him the champion of anybody whom he took to be a victim of tyranny. He was the sort of man who hurled perfectly healthy dogs over stiles.

The attitude of the top people in the high-Tory society of Britain to this trio of irreverent, colourful poets was predictable:

> I hate the whole race. I have the worst opinion of them. There is no believing a word they say – your professional poets, I mean – there never existed a more worthless set than Byron and his friends for example. Poets praise fine sentiments and never practise them; their praise of virtue and fine feeling is entirely from the imagination.
> Arthur Wellesley, first Duke of Wellington (1769–1852)

Childe Harold was published in 1812 and Byron 'awoke to find himself famous'. His poems were extremely popular both in Britain and on the Continent and he was reckoned by the Romantic-minded to be one of the leading spirits of the age. Then he married a pious heiress. The marriage was so incompatible that after a year she asked for a separation, first on the grounds that Byron was mad, then for an undisclosed reason. Byron agreed and left England in a fury. As Lady Byron had not disclosed her grounds for separation tongues were licensed to wag and it was generally believed that Byron had committed incest with his half-sister, Mrs. Augusta Leigh, and had inflicted upon Lady Byron 'every monstrous vice'. He became an object of horror and shame to the unromantically minded: a subject for cautionary sermons:

148

A denaturalized being who, having exhausted every species of sensual gratification, and drained the cup of sin to its bitterest dregs, is resolved to show that he is no longer human, even in his frailties, but a cool, unconcerned fiend.

John Styles, D.D.

Lord Byron's Works viewed in Connection with Christianity and the Obligations of Social Life

Other sermons preached by the popular Methodist preacher included *Immoral and Antichristian Tendencies of the Stage* and *The Temptations of a Watering-Place*. The Rev. John Styles lived in Brighton.

Shelley's private life was not quite such a sitting target, but he was still vulnerable, trailing round with his little free-love ménages, and despising authority:

He [Shelley] was a liar and a cheat; he paid no regard to truth, nor to any kind of moral obligation.

Robert Southey (1774–1843)

Poor Shelley always was, and is, a kind of ghastly object: colourless, pallid, tuneless, without health or warmth of vigour; the sound of him shrieky, frosty, as if a *ghost* were trying to 'sing' to us; the temperament of him, spasmodic, hysterical.

Thomas Carlyle (1795–1881)
Reminiscences

Mr. Shelley is a very vain man; and like most vain men, he is but half instructed in knowledge and less than half disciplined in reasoning powers; his vanity ... has been his ruin.

Quarterly Review

Poor Keats had the worst time of it. Until at least ten years after his death his poetry was disliked by almost everybody, including most of his fellow poets:

Here are Jonny Keats' *p-ss a bed* poetry, and three novels by God knows whom ... No more Keats, I entreat: flay him alive; if some of you don't, I must skin him myself: there is no bearing the drivelling idiotism of the Mankin.

Lord Byron (1788–1824)
Letter to John Murray, 12 Oct. 1820

Keats was particularly hateful to the powerful reviews because, unlike Byron and Shelley, he was not a 'gentleman', and the reviews were bitterly opposing the work of the newly emerging middle-class writers, then being encouraged by the liberal writer and editor, Leigh Hunt. A reviewer in *Blackwood's*, faced with a new book by Leigh Hunt, wrote that he felt like:

A man of fashion when he is invited to enter, for a second time, the gilded drawing room of a little mincing boarding-school mistress, who would fain have an *At home* in her house. Everything is pretence, affectation, finery and gaudiness. The beaux are attorney's apprentices, with chapeaux bras and Limerick gloves—fiddlers, harp-teachers and clerks of genius; the belles are faded fan-twinkling spinsters, prurient vulgar misses from the school, and enormous citizens' wives. The company are entertained with lukewarm negus, and the sounds of a paltry pianoforte.

Blackwood's

The reviewer-barons dubbed Leigh Hunt and his friends—including Keats—the Cockney School. The word 'cockney' was used in its early sense of 'suburban' rather than 'East London'.

In 1818 *Endymion* was published. In the preface Keats modestly described it as 'a feverish attempt rather than a deed accomplished', but it was violently attacked, particularly by *Blackwood's* who used it as the fourth part of a series of aggressive pieces about the Cockney School:

The Phrenzy of the 'Poems' was bad enough in its way; but it did not alarm us half so seriously as the calm, settled, imperturbable drivelling idiocy of 'Endymion'. ... Mr. Hunt is a small poet, but he is a clever man. Mr. Keats is a still smaller poet, and he is only a boy of pretty abilities, which he has done everything in his power to spoil ... We venture to make one small prophecy, that his bookseller will not a second time venture £50 upon anything he can write. It is a better and a wiser thing to be a starved apothecary than a starved poet; so back to the shop, Mr. John, back to 'plasters, pills, and ointment boxes,' etc. But for Heaven's sake, young Sangrado, be a little more sparing of extenuatives and soporifics in your practice than you have been with your poetry.

Believed to have been written by John Lockhart and
John Wilson ('Christopher North')
Blackwood's Magazine, Aug. 1818

Keats had trained to be a surgeon and was licensed to work as an apothecary.

Keats died three years later and both Byron and Shelley decided that the bad reviews of *Endymion* had killed him. This was unlikely—his tuberculosis was getting worse and his tortured passion for Fanny Brawne was hardly giving him the untroubled rest his condition needed—but Byron and Shelley flew to the attack. They attacked the wrong journal, as it happened; they went for the *Quarterly Review*. The *Quarterly* had given Keats a bad notice but couched in a much less offensive way. Perhaps they did not get *Blackwood's* in Italy, or perhaps the *Quarterly* was their old enemy, but the *Quarterly* became the villain:

Who killed John Keats?
'I', says the Quarterly,
So savage and Tartarly;
' 'Twas one of my feats'.
Lord Byron (1788–1824)
John Keats

150

Shelley did a more thorough job – the lame dog this time was a friend and colleague – and wrote for Keats the beautiful elegy *Adonais*. He laid it on thickly in the preface:

It may well be said that these wretched men know not what they do. They scatter their insults and their slanders without heed as to whether the poisoned shaft lights on a heart made callous by many blows or one like Keats's composed of more penetrable stuff ... Against what woman taken in adultery dares the foremost of these literary prostitutes to cast his opprobrious stone? Miserable man! You, one of the meanest, have wantonly defaced one of the noblest specimens of the workmanship of God. Nor shall it be your excuse that, murderer as you are, you have spoken daggers, but used none.

Percy Bysshe Shelley (1792–1822)
Preface to *Adonais*

Inevitably, the journals had the last word. *Blackwood's* replied:

A Mr. John Keats, a young man who had left a decent calling for the melancholy trade of Cockney-poetry, has lately died of a consumption, after having written two or three little books of verses, much neglected by the public. His vanity was probably wrung not less than his purse; for he had it upon the authority of the Cockney Homers and Virgils, that he might become a light to their region at a future time, but all this is not necessary to help a consumption to the death of a poor sedentary man, with an unhealthy aspect, and a mind harassed by the first troubles of versemaking. The New School, however, will have it that he was slaughtered by a criticism of the Quarterly Review – 'O flesh, how art thou fishified!' – We are not now to defend a publication so well able to defend itself. But the fact is, that the Quarterly finding before it a work at once silly and presumptuous, full of the servile *slang* that Cockaigne dictates to its servitors, and the vulgar indecorums which that Grub Street Empire rejoiceth to applaud, told the truth of the volume, and recommended a change of manners and masters to the scribbler. Keats wrote on; but he wrote *indecently*, probably in the indulgence of his social propensities.

Blackwood's Magazine

A gem of malignant snobbery.

Twenty-seven years after Keats's death an account of his life together with his collected poetry was published, in a climate of opinion slightly more favourable to his particular genius. The work was reviewed by Carlyle:

Fricassee of dead dog.

Thomas Carlyle (1795–1881)
Review of Monckton Milnes' *Life of Keats*

Two more Cockneys, who both worked on journals started by Leigh Hunt, were Charles Lamb and William Hazlitt:

Charles Lamb I sincerely believe to be in some considerable degree insane. A more pitiful, ricketty, gasping, staggering, stammering Tom-

151

fool I do not know ... Besides, he is now a confirmed, shameless drunkard; *asks* vehemently for gin and water in strangers' houses, tipples till he is utterly mad, and is only not thrown out of doors because he is too much despised for taking such trouble with him. Poor Lamb! Poor England, when such a despicable abortion is named genius!

Thomas Carlyle (1795–1881)

> Lamb had spent six months in a lunatic asylum when young. He had a bad stammer and was often drunk, but it is probable that only a little drink made him seem very drunk.

The *Quarterly Review* decided that it did not like William Hazlitt:

A mere ulcer; a sore from head to foot; a poor devil so completely flayed that there is not a square inch of healthy flesh on his carcass; an overgrown pimple, sore to the touch.

Quarterly Review

> The *Quarterly Review* was founded as the Tory answer to the Whig *Edinburgh Review*, to which Hazlitt contributed.

The reviews had become so influential in the small but powerful world of the educated middle class, and the bad reviews which they gave were so severe and destructive, that Sydney Smith, who was one of the *Edinburgh Review*'s co-founders, felt it necessary to write to the editor, Francis Jeffrey:

I certainly, my dear Jeffrey, in conjunction with the Knight of the Shaggy Eyebrows [Francis Horner], do protest against your increasing and unprofitable scepticism. I exhort you to restrain the violent tendency of your nature for analysis, and to cultivate synthetical propensities. What is virtue? What's the use of truth? What's the use of honour? What's a guinea but a d—d yellow circle? The whole effect of your mind is to destroy. Because others build slightly and eagerly, you employ yourself in kicking down their houses, and contract a sort of aversion for the more honourable, useful, and difficult task of building well yourself.

Rev. Sydney Smith (1771–1845)

But reviews and criticisms continued to be acrimonious and the reactions to them bitter. The celebrated poet, Mr. Wordsworth, did not approve of Hazlitt for artistic and personal reasons:

The miscreant, Hazlitt, contin··es, I have heard, his abuse of Southey, Coleridge, and myself, in the 'Examiner'. I hope that you do not associate with the fellow; he is not a proper person to be admitted into respectable society, being the most perverse and malevolent creature that ill-luck has thrown in my way. Avoid him, he is a — —.

William Wordsworth (1770–1850)
Letter to B. R. Haydon, April 1817

> Unhappily B. R. Haydon's correspondence does not reveal what sort of a —— Hazlitt was supposed to have been.

152

At the other end of the scale from the Cockneys and the rebels stood Thomas Babington Macaulay, later first Baron Macaulay: a professional writer from five o'clock in the morning until breakfast, and then successively barrister, Whig member of Parliament and senior civil servant. Macaulay read incessantly from the age of three, and forgot nothing. At the age of four, on being asked by a lady how his tummy-ache was, he piped, 'Thank you, madam, the agony is abated.'

As a member of Parliament he made many effective speeches:

I wish I was as cocksure of anything as Tom Macaulay is of everything.
William Lamb, Viscount Melbourne (1779–1848)
Preface to *Lord Melbourne's Papers*

Also attr. to William Windham (1750–1810), a statesman. Windham died when Macaulay was only ten years old, but the comment could well have applied to Macaulay at any time from the age of about four.

A favourite phrase of Macaulay's was 'as every schoolboy knows'. Examples of the sort of things which Macaulay was under the impression every schoolboy knew included 'who imprisoned Montezuma and who strangled Atahualpa' and 'the archbishops of Canterbury backwards':

He not only overflowed with learning, but stood in the slop.
Sydney Smith (1771–1845)
Quoted by Peter Quennell, *New Statesman*, 25 Aug. 1934

It seems clear that once Macaulay embarked upon conversation there was rarely anybody present sufficiently well equipped to stop him:

He was a most disagreeable companion to my fancy... His conversation was a procession of one.
Florence Nightingale (1820–1910)
Letter, quoted by Cecil Woodham-Smith: *Florence Nightingale*

Macaulay is well for a while, but one wouldn't *live* under Niagara.
Thomas Carlyle (1795–1881)
Quoted by Monckton Milnes: *Note-Book*

Macaulay is like a book in breeches... He has occasional flashes of silence, that make his conversation perfectly delightful.
Sydney Smith (1771–1845)
Quoted by Lady Holland: *Memoir*

This remark of Sydney Smith's was remembered by Harriet Martineau as 'Macaulay improves. I have observed in him, of late, flashes of silence.'

Macaulay's energy was prodigious. He turned out a stream of long critical essays for the *Edinburgh Review*, went to India for four years and, almost single-handed, wrote India's code of criminal law. His *History* was one of the most phenomenal publishing successes ever – the last two volumes earned him £20,000 in the first ten weeks – and it was immediately translated into twelve languages, including Russian, Bohemian and Persian. Carlyle was not impressed:

> At bottom, this Macaulay is but a poor creature with his dictionary literature and erudition, his saloon arrogance. He has no vision in him. He will neither see nor do any great thing.
>
> Thomas Carlyle (1795–1881)

A new crop of Ladies of Letters rose up in the nineteenth century and they were a different breed from the *salon*-society bluestockings of the previous age. There was Jane Austen:

> Mamma says she was then the prettiest, silliest, most affected, husband-hunting butterfly she ever remembers: and a friend of mine, who visits her now, says that she has stiffened into the most perpendicular, precise, taciturn piece of 'single blessedness' that ever existed, and that, till 'Pride and Prejudice' showed what a precious gem was hidden in that unbending case, she was no more regarded in society than a poker or a fire-screen, or any other thin upright piece of wood or iron that fills its corner in peace and quietness. The case is very different now: she is still a poker – but a poker of whom everyone is afraid.
>
> Mary Russell Mitford (1787–1855)
> Letter to Sir William Elford, Apr. 1815

Miss Mitford herself was noteworthy. She wrote plays, novels and a series of pieces on country life – published in the *Lady's Magazine* under the title 'Our Village' – which originated a new and leafy branch of literature. The genre was devastatingly satirized by Stella Gibbons in *Cold Comfort Farm*, but still flourishes.

Harriet Martineau started writing books on divinity, then became a successful popularizer of economic affairs, and anti-theological:

> Broken into utter wearisomeness, a mind reduced to these three elements: Imbecility, Dogmatism, and unlimited Hope.
>
> Thomas Carlyle (1795–1881)

Miss Martineau was delicate and very deaf. She was one of those frail nineteenth-century ladies who just managed to retain a slender hold on life and at the same time get through enough work to cripple a carthorse. She suggested to Carlyle that he made a lecture tour in England and subsequently managed it for him; perhaps unforgivably.

An American equivalent of the British literary lady was Margaret Fuller, journalist, author, Transcendentalist, social reformer and pioneer of women's rights. This last activity did not endear her to the many men of her day who held the view that as far as rights were concerned women were not historically, legally, morally or physiologically entitled to any:

> It was such an awful joke that she should have resolved – in all sincerity, no doubt – to make herself the greatest, wisest, best woman

of the age. And to that end she set to work on her strong, heavy, unpliable, and in many respects defective and evil nature, and adorned it with a mosaic of admirable qualities, such as she chose to possess; putting in here a splendid talent and there a moral excellence, and polishing each separate piece, and the whole together, till it seemed to shine afar and dazzle all who saw it. She took credit to herself for having been her own Redeemer, if not her own Creator.

Nathaniel Hawthorne (1804–1864)

There was a story that at a public meeting concerning Transcendentalism Miss Fuller rose in a moment of enthusiasm and cried, 'I accept the universe!' At which Carlyle growled, 'By God, she'd better!'

Another distinguished American writer was Harriet Beecher Stowe, ardent campaigner against slavery and author of *Uncle Tom's Cabin*:

A blatant Bassarid of Boston, a rampant Maenad of Massachusetts.

Algernon Swinburne (1837–1909)
Under the Microscope

Bassarid, Maenad = female votaries of the pagan god Dionysus. Clad in goat-skins and drunk, they helped with the orgies.

This rather unlikely line of abuse was prompted by an article which Mrs. Stowe had written in the September 1869 issue of the *Atlantic Monthly*, entitled 'The True Story of Lord Byron's Life', in which she committed to print the suspicion that Byron had had an incestuous affair with his half-sister. Mrs. Stowe had got together with Byron's widow, by then retired to Brighton and given to charitable works, and together they had decided to blacken the memory of the late Lord Byron and so discourage people from reading what was to them worthless, vile poetry. Swinburne, a great admirer of Byron's poetry, was infuriated. The ironic thing was that at the time when Mrs. Stowe was writing the article, her brother the Reverend Henry Ward Beecher, the most revered preacher of his day and a stern denouncer of vice and sin, was seducing Elizabeth Tilton, his neighbour's wife. The resultant court case produced the biggest scandal America had ever enjoyed.

In France, Lucile-Aurore Dupin, under her pen-name of George Sand, was turning out a seemingly effortless flow of passionate and lyrical novels:

A great cow-full of ink!

Usually attributed to Flaubert, who had far too much respect and affection for her to make such a comment. Baudelaire wrote 'She is above all and more than anything else, of a cow-like stupidity', but that is to do with density not fecundity. The nearest remark seems to be Nietzsche's description of her in *Roving Expeditions of an Inopportune Philosopher:* 'George Sand, or *Lactea ubertas.*' *Lactea ubertas*, a quotation from Quintilian, who coined the phrase to describe the highly prolific Livy, is usually translated 'milky abundance'.

155

The French were introducing an element of realistic human passion into their novels which some Englishmen found unhealthy:

> In the world there are few sadder, sicklier phenomena for me than George Sand and the response she meets with ... A new Phallus worship, with Sue, Balzac, and Co., for new prophets, and Madame Sand for a virgin.
>
> Thomas Carlyle (1795–1881)

> Eugène Sue was another in the long tradition of ship's doctors turned novelist, which ranged from Tobias Smollett to Richard Gordon. Sue wrote *The Wandering Jew* but was mainly known for his sensational novels of Paris low life.

> I took Eugène Sue's *Arthur* from the reading-room. It's indescribable, enough to make you vomit. You have to read this to realize the pitifulness of money, success, and the public. Literature has become consumptive. It spits and slobbers, covers its blisters with salve and sticking-plaster, and has grown bald from too much hair-slicking. It would take Christs of art to cure this leper.
>
> Gustave Flaubert (1821–1880)
> Letter to Louis Bouilhet, 1850

American literature was no great shakes at that time according to an English lady: too many newspapers and not enough education:

> The character of the American literature is, generally speaking, pretty justly appreciated in Europe. The immense exhalation of periodical trash, which penetrates into every cot and corner of the country, and which is greedily sucked in by all ranks, is unquestionably one great cause of its inferiority.
> ... Another obvious cause of inferiority in the national literature, is the very slight acquaintance with the best models of composition, which is thought necessary for persons called well educated.
>
> Frances Trollope (1780–1863)
> *Domestic Manners of the Americans*

If the French were too sexy, and the Americans too inferior, the English were too heathen:

> This great English people among so many good and solid qualities has one vice which spoils these very qualities ... From Shakespeare to Milton, from Milton to Byron, their beautiful and sombre literature is sceptical, judaic, satanic, to sum up anti-Christian.
>
> Jules Michelet (1798–1874)
> *L'Histoire de France*

The influential reviews were still, at the middle of the nineteenth century, fighting a rear-guard action against literature which was not orientated to a classical education; such as the work of Mr. Charles Dickens:

> He is a man with a very active fancy, great powers of language, much perception of what is grotesque, and a most lachrymose and melodramatic turn of mind—and this is all. He has never played any part

in any movement more significant than that of a fly ... on the wheel.

Saturday Review, Jan. 1857

> Unlike Keats, Dickens was a tremendous success with the public. The bad review in the *Saturday Review* did not cause him either to go broke or die.

Writers of philosophical works as well as novelists came under the critic's lash. Like Herbert Spencer, who evolved the theory of evolutionary philosophy, for which he invented the phrase 'the survival of the fittest':

The most unending ass in Christendom.

Thomas Carlyle (1795–1881)

> Sometimes quoted as 'The most immeasurable ass in Christendom', a more wounding phrase to a man of science. Spencer patented a special pin for binding sheets of music together. He also invented an invalid bed which worked well and a flying machine which did not work at all. It was while playing billiards with Spencer at the Savile Club that Robert Louis Stevenson is said to have propounded the maxim, 'proficiency in billiards is a sign of a mis-spent youth'.

Probably the most prolific novelist and playwright of the nineteenth century, for years the most popular writer of his day, was Edward George Bulwer-Lytton, later Baron Lytton, who managed to be a statesman as well:

Intrinsically a poor creature this Bulwer; has a bustling whisking agility and restlessness which may support him in a certain degree of significance with some, but which partakes much of the nature of *levity*.

Thomas Carlyle (1795–1881)

Bulwer-Lytton made a lot of money from his books, plus a little more from playing whist. He moved easily in fashionable circles and his most popular novel, *Pelham*, had as its eponymous hero a society dandy who startled London by forsaking the bright colours then worn by gentlemen in the evening to appear in black. This fashion was taken up by society and Britain's manhood has appeared on formal evening occasions ever since dressed like undertakers. Bulwer-Lytton was himself a dandy; he not only wrote of high life but lived it:

If he would but leave off scents for his handkerchief, and oil for his hair: if he would but confine himself to three clean shirts in a week, a couple of coats in a year, a beef-steak and onions for dinner, his beaker a pewter pot, his carpet a sanded floor, how much might be made of him even yet.

William Makepeace Thackeray (1811–1863)
Review of Lytton's Ernest Maltravers

> Thackeray himself was considered by some of his contemporaries to be something of a social climber, and a bit of a bore at dinner parties. John Ruskin wrote, 'Thackeray settled like a meat-fly on whatever one had got for dinner, and made one sick of it' (*Fors Clavigera*).

157

Benjamin Disraeli, although a Tory like Bulwer-Lytton and a fellow novelist and fellow dandy, thought that Bulwer-Lytton's high opinion of Bulwer-Lytton was remarkable enough to be used as a standard. Disraeli said of the diarist Charles Greville:

> The most conceited man I ever met, though I have read Cicero and known Bulwer-Lytton.
>
> Benjamin Disraeli (1804–1881)

In 1842 Tennyson published his *Poems* and was acknowledged to be the greatest living poet. In 1846 Bulwer-Lytton launched a powerful attack on Tennyson, stiff with resentment at a youngish, poor man writing poetry which was so different and so much more successful than his own work:

> If to my verse denied the Poet's fame,
> This merit, rare to verse that wins, I claim;
> No tawdry grace shall womanize my pen!
> Ev'n in a love-song, man should write for men!
> Not mine, not mine, (O Muse forbid!) the boon
> Of borrowed notes, the mock-bird's modish tune,
> The jingling medley of purloin'd conceits,
> Outbaying Wordsworth, and outglittering Keats,
> Where all the airs of patchwork-pastoral chime
> To drowsy ears in Tennysonian rhyme! ...
> Let School-Miss Alfred vent her chaste delight
> On 'darling little rooms so warm and bright!'
> Chaunt, 'I'm aweary,' in infectious strain,
> And catch her 'blue fly singing i' the pane.'
> Tho' praised by Critics, tho' adored by Blues,
> Tho' Peel with pudding plump the puling Muse,
> Tho' Theban taste the Saxon purse controuls,
> And pensions Tennyson, while starves a Knowles.
>
> Edward Bulwer-Lytton (1803–1873)
> *The New Timon: a Poetical Romance of London*

Just after the *Poems* were published Tennyson lost what little money he had in the collapse of a business he had invested in: a scheme for wood-carving by machinery. The poet went into such a decline at the hardships which resulted, including the postponement of his marriage, that his friends got together and persuaded the Prime Minister, Sir Robert Peel, to give Tennyson a civil-list pension of £200 a year; a considerable achievement as Sir Robert Peel had never heard of him.

Knowles was a poor schoolboy-poet, befriended by Southey, who got up a subscription to send the lad to a university. But Knowles died in 1817 at the age of nineteen.

Tennyson reacted immediately:

> We know him, out of SHAKESPEARE'S art,
>   And those fine curses which he spoke;
> The old TIMON, with his noble heart,
>   That, strongly loathing, greatly broke.

So died the Old: here comes the New.
  Regard him: a familiar face:
I *thought* we knew him: What, it's you,
  The padded man—that wears the stays—

Who kill'd the girls and thrill'd the boys,
  With dandy pathos when you wrote,
A Lion you, that made a noise,
  And shook a mane en papillotes ...

And once you tried the Muses too;
  You fail'd, Sir: therefore now you turn,
You fall on those who are to you,
  As Captain is to Subaltern ...

What profits now to understand
  The merits of a spotless shirt—
A dapper boot—a little hand—
  If half the little soul is dirt?

You talk of tinsel! why we see
  The old mark of rouge upon your cheeks.
You prate of Nature! You are he
  That spilt his life about the cliques.

A TIMON you! Nay, nay, for shame:
  It looks too arrogant a jest—
The fierce old man—to take *his* name
  You bandbox. Off, and let him rest.

Alfred, Lord Tennyson (1809–1892)
'*The New Timon, and the Poets*': *Punch*, 28 Feb. 1846

Tennyson seems to have been rather ashamed of his outburst, which was sent to *Punch* without his knowledge. He immediately wrote an apology, and two stanzas of recantation called 'An Afterthought', and never permitted the poem to be published in collections of his work.

At the age of seventy-five Tennyson accepted a peerage and became Alfred, Lord Tennyson. A critic peered into his clouded crystal ball and pronounced:

Mr. Tennyson is, after all, to be a peer, and the fact has gravely disconcerted and depressed many worthy people. Perhaps, however, Mr. Tennyson is the best judge of what will, in the long run, make for the reputation of his name ... Debrett and Burke may serve to keep the name of Tennyson alive when *In Memoriam* is forgotten.

Observer, 16 Dec. 1883

A close friend of Tennyson's, Edward FitzGerald, died the year that Tennyson was offered his peerage by Queen Victoria and Gladstone. FitzGerald, the translator of the *Rubaiyat of Omar Khayyam*, was one of the gentlemanly semi-pro's of nineteenth-century literature. He was a tranquil man:

Edward FitzGerald is the Prince of Quietists. Half the self-sacrifice, the self-denial, the moral resolution, which he exercises to keep himself easy, would amply furnish forth a martyr or a missionary. His tranquillity is like a pirated copy of the peace of God.

James Spedding (1808–1881)
Letter to a friend, 1 June 1835

FitzGerald was, as tranquil men of letters frequently were, a compulsive writer of very readable letters. In 1861 he wrote to an old friend describing his emotions on hearing of the death of Elizabeth Barrett Browning:

> Mrs. Browning's death is rather a relief to me, I must say: no more Aurora Leighs, thank God! A woman of real Genius, I know; but what is the upshot of it all? She and her Sex had better mind the Kitchen and the Children; and perhaps the Poor; except in such things as little Novels, they only devote themselves to what Men do much better, leaving that which Men do worse or not at all.

Edward FitzGerald (1809–1883)
Letter to W. H. Thompson, Master of Trinity College, Cambridge, 15 July 1861

At the time of writing, FitzGerald was virtually unknown. His translation of Omar Khayyam had sat in a magazine editor's tray for two years unheeded and had then been published as a pamphlet. As they used to say, 'It fell dead from the press.' But due to the efforts of Rossetti, Swinburne and Monckton Milnes, among others, it was later recognized for what it was, went through four editions, and the serene Fitz-Gerald ended his life a distinguished and respected figure. In 1889, six years after his death, and twenty-eight years after the letter about Mrs. Browning was written, the letter was published in the usual collection of a respected figure's literary remains: *Letters and Literary Review of Edward FitzGerald*.

Robert Browning, then aged seventy-seven and on his last visit to England – he died later in the year in Venice – saw the letter and immediately wrote a rejoinder, which he winged off to the *Athenaeum* magazine:

> I chanced upon a new book yesterday:
> I opened it, and where my finger lay
>   'Twixt page and uncut page, these words I read
>   – some six or seven at most – and learned thereby
> That you, FitzGerald, whom by ear and eye
>   She never knew, 'thanked God my wife was dead.
> Ay, dead! and were yourself alive, good Fitz,
> How to return you thanks would task my wits.
>   Kicking you seems the common lot of curs –
> While more appropriate greeting lends you grace:
> Surely to spit there glorifies your face –
>   Spitting – from lips once sanctified by Hers.

Robert Browning (1812–1889)
'To Edward FitzGerald': *Athenaeum*, 13 July 1889

Browning, like Tennyson, regretted his outburst. He sent a telegram to the editor of the *Athenaeum* asking him not to publish, but it is said that

160

the editor suspected what was afoot and delayed opening the telegram until the presses were rolling.

A spirited in-fighter in a number of literary punch-ups was the poet Algernon Swinburne. He was a curious figure: very frail, with a huge white face, green eyes, and a great mop of gingery hair like a rusty pot-scourer. He was epileptic and nervous, always either dancing about or sitting stock still. His own poetry came in for a deal of criticism on the grounds that it was blasphemous and immoral. Particularly immoral:

> I attempt to describe Mr. Swinburne; and lo! the Bacchanal screams,
> ... men and women wrench, wriggle, and form in an endless allitera-
> tion of heated and meaningless words, the veriest garbage of Baude-
> laire.
>
> Robert Buchanan (1841–1901)
The Fleshly School of Poetry
>
> Baudelaire, inspired by a number of colourful, and sometimes coloured,
> mistresses had written *Les Fleurs du mal* and, in 1857, had been prosecuted
> and convicted by the French government for immoral writings. For some
> odd reason the conviction was annulled in 1949.

Like Baudelaire and, later, D. H. Lawrence, Swinburne was deeply shocked by brother writers also attempting to illuminate the human sexual dilemma; particularly Walt Whitman, who did it in blank verse:

> Under the dirty, clumsy paws of a harper whose plectrum is a muck-
> rake, any tune will become a chaos of discords ... Mr. Whitman's
> Eve is a drunken apple-woman, indecently sprawling in the slush
> and garbage of the gutter amid the rotten refuse of her overturned
> fruit-stall; but Mr. Whitman's Venus is a Hottentot wench under the
> influence of cantharides and adulterated rum.
>
> Algernon Swinburne (1837–1909)

Friends brought to Swinburne's notice an American paper, *Frank Leslie's Illustrated Newspaper*, containing an interview with the poet and philosopher Ralph Waldo Emerson, in the course of which Emerson was quoted as saying that Swinburne was 'a perfect leper, a mere sodomite'. Swinburne wrote to Emerson asking for clarification.

Edmund Gosse, in his biography of Swinburne, recalled asking the poet whether he received a reply from Emerson:

> 'I did not!' Swinburne replied.
> 'You will take no more notice, I suppose?'
> 'I have just taken exactly such notice as a gentleman in my position
> was bound to take. I have written him another letter.'
> 'I hope your language was quite moderate.'
> 'Perfectly moderate! I merely informed him, in language of the
> strictest reserve, that he was a hoary-headed and toothless baboon,
> who, first lifted into notice on the shoulder of Carlyle, now spits and

splutters from a filthier platform of his own finding and fouling. That
is all I've said.'

Edmund Gosse (1849–1928)
Swinburne: Personal Recollections

But that was by no means all that he had said. Further extracts from
the letter which he sent to Emerson were more explicit in their imagery:

I am informed that certain American journalists, not content with providing filth of their own for the consumption of their kind, sometimes
offer to their readers a dish of beastliness which they profess to have
gathered from under the chairs of more distinguished men ...

I ... am not sufficiently an expert in the dialect of the cesspool
and the dung-cart to retort in their own kind on these venerable
gentlemen — I, whose ears and lips are alike unused to the amenities
of conversation embroidered with such fragments of flowery rhetoric
as may be fished up by congenial fingers or lapped up by congenial
tongues out of the sewage of Sodom ...

A foul mouth is so ill-matched with a white beard that I would gladly
believe the newspaper-scribes alone responsible for the bestial
utterances which they declare to have dropped from a teacher whom
such disciples as these exhibit to our disgust and compassion as per-
forming on their obscene platform the last tricks of tongue now possible to a gap-toothed and hoary-headed ape, carried at first into notice
on the shoulder of Carlyle, and who now in his dotage spits and
chatters from a dirtier perch of his own finding and fouling: coryphaeus or choragus of his Bulgarian tribe of autocoprophagous
baboons, who make the filth they feed on.

Algernon Swinburne (1837–1909)
Letter to Ralph Waldo Emerson, 30 Jan. 1874

coryphaeus, and choragus = cheer-leader, choir leader; autocoprophagous
= eater of own dung; Bulgarian = Bulgar was the origin of the word 'bugger'.

Emerson ignored this letter as well as the first. He was rather good at
turning away from the disagreeable.

It was about this time that Mr. Theodore Watts-Dunton, a strong-
willed and literary solicitor, rescued the frail poet from his boozing and
his birching, and led him off to 'The Pines', Putney. For the last thirty
years of his life Swinburne settled down to a routine of little walks, chats
with babies in prams, and a daily bottle of light ale:

Mr. Swinburne no longer writes poetry: he only makes a clattering
noise ... Swinburne has now said not only all he has to say about
everything, but all he has to say about nothing.

A. E. Housman (1859–1936)
Quoted in *A. E. H.* by Laurence Housman, 1937

Although A. E. Housman disliked much of Swinburne's poetry, the
two men had one talent in common: they could both produce, and
clearly enjoyed producing, what might be termed 'creative abuse'.
Others with the gift included Thomas Nashe, Robert Louis Stevenson
and H. L. Mencken.

162

Housman's invective was mostly directed against colleagues. Although famous as an original poet – *A Shropshire Lad* – he was primarily a classical scholar; he spent the greater part of his life as a textual critic, editing the works of Manilius, a somewhat arid poet of Rome's Golden Age. In the prefaces to his commentaries Housman gave some pungent examples of critic biting critic:

> It has become apparent what the modern conservative critic really is: a creature moving about in worlds not realised. His trade is one which requires, that it may be practised in perfection, two qualifications only: ignorance of language and abstinence from thought. The tenacity with which he adheres to the testimony of scribes has no relation to the trustworthiness of that testimony, but is dictated wholly by his inability to stand alone ... And critics who treat MS evidence as rational men treat all evidence, and test it by reason and by knowledge which they have acquired, these are blamed for rashness and capriciousness by gentlemen who use MSS as drunkards use lamp-posts, – not to light them on their way but to dissimulate their instability.
>
> A. E. Housman (1859–1936)
Preface to Manilius

For many years the Housman prefaces have been cherished by *aficionados* as being among the very finest examples of academic venom.

Many of his best slings and arrows were reserved for those colleagues who had been rash enough to attempt previous translations:

> Bentley is the first, and Scaliger second, among the conjectural emendators of Manilius ... if there was a third it would be Jacob ... yet the virtues of his work are quenched and smothered by the multitude and monstrosity of its vices. They say that he was born of human parentage; but if so he must have been suckled by Caucasian tigers ... Not only has Jacob no sense for grammar, no sense for coherency, no sense for sense, but being himself possessed by a passion for the clumsy and the hispid he imputed this disgusting taste to all the authors whom he edited; and Manilius ... is accordingly constrained to write the sort of poetry which might have been composed by Nebuchadnezzar when he was driven from men and did eat grass as oxen.
>
> hispid = bristly.   *Ibid.*

> The task of editing the classics is continually attempted by scholars who have neither enough intellect nor enough literature ...
> Frailty of understanding is in itself no proper target for scorn and mockery ... but the unintelligent forfeit their claim to compassion when they begin to indulge in self-complacent airs, and to call themselves sane critics, meaning that they are mechanics. And when, relying on their numbers, they pass from self-complacency to insolence, and reprove their betters for using the brains which God has not denied them, they dry up the fount of pity.
>
> A. E. Housman (1859–1936)
Preface to Juvenal

Laurence Housman rather blew the gaff on his brother in the short memoir, *A. E. H.*, which he wrote soon after the poet and critic's death. In it he recorded that A. E. Housman kept a little notebook in which he jotted down hurtful and disparaging phrases as they occurred to him. He applied the phrases later when suitable enemies presented themselves.

The achievements of the scholar-critics, who commented on the work of the ancient poets and picked and quarrelled away amongst themselves on precise points of translation, seemed to one modern poet to be out of proportion to the achievements of the poets being quarrelled over:

Those famous men of old, the Ogres—
They had long beards and stinking arm-pits,
They were wide-mouthed, long-yarded and great-bellied
Yet not of taller stature, Sirs, than you ...
So many feats they did to admiration:
With their enormous throats they sang louder
Than ten cathedral choirs, with their grand yards
Stormed the most rare and obstinate maidenheads,
With their strong-gutted and capacious bellies
Digested stones and glass like ostriches.
They dug great pits and heaped huge mounds,
Deflected rivers, wrestled with the bear
And hammered judgements for posterity—
For the sweet-cupid-lipped and tassel-yarded
Delicate-stomached dwellers
In Pygmy Alley, where with brooding on them
A foot is shrunk to seven inches
And twelve-pence will not buy a spare rib.
And who would judge between Ogres and Pygmies—
The thundering text, the snivelling commentary—
Reading between such covers he will marvel
How his own members bloat and shrink again.

Robert Graves (b. 1895)
Poems Selected by Himself: 'Ogres and Pygmies'

In France, Emile Zola was taking realistic writing a stage further and calling the result Naturalism. This was a semi-scientific approach which produced characters who were more case-histories than people. The stories were carefully documented with facts which shed light upon the reasons why the unfortunate characters were in their particular plight.

Thomas Hardy did not approve of naturalistic fiction:

The recent school of novel writers forget in their insistence on life, and nothing but life, in a plain slice, that a story must be worth the telling, that a good deal of life is not worth any such thing, and that they must not occupy the reader's time with what he can get at first hand anywhere around him.

Thomas Hardy (1840–1928)

164

The philosopher of the slice-of-life, naturalistic school was Hippolyte Taine, who believed that people were at the mercy of their environment and became what they were because of the physical conditions which surrounded them; after a visit to England he decided that English women had huge teeth and big feet because they ate a lot of meat and were forever striding across rain-sodden meadows.

Zola's writings were much concerned with brutal, squalid characters and the instincts and social conditions which had, in his view, made them so:

> His instinctive inclination to depict demented persons, criminals, prostitutes, and semi-maniacs ... his symbolism, his pessimism, his coprolalia, and his predilection for slang, sufficiently characterize M.Zola as a high-class degenerate. That he is a sexual psychopath is betrayed on every page of his novels ... His consciousness is peopled with images of unnatural vice, bestiality, passivism and other aberrations ... Every porter of a brothel is capable of relating a low debauch.
>
> Max Nordau (1849–1923)
> *Degeneration*

Nordau, a German doctor, was a writer and critic of moral and social issues. The two volumes of *Degeneration* were a slightly peculiar attempt to prove that geniuses were degenerate. Other comments in support of his theory included:

'Walt Whitman ... is morally insane ... a vagabond, a reprobate rake ... An American driveller.'

'Nietzsche ... belongs, body and soul, to the flock of mangy sheep.'

'Tolstoy ... a degenerate mystic.'

Count Leo Tolstoy may have been mystical, but he was hardly degenerate. He believed that works of art should promote high moral and religious principles and he was not at all in favour of another French school of writing, the art-for-art's sake, sensual, aesthetic romantics:

> The French critic Doumic in 'Les Jeunes' characterises the works of the new writers ... 'it is weariness of life, contempt for the present epoch, regret for another age seen through the illusion of art, a taste for paradox, a desire to be singular, a sentimental aspiration towards simplicity, an infantile adoration of the marvellous, a sickly tendency towards reverie, a shattering condition of nerves, – and, above all, the exasperated demand of sensuality. They are all productions of people suffering from erotic mania.'
>
> With but few exceptions this is a description of all French novels.
>
> Count Leo Tolstoy (1828–1910)
> *What Is Art?*

Two of the young poets who were working out new theories of what poetry should be doing were Paul Verlaine and Jean Rimbaud. They were close friends until Rimbaud shot Verlaine during a quarrel and went to prison for two years. Dorothy Parker said, in a girls' school of all places, 'Verlaine was always chasing Rimbauds.'

England enjoyed a wave of 'decadence' at about the same time. A 'decadent' poet was a welcome target to humorists and satirists—and *Punch*—and an object of loathing to conventional versifiers:

The erotic affairs that you fiddle aloud
Are as vulgar as coins of the mint.
And you merely distinguish yourself from the crowd
By the fact that you've put them in print.
For your dull little vices we don't give a fig,
It is this that we deeply deplore:
You were cast as a common or garden pig,
But you play the invincible bore.

Owen Seaman (1861–1936)
To a Boy Poet of the Decadence

The decadent movement, which more or less came to an end with Oscar Wilde, was so called after a French journal, *Le Décadent*, founded in 1886, which, whenever it ran short of literary reviews, printed *décadent* manifestos speaking highly of *langueur*, futility, and the enjoyment of any kind of novel sensation, such as an orgy.

The reading habit spread rapidly through all social classes during the nineteenth century, or rather spread downwards from the class which was formerly the only one to read, and the changing face of society—the sweep forward of education and the consequent drop in illiteracy, the gradual shortening of the working day, the rise of the lower middle class, the erosion of privilege and the spreading of power more thinly and widely, economic prosperity—brought about great changes in all areas of literature.

The factory workers had little time to read to begin with, but they had their penny Sunday newspaper, full of highly coloured, sensational news and stories to brighten up the Sabbath, and they could buy broadsheets from a shop or the chapman, penny plain or twopence coloured, which told of horrible murders, society scandals and assorted skulduggery.

The lower middle class had cheap novels which sold in weekly parts for a penny each, exciting tales with titles such as *Gentleman Jack, Ella the Outcast, Elmira's Curse*, which were so popular that they sold at the rate of twenty-four copies a week as compared with one a month of a book by Dickens or Bulwer-Lytton. They also bought large quantities of 'improving' works such as books on household management, manners and letter-writing.

The middle class had its circulating libraries, which increased in number and influence; it is said that the circulating libraries sometimes bought three-quarters of the entire printing of a popular novel and it was normal for one large circulating library to order two thousand copies of one book:

> We call ourselves a rich nation, and we are filthy and foolish enough
> to thumb each other's books out of circulating libraries!
>
> John Ruskin (1819–1900)
> *Sesame and Lilies*

During the first half of the century there were no public libraries; no collections of reference books and historical works on open shelves for writers to consult:

> What a sad want I am in of libraries, of books to gather facts from!
> Why is there not a Majesty's library in every country town? There
> is a Majesty's gaol and gallows in every one.
>
> Thomas Carlyle (1795–1881)
> *Journal*, 1832

> Carlyle, with Gladstone and others, solved his problem by founding the
> London Library in 1841, where subscribers could refer to books or borrow
> them. It still flourishes, and the superb facilities which it provides for re-
> search must be held to blame for the production of many volumes, includ-
> ing this one.

Free public libraries began in 1850, when an Act of Parliament authorized local authorities to provide free reading facilities to the public out of the rates. Municipal public libraries sprang up in most towns both in the U.K. and in the U.S.A., and were highly popular. One man was worried about the effect on youth of this unlimited access to books:

> Meek young men grow up in libraries.
>
> Ralph Waldo Emerson (1803–1882)
> *The American Scholar*

He went on to point out that libraries did not automatically educate those who spent time within them by a kind of osmosis:

> It is not observed that ... librarians are wiser men than others.
>
> Ralph Waldo Emerson (1803–1882)
> *Spiritual Laws*

Another philosopher was even more positive:

> A library makes me sick.
>
> Friedrich Nietzsche (1844–1900)
> *Ecce Homo*

> Nietzsche's nausea was induced by the fear that the inferior ideas pro-
> pounded in the books which surrounded him in libraries would inhibit
> the flow of his own superior thoughts.

During the nineteenth century an illusion grew that being a professional writer was as easy a way of earning a living and becoming famous as any, and easier than most. Editors and publishers were deluged with manuscripts from adolescents, social ladies, clerks, shop-assistants, lawyers and clergymen, as were famous authors and public figures.

Benjamin Disraeli evolved a standard reply to would-be authors who sent him unsolicited, and awful, manuscripts; a little masterpiece of balanced ambiguity:

> Many thanks; I shall lose no time in reading it.
>
> Benjamin Disraeli (1804–1881)
> Quoted by Wilfred Meynell: *Benjamin Disraeli*

Everybody, it seemed, wanted to be an author, or a critic, or a journalist, and a great number threw up their jobs and had a go. Very few had either the ability or the stamina to succeed:

> Innumerable are the men and women now writing for bread, who have not the least chance of finding in such work a permanent livelihood. They took to writing because they knew not what else to do, or because the literary calling tempted them by its independence and its dazzling prizes. They will hang on to the squalid profession, their earnings eked out by begging and borrowing, until it is too late for them to do anything else — and what then? With a lifetime of dread experience behind me, I say that he who encourages any young man or woman to look for his living to 'literature', commits no less than a crime.
>
> George Gissing (1857–1903)
> *The Private Papers of Henry Ryecroft*

Cheaper paper, more efficient printing presses, railway distribution and, since the Board Schools were started in 1870, a vast new lower class readership, tended to make new newspapers and publishing ventures aim at providing low-priced, mass-circulation reading-matter, bright and simple to understand:

> Bits of foolery, bits of statistics, bits of jokes ... Everything must be very short ... their attention can't sustain itself ... Even chat is too solid for them; they want chit-chat.
>
> George Gissing (1857–1903)
> *New Grub Street*
>
> A condemnation now applied to television audiences.

There was little enthusiasm amongst the newly literate for the kind of reading-matter enjoyed by men of letters:

> As I was lying on the green
> A little book it chanced I seen.
> Carlyle's 'Essay on Burns' was the edition —
> I left it laying in the same position.
>
> Anon. (nineteenth century)

The poet and critic Matthew Arnold was not happy about the level of literature enjoyed by the upper classes, whom he thought were no longer dilettantes and connoisseurs but Philistines and Barbarians.

On the other hand, Edith Sitwell did not think much of Matthew Arnold:

Aberdeen granite tomb ... with his chilblained mittened musings.
Edith Sitwell (1887–1964)
Alexander Pope

The thunderous criticisms of the great Quarterlies, which once could make or break – usually break – an author were now only distant rumblings, almost lost among the chirpings and twitterings of the dozens of new, lighter literary magazines which had sprung up. Although adverse criticism was no longer of the same depth, or inordinate length, that it had been in Keats's day, it was still thorough and it could still hurt. One notably wounded author was the novelist Amanda McKittrick Ros, who turned on her critic and gave literature a rare example of dog biting flea.

Amanda McKittrick Ros, who could be described as a female, prose McGonagall, was the wife of the stationmaster of a small Irish port, Larne, in Co. Antrim. Her first novel, *Irene Iddesleigh*, was reviewed by a humorous writer, Barry Pain, in the 19 Feb. 1898 edition of the magazine *Black and White* under the title 'The Book of the Century'. The review was adverse and supposedly funny (Pain made a serious mistake in accusing her of having no sense of humour when the whole joy of Miss Ros's writings was in her Olympian lack of it). Miss Ros, every formidable inch of her a fighter, lunged back at her critic in the introduction to her next novel:

This so-called Barry Pain, by name, has taken upon himself to criticise a work the depth of which fails to reach the solving power of his borrow'd, and, he'd have you believe, varied talent ...

I care not what Barry calls the book I have written. *I* care not for the opinion of half-starved upstarts, who don the garb of a shabby-genteel, and would feign feed the minds of the people with the worthless scraps of stolen fancies ...

When Barry was swelling his head with the idea he thought to press into universal persuasion, but in which he has experienced a defeat for at least once in his famous life-time, I wonder if he failed to experience a sense of shame, a sense of ignorance, strongly indulged in by his professional brothers, at the great presumption he manifested in laying before the public a page of such balderdash, only attributable to a ranting schoolboy; and one has just to read *Black and White*, page 249, of 19th February, 1898, to endorse my pungent remark ...

Never in the knowledge of man has there been such a downpour of expression, such a page of kindliness, as that found in *Black and White*, page 249, of 19th February, 1898, entitled '*The Book of the Century*,' by (I'm off in a swoon) – by (ah, the thought is too great, it is too much!) – by Bar – (Almighty Father, my brain is in a whizz!) – Barry – (I'm tremendous sick!) – P – (Holy of Holies!) – Pa – (the

heart's pulsations are about to stop!) – Pain! – (not a bit of them!
I've got relief, by heavens! relief at last!), and good-bye, Barry dear
...

Amanda McKittrick Ros (1860–1939)
Introduction to Delina Delaney

There was pages more of it.

Miss Ros, ever after, nurtured a hate against anybody unwise enough to venture an adverse opinion of her work, chasing up the reviews through friends:

> I would be glad to see the critique you mentioned which appeared in the 'Daily Express', no matter how bad the beast described his effortless effort to sting the Author, who loves to see she can wring from the critic crabs their biting little bits of buggery! Every critique you see, cut it out and let me have it, please.

Amanda McKittrick Ros (1860–1939)
Letter to Norman Carrothers
Quoted by Jack Loudan: O Rare Amanda!

Publishing had come a long way since the days of the Unspeakable Curll when it was the first refuge of ambitious scoundrels; by the end of the nineteenth century it had become the last refuge of gentlemen.

During the latter part of the eighteenth century many booksellers became more involved in copyright deals than in either printing or selling books, and in the nineteenth century, firstly in the U.S.A. and then in the U.K., new firms were founded whose sole interest was to act as literary entrepreneurs; they were 'publishers'.

The late nineteenth century added another figure to the literary scene: the literary agent:

> Mrs. Morland very wittily defined an agent as someone whom you pay to make bad blood between yourself and your publisher.

Angela Thirkell (1890–1961)
Pomfret Towers

Miss Thirkell, without benefit of agent, left £74,600.

Many publishers, if not all, were hostile to this new development, regarding an agent as an intrusion in the special, personal relationship between author and publisher. But publishers themselves, authors pointed out, were only an intrusion into the natural sequence of author–printer–bookseller:

> A publisher is simply a useful middle-man.

Oscar Wilde (1854–1900)
The Artist as Critic

The agent who caused all the fuss was Alexander Pollock Watt, the first man to go in for representing authors. In 1893 Mr. Watt issued the first literary agent's list, giving the names of the authors for whom he acted, together with a number of warmly worded letters attesting to his zeal and professional skill. Mr. William Heinemann, one of the new, young publishers – he was thirty years old and had founded his own company – spoke out in strong terms against Watt and what he stood for:

This is the age of the middleman. He is generally a parasite. He always flourishes. I have been forced to give him some little attention lately in my particular business. In it he calls himself the literary agent. May I explain his evolution?

Origin. You become the literary agent by hiring an office; capital and special qualifications are unnecessary ... You begin by touting among the most popular authors of the moment, and by being always at hand and glad of a job, you will soon be able to extract from them testimonials which, carefully edited, make up a seductive prospectus to send out broadcast. You must collect these testimonials with zest, just as the pill-doctor or the makers of belts electropathic ...

The Business. You commence by taking in a weekly paper, in which you follow very carefully every author who has hitherto been unsuccessful, who is just beginning to succeed, and who has found a friend in some publisher, whose endeavours and efforts and work have at last helped to bring him into recognition. You must lose no time in dispatching your circular to this author, telling him that he has been shamefully neglected in the past, that you can double, treble, increase his income tenfold, if he will only allow you 10 per cent of this income for doing so.　William Heinemann (1863–1920)
Athenaeum, 1893

Among the clients on Watt's list were Wilkie Collins, Arthur Conan Doyle, Rider Haggard, Thomas Hardy, Bret Harte and Rudyard Kipling. There were also six unsolicited testimonials from publishers, including ones from Richard Bentley and Son, and Longmans, Green. The firm of A. P. Watt and Son are still in business as literary agents; or were when they negotiated the contract for this book – with Messrs. William Heinemann Ltd.

Publishers may have seen themselves, as William Heinemann suggested, as avuncular figures, befriending their authors and sparing no effort on their behalf. But some nineteenth-century authors saw publishers in a somewhat bleaker light:

Those fellows hate us.
Charles Lamb (1775–1834)
Letter to Bernard Barton, 1823

Authors delighted in little anti-publisher stories:

Times have changed since a certain author was executed for murdering his publisher. They say that when the author was on the scaffold he said good-bye to the minister and to the reporters, and then he saw some publishers sitting in the front row below, and to them he did not say good-bye. He said instead, 'I'll see you again.'
J. M. Barrie (1860–1937)
After-dinner speech at the Aldine Club, U.S.A., 1896

One author did not see his publisher in any kind of light but through a red mist:

> Sir,
>
> I am weary of repeating that you are to accept *no* communications for me. I leave you no discretion. As for the infernally familiar style in which you have presumed to address me, I beg to inform you that I regard it as a fresh outrage committed by an impenitent thief.
>
> By all, to whom I name your name, you are despised or hated; but I doubt whether you ever made a more ruthless or persequent enemy than —
>
> Your obedient servant —
Frederick William Rolfe
>
> Frederick Rolfe, Baron Corvo (1860–1913)
Letter to his publisher, Grant Richards, 1899
>
> This typical burst of paranoia was brought on by Grant Richards forwarding Rolfe's letters to him instead of refusing to accept them from the postman.

Two novelists of widely different talents just about saw the nineteenth century out; Thomas Hardy, who chronicled Wessex and the struggle of man to make some kind of mark in an indifferent world:

> An abortion of George Eliot
>
> George Moore (1852–1933)

And Henry James, the American novelist and critic who became a naturalized Briton in 1915:

> Henry James was one of the nicest old ladies I ever met.
>
> William Faulkner (1897–1962)

James found Americans rather naive and he responded enthusiastically, both in his work and socially, to the more sophisticated life led by well-bred Europeans:

> Poor Henry, he's spending eternity wandering round and round a stately park and the fence is just too high for him to peep over and they're having tea just too far for him to hear what the countess is saying.
>
> W. Somerset Maugham (1874–1965)
> *Cakes and Ale*

He developed a delicate, elaborate, fastidious prose style which enabled him to express not merely what he meant but *exactly* what he meant:

> A magnificent but painful hippopotamus resolved at any cost... upon picking up a pea.
>
> H. G. Wells (1866–1946)
> *Boon*

172

James's novels began with simple plots of action, went on to describe adult passions through the eyes of children and finished up as extremely subtle and complex studies of character:

> The work of Henry James has always seemed divisible by a simple dynastic arrangement into three reigns: James I, James II, and the Old Pretender.
>
> Philip Guedalla (1889–1944)

Literature began to assume a slightly different shape within the culture of the twentieth century. Little literary movements were popular:

> A literary movement consists of five or six people who live in the same town and hate each other cordially.
>
> George Moore (1852–1933)

The Bloomsbury group, which was more a group of intellectual friends than a literary school, included philosophers and artists as well as writers. It met at Clive Bell's house in Gordon Square just before the war:

> The Young Men's Christian Association—with Christ left out, of course.
>
> Gertrude Stein (1874–1946)

The young men of the Bloomsbury group tended to be vegetarians and conscientious objectors. There was a story of a woman, white feather ready in her hand, who stopped one of the group in the early days of the war and demanded to know why he was not in uniform fighting for civilization. 'Madam,' he replied, '*I* am the civilization they are fighting for.'

To more muscular poets the Bloomsbury group seemed to be hopelessly pallid and narcissistic:

> Of all the clever people round me here
> I most delight in me—
> Mine is the only voice I hear,
> And mine the only face I see.
>
> Roy Campbell (1901–1957)
> *Home Thoughts on Bloomsbury*

Besides writing sinewy, aggressive poetry, Campbell, a South African, was a powerful man physically. He channelled his energies, at one time or another, into being a fisherman, bullfighter, horse-coper, soldier for Franco and B.B.C. producer.

A truly literary company, who came in with King George V, were the 'Georgian poets', who sang of the simple, cheerful, outdoor life. They included such poets of the open air as Walter de la Mare, John Masefield and W. H. Davies. They led a revival of interest in that kind of verse, and when E. V. Lucas's *Open Road* became the most popular anthology, a more study-bound writer wrote:

> One would think that poetry was a form of deep breathing. Even Mr. Chesterton seems to be suffering from a hearty degeneration of the fat.
>
> Philip Guedalla (1889–1944)

Both G. K. Chesterton and Hilaire Belloc wrote enthusiastically of striding out along dusty roads and quaffing ale at inns. Their joint heartiness at one period caused them to be described as:

> Two buttocks of one bum.
> T. Sturge Moore (1870–1944)

The early part of the century saw a good deal of experimental prose and poetry. Edith Sitwell was not impressed with the New Poetry from America:

> A school of American-Greek posturants, resembling not so much marble statues as a white-tiled bathroom, exuded a thin stream of carefully chosen, watery words. Added to that misfortune, we are now afflicted by the shrill moronic cackling of the Sur-realists — laying never so much as an addled egg — and the erotic confidences of rich young ladies, suffering less from an excess of soul than from an excess of distilled spirits.
>
> Edith Sitwell (1887–1964)
> *Alexander Pope*

The writers of prose were stunned by the publication, in 1922, of the most remarkable, and perhaps the most important, novel of modern times, James Joyce's *Ulysses*. Joyce's style was something of an enigma:

> My God, what a clumsy *olla putrida* James Joyce is! Nothing but old fags and cabbage-stumps of quotations from the Bible and the rest, stewed in the juice of deliberate, journalistic dirty-minded-ness.
>
> D. H. Lawrence (1885–1930)
> Letter to Aldous and Maria Huxley, Kesselmatte, 1928

Lawrence's shocked reaction to 'dirty-mindedness' was genuine. He saw himself as a reformer, trying to put an end to the stifling and arid code of sexual morality which had been imposed on the working classes by nonconformism at the beginning of the nineteenth century. He saw sex as a life-force, something beautiful and clean. The trouble was that at the time hardly anybody else did. When William Heinemann returned Lawrence's manuscript of *Sons and Lovers*, because he felt that the public were not quite ready for Lawrence's attitude to sex, Lawrence wrote to a friend expressing what he thought of the public:

> Curse the blasted, jelly-boned swines, the slimy, the belly-wriggling invertebrates, the miserable sodding rotters, the flaming sods, the

snivelling, dribbling, dithering, palsied pulse-less lot that make up England today. They've got white of egg in their veins, and their spunk is that watery it's a marvel they can breed. They *can* nothing but frog-spawn – the gibberers! God, how I hate them!

D. H. Lawrence (1885–1930)
Letter to Edward Garnett

Lawrence's definitive statement on sexual morality, *Lady Chatterley's Lover*, arguably the most discussed novel of the twentieth century if only because it was discussed by millions of people who did not normally discuss novels, came out in 1928, went back in again, and was not published in its full text until 1959 in the U.S.A. and 1960 in England.

The legal actions which then arose in both countries produced a number of thundering denunciations of the book's capacity for corrupting the then uncorrupted, if any. At one point the prosecution in the British trial, overwhelmed by memories of more spacious times, begged the jury to consider carefully whether it was the sort of book which they would care to let their servants read.

Of all the unfavourable reviews which the book attracted, perhaps the most piquant appeared in the American magazine *Field and Stream*:

Although written many years ago, *Lady Chatterley's Lover* has just been reissued by the Grove Press, and this pictorial account of the day-by-day life of an English gamekeeper is full of considerable interest to outdoor minder readers, as it contains many passages on pheasant-raising, the apprehending of poachers, ways to control vermin, and other chores and duties of the professional gamekeeper. Unfortunately, one is obliged to wade through many pages of extraneous material in order to discover and savour those sidelights on the management of a midland shooting estate, and in this reviewer's opinion the book cannot take the place of J. R. Miller's *Practical Gamekeeping*.

Ed. Zern (b. 1910)
Field and Stream: 'Exit Laughing'

By the end of the nineteenth century most schools had taken to teaching English literature, which produced a curious side-effect during the twentieth century; good books by dead authors were labelled 'classics', a term synonymous to schoolchildren with 'worthy and boring':

A classic ... something that everybody wants to have read and nobody wants to read.

Mark Twain (1835–1910)
Mark Twain's Speeches: 'Disappearance of Literature'

There go *Tom Jones, Sense and Sensibility, The Pickwick Papers, Vanity Fair* ...

A prophecy by Jeremy Bentham, in the early nineteenth century,

175

that poetry would eventually be no more important to society than a pin-table machine came true in the twentieth century:

> Publishing a volume of poetry is like dropping a rose-petal down the Grand Canyon and waiting for the echo.
>
> Don Marquis (1878–1937)
> *The Sun Dial*

There was no longer money in poetry:

> A publisher of today would as soon see a burglar in his office as a poet.
>
> H. de Vere Stacpoole (1863–1951)
> Robert Graves pointed out that 'there's no poetry in money, either'.

The twentieth century has seen a rapid decline in the sound and fury of literary controversy. Knives may still be concealed beneath cloaks in smiling academic circles but, whether due to the libel laws, or middle-class morality, or a chemical change in the modern spleen, little violent abuse or invective is offered in the ordinary world of writers, critics and readers. If a book gives grave offence nowadays it is put back on the shelf with a grimace; it is not, even metaphorically, hurled through the author's kitchen window. But a surprising number of people still care enough about books to buy them, and presumably read them, in the teeth of various other claims on their leisure time.

Perhaps the most helpful twentieth-century innovation for the casual book-buyer has been the invention of the 'best-seller':

> Best-sellerism is the star system of the book world. A 'best seller' is a celebrity among books. It is a book known primarily (sometimes exclusively) for its well-knownness.
>
> Daniel J. Boorstin (b. 1914)
> *The Image*

Booksellers' returns and the computer have freed the modern book buyer from the agonies of decision-making. Once a book has been declared a best-seller its sales accelerate—like the fresh-water polyp, the best-seller breeds from itself—and the book buyer can happily accept the judgement of the great majority:

> A best-seller is the gilded tomb of a mediocre talent.
>
> Logan Pearsall Smith (1864–1946)
> *Afterthoughts*

THEATRE

Theatre

During over two thousand years of busy and colourful life the theatre, more than any other of the arts, has attracted antipathy of every strength and form, from expressions of implacable hatred to petulant rebukes, arising from a variety of reasons ranging from burning conviction that the theatre was the breeding-ground of sin and the plague, to distaste for a poor performance.

A distinguished novelist reeled away, shuddering, from a brush with this curious world:

> It is a most unholy trade.
> Henry James (1843–1916)
> Letter to William Heinemann

To many people, from Plato on, the profession of acting lacked merit. It seemed to them that pretending to be somebody else and representing other people's agonies and ecstasies in the name of art was merely producing a kind of kitsch:

> Acting is the lowest of arts, if it is an art at all.
> George Moore (1853–1933)
> *Mummer-Worship*

This view of the profession was shared by one of the most popular actresses of her day:

> Surely, after all, acting is nonsense.
> Fanny Kemble (1809–1893)
> *Journal*, 15 April 1833

Whether acting was a lowly degree of art or just nonsense, it was rarely, to those of less than star status, the idle and glamorous existence which many people outside the profession believed it to be:

> It worries me to beat the band
> To hear folks say our life is grand;
> Wish they'd try some one-night stand—
> Ain't it awful, Mabel?
> John Edward Hazzard (1881–1935)
> *Ain't it Awful, Mabel?*

179

Until recent years it was held that acting was a perilous career for a young lady:

> It is nearly impossible for a woman to remain pure who adopts the stage as a profession.
>
> Clement Scott (1841–1904)
> *Life in the Theatre*

This statement, from a moralistic dramatic critic who deplored the works of Ibsen and Shaw, stirred up a controversy which raged happily for a while and drew a number of retorts, including one from a prolific writer and theatre-manager:

> This is a monstrous saying. No respectable woman on the stage! There are thousands of respectable women and only about six actresses.
>
> Robert Buchanan (1841–1901)

Guilt-stricken theatrical mums were reassured that the fault was not theirs:

> Actresses will happen in the best regulated families.
>
> Oliver Herford (1863–1935)

An ancient criticism of theatre was that acting had a corrupting effect upon actors. It was held that seeking applause was unhealthy:

> The appetite for applause grows tyrannical with indulgence.
>
> Anon.

And what was applause anyway?

> Applause is but a fart, the crude
> Blast of the fickle multitude.
> *Wit and Drollery*, 1645

Crude or not, applause was the actor and playwright's criterion of success with his audience and was frequently difficult to obtain. For instance, when a large proportion of the audience had been given complimentary tickets:

> Those who have free seats at the play hiss first.
>
> Chinese proverb

Other audiences notoriously difficult to please were those who attended a play during the wet and windy months of winter:

> Long experience has taught me that in England nobody goes to the theatre unless he or she has bronchitis.
>
> James Agate (1877–1947)
> *Ego 6*

And first-night audiences, which, according to an experienced American producer, were made up of two species of playgoer:

Theater habitués and sons of habitués.
Marc Klaw (1858–1936)

But a performer who mastered the lowly art and won dubious applause from difficult audiences could not only become rich and lead a lazy and glamorous life but could earn the respect of members of his or her own profession – some of them, at any rate:

Twinkle, twinkle, little star,
Who the hell do you think you are?
Quoted by Maggie Teyte (b. 1889)
Star on the Door

Miss Teyte, on tour as leading soprano with the Boston Opera Company, found the couplet scrawled on her dressing-room mirror with lipstick.

The modern concept of 'theatre', as distinct from colourful tribal rituals, had its beginnings in Greece in the sixth century B.C. Its immediate ancestor was the fun and games which grew around the worship of the god Dionysus, the poor people's god. As Dionysus was the god of wine these revels entailed a good deal of heavy drinking, dancing, and chasing about the hills in goat skins. But another aspect of the worship was the elaborate choral performances of hymns in honour of the god, which were called dithyrambs; these were sung and danced, to flute accompaniment, by a chorus of fifty. Then one day, according to legend, a poet named Thespis added himself to the cast, spoke a prologue and exchanged speeches with the leader of the chorus, thus becoming the first 'actor' and the originator of dialogue drama. Hence 'Thespian', a dramatic actor.

Telling a story by means of the interchange of dialogue rather than by chorus-singing proved such an improvement that the playing of 'tragedy', as it was called, was accepted officially as part of Greek religious celebration and in 534 B.C., in Athens, the world's first recorded drama competition took place. It was won, most suitably, by Thespis.

Comedy could well have derived from the other part of religious celebrations; the boozing and the orgy-making. Fertility was most important for both crops and people, and was traditionally invoked by wearing or exhibiting phalluses, the sign of male fertility, and by the exchange of spoken obscenities, the idea being that talking about procreation and the bits of the human body concerned with procreation would help the process to be successful. These revels also traditionally contained a good deal of abuse of figures of authority and participants dressed themselves up to represent dwarfs, hunchbacks and other victims of physical distress on the principle that the evil spirits who bestowed those favours would reckon that they had done enough and go elsewhere. All this became a dramatic form, and 'comedy', from the Greek word *komos*, 'a revel', was accepted as part of the Athens festivities in 486 B.C.

From its very beginning theatre invoked disapproval. In what must be the first backstage visit on record the great Greek legislator Solon, one of the 'Seven Wise Men of Greece', went to see one of Thespis' performances and called round to see the actor afterwards:

> Thespis, at this time, beginning to act tragedies, and the thing, because it was new, taking very much with the multitude, though it was not yet made a matter of competition, Solon ... went to see Thespis himself, as the ancient custom was, act; and after the play was done, he addressed him, and asked him if he was not ashamed to tell so many lies before such a number of people; and Thespis replying that it was no harm to say or do so in a play, Solon vehemently struck his staff against the ground: 'Ay,' said he, 'if we honour and commend such play as this, we shall find it some day in our business.'

Plutarch (*c.* A.D. 46–*c.* 120)
Lives

The moral implications of drama bothered many of Greece's wise men. Was it right for an actor to represent a villainous man? Was it right for an actor to represent any man apart from himself, i.e. to pretend to be something which he was not? The Greek word for an actor, *hupokritēs*, has now become the pejorative word 'hypocrite', although the old meaning of the word survived until the last century:

> Someone inquiring for cottage lodgings asked if she could not be taken in at a certain cottage. The reply was, 'Oh, no! they have got two or three of the *Hypocrites* staying there.' These lodgers proved to be some members of a travelling theatrical company.

Letter from the Rector of Little Chart, near Ashford, Kent
Notes and Queries, 14 July 1906

Plato was much bothered by the ethics of drama and acting, which went against his own philosophy that 'one man plays one part only':

> And therefore when any of these pantomimic gentlemen, who are so clever that they can imitate anything, comes to us and makes a proposal to exhibit himself and his poetry, we will fall down and worship him as a sacred, marvellous and delightful being; but we must also inform him that in our State such as he are not permitted to exist; the law will not allow them. And so when we have anointed him with myrrh, and set a garland of wool upon his head, we shall send him away to another city.

Plato (*c.* 427–*c.* 347 B.C.)
Republic

Another form of performance, though it was hardly drama, was 'mime'. Mime had no connection with religious revelry, in fact it made a speciality of burlesquing the gods, but seemed to arise from the need of the underprivileged to mock figures of authority and so cut them down to size. It began as a simple kind of street-corner performance involving not only the usual conjurers, jugglers and acrobats but also cheerfully obscene sketches lampooning the gods, the magistrates, or anybody worth cocking a snook at. The leader of the troupe was an actor who could impersonate the personages lampooned, hence our word 'mimic'. A troupe of *mimi*, often a family, travelled light; all they needed was a few cloaks and props and a curtain they could hang from a pole, and they could wander from town to town, or country to country. Mime, in the historical sense of rough, vulgar, underpaid, mickey-taking entertainment, proved to be the most imperishable form of theatre.

In the space of about three hundred years the Greeks inaugurated drama and developed both comedy and tragedy to a high degree of excellence.

Then came the Romans and for seven hundred years the drama steadily sank, to disappear completely beneath the surface in the sixth century A.D.

There was some interest in plays to begin with, such as the comedies of Plautus (254–184 B.C.) and Terence (*c.* 195–159 B.C.), but the circuses and the games were more to the Roman taste and virtually no plays were written for performance after about 100 B.C., and those that had been written were adaptations of Greek originals; not one play has survived with an original plot invented by a Roman playwright.

In Republican Rome the mime was the most popular form of theatre, enjoyed by the poor sections of the city because of its irreverence and bawdiness. During the Feast of Flora the mime-actresses traditionally performed naked and the troupes of travelling *mimi*, 'birds of passage' as one writer described them, were notoriously made up of part-time whores and thieves.

This was the theatre that the Christian Fathers and the other early ecclesiastical authors pronounced upon:

> Away then with these Lewd, Ungodly Diversions, and which are but Impertinence at the best. What part of Impudence either in Words or Practice, is omitted by the Stage? Don't the Buffoons take almost all manner of Liberties, and plunge through Thick and Thin, to make a Jest?
>
> St. Clement of Alexandria (*c.* A.D. 150–*c.* 215)
> *Works*

The *mimi* not only let fly at the old pagan gods but also at the new and swiftly growing Christian religion. Clearly, it was Devil's work:

> A certain Woman went to the *Play-house*, and brought the Devil
> Home with her. And when the Unclean Spirit was press'd in the
> *Exorcism*, and ask'd how he durst attack a Christian; I have done
> nothing, says he, but what I can justify; for I seiz'd her upon my
> own Ground.

Tertullian (b. *c.* A.D. 150–160)
De Spectaculis

> What tho' the Performance may be in some Measure pretty and enter-
> taining? ... the Devil throws in a Cordial Drop to make the Draught
> go down ... Look upon it only, I say, as Honey from the Bowels
> of a Toad, or the Bag of a Spider.

Ibid.

One of the problems which bedevilled early Christian writers, and later ones, was that although they knew in their bones that Christ and His disciples must have hated the theatre of their day and everything connected with it, nobody actually said so in the Bible. St. Cyprian had a brave go at explaining away this omission:

> Let mere Modesty supply the *holy Text:* And let *Nature* govern where
> *Revelation* does not reach. Some Things are too black to lie upon
> *Paper*, and are more strongly forbidden, because unmention'd. The
> Divine Wisdom must have had a low Opinion of *Christians*, had it
> descended to Particulars in this Case. Silence is sometimes the best
> Method for Authority. To forbid often puts People in Mind of what
> they should not do.

St. Cyprian (*c.* A.D. 200–258)
Works

The state of theatre became even worse under the later Empire and the fifth-century historian Zosimus blamed the introduction of 'panto-mime' for the decline and fall of the Empire (others have blamed the use of lead-lined cooking pots and failure to invent the stirrup). A pantomime was a solo performance by a masked and cloaked dancer, accompanied by an orchestra and a choir, and it was Rome's sole original contribution to the theatre. Successful *pantomimi* became perfumed, pampered darlings of the crowd and very rich, although Nero's favourite, Paris, tactlessly out-danced his master and was promptly put to death. The modern word 'mime' comes from the silent performance of a *pantomimus*, not, confusingly, from the Greek and Roman *mimi* who used dialogue.

Permanent stone and brick theatres were built throughout the Roman Empire with complicated stage machinery, canvas awnings to provide shade, even fine sprays of scented water to cool plebeian brows, but the plays were trivial: crude rustic farces, spectacular productions about nothing in particular and obscene mime-plays. Under the Emperor Elagabalus (or Heliogabulus, A.D. 204–222), a young man of conspicuous nastiness, scenes of rape and fornication were not acted but actually performed and, provided the local magistrate had a condemned criminal available, executions actually took place on stage:

The *Theatres* — those *Cages of Uncleanness,* and publick Schools of Debauchery.

St. Augustine (354–430)
De Consensu Evangelistarum

By the fifth century the state of the theatre was so abysmal that the Christian Church, now powerful enough to take action, excommunicated all actors and actresses. And in the early part of the sixth century the Emperor Justinian officially closed all theatres in the Roman Empire, or what was left of it. The last reference to theatres in the Western world was dated A.D. 533. There were to be no more public plays, as distinct from civic or religious festivals, for a thousand years. The barbarians overwhelmed the continent of Europe and the massive theatres were shut down, torn down, or turned into fortresses and granaries.

During the dark centuries of confused warfare, plague and famine small groups of performers wandered from village to village giving displays of singing, dancing, conjuring, tumbling and buffoonery. Some of these medieval minstrels, or *jongleurs*, were highly skilled and ended up permanently attached to a royal court or a noble household while others were little more than wandering thieves.

Some of the jollier monasteries enjoyed a visit from a troupe, but the more austere churchmen would not entertain the detested *mimi*:

It is better to please God than the actors; it is better to have a care for the poor than for the Mimes.

Alcuin (735–804)
Epistles, XXII

An idle, light, evilly deceitful, and proud fellow who whispers insulting jests basely and obscenely and rightly called by the people by the name of Mimmus.

Milo (*c.* 850)
Life of St. Amandus

It was ironic that the Church, which had attacked drama unswervingly, and ultimately successfully, brought drama back into existence again.

In the tenth century an experiment was authorized in France to 'strengthen faith in the unlearned vulgar' by acting out the Easter story in church in the form of a sung play. The Liturgical Dramas, as they are now known, were extremely successful and the practice spread throughout Europe, only dying away in England with the Reformation.

Liturgical dramas were extended to performances at Christmas as well as at Easter and in the Christmas stories it became a tradition for the actor playing the part of Herod to give a boisterous, extrovert performance:

> O, it offends me to the soul to hear a rombustious periwig-pated fellow tear a passion to tatters, to very rags, to split the ears of the groundlings, who for the most part are capable of nothing but inexplicable dumb-shows and noise. I would have such a fellow whipped for o'erdoing Termagant. It out-herods Herod.
>
> William Shakespeare (1564–1616)
> *Hamlet:* Act III, sc. ii

By the end of the twelfth century liturgical drama had developed to such an extent that churches were too small for the productions, and so the performances were given in the open air, usually at the church porch. From there they moved to market-places; the parts were played by villagers instead of priests and the words were spoken in the vernacular.

The result of this was the rise of a new form of drama; not so much a play as a flamboyant parade of episodes from a Bible story – the medieval Mystery Play.

Mystery plays, and the stories about saints called Miracle plays, were performed at Whitsun and on the feast of Corpus Christi. Each episode was self-contained, with its own cast and setting, and these were either staged around the town square so that citizens made their way from one episode to the next, or mounted on wagons so that the citizens stayed put and the episodes came and went in front of them. Each episode was staged by a different craftsman's guild and the actors were paid. An example of how remote this drama was from the Church authorities is to be found in the scale of fees paid; one year Noah received 10d. but God only got 8d.

A tremendous amount of zest went into these productions, which lasted as long as ten hours at a stretch and sometimes spread over three days. Even on the wagons the scenery was elaborate and vivid, often on two levels, with complicated machinery producing wondrous effects; the devils were played by comics and tumblers; saints were visibly tortured, teeth drawn by tongs, limbs roasted; cardboard breasts were sheared off; hell belched real flames; gunpowder banged and fizzed away everywhere.

Some of the parts, such as Belial the Spirit of Evil, called for an actor with not only a talent for playing character but also strong nerves:

> He that schal pleye Belyal loke that he have gunne-powder brennynge In pypys in his handis & in his eris & in his ars whanne he gothe to battel.
>
> Ms. note in *The Castle of Perseverance* (fifteenth century)

A late-medieval development of the Mystery cycles moved drama even further away from religion by dropping the Bible stories in favour

186

of stories which gave a more general moral instruction. These were not great pageants but static, wordy plays whose characters had names like Ignorance, Good Deeds, Bad Angel. *Everyman* is the best known of these productions, which were called Morality plays:

> Their very name is like a yawn.
>
> Anon.

The secularization of drama was completed by the success of Interludes, short dramatic pieces played at court, and in country houses, probably between the immense and prolonged courses of early-Tudor meals. Interludes had nothing to do with the Bible or with moral instruction, they were purely pieces of entertainment and could well have been the real starting point of English drama.

An Interlude was performed at court to divert Queen Elizabeth in the second month of her reign. She was not amused:

> The sam day at nyght at the quen['s] court ther was a play a-for her grace, the wyche the plaers plad shuche matter that they wher commondyd to leyff off and continently the maske cam in dansyng.
>
> Henry Machyn (1498?–1563?)
> Diary: Jan. 1559

> The Queen could well have taken offence at some satirical remark about the Church. Some of the best Interludes then written were by John Heywood, one of the first English dramatic writers. He had been a minstrel to Henry VIII and a court jester to Edward VI and Mary. He was a Catholic. The danger in making a satirical remark about the Church under the Tudors was that a jibe at, say, the Archbishop of Canterbury could win him a purse of gold from Henry, lose him his ears under Edward, earn him a pension from Mary and then get him sent to the Tower by Elizabeth. In fact, Heywood prudently went abroad after Queen Mary's death 'for the security of his person, and the preservation of his religion'.

By the late 1400s England had a number of acting troupes, attached to a nobleman's household and wearing his livery. When they were not required by his lordship they usually went on a profitable tour of the countryside, setting up and playing in halls, barns and innyards.

There was also a large number of more disreputable groups – much more like the old *mimi* – who slept rough between performances and had no master.

By the time of Elizabeth 'masterless men' had become a considerable problem. A plague of vagrants – soldiers and retainers adrift after the break-up of the great feudal households, monks, clerks, farm labourers homeless from the dissolution of the monasteries, beggars, poor scholars – infested the highways and made travel very dangerous.

In 1572 Elizabeth tightened up the already severe vagrancy laws with a famous statute:

All Fencers Bearewardes Comon Players in Enterludes and Minstrels, not belonging to any Baron of this Realme or towards any other honorable Personage of greater Degree ... shall wander abroade and have not Lycence of two Justices of the Peace at the leaste ... to be Rogues Vacabounds and Sturdye Beggers ... on first conviction to bee grievouslye whipped, and burnte through the gristle of the right Eare with an hot Yron of the compasse of an ynche about.

Statute 14 Elizabeth, cap. 5, 1572

This statute was gleefully quoted by Puritans as a royal proclamation that all actors were rogues and vagabonds, but modern commentators believe that the intention of the edict was to provide the means of setting up a properly regulated acting profession: 'Elizabeth's edict of 1572 ... was not a hostile measure but protective and salutary ... It was to confer on James and Richard Burbage a security that would enable them to get the best out of Shakespeare. It was to confer on Shakespeare a security that would enable him to get the best out of Richard Burbage: a conjunction to which we owe much' (W. Bridge-Adams, *The Irresistible Theatre*, 1957). The first royal patent for performers of plays, made possible by the edict, was obtained for James Burbage by his patron, the Earl of Leicester, in 1574.

For most of her reign, until she grew old and impossible to please, Queen Elizabeth shared with most of her subjects a delight in watching the performance of plays and masques, and she did much to protect the players against increasing pressure to limit their activities or to abolish them entirely.

The prosperous merchants of the City of London were implacably opposed to the colourful, rowdy inn-yard performances to which their clerks, apprentices and employees flocked, and they continually passed ordinances prohibiting the staging of plays within the city limits. When these failed to bite they imposed severe restrictions on play-acting, with a scheme of fines for transgressions.

And so it was outside the City of London limits and the Lord Mayor's restrictions that, in 1576, a stage-struck joiner, James Burbage, who was also an actor with the Earl of Leicester's company and a property developer of genius, took a lease of land and built the world's first public, private-enterprise theatre, The Theater.

The Theater was a huge wooden building, open to the skies, seating over three thousand people. Burbage built it with money borrowed from his father-in-law on a parcel of land near what is now Holywell Lane, off Shoreditch High Street, just north of Liverpool Street Station. He also built twenty-one houses on the site.

Within a few months another theatre was built nearby, in Curtain Road which runs off Holywell Lane, called The Curtain.

The success of both the playhouses brought immediate fulminations from Puritan pulpits:

> Look but upon the common plays in London, and see the multitude that flocketh to them and followeth them. Behold the sumptuous theatre houses, a continual monument of London's prodigality and folly. But I understand they are now forbidden because of the plague. I like the policy well if it hold still, for a disease is but lodged or patched up that is not cured in the cause, and the cause of plagues is sin, if you look to it well: and the cause of sin are plays: therefore the cause of plagues are plays.

Thomas White (1550?–1624)
A Sermon Preached at Pawles Crosse on Sunday the thirde of November 1577 in the .Time of the Plague

> This is the earliest surviving attack on the newly built playhouses. It was first preached on 9 Dec. 1576. It was presumably repeated the following year by popular request and then published. The playhouses were closed whenever the plague became particularly lethal. Although playhouses, or any places where crowds herded together, must have been a hazard to health the Rev. Thomas White's concluding syllogism owed more to puritan zeal than to logic.

The great era of Elizabethan drama had not yet begun and the performances were usually a mixture of vaulting, rope-dancing, fencing, singing and the production of a Morality, or an Interlude, or one of the rubbishy plays then current, all 'bombast and buffoonery', like *Appius and Virginia* and *Cambyses*.

Admission was a penny – not all that cheap for a Tudor working man – and another penny bought a seat on a bench. A third penny provided a better seat up in the stands. Noblemen sat on the stage.

Performances took place in the afternoon. A flag was flown on days when performances were given and the signal that the show was about to begin was three blasts on a trumpet:

> Will not a filthy play, with the blast of a trumpet, sooner call thither a thousand, than an hour's tolling of a bell bring to the sermon a hundred? . . . If you resort to the Theater, the Curtain, and other places of plays in the city, you shall on the Lord's day have those places, with many others that I cannot reckon, so full as possible they can throng . . . For reckoning with the least, the gain that is reaped of eight ordinary places in the city, which I know, by playing but once a week (wheras many times they play twice or sometimes thrice) it amounteth to two thousand pounds by the year.

John Stockwood (d. 1610)
A Sermon Preached at Paules Crosse, 1578

> The Rev. John Stockwood, preaching a year after the Rev. Thomas White from the same pulpit, put his finger on two aspects of the theatre which particularly infuriated Puritans: the size of audiences when compared with their own congregations and the profits which theatres earned.

A trip to one of the new playhouses was then a colourful and slightly adventurous excursion to beyond the city limits, to a fringe area of brothels, tumbledown lodging-houses, absconded apprentices and fugitives from creditors. Once inside there was the jostling for a good place, apples and nuts to eat and ale to drink.

The Puritan movement, gaining in strength, was totally opposed to this kind of escape from life's serious purpose and one of their early pamphleteers, Philip Stubbs (or Stubbes), waded into the playhouses and the sort of conduct he believed that they gave rise to:

> Do they not maintain bawdry, insinuate foolery, and renew the remembrance of heathen idolatry? Do they not induce whoredom and uncleanness? Nay, are they not rather plain devourers of maidenly virginity and chastity? For proof whereof but mark the flocking and running to Theaters and Curtains, daily and hourly, night and day, time and tide, to see plays and interludes, where such wanton gestures, such bawdy speeches, such laughing and fleering, such kissing and bussing, such clipping and culling, such winking and glancing of wanton eyes, and the like is used, and is wonderful to behold. Then these goodly pageants being ended, every mate sorts to his mate, every one brings another homeward of their way very friendly, and in their secret conclaves (covertly) they play the sodomites, or worse.

Philip Stubbs (*fl.* 1583–1591)
The Anatomie of Abuses, 1583

> Unfortunately Stubbs did not state what behaviour he considered to be worse than playing the sodomite. In the preface to the first edition Stubbs declared that he was not against all plays but only those that went too far, and that some plays served a useful and moral purpose. However, the book sold so well on the strength of its bitter attacks that Stubbs withdrew this note of moderation from the second edition and the book went smartly through four large editions in two years.

Queen Elizabeth had been on the throne nearly thirty years, protecting the players and their mainly crude and trivial plays from extinction, when the standard of drama rose spectacularly. John Lyly helped pave the way with his graceful and sophisticated comedy and Thomas Kyd wrote a number of successful tragedies of revenge, but the great age of English drama could be said to have begun with the production in 1587, eleven years after Burbage opened The Theater, of Christopher Marlowe's *Tamburlaine the Great*.

Marlowe, perhaps more a poet and scholar than a dramatist, transformed the plodding, naive rhymes then current in plays into blank verse of great power and beauty. Marlowe's work was much admired by his contemporaries – Jonson spoke of his 'mighty line' – but a modern critic thought otherwise:

> He is the true Elizabethan blank-verse beast, itching to frighten other people with the superstitious terrors and cruelties in which he does

not himself believe, and wallowing in blood, violence, muscularity of expression and strenuous animal passion as only literary men do when they become thoroughly depraved by solitary work, sedentary cowardice, and starvation of the sympathetic centres. It is not surprising to learn that Marlowe was stabbed in a tavern brawl: what would be utterly unbelievable would be his having succeeded in stabbing anyone else.

George Bernard Shaw (1856–1950)
Dramatic Opinions and Essays

While *Tamburlaine* was delighting audiences with its language and majesty, a young lad who was to be England's greatest dramatic genius was (some say) holding horses' heads for theatre-going gentry, or (some say) being call-boy, or (probably) working as a hack-writer, at either The Curtain or The Theater.

William Shakespeare seems to have arrived in London in 1586. Very little is known about this period of his life (or any other period), but it is thought that he turned up in the capital at the age of twenty-two having had to leave his home in Stratford-upon-Avon to avoid arrest on a charge of deer-poaching. It is generally agreed that during the years 1586–1591 he did a certain amount of hack-work for the management, and became an actor.

The custom then was for the manager of a players' company to buy a play outright—the prices were low, averaging from £6 to £10— and then have it doctored to his requirements by a team of hack-writers. It was probably marginally more profitable to alter other writers' plays than write originals, but the articulate, boozy, hard-living, often miserably poor poets—mostly 'university wits'—often collaborated and produced new pieces: Marlowe and Thomas Nashe wrote *Dido* together, Ben Jonson, George Chapman and John Marston all had a hand in *Eastward Ho!* (and all went to prison for it), Thomas Dekker, John Ford and Samuel Rowley wrote *Witch of Edmonton*; which made it difficult for scholars in later centuries to determine who added what to whose original play.

In 1592 the agreeable young actor had a play which he had written produced by Lord Strange's company of players. It was *King Henry the Sixth, Part One*, played at the new Rose Theatre (and noted in the manager Philip Henslowe's diary as *Harey the vj.*). *Part Two* and *Part Three* followed during the year; all were successful.

That a fellow hack should turn successful actor and then come out with a new play of his own was deeply offensive to an embittered colleague:

There is *an upstart crow beautified with our feathers*. That with *his tyger's heart wrapt in a player's hide*, supposes he is as well able to *bombast out a blank verse* as the best of you, and being *an absolute*

Johannes Factotum, is, in his own conceit, the only Shakescene in a country.

Robert Greene (1558–1592)
Groatsworth of Wit Bought with a Million of Repentance

bombast = to pad out.

His tyger's heart wrapt in a player's hide was a parody of a line in the third part of *King Henry the Sixth*, Act I, sc. iv: 'O, tyger's heart wrapt in a woman's hide!' This, in its turn, had been lifted by Shakespeare from *Wounds of Civill Warr*, a dull play written by a syndicate made up of Greene, Thomas Lodge and George Peele.

By the turn of the century Shakespeare had almost given up acting, at which he had only been 'moderate'. He was writing two plays a year which brought him much patronage, he was well off, a force in the theatre, and he was planning to live in the estate he had bought in Stratford.

Although he was respected by his fellow dramatists he does not seem to have been popular with them. In an age of elaborate, flowery compliment-making the only comments on record about Shakespeare are brief and moderate and he seems to have been unknown outside his own small theatrical circle:

In the long series of letters from John Chamberlain to Dudley Carleton, scattered over the whole period from 1598 to 1623—letters full of news of the month, news of the Court, the city, the pulpit, and the bookseller's shop, in which Court masques are described in minute detail, authors, actors, plot, performances, reception and all— we look in vain for the name of Shakespeare.

James Spedding (1808–1881)

Spedding was researching for his Life of Bacon.

It seems likely that Shakespeare 'practised frugality' even when he was well-off enough to live more gregariously; that when the 'poets' were livening things up in the tavern he would be the one who murmured the contemporary equivalent of 'I won't have another, thank you – rather a lot of work to do'.

The turn of the century was Shakespeare's most creative period and in his work, for instance in *Julius Caesar*, there is evidence of his concern about the absolute power wielded by the ageing Queen Elizabeth, which he respected for its potency and splendour yet disliked for its old-fashioned tyranny. Like most Englishmen of the time he was entirely patriotic and, like many, believed that despots were no longer good enough.

George Bernard Shaw thought that Shakespeare was politically naive:

It is impossible for even the most judicially minded critic to look without a revulsion of indignant contempt at this travestying of a great man [Julius Caesar] as a silly braggart, whilst the pitiful gang of mischief-makers who destroyed him are lauded as statesmen and patriots. There is not a single sentence uttered by Shakespear's Julius Caesar that is, I will not say worthy of him, but even worthy of an average Tammany boss. Brutus is nothing but a familiar type of English suburban preacher: politically he would hardly impress the Thames Conservancy Board.

George Bernard Shaw (1856–1950)
Saturday Review, 29 Jan. 1898

Shaw's personal feud with The Bard, which was good journalism if nothing else, did not extend to the production. He went on to say, 'Caesar's nose was good: Calpurnia's bust was worthy of her.'

By the year 1600, Paris had one theatre but London had six. The Elizabethan theatre was at its height; it has been estimated that one Londoner in eight went to the theatre once a week.

The Puritan's were appalled and the City of London made repeated efforts to get the Privy Council to close down the playhouses; even those outside the city limits:

1. They are a special cause of corrupting their youth containing nothing but unchaste matters, lascivious devices, shifts of cozenage, and other lewd and ungodly practices ...
2. They are the ordinary places for vagrant persons, masterless men, thieves, horse-stealers, whoremongers, cozeners, coney-catchers, contrivers of treason and other idle and dangerous persons to meet together ...
3. They maintain idleness in such persons as have no vocation, and draw apprentices and other servants from their ordinary works ...
4. In the time of sickness it is found by experience that many, having sores and yet not heart-sick, take occasion thereby to walk abroad and to recreate themselves by hearing a play. Whereby others are infected ...

Letter from the Lord Mayor and Aldermen to the Privy Council
28 July 1597

These moves were carefully blocked by the Privy Council according to the Queen's wishes. Carefully, because it was a delicate game of power; the Queen needed the City's resources behind her and could not afford to ride rough-shod over the Lord Mayor's requests and the Lord Mayor dared not let himself get into a position where he openly opposed the Queen's wishes. The Privy Council's invariable last resort was to point out to the Lord Mayor that the Queen liked her court plays and the players must have practice before appearing before her. The City never found an answer to that one.

So James Burbage, in 1597, bought part of an old convent at Blackfriars and built the Blackfriars Theatre, an enclosed theatre where his company – including Shakespeare – could play in the winter when the weather made productions in the huge, open wooden O's impossible. This was the first of the public indoor theatres, which were called – confusingly – private theatres.

For the first eight years the theatre was leased to one of the phenomena of the period—a company of child actors. The Elizabethan
audience's fascination with watching moppets in miniature costume
lisping their way through pastoral comedy and high tragedy was not
shared by all grown-ups:

> ROSENCRANTZ: There is, sir, an eyrie of children, little eyases, that cry
> out on the top of question and are most tyrannically clapped for't.
> These are now the fashion, and so berattle the common stages
> (so they call them) that many wearing rapiers are afraid of goose-
> quills and dare scarce come thither.
>
> William Shakespeare (1564–1616)
> *Hamlet:* Act II, sc. ii

The children's companies were made up mostly from choristers
attached to cathedrals and college churches. Likely performers were
spotted by scouts and compulsorily trained to perform in masques and
various court productions under an edict of the Queen (1585). It seems
that Henry Evans, who had the lease of the Blackfriars Theatre to
present the Children of the Queen's Revels, overdid his recruiting and
was reprimanded for moppet-running:

> Was censured by the Right Honrable Courte of Starr Chamber for
> his vnorderlie carriage and behauiour in takinge vp of gentlemens
> childeren against their wills and to ymploy them for playes.
>
> 43 Elizabeth, 1601

> Evans, and a certain James Robinson, kidnapped a boy, Henry Clifton,
> on his way to school and locked him up in the theatre, commanding him
> to learn a play by heart. But they had unwittingly nabbed a gentleman's
> son and the distraught father was able to obtain a warrant for the release
> of his only son and heir, and to lodge a complaint with the Star
> Chamber.

When the Queen was old a large group of men, including Shakespeare, could not wait for her to die—in 1600 a book of poems to celebrate her was published to which he was the only major poet not to
contribute—and she was regarded by them as a bigoted old harridan
of a dictator with no longer any real interest in the arts. They looked
forward eagerly to the reign of James I, when everything was going
to be better for them.

Queen Elizabeth died in 1603 and James, who at least thought himself to be cultured, came to the throne and drama prospered. Shakespeare wrote many of his greatest plays after 1603 and his company
did much better under James in terms of performances given and
money received than ever they did under Elizabeth. But it did not last
and suddenly the great age of English drama was over. It was astonish-
ingly short; all the plays of Marlowe, Shakespeare, Ben Jonson, Heywood, Webster, Massinger, and Beaumont and Fletcher were written
within a period of thirty-eight years.

An indication of Stuart taste in theatrical performance was the development by James of the court masque. Under Elizabeth the masques had been pretty tableaux put on as graceful compliments to the monarch. Under the Stuarts they became probably the most lavish, artificial, expensive charades ever devised.

Inigo Jones went off to Italy where that kind of court spectacle had been employing the talents of leading Renaissance architects and artists and returned with note-books stuffed with drawings of elaborate stage-machinery and scenic novelties.

The court's favourite masque writer was Ben Jonson. The poet watched glumly as Inigo Jones draped the acting area with glittering cloths, enclosed the players within a proscenium arch – an Italian innovation which made magical scene changes possible – built boats on wheels and castles and mansions which glided on and off, installed clouds on wires which rose and sank carrying a complement of posing ladies-in-waiting. Finally the poet burst angrily into print:

> O showes! Showes! mighty showes!
> The eloquence of Masques! What need of prose,
> Or verse or sense, t'express immortal you?
> You are the Spectacle of state!
>
> Ben Jonson (1572–1637)
> *Expostulation*

Jonson survived Shakespeare by twenty-one years. He saw the decline of the huge public theatres in favour of small private theatres. These charged much more for admission and were vastly more profitable to the management; it was said that a private theatre took a thousand pounds more in a year than two public playhouses. But the higher prices excluded the 'groundlings', the apprentices, workmen and clerks who were the backbone of the Elizabethan audience, and the theatres came to depend on the custom of lords and ladies of the court and merchants and their wives with social ambitions. The taste of the new audiences was for heavy and gory Tragedies of Revenge and comedies in which the old Elizabethan bawdiness was replaced by a kind of sly lasciviousness.

King James died in 1624 and the new King, Charles I, inherited a theatre against which Puritan opposition was mounting. James had changed the system of licensing players so that all licences were issued by the King. No doubt he needed the money, but in political terms it meant that all players were now the King's men and targets for anti-monarchic feeling. A touring company's licence did more than authorize the troupe to play in any town they visited, it gave them the right to demand that the town provide a suitable hall. Many strongly Puritan towns like Banbury, Exeter and Leicester paid off the actors rather than have their towns tainted.

195

In 1629 Jonson was getting on in years. He was suffering from the palsy and dropsy, and he was short of money. Charles had proved less benevolent than James and less inclined to pay the poet his pension on time. So Jonson wrote a new play, *The New Inn*. It was a disastrous failure on the first night, the audience leaving before the play was over. The ignominy of this treatment from an audience whose judgement he no longer respected caused the poet to publish an ode to himself:

> Come, leave the loathèd stage,
>   And the more loathsome age;
> Where pride and impudence, in faction knit,
>   Usurp the chair of wit!
> Indicting and arraigning every day
>   Something they call a play.
> Let their fastidious, vain
> Commission of the brain
> Run on and rage, sweat, censure, and condemn;
> They were not made for thee, less thou for them.

Ben Jonson (1573–1637)
Ode to Himself

A number of cavalier poets sprang to the defence of the 'loathsome age' and published poetic answers to Jonson. The most effective of these came from Owen Felltham, a literary chaplain so fervently Royalist that after the execution of Charles I he wrote of his late monarch as 'Christ the Second'. His piece began:

> 'Come leave this sawcy way
> Of baiting those that pay ...'

Jonson reaped some benefit from the to-do. The King made him a present of a hundred pounds and increased his pension from marks to pounds, adding an annual 'terce of canary' (terce=an old wine measure equivalent to a third of a pipe; about forty-two gallons). The pension and the wine made Jonson the first unofficial Poet Laureate. The first real Poet Laureate seems to have been Dryden.

The majority of people probably agreed with Jonson that the age was loathsome, or at any rate unsettled and worrying. The gap between the King and Parliament was widening and the population was nervy of any move which might indicate a royal leaning towards continental practices.

The temperature was not lowered by the appearance at the Blackfriars Theatre in 1629 of a company of French players. That was provocative enough, but the cast included women:

> I rejoice to saye they were hissed, hooted, and pippen-pelted from the stage, so as I do not thinke they will soone be ready to trie the same againe.

Thomas Brande
Letter, 8 Nov. 1629

pippen=apple.

The Puritan hatred of the drama, which the players could write off as the view of a semi-lunatic fringe when Shakespeare was a young actor, was now shared by the majority of sober-minded citizens, although the anti-theatre feeling was now on social and political, as well as religious, grounds. Attacks by pamphlet and from pulpit increased in ferocity, coming to a head in 1633 with the publication of an extraordinary book, *Histrio-Mastix, the Players Scourge*, by William Prynne.

Histrio-Mastix ran to over a thousand pages, adding little new in the way of arguments but amassing all previous attacks and bringing together everything ever written which could be construed as an unfavourable comment on plays and players. Many of the classical texts he quoted said nothing at all about plays or players, but Prynne felt that they helped his case so in they went. The margins of each page were so stuffed with references and quotations that Milton, in *Colasterion*, dubbed him 'marginal Prynne'. Altogether he quoted from the works of seventy-one of the Early Fathers, and he referred to fifty-five Synods: a bishop worked out that to read all the sources referred to would take a man over seventy years.

It was a work of blind zeal; perhaps the most intolerant and prejudiced piece of Puritan extremism in the language:

On actors:

Actors (the Divel's chiefest Factors) rake earth and hell itself ... for unparalleled villainies, that so they may pollute the Theatre ... the very filth and off-scouring, the very lewdest, basest, worst and most perniciously vicious of the sonnes of men.

On plays:

Idle, frothy, superfluous, unprofitable; as vaine, as empty, as vanity it selfe ... The beholding of one lascivious Stage-Play, though with prejudice, disaffection, and an absolute resolution against it, is able to corrupt and vitiate the very best spectators that resort unto it.

On the performance of the French actresses at Blackfriars:

An impudent, shamefull, unwomanish, graceless, if not more than whorish attempt.

On lady playgoers:

Because we now have many wanton females of all sorts resorting daily by troopes unto our Playes, our Play-houses, to see and to be seene, as they did in Ovid's age; I shall only desire them (if not their Parents and Husbands) to consider, that it hath evermore been the notorious badge of prostituted strumpets and the lewdest Harlots, to ramble abroad to Playes, to Play-houses; whither no honest or chast or sober Girles or Women, but only branded Whores and infamous Adulteresses did usually resort in ancient times: the Theater being then made a common Brothell: and that all ages, all places have constantly suspected the chastity, yea branded the honesty of

197

those females who have been so immodest as to resort to Iheaters, to Stage-playes, which either finde or make them Harlots.

William Prynne (1600–1669)
Histrio-Mastix, the Players Scourge

Prejudice was not always all on the one side. Although the book came out either the day before, or just after, the Queen Consort, Henrietta Maria, had acted in an amateur performance at court of Walter Montagu's *Shepherd's Paradise* and could hardly have been intended as an attack on her, the King's advisers decided to treat it as such and made a Star Chamber matter of it. Prynne was arrested and sentenced to be imprisoned for life, to lose his degree – he was a barrister – to be fined £5000, and to be deprived of his ears in the pillory, one ear at Charing Cross and the second at Westminster.

Cooped up in the Tower of London, he continued to write pamphlets attacking the Anglican Church, smuggling them out to be published. After three years, an anonymous pamphlet *News from Ipswich* was traced back to Prynne and he was up again in front of the Star Chamber and sentenced to another stretch of life imprisonment, another fine of £5000, branding with the letters S.L. – for seditious libeller – and, as fragments of ear were discernible beneath his hair, to have the last fragments sliced away. His books were to be burnt beneath his nose while he stood in the pillory. Prynne was – to put it mildly – a voluminous writer; his output exceeded two hundred fat volumes. A contemporary wrote that when the pile of books was set on fire Prynne was nearly asphyxiated.

On 2 September 1642, eleven days after King Charles raised his standard at Nottingham, the Long Parliament issued a solemn Ordinance of the Lords and Commons banning all stage-plays. This order, which closed the theatres for eighteen years, marked the end of the great Elizabethan and Jacobean era of public drama:

Whereas public sports do not well agree with public calamities, nor public stage-plays with the seasons of humiliation, this being an exercise of sad and pious solemnity, and the other being spectacles of pleasure, too commonly expressing lascivious mirth and levity: it is therefore thought fit and ordained by the Lords and Commons in this Parliament assembled, that while these sad causes and set-times of humiliation do continue, public stage-plays shall cease and be forborne.

Ordinance of Parliament, 2 Sept. 1642

Parliament also banned Christmas.

Once again, when theatre seemed to be almost dead it survived through reverting to the *mimi* style of performer and performance. A popular actor named 'the incomparable' Robert Cox invented a kind of theatrical hodge-podge of music, dancing, mime, and short comedy sketches, which he could present under the pretence that it was a demonstration of rope-dancing. The sketches were compounded from funny scenes from Shakespeare, Marston, Shirley and others, and were called Drolleries. He wrote a number of original sketches himself, and an essential part of these Drolleries was their *mimi*-like, and most un-

Puritan, bawdiness (there is a print showing Cox, in his *Simpleton the Smith*, doing imaginative things with a long French loaf. Cox's publisher, Kirkman, wrote, 'I have frequently known several of the female spectators ... to long for it').

Although the Drolleries were 'the delight of the city, the country, and the universities' they were not drama. And no significant theatrical event occurred until 1656, fourteen years after the theatres were closed, when the dramatist and poet laureate Sir William Davenant put on *The Siege of Rhodes* at Rutland House. This was a noteworthy production, not only because Sir William Davenant had managed to duck under the ropes by filling his play with music and calling it a 'Moral Representation', but because it was the first opera staged in England; it introduced wings and scenery painted in perspective; and it featured the first English actress – although she is usually discounted because she was an amateur, she only acted the once, and she had to read her part from a book. Her name was Mrs. Edward Coleman.

In 1660, after eighteen years, the ban on theatres was lifted. King Charles II arrived in London on 29 May, and on 21 August he issued licences for the raising of some companies of actors to play in London. But, Stuart-like, he only required two companies to provide for his pleasure in London. These two companies, under patents granted to Sir William Davenant and Thomas Killigrew, had the complete monopoly of playing legitimate drama in the capital – an awkward and unmanageable situation which lasted until 1843.

The term 'Restoration theatre' conjures up a picture of Good King Charles's Golden Days, Nell Gwynn gaily waving a basket of oranges and the good citizens of London crowding into the theatres to enjoy a play after the grim austerities of the Commonwealth. In fact Davenant and Killigrew had the greatest difficulty in filling their two theatres. The 'good citizens' had lost the habit of theatregoing and the days when nearly everybody from apprentice hatter to statesman looked upon drama as part of his life were gone for ever.

The new audiences were different, and they went to the theatre for different reasons:

Here lords come to laugh, and to be laughed at for being there and seeing their qualities ridiculed by every worthless poet. Knights come hither to learn the amorous smirk, the *alamode* grin, the antic bow, the new-fashioned cringe, and how to adjust their phiz to make themselves as ridiculous by art as they are by nature.

Hither come the country gentlemen to shew their shapes, and trouble the pit with irrelevancies about hawking, hunting, their handsome wives and their housewifery. There sits a beau like a fool in a frame, that dares not stir his head nor move his body for fear of incommoding his wig, ruffling his cravat, or putting his eyes or mouth out of the order his *maître de danse* set it in; whilst a bully beau

199

comes drunk into the pit, screaming out, 'Damn me, Jack, 'tis a confounded play, lets to a whore, and spend out time better.'

Here the ladies come to show their clothes, which are often the only things to be admired in or about 'em; some of them having scabbed or pimpled faces wear a thousand patches to hide them, and those that have none, scandalize their faces by a foolish imitation ...

That beau there is known by the decent management of his sword-knot and snuff-box; a poet, by his empty pockets; a citizen, by his horns and gold hat-band; a whore, by a vizor-mask and a multitude of ribbons about her breast; and a fool by talking to her.

Tom Brown (1663–1704)
Amusements, Serious and Comical

Pleasing a crowd of court hangers-on and bully-boys called for some new approaches in playwriting; not all of which were wholly admired:

I am come newly from my Lord of Orrery's new play called The Widow, whose character you will receive from better hands. I will only say that one part of it is the humour of a man that has great need to go to the close stool, where there are such indecent postures as would never be suffered upon any stage but ours, which has quite turn'd the stomach of so squeamish a man as I am, that am used to see nothing upon a theatre that might not appear in the ruelle of a fine lady.

Henry Savile (1642–1687)
Letter to Sir George Savile, 4 May 1665

ruelle=a morning reception of distinguished persons held by a lady of fashion in her bedroom.

It was an age in which audiences wanted to be entertained in the French manner, with artificial comedies of manners and grand dramas.

There was no place for reality. Particularly, it seems, in comic pieces:

Gall in *mirth* is an *ill mixture*: and sometimes *truth* is *bitterness*. I would wish any man to be *pleasingly merry*: but let him beware, he bring not *Truth* on the *Stage*, like a *wanton* with an edged *weapon*.

Owen Felltham (1602?–1668)
Resolves

The playwrights came up with two ways of meeting their customers' needs: heroic drama and licentious comedy. Heroic drama, in verse, full of jaw-cracking speeches and bombast, was perfected by John Dryden in plays like *The Conquest of Granada*, but died an unheroic death after being satirized by George Villiers, second Duke of Buckingham, in his play *The Rehearsal* (1671).

The comedies, mostly arabesques on the theme of sexual conquest, had a longer life. Mrs. Aphra Behn, addressed poetically as Astraea,

200

developed the Spanish-style 'comedy of intrigue' and turned out sex comedies successfully for seventeen years:

> The stage how loosely does Astraea tread
> Who fairly puts all characters to bed —
> Alexander Pope (1688–1744)
The Dunciad

Mrs. Behn summed up the difficulties which dramatists met with when trying to please their difficult customers with heroic drama and mannered comedy:

> Long, and at vast Expense, th'industrious Stage
> Has strove to please a dull ungrateful Age:
> With Heroes and with Gods we first began,
> And thunder'd to you in heroick Strain:
> Some dying Love-sick Queen each Night you injoy'd,
> And with Magnificence at last were cloy'd ...
> In humble Comedy we next appear.
> No Fop or Cuckold, but slap-dash we had him here;
> We show'd you all, but you malicious grown,
> Friends vices to expose, and hide your own,
> Cry, damn it — This is such, or such a one.
> Yet nettled, Plague, what does the Scribbler mean
> With his damn'd Characters and Plot obscene?
> Mrs. Aphra Behn (1640–1689)
Prologue to *The Emperor of the Moon*

Davenant and Killigrew, harassed by dwindling audiences, tried to win back the crowds with Italian-style scenery and dazzling stage effects. Both Davenant's theatre in Lincoln's Inn Fields and Killigrew's in Bridges Street, Drury Lane, had proscenium arches. They became the first theatres in England to mount spectacular productions:

> There's not a player but is turn'd a scout;
> And every scribbler sends his envoys out
> To fetch from Paris, Venis, or from Rome,
> Fantastic fopperies to please at home;
> And that each act may rise to your desire,
> Devils and witches must each scene inspire.
> Wit rolls in waves, and showers down in fire;
> With what strange care a play may now be writ,
> When the best half's compos'd by painting it,
> And in the air or dance lies all the wit.
> Prologue to *Tunbridge Wells*, 1678

The Restoration age found the plays of Shakespeare barbarous and totally lacking in the Neo-Classical virtues which they had learnt to admire from the French court:

201

So the managers and poets took scissors and pens and set about making Shakespeare more palatable:

Davenant produced a new concept of *Macbeth*, 'being drest in all it's Finery, as new Cloath's, new Scenes, Machines, as Flyings for the Witches; with all the Singing and Dancing in it – it being all Excellantly perform'd, being in the nature of an Opera'.

Thomas Betterton had a go at *A Midsummer Night's Dream* and came up with a fantastically elaborate production he called *The Fairy Queen*. This had a musical score and included a Grand Dance of twenty-four Chinese, a monkey ballet, and swans that were translated into fairies.

The memorably named dramatist Nahum Tate (his father's name was Faithful Teate) reworked *King Lear* so that everything ended happily, with Cordelia married to Edgar.

Thomas Shadwell rewrote *Timon of Athens* and proudly announced in the prologue, 'I can truly say I have made it into a play.'

Dryden's brother-in-law, the Hon. James Howard, sorted out *Romeo and Juliet* so that they lived happily ever after.

Etc. etc. ...

In the early days of the Restoration, England was the only country in Europe where women's parts were still played by men:

His Majesty being at a Representation of *Hamlet*, and thinking the Entry of the *Queen*, in that play, a little too tedious, one of the Actors most humbly acquainted the Audience that the QUEEN *was not quite shaved.*

Thomas Betterton (1635?–1710)
The History of the English Stage

The Queen was played on that evening by Edward Kynaston (1640?–1706), the last great male actor of female roles. He was so impressive as a woman that Ladies of Quality took him riding in their open coaches to show him off in his stage clothes.

In the year 1660, a few months after Charles was restored to the throne, English professional actresses began to take over female parts.

Who the first English professional actress was, if it was not Mrs. Coleman who spoke or sang her lines in Davenant's operatic *Siege of Rhodes* in 1656, has not been finally settled. Nominees include Anne Marshall, Margaret Hughes and Mrs. Norris. Whoever she was, she played Desdemona at Killigrew's temporary theatre in Gibbon's Tennis-Court, Clare Market, on 8 December 1660.

202

Six years later a diarist reported on the effect that actresses had had:

Very seldom at any time, going to the publique *Theatres*, for many reasons, now as they were abused, to an atheisticall liberty, fowle & undecent; Women now (& never 'til now) permitted to appeare & act, which inflaming severall young noble-men & gallants, became their whores, & to some their Wives, wittnesse the *Earle of Oxford*, Sir R: Howard, Pr: Rupert, the E: of Dorset, & another greater person than any of these.

John Evelyn (1620–1706)
Diary, 1666

The diarist's gossip was not very accurate. Sir Robert Howard's mistress, whom he later married, was not an actress. Prince Rupert's was; she was the early actress Margaret Hughes, and bore the Prince a daughter in 1673. The Earl of Dorset did not have an actress-mistress but his son did: Nell Gwynn. The King's actress-mistress at that time was Moll Davis.

Whoring, with a view to eventual marriage, was widespread and most actresses who added to the gaiety of the nation on-stage were, in the main, open to a reasonable offer for their attentions off-stage. Almost all professional actresses from Nell Gwynn downwards had rich protectors, and this was inevitable in the society of the time. No girl born into a respectable family, good-looking, possessed of some spirit and a modest fortune, would have considered becoming an actress. Nor would she have been much interested in becoming a rich man's mistress – as a career. But an attractive, spirited girl without the protection of either family or fortune was totally vulnerable. Her lot was either to become the wife of the bailiff, or the curate, or – if her spirit was too strong – to find herself a rich protector. And a career on the stage was the most effective way of meeting the richest and noblest predators.

But there were exceptions. One of the earliest actresses to devote all her energies to acting was the virtuous Mrs. Bracegirdle (1663?–1748), whose remains were deservedly interred in the east cloisters of Westminster Abbey. A contemporary, Antony Aston, described her in *Brief Supplement to Colley Cibber* as 'of a lovely height with dark brown hair and eyebrows... and whenever she exerted herself, had an involuntary flushing in her breast, neck, and face'. Despite a great number of attempts on her virtue, including a kidnapping which happily was frustrated, Mrs. Bracegirdle – perhaps buttressed by her name – remained, by most accounts, unsullied.

Lord Macaulay was unimpressed:

She seems to have been a cold, vain, and interested coquette, who perfectly understood how much the influence of her charms was increased by the fame of a severity which cost her nothing, and who

could flirt with a succession of admirers in the just confidence that
no flame which she might kindle in them would thaw her own ice.

Thomas Babington Macaulay (1800–1859)

History of England

Mrs. Bracegirdle's chief acting triumphs were achieved in Congreve's
plays and there were insinuations at the time that Congreve had managed
to thaw the ice on some discreet occasions. He left her £200 in his will.

As the seventeenth century drew to its close, theatre audiences continued to dwindle alarmingly:

But against this Evil, the provident Patentees had found out a Relief
∴ *viz.* Never to pay their People, when the Money did not come
in; nor then neither, but in such Proportions, as suited their Con-
veniency. I my self was one of the many, who for six acting Weeks
together, never received one Day's Pay; and for some Years after,
seldom had above half our nominal Sallaries.

Colley Cibber (1671–1757)

An Apology for the Life of Mr. Colley Cibber, Comedian

The two Patent companies tried amalgamating, but that made little
difference when they were committed to producing a reasonable
number of dramas and the only entertainment which would fill their
houses was rope-dancing and troupes of wild animals.

With virtually no provincial theatre as alternative employment, the
actors went through a lean period:

Peel'd, patch'd, and piebald, linsey-woolsey brothers,
Grave Mummers! sleeveless some and shirtless others.

Alexander Pope (1688–1744)

The Dunciad, Bk. III, l. 115

linsey-woolsey = a coarse, inferior woollen material.

Cardonnell 'Scum' Goodman, a leading actor, shared his shirt with a
colleague, Griffin. A sword fight broke out one evening when Goodman
had a rendezvous with a lady of the town and tried to take the shirt out
of turn. He tried to supplement his income by becoming a highwayman
but was caught immediately. He then became the lover of Charles II's
discarded mistress, the Duchess of Cleveland, by whom he had a son, but
that broke up when he was apprehended for trying to poison two of the
Duchess's sons, and fined. Eventually a syndicate paid him a pension to
live abroad, where to everybody's relief he died.

There was more trouble on the way for actors and patent-holders.
What is now called Restoration Comedy was, at its best, a brilliant
contribution to the repertoire of drama. It emerged as a true child of
the Restoration period, witty, gay, artificial and utterly amoral. The
trouble was that it took a long while to emerge and by the time it had
reached its heights the times had changed; there had been a bloodless
revolution and the era was now William and Mary; a different mood
was beginning to prevail and the nonconformist conscience was on the
march.

A growing dissatisfaction amongst soberer members of the community over the production of what they believed to be wicked, blasphemous, grossly immoral plays acted by degenerate people in dens of iniquity was brought to a head in 1698 with the publication of a swingeing attack by a nonconformist clergyman, Jeremy Collier. Collier's *A Short View of the Immorality and Profaneness of the English Stage*, which ran to over two hundred pages, made a great impact, resulting in a snowstorm of pamphlets defending and counter-attacking and countering the counter-attacks.

Collier quoted heavily from the works of the Christian Fathers, passing lightly over the fact that the Fathers were condemning the unspeakably awful happenings in the Roman theatre of their day, and he tended to weaken his case by inserting little home-made dramatic criticisms of his own. He dismissed The Bard briefly:

> As for *Shakespear*, he is too guilty to make an Evidence: But I think he gains not much by his Misbehaviour: He has commonly *Plautus's Fate*, where there is most Smut, there is least Sense.
>
> Jeremy Collier (1650–1726)
> *A Short View of the Immorality and Profaneness of the English Stage, &c.*

He was also something of a snob:

> I can't think it any *Excellence of good Manners* to expose the *Nobility* in their *Robes*, to put Contempt among their Titles.
>
> Ibid.

Many agreed with Collier's view of the low standard to which theatre had sunk but disagreed with him as to the cause. One writer blamed the debased taste of the audiences:

> What a wretched Pass is this wicked Age come to, when *Ben. Johnson* and *Sh'akespear* won't go down with 'em, without these Baubles to recommend 'em, and nothing but *Farces* and *Grimaces* will go down ... In short, Mr *Collier* may save himself the trouble of writing against the Theatres, for, if these lewd Practices are not laid aside, and Sense and Wit come in play again, a Man may easily foretell, without pretending to the Gift of Prophesie, that the Stage will be short-liv'd.
>
> Tom Brown (1633–1704)
> *Letter to Mr. Moult*

A thoughtful comment from one of the more boozy and bawdy Grub-Street hacks; himself a main target of the many societies for the reformation of manners then springing up.

John Dryden, by then old and frail, blamed the state of affairs firmly on the influence of Charles II's court:

> Perhaps the Parson stretched a Point too far,
> When, with our Theatres he wag'd a War.
> He tells you, that this very moral Age
> Receiv'd the first Infection from the Stage.

But sure, a banish'd Court, with Lewdness fraught,
The Seeds of open Vice returning brought.

John Dryden (1631–1700)
Prologue to *Pilgrim*

Whether Collier's *Short View* contributed to the hardening attitude towards moral laxity in the theatre or merely reflected it, the book marked the end of the free-wheeling theatre of the Elizabethans and Stuarts, where nothing was considered immoral except atheism and sedition, and the entry into theatre of middle-class morality.

Italian opera became the toy of fashionable society at the beginning of the eighteenth century, with the price of admission rising as high as a guinea. Antipathy towards this alien pleasure for the élite was one of the factors prompting John Gay to write *The Beggar's Opera*, an entirely British theatrical innovation in that it was not an opera at all but a play, a satire on the court political circle, with interpolated ballads sung to well-known airs.

Another British innovation was 'pantomime', a development of the old silent mime plays into lavish, colourful productions with music, dancing, singing, a strong plot and elaborate changes of scene.

Ten per cent of all plays put on were by Shakespeare. Most of them were cut and heavily adapted, a notable case being *The Taming of the Shrew* which was rendered into prose, changed about a bit and produced as *Sauny the Scot*. This in its turn was given a simpler plot, twenty-three songs, and presented as an opera, *A Cure for a Scold*. The plays were not only truncated, rewritten and altered, they were also stuffed. A custom grew of interpolating quite random musical items between the various acts:

> Macbeth: With all Songs, Dances and other Decorations proper to the Play; and several additional entertainments. viz.
> After the 1st Act, the Musette by Y. Rainton and Miss Robinson.
> After the 2nd, the 8th of Corelli's Concertos;
> After the 3rd, a Wooden Shoe Dance by Mr. Sandham's Children;
> After the 4th, a Dutch Skipper by Mr. Sandham;
> After the 5th, La Peirette by Mr. Roger the Peirror and Mrs. Brent.
>
> Advertisement in *Daily Post*, 5 May 1726

And that was not all. After the main play came one or more 'afterpieces'; light comedies or farces, with titles like *The Intriguing Chambermaid*, *The Lying Valet*, *The Virgin Unmasked*. After-pieces were an eighteenth-century innovation, and were probably introduced to attract the middle classes, who were still at their work when the theatre performances began at six o'clock. The managers made an arrangement whereby seats were half-price after the third act of the main play, thus encouraging the business men and lawyers to drop in to the theatre to see the last two acts of the drama plus another short, but complete, comedy.

Scenery was often elaborate, especially for spectacular productions of pantomime. It slid on-stage in a system of wooden grooves (a stage-direction would say: Let in the forest in the second grooves). A curtain was usually lowered between the acts, but between scenes the scenery was changed in full view of the audience. Actors in consecutive scenes stood about the stage during scene-changes to give a kind of continuity.

Principal actors took up a commanding position down-stage and addressed their lines to the audience. Lesser actors hovered about up-stage, listening hopefully for their cue and whiling away the time:

> On the *Stage*, not only the Supernumeraries, as they call them, or Attendants, seem regardless of the great Concern of the *Scene*, and, even the *Actors* themselves, who are on the *Stage*, and not in the very principal Parts, will be whispering to one another, or bowing to their Friends in the Pit, or gazing about.
>
> Thomas Betterton (1635?–1710)
> *The History of the English Stage*

> This publication of 1741, like many so-called autobiographies of actors was, not written by the actor but by a ghost-writer.

Actresses tried to cultivate a sing-song way of speaking, supposedly borrowed from the French classical stage. Actors, particularly in tragedy, tended to rant. This was another hangover from the French-inspired heroic tragedies of the Restoration whose stately alexandrine verse defied any kind of naturalistic delivery and required the actor to declaim loudly and ponderously. Perhaps the last great actor of the old school was James Quin (1693–1766), a majestic declaimer:

> Heavy and phlegmatic, he trod the stage,
> Too proud for tenderness, too dull for rage.
> Charles Churchill (1731–1764)
> *The Rosciad*

Theatrical costume for historical pieces was traditional, and quite meaningless: Quin invariably played James Thomson's *Coriolanus* in a hat with high plumes, a wig, a flared ballet skirt and a truncheon. Since Elizabethan times it had been customary for managements to dress their actors handsomely; the Elizabethan impresario Philip Henslowe recorded in his diary that he paid £6.13/– for Mrs. Frankford's gown in Thomas Heywood's *A Woman Killed With Kindness*, which is more than he paid Heywood for writing the play. Managements who fell down on their obligations were gently reminded of them:

King Duncan has not had a habit for the last century; Julius Caesar was as ragged as a colt, and his guards were a ragged regiment. Only the parts played by the managers were well dressed.

Newspaper review of a performance in 1723
quoted by H. Barton Baker: *History of the London Stage*

Perhaps due to a changing society as well as a changing theatre an increasing number of people with a little money to spare seemed prepared to spend it on going to see a play, and a number of new troupes of strolling players appeared, operating within a circuit of towns in the provinces. This led to the building of the first provincial theatres, at Bath in 1705, Bristol in 1729 and Ipswich in 1736.

The new plays offered were certainly no longer coarse and immoral but they were pretty feeble. Tragedies were written in the classical manner befitting the Augustan Age of Letters, full of literary allusions and windy oratory:

> Then crushed by rules and weaken'd as refin'd,
> For years the power of tragedy declin'd;
> From bard to bard the frigid caution crept,
> Till declamation roar'd while passion slept.

Samuel Johnson (1709–1784)
Prologue for opening of Garrick's management at Drury
Lane, 15 Sept. 1747

The comedy which replaced the genius of playwrights like Wycherley, Congreve and Vanbrugh was 'sentimental'; virtue eventually triumphing after a great deal of moralizing and sorting out of tedious misunderstandings. Mrs. Centlivre, Sir Richard Steele and Colley Cibber were prominent in establishing this pure but comparatively witless genre.

The only drama with any sort of edge to it was political satire. The growth of party-politics had given citizens as big a thirst for political gossip and scandal as they already had for social tittle-tattle. The Whig prime minister, Sir Robert Walpole, made a large and vulnerable target. At the opening night of Gay's *The Beggar's Opera* he was observed to smile bleakly through the sallies, but he caused the sequel, *Polly*, to be suppressed before production.

Then Henry Fielding, a young lawyer playwright with a strong distaste for the political chicanery and corruption which was then normal practice, took over the little Haymarket theatre, assembled a company of actors, and wrote a number of political satires:

> A broken wit collected a fourth company, who for some time acted
> Plays in the Hay-market ... He knew ... that as he was in haste
> to get money it would take up less time to be intrepidly allusive,
> than decently entertaining; that to draw the mob after him, he must
> rake the channel, and pelt his superiors; that to shew himself some-

body he must come up to Juvenal's advice, and stand the consequence ... upon this principle, he produced several frank and free
farces that seemed to knock all distinctions of mankind on the head.
Religion, laws, government, priests, judges, and ministers, were all
laid flat ...

Colley Cibber (1671–1757)
An Apology for the Life of Mr. Colley Cibber, Comedian

The first of these frank and free farces was *Pasquin*, which was almost
as big a success with the town as *The Beggar's Opera* and was even more
explicit in mocking and deriding Walpole. *The Historical Register* and
The Golden Rump went even further.

And so, in 1737, Walpole put through Parliament a Bill to put the
theatre under strict control. The Licensing Act of 1737 made provincial
strolling companies illegal (they took no notice) and imposed the first
real censorship on plays, requiring that all new plays had to be read
and licensed by the Lord Chamberlain. Previously a play was usually
only denied a licence if it contained seditious or anti-Christian matter.
The Lord Chamberlain was now given powers to suppress a play if
it contained anything at all of which he disapproved, such as ridicule
of the administration. This censorship could be effectively enforced,
so Fielding left the world of theatre and wrote *Tom Jones*.

And at the insistence of the theatre-hating city. M.P. who promoted
the Act, Sir John Barnard, the playing of legitimate drama was to be
strictly confined to the two Patent Theatres.

Ingenious and devious schemes were immediately put into effect by
'pirate' managements to squeeze through loopholes in the wording of
the Act.

A popular trick was to transform a drama's dialogue into vaguely
rhyming couplets, insert half a dozen songs and call the resulting pud
ding a 'burletta'. Burlettas – musical farces – were not classified as
drama and therefore could be played anywhere.

Henry Giffard, manager of the theatre in Goodman's Fields, blandly
advertised a concert of music to be given in two parts, with a free
dramatic sketch during the interval. The 'sketch' was a full production
of *The Winter's Tale*, revived for the first time for over a hundred
years.

On 19 October 1741, Giffard's 'Concert of Vocal and Orchestral
Music' had as its free middle bit *The Life and Death of King Richard III*.
And playing the lead was a young actor from Giffard's theatre in
Ipswich trying his luck in London: David Garrick.

Garrick was an immediate success. He was exactly what the mid-
eighteenth-century British theatre was most in need of: an actor who
could ease theatre out of its old habits, and a figure who could stand
as a central artistic authority. Garrick managed this. He also managed

to demonstrate that an actor-manager could make a tremendous amount of money; his wealth was second only to that of the Elizabethan actor Edward Alleyn, who left enough to found Dulwich College, but Alleyn did have a head start; he married the step-daughter of the very rich impresario Philip Henslowe and became his business partner.

One of Garrick's great achievements was to change the mannered and declamatory style of acting into something more realistic. Macklin, the Irish actor and a friend of Garrick's, had pioneered the natural method of speaking and moving, notably when he played Shylock – normally played as a comic character in a red scratch wig – but it needed Garrick's genius to make audiences accept an 'easy and familiar, yet forcible style in speaking' and 'concurring expressions of the features from the genuine workings of nature' instead of eye-rolling and bellowing. The old-style actor James Quin remarked glumly:

> If the young fellow is right, I and the rest of the players have been all wrong.
>
> James Quin (1693–1766)

Garrick was proved to be right. Henry Fielding described the difference between the two acting styles in a famous ironic passage:

> 'Indeed, Mr. Partridge,' says Mrs. Miller, 'you are not of the same Opinion with the Town, for they are all agreed, that Hamlet is acted by the best Player who was ever on the Stage.'
>
> 'He the best Player!' cries Partridge with a contemptuous Sneer, 'why I could act as well as he myself. I am sure if I had seen a Ghost, I should have looked in the very same Manner, and done just as he did ... the King for my Money; he speaks all his Words distinctly, half as loud again as the other. – Anybody may see he is an Actor.'
>
> Henry Fielding (1707–1754)
The History of Tom Jones, a Foundling, Book XV, Chap. 5

In 1747 Garrick became co-manager of Drury Lane theatre and began instituting a number of badly needed reforms. He reorganized rehearsals and required that actors turned up for them, rehearsed, and had some grasp of their lines. He paid some attention to improving the lighting of the theatre – it was customary to light the stage and the auditorium as though they were part of the same room – by concentrating more light on the stage by means of more carefully designed floats (long tanks of oil in which lines of wicks were floated), and banks of candles on ladders in the wings. He dressed his productions more richly but not, alas, more suitably; that had to wait until the nineteenth century.

Since the Restoration it had been the pleasure of gentlemen of quality to roam about back-stage. Dr. Johnson went behind the scenes a few times at the invitation of his friend Garrick, but discontinued the practice for personal reasons:

210

I'll come no more behind your scenes, David; for the silk stockings and white bosoms of your actresses excite my amorous propensities.

Samuel Johnson (1709–1784)
Boswell's Life

Garrick told this story to the philosopher Hume, who told it to Boswell. The story may have been watered down during its journey. The politician John Wilkes also heard the story from Garrick, but according to Wilkes what Johnson actually said was 'the silk stockings and white bosoms of your actresses do make my genitals to quiver'.

Garrick put a stop to the practice of selling tickets to allow gallants to visit the dressing-rooms and also to the extremely tedious tradition of permitting important people to sprawl and doze in seats on the stage. He also wrote a great many adaptations, prologues and odes:

I have blushed at Paris, when the papers came over crammed with ribaldry, or with Garrick's insufferable nonsense about Shakespeare. As that man's writings will be preserved by his name, who will believe that he was a tolerable actor? ... Garrick's prologues and epilogues are as bad as his Pindarics and pantomimes.

Horace Walpole (1717–1797)
Letter to George Montagu, Strawberry Hill, 16 Oct. 1769

Garrick had enjoyed a stormy love-affair with Peg Woffington when he was a young actor, but after his marriage his relations with his leading ladies were entirely professional, and acrimonious. Offstage Garrick was vain, socially ambitious – he 'dearly loved a lord' – thrifty, temperamental and altogether a little bit tiresome:

On the stage he was natural, simple, affecting.
'Twas only that when he was off he was acting.

Oliver Goldsmith (1728–1774)
Retaliations

Theatre continued to expand throughout the eighteenth century. There was a boom in theatre-building both in London (mostly 'summer theatres' where drama was legally permitted between seasons, and opera-houses) and in the provinces; by the end of the century there were over a hundred theatres scattered throughout Britain. With this went a population-explosion in the acting profession.

The humblest actors were the strolling players who went about the country fitting-up and playing in booths, haylofts and barns. It was a wretchedly poor existence:

The strolling tribe; a despicable race.

Charles Churchill (1731–1764)
Apology

Churchill's satires on the stage, The Rosciad and Apology, were hugely successful, making him much feared by actors, and making him enough money to pay his debts and buy himself 'a blue coat with metal buttons'. One line about the actor Tom Davies, 'He mouths a sentence as curs mouth a bone', so upset Davies that he left the stage and opened a

211

bookshop. Dr. Johnson remarked (*Life*, 20 March 1778), 'But what a man is he who is to be driven from the stage by a line? Another line would have driven him from his shop.'

The backbone of the profession was the provincial 'circuit' or 'stock' companies which played two or three nights in one theatre and then moved on to another. This was the training ground where actors and actresses learnt their craft and found out whether they were any good at it. The companies had enormous repertoires of up to a hundred plays and played a different play every night, each actor tending to specialize in one kind of part, e.g. Heavy Lead, or Juvenile Tragedian, or lower down the scale, Walking Villager, or Singing Chambermaid:

> JOHNSON: 'Players, Sir! I look upon them as no better than creatures set upon tables and joint-stools to make faces and produce laughter, like dancing dogs.'
>
> Samuel Johnson (1709–1784)
> Boswell's *Life*
>
> Johnson held firmly to the view that all acting, even Garrick's, was 'no better than mere mimickry'.

A 'circuit company' player with some sort of talent soon gravitated to London, as Garrick did, where he could become a 'star' performer, have his pay augmented with benefit performances and take to management. But few actors and actresses had that sort of talent. An odd assortment of people seem to have drifted into the acting profession and then either drifted out again or survived through good looks, personality, doggedness, or the ability to camouflage their lack of professional skills.

A dip into *The Thespian Dictionary*, a contemporary biography of eighteenth-century actors and actresses, gives an idea of the kind of talent which audiences were accustomed to putting up with:

> BROWN, (MR.): actor. His memory was frequently treacherous; but he had, on this occasion, a peculiar *laugh* which always put the audience into good-humour, and gave himself sufficient time for recollection. There have been and still are several performers of this name.
>
> BURTON, (MR.): actor. He joined Mr. Strickland's company at Market Street, Herts; where he appeared for the first time in the character of David (*Rivals*) ... we say appeared, for though extremely perfect in his parts, fright had prevented all utterance, and his brother performers, anticipating the meaning of his motions, were obliged to declare to the audience what they knew he *intended to say*.
>
> BRUNTON, (ELIZABETH): actress, made her first appearance in London for her sister's benefit, in Miss Hoyden (*Man of Quality*), at Covent Garden, about 1788. Her terrors for some time deprived her of utterance.

212

CRAWFORD, (MR.) : actor. This gentleman had a most unfortunate New-castle *burr* in his throat, but was totally unconscious of it himself ... He was encored in the — 'Approach me in the Russian Bear! &c.' which he took for applause.

FARREL, (CHARLES): actor. He excelled in Harlequin, and at the advanced age of seventy-five danced the highland broad dance; the sword wounding him in the thigh, from a false step perhaps, did not make him desist, and though the blood streamed on the stage, he persevered.

THORNTON, (HENRY): As an actor, he boasts of that merit which con-stitutes a good country performer, for he can bustle through a part with considerable ease, though unacquainted with the author's words.

Walter Donaldson, in *50 Years of Green Room Gossip*, recalled an instance of Thornton's ability to avoid total disaster:

'One night at Gosport, while representing Biron in the tragedy of *Isabella*, he died without giving the letter which unravels the plot; and as he lay prostrate in the last scene, one of the performers on the stage whispered to him, "Mr Thornton, the letter — the letter!" Thornton then rose up, took the letter out of his bosom, and said, "One thing I had forgot through a multiplicity of business. Give this letter to my father; it will explain all," and laid down again in the arms of death.'

COOKE, (GEORGE FRED.) : actor. This actor, during his theatrical career, has experienced both the frowns and smiles of fortune; he is con-sequently soon conquered by the Tuscan grape.

The Thespian Dictionary, or, Dramatic Biography, 2nd ed. 1805

Cooke, in fact, was a very fine actor, highly thought of by his colleagues. After his death Kean arranged for his grave to be shifted and during the move stole one of the corpse's toe-bones. He kept it as a relic of 'the greatest of actors' until Mrs. Kean got hold of it and threw it away. But Cooke was not merely prone to an occasional tussle with the Tuscan grape, he was one of the acting profession's most spectacular drunks. He died in the Mechanic Hall, New York, in 1811, and two years later a biography appeared. Lord Byron wrote in a letter: 'There is an American life of G. F. Cooke ... deceased, lately published. Such a book! — I believe since *Drunken Barnaby's Journal*, nothing like it has drenched the press ... Two things are rather marvellous: first that a man should live so long drunk, and next that he should have found a sober biographer.' Cooke willed his skull to an American friend, a Dr. Francis, who later gave it to a troupe of players for use in the graveyard scene in *Hamlet*. So it is quite possible that somewhere, in the U.S.A., George Frederick Cooke is still occasion-ally putting in an appearance.

Plays, like actors, increased in number rather than in quality during the century and perhaps they reflected the taste of their now enormous but relatively indiscriminate audience:

There is a total extinction of all taste: our authors are vulgar, gross, illiberal: the theatre swarms with wretched translations, and ballad operas, and we have nothing new but improving abuse.

Horace Walpole (1717–1797)
Letter to George Montagu, Strawberry Hill, 16 Oct. 1769

Comedy still continued to consist of perky farce and sentimental comedy, yet from this plateau of mediocrity arose two peaks: one was Oliver Goldsmith, whose *She Stoops to Conquer* and *The Good-Natured Man* were far removed from, and satires on, sentimental comedy; the other – a peak of Everest-like proportions – was Richard Brinsley Sheridan, arguably the best playwright England (and Ireland) had produced since Shakespeare, whose *The School for Scandal* is generally acknowledged to be the masterpiece of the English comedy of manners. In a hundred years of comedy: two geniuses, the rest nowhere.

Serious drama was almost uniformly awful; dull and stilted. One hugely successful tragedy was *Douglas*, by the Rev. John Home, a Scottish minister. It contained a long speech beginning 'My name is Norval', which was a show-piece for elocution students until late in the nineteenth century. At the play's opening night in Edinburgh, in 1756, the patriotic excitement was so intense that a voice cried out from the pit:

> Whaur's yer Wully Shakespeare noo?
>
> Anon. Scottish theatregoer

Shakespeare was there all right – the percentage of plays produced which were written by Shakespeare rose during the century from ten to twenty-five per cent – but they were not presented as written; they still underwent the cutting-down and cheering-up process. And King George III was hardly the man to lead his nation back to a true appreciation of her greatest dramatic genius:

> 'Was there ever,' cried he, 'such stuff as great part of Shakespeare? only one must not say so! But what think you – What? – Is there not sad stuff? What? – What?'
>
> Madame D'Arblay (Fanny Burney) (1752–1840)
> *Diary*, Windsor, 16 Dec. 1785

The state of English drama at the end of the eighteenth century was summed up by a German writer:

> English plays,
> Atrocious in content,
> Absurd in form,
> Objectionable in action,
> Execrable English theatre!
>
> Goethe (1749–1832)

At the turn of the century the English theatre was dominated by the awesome figures of the great tragedienne Sarah Siddons and her brother John Philip Kemble, children of Roger Kemble, a hairdresser turned strolling player. Mrs. Siddons, acknowledged to be the greatest player of tragedy (female) that England had ever produced, was a stately, goddess-like figure who managed, with her brother John Philip,

214

to make popular a grand-opera-without-words kind of acting which must have sent Garrick spinning in his grave.

John Philip Kemble, a failed-priest turned actor, had a somewhat formal style of playing:

> Kemble turned his head so slowly that people might have imagined he had a stiff neck, while his words followed so slowly that he might have been reckoning how many words he had got by heart.
>
> Leigh Hunt (1784–1859)
> *Dramatic Essays*, ed. William Archer
>
> Leigh Hunt was the first regular drama critic of any importance.

A friend wrote 'even in his most convivial hours he was solemn and funereal' and Sir Walter Scott said that 'natural bursts of passion are not his forte'. By all accounts he was hardly what is nowadays called a fun-person:

> Frogs in a marsh, flies in a bottle, wind in a crevice, a preacher in a field, the drone of a bagpipe, all yielded to the inimitable soporific monotony of Mr. Kemble.
>
> George Coleman (the younger) (1762–1836)
>
> Coleman's opinion of Kemble was no doubt coloured by the initial failure of Coleman's *The Iron Chest*; Kemble played the lead.

Kemble's successor was a totally different kind of actor. Edmund Kean was as romantic and unstable as Kemble had been classical and disciplined. Almost everything about him had a whiff of the bizarre. Not only is it not known who was his father, it is not really certain who his mother was. Whereas, a little surprisingly, Kemble had a bout or two with the 'Tuscan grape' Kean was almost as spectacular a drunk as George Frederick Cooke and was also an incautious amorist; a notorious affair with the wife of an Alderman Cox ended in a court action (for what was then called 'Criminal Conversation') and booing from the pit. Kean picked acting up where Garrick left off and pushed it into the nineteenth century, breaking away at last from the cold hand of classicism which had gripped drama for so long.

Not everybody approved:

> Well, I went to see Mr. Kean, and was thoroughly disgusted. This monarch of the stage is a little insignificant man, slightly deformed, strongly ungraceful, seldom pleasing the eye, still seldomer satisfying the ear—with a voice between grunting and croaking, a perpetual hoarseness which suffocates his words, and a vulgarity of manner which his admirers are pleased to call nature.
>
> Mary Russell Mitford (1787–1855)
> *Letters*, 5 July 1814

The booing of Kean because of his indiscretions with the Alderman's wife was far from being an isolated instance of this kind of audience participation. This 'many-headed monster of the pit', as Alexander

215

Pope called the audience, was traditionally rowdy and vociferous. Managers were expected to fawn and cringe to patrons at all times and when the management did something to displease them they had no hesitation in rioting and breaking up the theatre. When Covent Garden theatre burnt down in 1808, almost ruining Kemble and his sister, it was rebuilt and higher prices were charged. The audiences rioted for two months, chanting 'O.P! O.P!' (Old Prices) throughout the attempted performances until Kemble was forced to apologize humbly and submit.

It was in such an audience that Charles Lamb sat on 10 December 1805, to watch the opening night of his farce *Mr. H.* The following day he reported to a friend how his play had been received:

> Damn 'em, how they hissed! It was not a hiss neither, but a sort of frantic yell, like a congregation of mad geese, with roaring something like bears, mows and mops like apes, sometimes snakes, that hiss'd me into madness. 'Twas like St. Anthony's temptations. Mercy on us, that God should give his favourite children, men, mouths to speak with, to discourse rationally, to promise smoothly, to flatter agreeably, to encourage warmly, to counsel wisely: to sing with, to drink with, and to kiss with: and that they should turn them into mouths of adders, bears, wolves, hyenas, and whistle like tempests, and emit breath through them like distillations of aspic poison, to asperse and vilify the innocent labours of their fellow-creatures who are desirous to please them! God be pleased to make the breath stink and the teeth rot out of them all therefore!
>
> Charles Lamb (1775–1834)
> Letter to Thomas Manning, 11 Oct. 1805
>
> Lamb later confessed that he had joined in and hissed and booed as loudly as any of them because he was desperately afraid of being taken for the author.

It was not the sort of audience to attract the work of distinguished men of letters:

> I do not think the character of the audience in London is such that one could have the least pleasure in pleasing them. One half come to prosecute their debaucheries, so openly that it would disgrace a bagnio; another set to snooze off their beef-steaks and port wine; a third are critics of the fourth column of the newspaper; fashion, wit, or literature there is not.
>
> Sir Walter Scott (1771–1832)
> Letter to a friend, 1819
>
> Scott's friend had asked him whether he had considered writing a play.

Lord Byron wrote several verse plays which were produced but not enjoyed and Shakespeare was continually produced, in eye-stunning productions which went in heavily for live horses, fire, enormous casts and spectacular scenery, but the staple drama of the time—in fact for most of the nineteenth century – was melodrama, a French form instituted by Pixiécourt. Melodrama consisted of violent action, treacly sentiment and a quick happy ending, all bound together with mood-setting incidental music and snatches of song and dance. It was just the kind of romantic, thrilling, intellectually inert pabulum which the public wanted for its entertainment, and various forms were played in every kind of theatre from Drury Lane to the 'penny gaffs' (the poorest possible type of fit-up theatre. Also known as 'blood-tubs'). The titles of some of the melodramas convey their flavour:

The Bleeding Nun of Lindenberg.
The Dog of Montargis (with a sword fight to music and a dog hero).
Footpad Joe, the Terror of Charing Cross.
The Spectre Bride and the Demon Nun (nuns were popular).
The Blood-Red Knight (real horses).
The Burning of Moscow (real flames).

There was now a mounting agitation to persuade the government to do something to stimulate a flagging theatre, a movement led by the finest actor of the time, William Charles Macready. Macready was the first 'gentleman' actor – he only went on the stage because his father had been put into a debtor's prison – and he detested acting and actors. The only other major figure in the theatre with the same attitude towards the job was John Philip Kemble's niece, Fanny Kemble, who became an actress to save her father from bankruptcy. A youngish poet did not enjoy seeing them act together:

> The squalor of the place, the faint earthy orange smell, the dimness of the light, the ghostly ineffectualness of the sub-actors, the self-consciousness of Fanny Kemble, the harshness of Macready, the unconquerable difficulty of the play, altogether gave me sensations of wretchedness during the performance of Othello the other night.
>
> Matthew Arnold (1822–1888)
> Letter to Arthur Hugh Clough, 6 Mar. 1848

Fanny Kemble did not enjoy acting with Macready in that production of *Othello*. In a letter to her friend, Harriet St. Leger, she wrote:

> He growls and prowls, and roams and foams, about the stage, in every direction, like a tiger in his cage, so that I never know on what side of me he means to be; and keeps up a perpetual snarling and grumbling like the aforesaid tiger, so that I never feel quite sure that he *has done*, and that it is my turn to speak ... my only feeling about my acting it with Mr Macready is dread of his personal violence. I quail at the idea of his laying hold of me in those terrible passionate scenes; for in *Macbeth* he pinched me black and blue, and almost tore the point lace from my head. I am sure my little finger will be re-broken.
>
> Fanny Kemble (1809–1893)
> Letter, 23 Feb. 1848, published in *Records of Later Life*

217

Violence was never far away from Macready. He was quarrelsome and had a vicious temper. He once rushed in on his manager, the untrustworthy Bunn, and attacked him. Bunn managed to bite Macready's little finger and obtain damages for £150. Later, during an American tour, Macready quarrelled so bitterly with the American actor Edwin Forrest that partisan supporters came to blows and twenty-two people died.

Perhaps because of his scorn for the 'glitter-and-tinsel' aspect of his profession Macready brought a cool, intellectual approach to acting; he began to rescue Shakespeare from the manglings which the plays had been subjected to since Restoration times, he put less emphasis on scenery and effects and more on the text of the play and he did much to put a little discipline into play production by instituting measures like full rehearsals for the entire cast, including the crowd-players. At that time the leading actor didn't usually bother much how the smaller players played their parts, as a young actor/stage-manager discovered when he received a letter from the great Edmund Kean:

St John's Wood, Nov. 8, 1829

Sir — I shall not require rehearsals for my plays; but be particular in your selection of Wilford. He is all-important to me. I will run through the library scene with him when I come down. He must be young, mind.

Yours obediently,
E. Kean.

When Kean arrived, he sent for me to his dressing-room. 'You are rather tall, sir.'
Rejoinder: 'Yes, sir, what do you wish me to do?'
Kean: 'Why, in the Library scene, sink gradually on your right knee, with your back to the audience. When I place my hand on your head to curse, mind you keep your eyes fixed on mine.'
(No very easy task to look steadily into such eyes.)
'Is that all, sir?'
Kean: 'Yes — do whatever you like after that; it will be all the same to me.'

Edward Stirling (1807–1894)
Old Drury Lane

Macready had a genuine desire to reform the general sloppiness of traditional production practices. His influence helped to promote a new government measure to help the state of the profession, the Act for Regulating Theatres, 1843. Although this gave the Lord Chamberlain even tighter powers of censorship it also controlled the structure and safety regulations of theatres, in an attempt to disturb the inevitability with which theatres burnt to the ground, and it broke at last the two monopolies granted by Charles II, thus freeing Shakespeare to any management who wanted to produce him. Many did and rapidly went bankrupt.

By the middle of the nineteenth century two influences were being felt which were going to dominate drama by the end of the century. The first of these was the 'well-made play', originated in France by Eugène Scribe. Plots had always been considered unimportant until then. Playwrights freely stole and borrowed them from each other and they were used rather like an old piece of string upon which to thread the big scenes. Scribe showed that there was much more that a plot could do than that; that a skilfully wrought plot, with its twists and turns and surprises, could produce theatrical effects just as satisfying to an audience as displays of passion and gore.

The other influence, perhaps a reaction to both the colourful fantasies of romantic melodrama and the unworldliness of classical tragedy, was a move towards making drama more relevant to real life.

A beginning was made with scenery when, in 1836, box-sets consisting of three apparently solid walls and a ceiling-cloth began to be used for interiors instead of a painted back-cloth and wings.

Charles Kemble became the first man to try to get some sort of historical reality into the scenery and costumes of Shakespearian productions – thus, perhaps, putting himself into the financial trouble that forced his daughter Fanny to become an actress.

This theatrical antiquarianism was carried to the extreme by Edmund Kean's son Charles in a series of massive productions at the Princess's theatre from 1851 to 1859. Charles Kean's productions of Shakespeare were rather like Cecil B. de Mille's films about the Bible; the settings, costumes and spectacle were the point of the operation: what met the ear was less impressive:

> In such a melodrama as 'The Corsican Brothers' he [Charles Kean] was very effective; but nothing would be more exasperating now than to sit through his performance of a part like Richard, and hear his wooden intonation in this fashion —
>
> 'Dow is the widter of our discodtedt
> Bade glorious subber by the sud of York.'
> David Masson (1822–1907)
> *Memories of London*

Kean's mighty, pedestrian productions of Shakespeare – he filled the stage with extras at every opportunity the text offered; the crowds were split into little groups, each controlled by a kind of shop-steward – were interspersed with productions in a similar vein of the more staid romantic melodramas. The success of Kean's idea of drama, which was called 'gentlemanly' medodrama, was an indication of the changing taste of theatregoers. The Victorian middle-class preoccupation with what was 'respectable' and what was not meant that the crude, vulgar old Blood-Tub melodrama moved away from the West End of London to south of the river – hence the jocular phrase 'transpontine drama' used to describe it – to be replaced by a more genteel form of theatre.

The audience at Charles Lamb's first night might have been frightening, but at least they cared enough about what was happening on the stage to express their disapproval. The Victorian audience did not, it seems, care enough even to show approval. An author wrote in 1859:

> Audiences now-a-days are more numerous than ever; but they sit, for the most part, in silent admiration ... The stalls, boxes, and even the pit, are too genteel to clap their hands.

Quoted by Allardyce Nicoll:
British Drama, Vol. V

Theatre auditoriums had kept pace with the increasingly middle-class tone of production. About 1817 gas lighting was introduced, which was easier on the audience's eyes and slightly reduced the size of the grimace an actor needed to make for it to be seen. In 1820 the rows of benches in the pit were moved to the back and the area was furnished more comfortably, the price raised, and the seats called Orchestra Stalls. In 1822, the first Dress Circle was introduced. All that was needed to make the theatre a fit place for a genteel Victorian theatre-goer was a carpet and an antimacassar; these came in 1865.

In that year a leading actress, Mary Wilton, took over the Queen's, a dilapidated old Blood-Tub of a theatre off Tottenham Court Road, known in the trade as the Dust Hole (it later became the Scala, noted for its annual flight of *Peter Pan*). She redecorated it, installed a carpet, and gave it an elegant décor. 'The stalls', she wrote later, 'were pale blue, with lace antimacassars over them; the first time such things had ever been seen in a theatre.'

Miss Wilton and Squire Bancroft, later to become her husband, gave the theatre more than drawing-room home comforts; they produced the plays of T. W. Robertson, an epoch-making run of plays, like *Society*, *Ours*, *Caste*, which, artificial and fundamentally trivial though they were, were the nearest any playwright had ever got to representing ordinary people in ordinary domestic circumstances. This effort to reach a new sort of reality was named 'cup-and-saucer drama' (a similar effort in the 1950s was called 'kitchen-sink drama').

But significant trends do not necessarily make for good theatre and by the 1870s drama in England was little healthier than it had been at the beginning of the century. The West End audiences, now too sophisticated for 'transpontine drama', were quite satisfied with a diet of revivals of old favourites, thin comedies mostly stolen from French playwrights and occasional attempts at realism; bad plays acted by very good actors.

In 1873 Matthew Arnold was moved to cry:

We have no drama at all.
Matthew Arnold (1822–1888)

A later man-of-the-theatre described the period as:

Slovenly chaos.
Harley Granville Barker (1877–1946)
The Eighteen-Seventies

The logical development in a situation where the sole attraction in the theatre was the leading actor's performance was for the leading actor to take over the whole production. So began the era of the grand actor-managers.

The actor-manager's power was absolute in his domain. He leased, and frequently owned, his theatre, hired and fired his cast, was in complete financial control of every aspect of the production, chose the plays, was his own producer, took the star role, chopped the play about and generally ensured that his own performance dominated everything:

ACTOR-MANAGER: One to whom the part is greater than the whole.
Ronald Jeans (b. 1887)

One of the greatest of these splendid figures was Henry Irving, the first actor to be knighted. He gave much thought to modernizing the mechanics of production; he controlled stage-lighting more effectively and used lighting for dramatic effect on stage. He adopted the idea put forward by the Italian Renaissance architects and pioneered by Wagner of darkening the auditorium during performances. And, for the first time, he had a curtain lowered between scenes so that audiences were no longer distracted by scene-changes.

Other technical improvements were gradually taking place. The Duke of Saxe-Meiningen, a rich and princely Duke with an English actress wife and a passion for the theatre, had been interested in the way Charles Kean had organized his crowd-scenes and how the English box-sets had made scenery three-dimensional. Back home in his court theatre he introduced a number of innovations which had an influence throughout Europe, notably more realistic settings and 'ensemble-playing'. This last was a startling breakthrough. Up until then the leading actors tended to declaim their lines straight at the audience while the supporting characters kept in the background, preferably, as we know from Edmund Kean, with their backs to the audience. In 'ensemble-playing' – which is now normal modern practice – actors had to learn to ignore the audience and talk to whoever the play required them to be talking to. And the other actors had to pretend to be listening. This was a big step forward for realism in drama, leading to theatres tearing out the old system of wooden grooves and building their sets as solid boxes, dressed with real furniture and practical props.

The Duke also persuaded his leading performers to accept small supporting parts in occasional productions, a triumph of art over ego which only a very rich Duke could have accomplished.

Comedy, which by its nature always needed to be more realistic than tragedy, was given a boost and the last quarter of the century saw a boom in light 'boulevard' comedy on the London stage; well-dressed, charming, upper-class plays summed up by Bernard Shaw as:

> A tailor's advertisement making sentimental remarks to a milliner's advertisement in the middle of an upholsterer's and decorator's advertisement.
>
> George Bernard Shaw (1856–1950)

But, as had happened over a hundred years previously, from the mediocrity rose a comedy writer of genius, Oscar Wilde.

A literary man found Wilde's *A Woman of No Importance* a little baffling:

> It was rather amusing as it was a complete mass of epigrams, with occasional whiffs of grotesque melodrama and drivelling sentiment. The queerest mixture! Mr. Tree is a wicked Lord, staying in a country house, who has made up his mind to bugger one of the other guests — a handsome young man of twenty. The handsome young man is delighted; when his mother enters, sees his Lordship and recognises him as having copulated with her twenty years before, the result of which was — the handsome young man ... It seems an odd plot, doesn't it?
>
> Lytton Strachey (1880–1932)
> Letter to Duncan Grant, 2 June 1907

Realism in serious drama was taken to an extreme on the Continent by Emile Zola's 'slice of life' naturalism in adaptations of such novels as *Thérèse Raquin* and *L'Assommoir*, and developed by Strindberg and Henrik Ibsen into a new drama concerned with exploration of human nature and the realities of society.

Misgivings were expressed:

> The modern theatre is a skin disease, a sinful disease of the cities. It must be swept away with a broom; it is unwholesome to love it.
>
> Anton Chekhov (1860–1904)
> Letter to I. L. Scheglov, Moscow, 7 Nov. 1888

The 'play of ideas' took a long time to get off the ground in London. Henry Arthur Jones and Pinero made a start by venturing into what was then thought of as 'unpleasant areas' and writing plays which touched upon social problems. Although these were written more with the object of producing effective theatre than stimulating reforms, Jones and Pinero, with T. W. Robertson, were the first stirrings of a dramatic revival in England.

George Bernard Shaw, among others, tried hard to persuade theatre managers to produce Ibsen, but without success, which is understandable; the managers conducted their business according to the maxim formulated by Dr. Johnson in his *Prologue at the Opening of Drury Lane* —

222

'The drama's laws, the drama's patrons give, for we that live to please, must please to live':

> What can be hoped of an art which must necessarily depend on the favour of the public – of such a public, at least, as ours? Good work may, does sometimes, succeed. But never with the degree of success that befalls twaddle and vulgarity unrelieved. Twaddle and vulgarity will always have the upper hand.
>
> Max Beerbohm (1872–1956)
> *Saturday Review*, 5 Sept. 1908

The theatre managers knew their audiences. The boiled-shirt and sables set were happy enough with society – God was in His Heaven, the Queen was on the throne, cook was in the kitchen and trade was booming – and the cloth-cap and bonnet contingent went to the theatre for a bit of excitement and a bit of a giggle. Neither were keen on paying money to be told that society was a mess of lies, self-righteousness and bent ethics:

> There is no sadder spectacle of artistic debauchery than a London theatre; the overfed inhabitants of ... the stalls hoping for gross excitement to assist them through their hesitating digestions; an ignorant mob in the pit and gallery forgetting the miseries of life in imbecile stories.
>
> George Moore (1852–1933)
> *Mummer-Worship*

There was little hope of winning over the actor-managers to the 'play of ideas'. Beerbohm Tree, romantic, inventive and charming, produced *An Enemy of the People*, with what the translator William Archer called 'a monstrously mutilated text' but was more interested in presenting a series of sumptuous, 'coffee-table' productions of Shakespeare. The splendours included a great ship tossing on waves in *The Tempest*; a thatched cottage among trees, a working waterfall and a gently flowing stream in *The Winter's Tale*; an enormous set-piece showing the signing of Magna Carta in *King John*; and real bunny-rabbits nibbling real grass in *A Midsummer Night's Dream*. Some of the sets were so complicated that there was a wait of forty-five minutes between scenes.

Tree also played *Hamlet*, a performance which another man of the theatre pronounced:

> Funny without being vulgar.
> W. S. Gilbert (1836–1911)

The great Henry Irving was totally uninterested in the work of contemporary dramatists; his mannered, hypnotic style of acting, his odd walk – Oscar Wilde said 'His left leg is a poem' – and his rather thin voice which had a faint, built-in bleat, made him most effective in the moodier Shakespearian roles and in melodrama. In his expensively staged productions his practice was to pare subsidiary roles down to the bone so that his own leading role stood out strongly. This editing also gave him time for the lengthy pauses and impressive movements of which he made a feature. He cut two thousand lines out of *Cymbeline*.

This was the production which infuriated George Bernard Shaw. Shaw bitterly resented the way managers were refusing to acknowledge that the 'play of ideas' had a future and was important and continued to clutter up the theatres with vast and, as far as contemporary social problems were concerned, irrelevant revivals:

> Cymbeline is for the most part stagey trash of the lowest melo-dramatic order, in parts abominably written, throughout intellectually vulgar, and judged in point of thought by modern intellectual standards, vulgar, foolish, offensive, indecent, and exasperating beyond all tolerance. There are moments when one asks despairingly why our stage should ever have been cursed with this immortal 'pilferer' of other men's stories and ideas, with his monstrous rhetorical fustian, his unbearable platitudes, his pretentious reduction of the subtlest problems of life to commonplaces against which a Polytechnic debating club would revolt, his incredible unsuggestiveness, his sententious combination of ready reflection with complete intellectual sterility, and his consequent incapacity for getting out of the depth of even the most ignorant audience, except when he solemnly says something so transcendently platitudinous that his more humble-minded hearers cannot bring themselves to believe that so great a man really meant to talk like their grandmothers. With the single exception of Homer, there is no eminent writer, not even Sir Walter Scott, whom I can despise so entirely as I despise Shakespeare when I measure my mind against his. George Bernard Shaw (1856–1950)
> *Saturday Review*, 1896

But Ibsen arrived. Mainly played in little experimental theatres, and in dubious translations, the plays made an extraordinary impact. Besides upsetting the theories of drama which the critics had evolved for themselves, the plays touched nerve-ends in the audience's conscience, and great cries of rage rang out in the review columns and correspondence pages of the press.

It is unlikely that any playwright's work has ever met with quite such red-necked, foam-flecked abuse as did Ibsen's:

A Doll's House. The Novelty theatre. 7 June 1889.

> Unnatural, immoral ... *People*
> Morbid and unwholesome ... *Observer*

Rosmersholm. The Vaudeville theatre. 23 Feb. 1891.

> These Ibsen creatures are 'neither men nor women, they are ghouls'
> ... *Gentlewoman*

Ghosts. The Royalty theatre. March 1891.

> An open drain; a loathsome sore unbandaged ... *Daily Telegraph*
> Garbage and offal ... *Truth*
> Repulsive and degrading ... *Queen*
> Foul and filthy ... *Era*

Hedda Gabler. The Vaudeville theatre. 20 April 1891.

> A bad escape of moral sewer-gas ... *Pictorial World*
> Photographic studies of vice and morbidity ... *Saturday Review*

The Master Builder. The Trafalgar Square theatre. 20 Feb. 1893.

> Hopeless and indefensible ... *Globe*
> Three acts of gibberish ... *Stage*
> Sensuality ... irreverence ... simply blasphemous ... *Morning Post*
>
> Quoted by Michael Meyer (b. 1921)
Henrik Ibsen: Vol. 3, 'The Top of a Cold Mountain'
>
> A brief, edited selection from pages of vituperation.

In the late 1890s George Bernard Shaw stopped being a propagandist for Ibsen and became a playwright himself. In his first plays he deliberately jumped in at the deep end and wrote about social evils like prostitution, slum landlordism and religion – the unpleasantest of the genteel playgoer's 'unpleasant' areas – in order to shake people into thinking while they were in the theatre instead of just sitting back gawping.

Mrs. Warren's Profession, written in 1893, was not publicly performed in England until the 1920s because of a suspicion in the Lord Chamberlain's department that it was about incest, but it was produced in New York in 1905 where it enjoyed a reception of Ibsen-like ferocity:

> Superabundance of foulness ... wholly immoral and degenerate ...
> *New York Herald*
> Offensive ... contemptible ... abominable ... *New York Post*
> Decaying and reeking ... *New York Times*
> A dramatized stench ... *New York Sun*
>
> Anthony Comstock, the American professional reformer and secretary of the Society for the Suppression of Vice, denounced Shaw as an 'Irish smut-dealer' and after the first performance arranged for the arrest of everybody, from the owner of the theatre to the entire cast.

Literary men, like the young lyric poet Alfred Noyes who wanted to preserve the high moral tone of Victorian writings, found Shaw appalling:

> Intellectually he is beneath contempt ... Are we not a little tired of this blatant self-puffery? ... The vulgarity ... that indecent familiarity with himself, the self-complacent vanity ... It would be an unkindness to cut his capers short too soon, if they amuse him. But it is our duty to the great and famous dead ... to say that Mr. Shaw's capers are vulgar, fatuous and extremely wearisome.
>
> Alfred Noyes (1880–1958)

It seemed to many that the walls of respectability were being breached by these disturbing plays. The potential damage which the new drama could wreak upon impressionable minds was discussed in 1909 by a Select Committee set up to enquire into the effectiveness of the censorship system. Doubts were expressed as to whether the new drama could be called art. In an extraordinary session of questioning, A. B. Walkley, the distinguished drama critic of *The Times*, expressed doubts as to whether any drama was worth bothering about to any extent; or, indeed, any form of art:

MR. WALKLEY: I venture to think that the importance of all art, and more especially the importance of the drama, is apt to be somewhat overrated nowadays ...

MR. HARCOURT: I understand in general terms that you think that the importance of the drama is very greatly exaggerated; then you go on to say that the importance of all art in this country is very greatly exaggerated?

MR. WALKLEY: Yes.

MR. HARCOURT: Do you really think that is the case – that the British nation are an excessively artistic nation?

MR. WALKLEY: Indeed I do not, but I think there is a great deal of exaggerated talk about it, inflated talk, a great deal of cant about art, and more now than ever before; and partly that cant, that exaggerated way of talking about it, and partly the author's own natural prepossessions in favour of art, have created a false standard and a false state of opinion.

MR. HARCOURT: Do you feel any sense of humiliation in concerning yourself as a critic with this unimportant art?

MR. WALKLEY: No; one must live.

Proceedings of the Joint Select Committee

Mr. Walkley was not entirely dependent upon the unimportant art of drama for his daily crust; during the daytime he was a senior civil servant in the General Post Office. The Select Committee, under the chairmanship of the Rt. Hon. Sir Herbert Samuel, called upon many illustrious authors and playwrights to give their views about censorship and some splendid performances resulted. Chesterton thought that he could trust himself to the judgement of a number of men, e.g. a jury but not to one man. Shaw used shock tactics and described himself as 'an immoral author', to the delight of the newspapers.

Shaw continued his policy of cheerfully telling the truth as he saw it, however unpalatable it was to the complacent and the unthoughtful. Soon after the First World War broke out he gave his view on how it should be brought to a finish. In *Common Sense About the War*, published as a supplement to the *New Statesman*, which he helped to found, he proposed that the soldiers on both sides shoot their officers and go home. This provoked H. G. Wells to call Shaw:

An idiot child screaming in a hospital.

H. G. Wells (1866–1946)
Daily Chronicle, Dec. 1914

Wells worked for a time preparing anti-German propaganda. He had hopes that the war would eventually be a good thing for the world.

When the war was over Shaw travelled a good deal. He visited the Soviet Union and spoke highly of the good things that were happening over there, to the fury of those Englishmen to whom the word 'communist' meant a bearded foreigner in a black hat carrying a round bomb:

> George Bernard Shaw, most poisonous of all the poisonous haters of England; despiser, distorter and denier of the plain truths whereby men live; topsyturvey perverter of all human relationships; menace to ordered social thought and ordered social life; irresponsible braggart, blaring self-trumpeter; idol of opaque intellectuals and thwarted females; calculus of contrariwise; flippertygibbet pope of chaos; portent and epitome of this generation's moral and spiritual disorder.
>
> Henry Arthur Jones (1851–1929)
> *My Dear Wells*, Letter XIX

> Jones, a prolific dramatist – over 150 plays produced – was an excellent craftsman who had done much to raise the level of actor-manager drama. In early life he had dabbled lightly in socialism but he rebounded to the other extreme when it seemed to him that socialism might result in rich dramatists becoming less rich. He then devoted himself to writing terrific diatribes against H. G. Wells, Shaw and other exponents of Advanced Ideas. In *My Dear Wells* (1921) occurred what was then believed to be the longest sentence in the English language. Shaw reviewed the book and wrote, 'Read the sentence beginning with "Know that this is your appointed lot" ... It contains more than 800 words, and stops then only because the printer, in desperation, bunged in a full-point. I read that sentence to my wife, and at the end we found ourselves cheering with excitement.'

Shaw's plays were not regularly performed in public until he was over forty, but by the 1920s he was England's finest dramatist and the best-known living playwright in the world.

To many middle-aged people he remained the disturber of their peace; the man whose works had brought about the breakdown of social barriers, the desire of women to be treated as people, industrial unrest and a lack of the long, hot summers they used to have:

> On another occasion, when I was sixteen, I tried to win back his long-lost faith in me, by telling him about some books that I was reading. I told him that I had just read a book by Bernard Shaw. My father stopped still in the path where we were walking and said: 'I have heard of other people having children like that, but I have always prayed God I might be spared.'
>
> Stephen Spender (b. 1909)
> *The Old School:* Ed. Graham Greene

The era of the actor-managers ended with the First World War. After the war property prices rose steeply and the theatres were bought by groups of investors who sub-let to theatrical production-companies.

Play production was now in the hands of a Producer, who worked for, or was, the management. He organized the production and controlled the finances. The play was staged by the Director:

> A person engaged by the management to conceal the fact that the players cannot act.
>
> James Agate (1877–1947)

Ever since Thespis plays had been directed by the author or the leading actor. The first director in the modern sense, who was neither of these, was the Duke of Saxe-Meiningen. In the twentieth century directing became a separate profession.

Drama between the wars was a mixture of adventurous theatre, such as Pirandello's exploration of the areas of drama beyond realism and the well-make play, the political drama of writers like Clifford Odets and the left-wing semi-amateur drama groups like London's Unity Theatre, together with a commercial theatre consisting largely of long runs, matinée-idols, tea-trays in the intervals, thrillers, farces and musicals—an English form in which America was soon to excel:

> What are the plays of today? They're either so chock-full of intellect that they send you to sleep,—or they reek of sentiment till you yearn for the smell of a cabbage.
>
> Alfred Sutro (1863–1933)
> *The Man in the Stalls*

A fresh interest in Shakespearian production blossomed in the first half of the twentieth century; a tribute to a genius able not only to withstand the indignities which the plays suffered from the Restoration onwards but also to survive being taught as a compulsory subject in schools:

> Like most schoolboys, I had been sickened of Shakespeare by education ... All too well did I know and was able to repeat on paper what the Rialto was: I could define an argosy to any teacher's delight and could be profound about Arden, Ducdame, and the Symbolic value of Ariel and Caliban ... By the age of eighteen I was allergic almost beyond hope of therapy.
>
> Ivor Brown (1891–1974)
> *Shakespeare*

Most actors liked playing Shakespeare, perhaps because the plays were written by an actor as acting material rather than as dramatic literature, but a distinguished American actress added a cautionary footnote:

> Playing Shakespeare is very tiring. You never get to sit down, unless you're a King.
>
> Josephine Hull (1886–1957)

Abuse and invective on the scale of that generated by the work of Ibsen and Shaw will probably never happen again; the theatre now occupies a different position in society's priorities and society itself has changed. It is difficult to arouse our present society to anger about anything.

There was a brief flurry, perhaps, at the theories and practices of Bertholt Brecht:

> I don't regard Brecht as a man of iron-grey purpose and intellect, I think he is a theatrical whore of the first quality.
>
> Peter Hall (b. 1930)

228

The state of alienation known as Brechtian, but what we used to call bored stiff.

John Coleman (b. 1927)

Brecht: If it hadn't been for Adolf Hitler he'd still be behind the bacon counter in Oberammergau.

Anon. actor

Style in drama criticism changed; it became more a part of the slighter, defter journalism of today. It acquired manners, as well as mannerisms, but no doubt is as difficult a form as it ever was:

To many people dramatic criticism must seem like an attempt to tattoo soap bubbles.

John Mason Brown (b. 1900)

It has been said that the first duty of a critic writing for a journal is to be entertaining; certainly disapproval is more usually expressed these days with wit than with malicious invective.

The archetype of the modern critical witticism, which corresponds to Aristotle's definition of wit as 'educated insult', was probably the line coined by an American humorist and critic as a comment on the performance of the actor Creston Clarke in *King Lear*:

He played the King as though under momentary apprehension that someone else was about to play the ace.

Eugene Field (1850–1895)
Denver Tribune, c. 1880

Another early example was a novelist's comment after enduring the opening night of *Peter Pan* in 1904:

Oh for an hour of Herod!
Anthony Hope (1863–1933)

> The sentiment had been expressed before. At the beginning of the nineteenth century the child actor Betty, the 'Infant Roscius', made such a lucrative impact on the public that the stage became infested with a multiplicity of diminutive prodigies, causing the actress Mrs. Jordan (mistress of the Duke of Clarence, later King William IV) to exclaim, 'Oh, for the days of King Herod!' (*Anecdotes of Actors*, Mrs. Mathews, 1844).

The witty critique was perfected by New York critics who belonged to, or wouldn't be seen dead at, the famous round table of the Algonquin Hotel. They developed a technique of bitchy phrase-making which has endured ever since:

Katherine Hepburn ran the whole gamut of emotions, from A to B.

Dorothy Parker (1893–1967)

Tallulah Bankhead barged down the Nile last week as Cleopatra — and sank.

John Mason Brown (b. 1900)
Reviewing *Antony and Cleopatra*

229

I always said that I'd like Barrymore's acting till the cows came home. Well, ladies and gentlemen, last night the cows came home.

George Jean Nathan (1882–1958)

I have knocked everything but the knees of the chorus-girls, and Nature has anticipated me there.

Percy Hammond (1873–1936)

Hook and Ladder is the sort of play that gives failures a bad name.

Walter Kerr (b. 1913)

A formula which has been much used since in various forms, i.e. Clive Barnes on *Oh! Calcutta!*, 'the sort of show that gives pornography a bad name'.

It was one of those plays in which all the actors unfortunately enunciated very clearly.

Robert Benchley (1889–1945)

Of the acting of Miss Bergere's company, one may not speak candidly unless one is in a trench.

Alexander Woolcott (1887–1943)

In an article in the magazine *Smart Set*, 1921, another critic, George Jean Nathan, described Woolcott's reviews as resembling 'either a gravy bomb, a bursting gladiolus, a palpitating *missa cantata*, an attack of psychic hydrophobia, or a Roman denunciation'.

Other Woolcott lines included:

The scenery was beautiful, but the actors got in front of it. The play left a taste of lukewarm parsnip juice.

There is a body of opinion which holds that the live theatre is now on its death-bed; that it is an anachronism in an electronic age. It is pointed out that property values and production costs have risen so high that theatres cannot hope to be financially self-supporting and that the number of theatres in Britain has dropped from seven hundred during the nineteenth century to under two hundred. It is further argued that the cinema and television fulfil whatever need there is for drama.

But these are familiar demons. The first public theatre of all, erected by Burbage, was a piece of speculative property development and the history of the bricks-and-mortar of theatre is studded with woeful tales of bankrupt proprietors. The managements, too, were rarely stable for very long. It seems unlikely that the investments of present-day Broadway and Shaftesbury Avenue impresarios are any more precarious than those of the early eighteenth- and nineteenth-century managements, many of whom only lasted a season before being beggared: some only lasted one production. Limited liability and the system by which productions are financed by a syndicate of backers save modern managers from the threat of the debtor's cell, and from the kind of complicated and frantic financial machinations which Sheridan was forced into to

230

keep Drury Lane afloat. Modern theatre needs a government subsidy to keep it lively, but then the great age of Elizabethan theatre flourished under royal and noble patronage; it is unlikely that Shakespeare could have retired to New Place solely on his cut of the box-office takings.

The phenomenal popularity of the cinema meant that a sizeable number of playgoers who went to the theatre because it was somewhere to go were lured away from plays to films, leading to the closure of many theatres. But these customers were, in turn, lured away from the cinema by an even more convenient form of 'convenience' entertainment, television, and a whole string of cinemas were closed. The trend began to change in the 1960s and by the 1970s a number of new theatres had been opened, and more are opened every year, some being converted from old cinemas.

The theatre, having survived two thousand years of assorted troubles like excommunication, total suppression, creative malnutrition, poverty, political antipathy and dismal mismanagement, is hardly likely to succumb suddenly to the rival forms of cinema, radio and television; if only because however good is a film, or a play on the radio or television, it remains a film, or a radio-play or a television-play; it is not theatre. In the theatre the audience is part of the performance; the actor affects the audience, but the audience's reaction also affects the actor's performance, and this interplay cannot be synthesized.

The primitive urge which some people have to stand up in front of a crowd and entertain it and the pleasure which others have of being entertained in this fashion show no signs of having been bred out of the human race. The standard of acting on the British stage after the Second World War was probably as high as it has ever been in the history of the theatre; knighthoods abounded, and for the first time an actor, Lord Olivier, sat in the House of Lords. And John Osborne's *Look Back in Anger*, produced in 1956, marked the beginning of a quite new form of theatre: plays written by, and appealing to, young people.

This theatre of the young, or at least young-minded, rapidly grew and galloped off in all directions; there was the Off-Broadway movement in New York, student theatre, Portable theatre, performances in pubs, on buses, Street theatre, Lunchtime theatre; much of it showing a *mimi*-like virility in the way in which it derided authority and milked the sacred cows of society for laughs:

Comedy is the last refuge of the nonconformist mind.
Gilbert Seldes (b. 1893)
The New Republic, 20 Dec. 1954

The post-war years brought a widening of the whole theatrical experience. Realism came to the fore again in Kitchen-Sink drama. Christopher Fry had great success with verse drama. There was Theatre of Cruelty and Theatre of the Absurd, and many other excursions into virgin country. Perhaps the most startling innovation was a complete reversal of the early theatre's preoccupation with rich costumes in the production *Oh! Calcutta!*, a revue in which the cast went stark naked.

There might be some aesthetic advantage in actors playing drama without the constraint of clothing, but it seems that this freedom gives dancing an unwelcome imprecision:

> The trouble with nude dancing is that not everything stops when the music stops.
>
> Sir Robert Helpmann (b. 1909)
>
> Sir Robert was asked for a comment after the New York opening of *Oh! Calcutta!*

Richard Rodgers and Oscar Hammerstein, who did more than anyone to bring new life and form to American musicals, had no affection for people who insisted that theatre was dying. In *Me and Juliet* they hit back. The scene was a theatre lobby during an intermission. In a 'conversation-piece' in song a group of cheerful playgoers took up arms against a sea of troubled pessimists:

> PESSIMISTS: Oh, the theatre is dying, the theatre is dying,
> The theatre is practically dead.
> Someone every day writes,
> We have no more playwrights,
> The theatre is sick in the head ...
> OTHERS: But actors keep acting, and plays keep attracting,
> And seats are not easy to buy;
> And year after year
> There is something to cheer—
> PESSIMISTS: We'd much rather have a good cry.
> OTHERS: Why the hell don't *you* lie down and die!
>
> Music: Richard Rodgers (b. 1902)
> Lyric: Oscar Hammerstein (1895–1960)
> *Me and Juliet*

ART

Art

Art in England has traditionally been regarded with less enthusiasm than it has been in warmer, Mediterranean countries:

> I hate all Boets and Bainters.
>
> George II (1683–1760)
> Quoted by Lord Campbell,
> *Lives of the Chief-Justices*

Royal patronage of the home product, when it existed, became more cautious over the centuries:

> Artists in England are paid too much.
>
> Prince Albert (1819–1861)
> Quoted by B. R. Haydon,
> Letter to Seymour Kirkup, Aug. 1844

And many prominent Englishmen shared the royal indifference:

> May the Devil fly away with the fine arts!
>
> Thomas Carlyle (1795–1881)
> *Latter-Day Pamphlets*, No. 8

Protests against art in other countries included one from a Greek comedy playwright:

> Who of the gods first taught the artist's craft
> Laid upon the human race the greatest curse.
>
> Antiphanes (408?–334? B.C.)
> *Kanpheus:* Frag. L. i.

A modern musician said of the U.S.A.:

> All the arts in America are a gigantic racket run by unscrupulous men for unhealthy women.
>
> Sir Thomas Beecham (1879–1961)

And a Nazi wrote:

> The most perfect shape, the sublimest image that has been recently created in Germany has not come out of any artist's studio. It is the steel helmet.
>
> S.S. Officer Count Baudissin
> Quoted by Paul Ortwin Rave, *Kunst und Diktatur im Dritten Reich*
>
> In 1933 the Nazi Party appointed Count Baudissin director of the Folkwang Museum.

235

A witty, cantankerous, American-born painter believed that conditions had always been the same for painters:

> Listen! There never was an artistic period.
> There never was an Art-loving nation.
> James McNeill Whistler (1834–1903)
> *Ten O'Clock*

Two of the main divisions of art have been defined in simple terms:

> Sculpture: mud pies which endure.
> Cyril Connolly (1903–1974)
> *Enemies of Promise*

> PAINTING, n. The art of protecting flat surfaces from the weather and exposing them to the critic.
> Ambrose Bierce (1842–1914?)
> *The Devil's Dictionary*

And a point has been made about professional painters:

> Most of those who call themselves artists are in reality picture dealers, only they make the pictures themselves.
> Samuel Butler (1835–1902)
> *Note-Books*

There has been a good deal of comment written about art itself. Its practical value:

> All art is quite useless.
> Oscar Wilde (1856–1900)
> Preface to *The Portrait of Dorian Gray*

Its effect on those who practise it:

> Art is a vice, a pastime which differs from some of the most pleasant vices and pastimes by consolidating and intensifying the organs which it exercises.
> Walter Sickert (1860–1942)
> *A Free House*

And its function:

> What is art? Prostitution.
> Charles Baudelaire (1821–1867)

One point which has dismayed many laymen has been the free use which artists have made of the naked human figure:

> Art is art, and nothing can be done to prevent it. But there is the Mayoress's decency to be considered.
> The Mayor of a Lancashire town on being presented
> with a pair of nude statues for his Town Hall
> Quoted by James Agate (1877–1947)
> *Ego*

The feeling grew up in Victorian times that there was something raffish about art; it was not respectable:

As my poor father used to say
In 1863,
Once people start on all this Art
Good-bye, moralitee!
A. P. Herbert (1890–1971)
Lines for a Worthy Person

Since artists of the Romantic era went about playing the role of Wild Men of Genius, there has been a deeply held conviction that to have one in the family was asking for trouble:

The true artist will let his wife starve, his children go barefoot, his mother drudge for his living at seventy, sooner than work at anything but his art.
George Bernard Shaw (1856–1950)
Man and Superman

It was believed that creative people were not quite like normal folk, and were much more difficult to cope with:

Authors and actors and artists and such
Never know nothing, and never know much.
Sculptors and singers and those of their kidney
Tell their affairs from Seattle to Sydney.
Playwrights and poets and such horses' necks
Start off from anywhere, end up at sex.
Diarists, critics, and similar roe
Never say nothing and never say no.
People Who Do Things exceed my endurance;
God, for a man that solicits insurance!
Dorothy Parker (1893–1967)
Bohemia

There was never much prestige attached to being a professional artist; only to being a rich and fashionable professional artist. Art was one of those callings, like the theatre and the merchant navy, which even comparatively poor parents hoped their sons would not go in for. The social position was lowly, usually hovering somewhere between that of a shopkeeper and a curate.

When Tennyson wrote his poem telling about the poor village maiden who fell in love with a lad whom she took to be as poor as herself, he gave the lad an occupation which he knew his Victorian readers would recognize as being a humble one:

He is but a landscape painter
And a village maiden she.
Alfred, Lord Tennyson (1809–1892)
The Lord of Burleigh

After the wedding the unfortunate maiden discovered to her horror that her husband was not common like her but a real lord, who did a bit of

237

landscape painting for fun. Overwhelmed by having to run the Big House and be called by an illustrious name 'unto which she had not been born' she rapidly bore her husband three fair children and expired.

But Oscar Wilde did not believe that art should be assessed too low down the scale:

> There are moments when art attains almost to the dignity of manual labour.
>
> Oscar Wilde (1856–1900)

The great critic John Ruskin thought it wrong for artists to aim too high socially. Not that he was afraid that they would pick their teeth with their patron's butter-knife, or keel over dead-drunk into the mashed potatoes; he was just wary of the corrupting effect that polite company might have on the purity of their genius:

> An artist should be fit for the best society and keep out of it.
>
> John Ruskin (1819–1900)

As far as most artists of the Impressionist period and after were concerned, purity did not figure much in the relationship between them and their work:

> Art isn't something you marry, it's something you rape.
>
> Edgar Degas (1834–1900)

If, since then, the myth has grown that artists are necessarily somewhat peculiar it is at least a point of view shared by many artists themselves:

> What garlic is to salad, insanity is to art.
>
> Augustus Saint-Gaudens (1848–1907)
>
> In spite of his name Saint-Gaudens, a sculptor, was an Irishman brought up in America. His dignified statues of Abraham Lincoln and General Sherman (on a horse) brought him election to the American Hall of Fame.

The seeds of this nineteenth-century concept of the Great Artist as Semi-Lunatic were probably sown during the period of the Italian Renaissance when Leonardo da Vinci claimed that there was a bit more to art than slapping colour on to wet plaster as instructed. He argued that painting was *cosa mentale*, 'a spiritual thing'; and the Bible clearly stated – Hosea ix. 7 – 'the spiritual man is mad'.

During the early Middle Ages, before the emergence of well-organized craftsmen's guilds, most of the best painters seem to have been originally trained as goldsmiths. There was little demarcation then between the various forms of decorative art, and an 'artist' was a craftsman who was prepared, at the right price, to set stones, cast bronze, carve a crucifix, work precious metals, design a flag or paint something on a wall. By the later Middle Ages the guilds seem to have sorted things out a little, but pure painting was not reckoned to be very important; painters in London were an off-shoot of the Saddlers' Guild, elsewhere they usually came under the Painters' and Stainers' Guild. Most professional painting undertaken by guild craftsmen was probably painting patterns on peoples' living-room walls and decorating their furniture but some of these artisan artists had real talent for drawing and so were called upon to paint people. The development of pure painting was also furthered by the work of amateurs, talented monks like St. Dunstan, Abbot of Glastonbury.

The wall paintings painted by talented 'house-painters' were not always anonymous decorations; many medieval pictures were signed by the artist, who sometimes added an inscription pointing out what a good artist he was, and a few successful painters were taken into their patron's household and given some sort of office; usually *valet de chambre*. But this was almost certainly because the painter himself was a buffoon, or a wit, or was in some way socially acceptable. A professional painter or sculptor, whatever his genius, still had only the status of a guild-trained workman.

By the time of the Italian Renaissance the difference between the creative artist and the skilled craftsman was clear, and the rediscovery of classical literature had revealed that artists were treated with considerable respect in the Rome of Cicero, so the artists of Italy, led by Leonardo da Vinci, went into battle with words and pamphlets. They argued, with great force, that art had transcended its original functional purpose and that a guild training – How to Grind Your Colours, How to Clean Your Brushes – was totally inadequate to the requirements of a Renaissance artist who needed to be familiar with anatomy, mathematics, classical literature, the Bible and other gentlemanly studies. And so, by the year 1500, it was recognized that painting and sculpture were Liberal Arts and artists could be accepted as intelligent and reputable members of society.

This did not mean that artists were free to paint away at what they liked. Some were attached to rich merchants' households, but most were engaged on a tight contract to produce exactly what the client ordered in exchange for their expenses plus so much per hour for their skill.

A few patrons, like Borso d'Este, Duke of Ferrara, paid their artists at a flat rate of so much a square foot.

Much of Renaissance art was religious in theme, if not always in inspiration. Some of it was commissioned by wealthy families with bad consciences – a number of massive fortunes were built on such unChristian practices as piracy and usury – and then presented to the Church as a gesture of atonement. Whether the inspiration was wholly religious, as with painters like Fra Angelico and Giotto, or whether

239

it was just another job, as it probably was with secular artists like Titian, Giorgione, even Leonardo, the 'Madonna Market' was a lucrative and important outlet for artists. And the Church itself was a valuable patron, rich and powerful enough to command the best work. The Church firmly believed in using pictures and images as an aid to piety: religious art was, according to Pope Gregory, the Bible of the Illiterate.

A Protestant, later, was unimpressed:

> I question if Raphael himself could ever have made one convert, though he had exhausted all the expression of his eloquent pencil on a series of popish doctrines and miracles.
>
> Horace Walpole (1717–1797)
> Preface: *Anecdotes of Painting*

The Catholic Counter-Reformation in the sixteenth century, following upon the Reformation of Luther and Calvin, resulted in churches becoming even more colourful and splendid. It was as though the Catholic Church had decided that if Luther was going to make his brand of religion 'penny plain' then Catholicism was going to be decidedly 'twopence coloured'. The outcome was more religious art and the development of Baroque architecture for churches, where architectural form, painting and sculpture were all blended together into a rich, exuberant, emotional tribute to the Glory of God.

It was all a bit different in England. In the year 1509, when Michelangelo was painting the roof of the Sistine Chapel, Henry VIII became King of England. And when Henry broke away from the Roman Catholic Church any hopes of England developing a tradition of religious patronage evaporated.

Furthermore, a great deal of the religious art which English artists had produced through the Middle Ages was sold off, looted, and otherwise dispersed at the dissolution of the monasteries. And few of the religious pictures, statues and stained-glass windows which survived that onslaught escaped, intact, from seventeenth-century puritanism. In 1643, Parliament ordered that 'idolatrous' images in churches should be defaced. This gave a number of Puritan fanatics an opportunity of demonstrating their opinion of religious art with the aid of long ladders and sledge-hammers:

> Sudbury, Jan. 9, 1643. We broke down 10 mighty great Angels in Glass, in all 80.
> Haverhill, Jan. 6. We brake down about a hundred superstitious Pictures; and seven Fryars hugging a Nunn; and the picture of God and Christ, and divers other very superstitious.
> Clare, Jan. 6. We brake down 1000 Pictures superstitious; I brake down 200; 3 of God the Father, and 3 of Christ, and the Holy Lamb, and 3 of the Holy Ghost like a Dove with Wings; and the 12 Apostles were carvd in Wood, on the top of the Roof, which we gave orders

to be taken down; and the Sun and Moon in the East Window, by the King's Arms, to be taken down.

Dunstall, Jan. 23. We broke down 60 superstitious Pictures: and broke in pieces the Rails; and gave orders to pull down the Steps.

Otley, Feb. 27. A Deputy brake down 50 superstitious Pictures; a Cross on the Chancel, 2 Brass Inscriptions; and Moses with a Rod, and Aaron with his Mitre, taken down: and 20 Cherubims to be broke down.

William Dowsing (1596?–1679?)

Suffolk Journal (1643–4)

Dowsing was the most notorious of the professional iconoclasts. After battering his way through Suffolk he began upon Cambridge University, quite unlawfully smashing windows in private rooms and libraries, and digging up floors. He made a little money on the side by fining colleges forty shillings each for the mess which he himself left.

Isaac D'Israeli quoted a report that during the eighteenth century a group of English artists offered to decorate the insides of churches free of charge. The offer was refused by the authorities.

Denied the incentive and patronage of religion from the days of Henry VIII, paintings might almost have ceased to exist in England but for one sort of picture which the English, far more than any other nation, have always loved. The portrait:

A portrait is a picture in which there is something wrong with the mouth.

Eugene Speicher (1883–1962)

Speicher was a successful American portrait painter.

There are only two styles of portrait-painting; the serious and the smirk.

Charles Dickens (1812–1870)

Nicholas Nickleby

Every time I paint a portrait, I lose a friend.

John S. Sargent (1865–1925)

Sargent was a highly successful painter of bravura portraits of the rich. Osbert Sitwell wrote that 'looking at his portraits, they understood at last *how* rich they were'.

Roger Fry wrote in the *Nation* in 1929, 'he was stinking and undistinguished as an illustrator and non-existent as an artist'.

Millais once confessed that the only thing he enjoyed about portrait-painting was putting the high-lights on the boots of his subjects.

Quoted by James Agate (1877–1947)

Ego

Millais was one of the founders of the Pre-Raphelite Brotherhood, but he turned fashionable portrait painter. Enjoyable the work may not have been, but it was certainly rewarding: he became President of the Royal Academy and a baronet.

The Englishman's fervent wish to have his face painted for posterity was shared by Royalty. For two hundred years after Henry VIII came to the throne, English monarchs caressed and enriched their favourite court painters. The royal artist had a busy time. He not only provided a stream of assorted royal portraits to be given away to other courts, or to favourite courtiers, or to humbler subjects in lieu of the repayment of a debt, but he was also used to paint portraits of prospective royal brides to give the king an idea of what he was in for, e.g. Holbein's portraits of the Duchess of Milan and Anne of Cleves. In between times he was expected to do some heraldic work, design silverware, touch up the royal barge and carriages and produce sketches for royal tents, pavilions and funeral equipment.

But the great court painters of England were not Englishmen. From the reign of Henry VIII to the middle of the eighteenth century all the celebrated royal portraitists were German or Dutch: Hans Holbein – German. Rubens – Flemish. Van Dyck (knighted by Charles I) – Flemish. Peter Lely (knighted by Charles II) – born in Germany of Dutch parentage. Godfrey Kneller (knighted by William III, created a baronet by George I) – German.

This lack of patronage for home talent was probably mostly due to the lack of outstanding sculptors, and painters in oils – the English were traditionally better at other things, like stained-glass windows, illuminated manuscripts, and miniatures painted on ivory or vellum – but it also must have been affected by the Tudor and Elizabethan fascination with travel, and with the riches of other countries.

When the great nobles of the seventeenth century decided to mark their wealth and power by amassing vast collections of art treasures there was little in England to interest them and they began to buy up foreign pictures, statues, and *objets d'art*; a kind of semi-looting operation for which this country became notorious:

> Wealthy England has amassed the treasures of the whole world in her collections; none too creative herself, she has carted away the metope of the Acropolis and the Egyptian colossi of porphyry or granite, the Assyrian bas-reliefs, knotty plastic works of ancient Yucatan, smiling Buddhas, Japanese wood-carvings and lacquer-work, the pick of continental art and a medley of souvenirs from the colonies: iron-work, fabrics, glass, vases, snuff-boxes, book-bindings, statues, pictures, enamel, inlaid escritoires, Saracen swords, and heaven alone knows what else; perhaps everything in the world that is of any value.
>
> Karel Capek (1890–1938)
> *Letters from England*

The pioneer English art collectors were men of great power in the land. Perhaps the first was Thomas Howard, second Earl of Arundel, who started in 1615. Another was the Duke of Buckingham, who probably influenced King Charles I to begin a collection. Both the King and Prince Henry collected on the grand scale; the King's treasures included the Raphael cartoons and the entire art collection of the Duke of Mantua. Naturally enough these collectors were too busy doing other things to do their collecting themselves; the finding, selecting and buying of the items were delegated to lesser mortals, frequently consular officials, or ambassadors with a good eye for art, like Sir Thomas Roe. The Earl of Arundel employed a professional scout, the Rev. William Petty, to scour the Continent for shippable loot. It was an adventurous calling and several times the reverend gentleman nearly lost his life; on one occasion he was nearly executed as a spy, and on another the small boat in which he was transporting a consignment of classical statues from the island of Samos was overwhelmed by stormy seas and foundered (the statues sank but, happily for him, the Rev. William Petty floated).

The influence of these collections of European art on England must have been considerable – although the collections were private, a nobleman's art gallery, statues, cabinets, and, indeed, his houses, were always, with certain reservations, open to view – and the domination of English art by imported art was further accentuated by the growing popularity of the Grand Tour.

Wealthy families had for some time realized that having a little Greek and a lot of Latin flogged into their sons at school was an incomplete training for a brilliant career and had taken to sending their young men on a year or two's tour of the Continent, under supervision, to give them some kind of worldly Further Education. During the Civil War this traffic had increased for obvious reasons, and the Restoration, with its warm regard for continental practices, had further encouraged the flow. By the eighteenth century the number of Englishmen embarking on the Grand Tour, as it was by then known, had reached flood proportions, comprising not only young sprigs of the nobility, but scholars, poets, merchants, ladies of means, squires, artists; in fact, everybody who could rake up the money. And most of them tried to bring back souvenirs of the classical art which they, one up on those who stayed at home, had seen at first hand. The antique dealers of Europe had a saying 'If the Colosseum were portable, the English would carry it away', and happily sold them anything which could be picked up, dug up, or prised loose. A great number of these dealings were conducted according to the old legal maxim 'let the buyer beware'.

> Here are several professed antiquaries who are ready to serve anybody who desires them ... their trade is only to sell. They have correspondents at Aleppo, Grand Cairo, in Arabia, and Palestine, who send them all they can find, and very often great heaps that are only fit to melt into cans and kettles ... Those that pretend to skill generally find out the image of some saint in the medals of the Greek cities. One of them, showing me the figure of a Pallas with a victory in her hand on a reverse, assured me it was the Virgin holding a crucifix.

The same man offered me the head of a Socrates on a sardonyx, and to enhance the value gave him the title of St Augustine.

Lady Mary Wortley Montagu (1689–1762)
Letter to the Abbé Antonio Conti, Constantinople, 29 May 1717

In another letter Lady Mary wrote that the English Grand Tourists had earned themselves 'the glorious title of Golden Asses all over Europe'.

The Golden Asses were also milked at home. The great collections of Italian and French art in stately homes, together with the influx of smaller pieces brought back from the tour and proudly hanging in the sitting-rooms of manor houses, town houses and country seats, themselves frequently just rebuilt or refronted in the classical taste, had generated such a fashion that by the early eighteenth century it was the only sort of art that polite society would buy in England. This dubious trade in imported pictures infuriated William Hogarth:

> Picture jobbers ... are always ready to raise a great cry in the prints whenever they think their craft is in danger, and indeed it is their interest to depreciate every English work, as hurtful to their trade of continually importing shiploads of dead Christs, Holy Families, Madonna's, and other dismal dark subjects, neither entertaining nor ornamental; on which they scrawl the terrible cramp names of some Italian masters, and fix on us poor Englishmen the character of *universal dupes*. If a man, naturally a judge of painting, not bigoted to those empirics, should cast his eye on one of their sham virtuoso-pieces, he would be very apt to say: 'Mr. Bubbleman, that grand Venus (as you are pleased to call it) has not beauty enough for the character of an English cook-maid.' Upon which the quack answers, with a confident air, 'O Lord, sir, I find that you are no connoisseur— that picture, I assure you, is in *Alesso Baldovinetto's* second and best manner, boldly painted, and truly sublime; the contour gracious; the air of the head in the high Greek taste; and a most divine idea it is.' Then spitting on an obscure place, and rubbing it with a dirty handkerchief, takes a skip to the other end of the room and screams out in raptures, 'There is an amazing touch! A man should have this picture a twelve-month in his collection before he can discover half its beauties.' The gentleman (though naturally a judge of what is beautiful, yet ashamed to be out of the fashion in judging for himself) is struck dumb with this cant; gives a vast sum for the picture; very modestly confesses that he is indeed ignorant of painting, and bestows a frame worth fifty pounds on the frightful thing, not worth as many farthings.

William Hogarth (1697–1764)
Letter to the St. James's Evening Post, 7 June 1737

Hogarth was a very successful English artist, ending up with his coach-and-four, but he was primarily an engraver rather than a painter; even fairly poor cottagers could afford to buy a print, so his work was marketed to a vastly wider public than polite society. He came from a poor background and achieved an astonishing amount during his career without any kind of classical training or easy patronage. He transformed the continental 'conversation piece' into relaxed, informal family portraits. He invented the series of anecdotal pictures which together told a complete, and usually moralistic, story, e.g. *A Rake's Progress, Marriage à la Mode*. He had the idea of hanging some of his pictures on the staircase of a hospital so that the public could see them, thus anticipating public exhibitions. He was mainly responsible for getting the government to pass an Act, 'Hogarth's Act', which gave the designer the copyright in his work to protect him against piracy. And all his life he hated and fought against art patronage and connoisseurship, and what he called 'foreign rubbish'.

It was a bleak time for English painters generally. There was a certain amount of decorative work to be done on the new houses which were springing up, but most of the top jobs were given to foreign painters; Sir James Thornhill, the royal sergeant-painter, was glad to paint the dome of St. Paul's, at considerable risk to his life, for forty shillings a square yard. Young painters once learned their craft as assistants to fashionable portrait painters who used to employ anything up to two hundred of them to do the donkey work of painting in the trees, drapery, sky, furniture, etc., on an assembly-line basis; with the death of Sir Godfrey Kneller there.were few English artists rich enough to employ more than a 'drapery man', and there was very little other tuition to be had:

> The present State of this art in Britain does not afford sufficient education to the painter. We have but one Academy meanly supported by the private subscriptions of the student, in all this great metropolis. There they have but two figures, a man and a woman, and consequently there can be but little experience gathered. The subscribers to this lone Academy pay two guineas a season which goes to the expense of the room and the lights.
>
> *The London Tradesman*, 1747

> This was probably the somewhat run-down establishment owned by Sir James Thornhill. Hogarth was a pupil there briefly. He took away little of benefit to his artistic development but he eloped with Sir James's daughter, Jane, with whom he enjoyed an admirable marriage; later he inherited the school.

The demand for portraiture was as brisk as ever, particularly amongst the swelling middle class, but for the artist it was dreary hack work:

> I am unwilling to sink into a portrait manufacturer.
>
> William Hogarth (1697–1764)
> Autobiographical sketch published by John Ireland, 1798

Having one's portrait painted in those days was as ordinary an experience as, in this century, having one's portrait taken by the High Street photographer, and a great deal of mid-eighteenth-century portraiture was totally undistinguished:

> At a distance one would take a dozen of their portraits for twelve copies of the same original ... Excepting the single countenance

or likeness they have all the same neck, the same arms, the same colouring and the same attitude. In short these pretended portraits are as void of life and action as of design in the painter.

J. B. le Blanc (1708–1781)
Letters on the English and French Nations, 1747

As so often happens, the times produced the man: Joshua Reynolds, the greatest academical painter England has produced.

Reynolds, unlike Hogarth and many others who came from the ranks of tradesmen, was brought up in an atmosphere of learning. After studying the work of artists of the Italian Renaissance he settled in London and rapidly became fashionable amongst the whig aristocracy for his portraits executed in the Grand Manner. At last the connoisseurs and the rich dilettanti had found an Englishman whose art was socially acceptable: his cult of classicism almost exactly represented the aesthetic taste of the middle of the eighteenth century. And he himself was socially acceptable; friendly, urbane, gregarious – he founded the Literary Club whose meetings Dr. Johnson so enjoyed – but a little difficult to argue with on matters of art:

> When they talk'd of their Raphaels, Correggios, and stuff,
> He shifted his trumpet, and only took snuff.

Oliver Goldsmith (1728–1774)
Retaliations

> The ear-trumpet was necessary because Reynolds had damaged his hearing in Rome when trying to copy a Raphael in a particularly draughty corridor of the Vatican: which might account for his rather muted enthusiasm for Raphael's work.

In Reynolds's Grand Manner of portraiture he arranged his sitters in a setting redolent of antiquity, making use of broken stone walls, pillars, views of distant plains, and so on, and his sitters sat in attitudes well known from the works of the old masters. Classical clothing was favoured for the gentlemen, although the ladies were permitted to wear a nightdress-like garment, timeless in its cut.

This was an educated taste; it was gentleman speaking to gentlefolk through a series of symbols and allusions familiar only to those who had benefited from a classical education. Just as the polite literature of the time was studded with lines like 'Sister of Ebon-scepter'd Hecat, hail!' (The Pleasures of Melancholy by Thomas Warton) and 'A purple shred of some rich robe, prepared erst by the Muses or th'Aonian Maid, to deck great Tullius or the Mantuan Bard' (Education by Gilbert West), so Reynolds and other painters in the Neo-Classical manner worked into their pictures a few quotations from the old masters for those in the know to recognize.

Reynolds's portrait of the Marlborough family (fee 700 guineas) was graced with many echoes from the past:

The composition abounds with every absurdity, and as to the plagiarisms they are really capital. The Correggio character in some, the Carlo Maratti in others, with those negative characters which the painter has given to the remaining part of the group, added to the servile character of the draperies of Van Dyck, and others again in the manner of Rembrandt, make it the worst of all oil Olios that ever was exhibited, although meant as a very capital performance.

Rev. Henry Bate (1745–1824)
Morning Post, 1778

The Rev. Henry Bate was a pleasure-loving and highly colourful parson-cum-journalist who brightened up London life. Johnson thought that he lacked merit but had courage.

Curiously, because Reynolds employed a number of assistants who should have been able to correct the fault, he never mastered the technique of preparing his colours, consequently the carmine in the cheeks of his portraits began to fade almost before the paint was dry:

The complexions of the figures too are most cadaverously insulted. It is well known that the two principals were always troubled with the gripes, but nevertheless it was cruel of Sir Joshua to physic them to that unmerciful degree to bring them down to the deadly tone of his palette.   Ibid.

When Sir Joshua Reynolds died
All Nature was degraded;
The King drop'd a tear into the Queen's Ear
And all his Pictures Faded.

William Blake (1757–1827)
Annotations to Sir Joshua Reynolds's Discourses

Horace Walpole suggested that the portraits should be paid for by annuities so long as they lasted.

This period saw a remarkable change for the better in the lot of British artists. Reynolds, by his character as much as by his painting, had brought prestige to the profession and the market for paintings was brisk.

The next step towards pulling the profession together was to persuade the king that it was time that the country had an official academy, a fountain-head which would issue guide-lines on questions of taste, train the young, discourage the growing tendency among some painters to paint from personal emotions rather than with academic detachment, and generally promote the classic ethic that the purpose of art was to elevate moral standards. Inevitably Reynolds, visibly the Grand Artist of Great Britain, was put forward as its first president. George III agreed – somewhat reluctantly; he was not an admirer of Reynolds's work – and in 1768 Reynolds became the first president of the new Royal Academy. In 1769 he was made Sir Joshua Reynolds.

Ironically, now that home-produced Neo-Classical art was an established taste, with the Royal Academy behind it, the spirit of the age began to move onwards towards something new – Romantic art.

One of the first rifts in the lute occurred when the American-born painter of 'history' pictures, Benjamin West, announced that he was going to paint a canvas depicting the death of General Wolfe at the siege of Quebec with everybody in the picture dressed in the sort of clothes they wore on the battlefield. It is difficult, two hundred years later, to appreciate what a bombshell this was, but to West's fellow members of the Royal Academy it was rank heresy; the rule was quite plain: all serious subjects, whether in poetry, drama, sculpture or painting, could only be decently portrayed by clothing them in the trappings of ancient Rome or Greece. Sir Joshua Reynolds hurried round to make West see reason, taking the Archbishop of York with him for added weight, but West – who had a talent for anticipating the turns and twists of fashion – argued back:

> The event to be commemorated happened in the year 1759, in a region of the world unknown to the Greeks and Romans, and at a period of time when no warriors who wore such costume existed. The subject I have to represent is a great battle fought and won, and the same truth which gives law to the historian should rule the painter.
>
> Benjamin West (1734–1820)
> John Galt: *Life and Studies of Benjamin West*

Reynolds prophesied gloomily, and correctly, that the picture would occasion a revolution in art. *Death of Wolfe* was exhibited at the Royal Academy in 1771 and was a huge success, earning West over £15,000 in royalties from the engraving rights alone. Many of his die-hard colleagues thought his treatment of his subject inexpressibly vulgar, notably James Barry, R.A. Barry sought to put the matter right by exhibiting his own version, *Death of General Wolfe*, in which everybody was naked. The picture was not a success.

Perhaps the most violent attack on the Grand Manner of painting as taught at the Academy, and certainly the strongest personal attack on Sir Joshua Reynolds and his teachings, came from the poet, mystic, engraver and painter, William Blake. A more recent artist made the point:

> Art is either plagiarism or revolution.
> Paul Gauguin (1848–1903)

If Reynolds could be said to represent the art plagiarists then Blake could certainly represent the revolutionaries. Reynolds had given a series of important lectures to the Academy which encapsulated the classical attitudes towards art. These were published under the title *Sir Joshua Reynolds's Discourses*. About 1808 Blake went through the book making marginal comments.

248

Blake's opening remark set the tone:

> This Man Was Hired to Depress Art. This is the opinion of Will Blake.
>
> William Blake (1757–1827)
Annotations to Sir Joshua Reynolds's Discourses

He went on to mention the time he spent studying in the Academy schools:

> Having spent the Vigour of my Youth & Genius under the Oppression of Sr Joshua & his Gang of Cunning Hired Knaves Without Employment & as much as could possibly be Without Bread, The Reader must Expect to Read in all my Remarks on these Books Nothing but Indignation & Resentment.
>
> Ibid.

Reynolds spoke highly of the skill with which the Venetian painters like Titian, Veronese and Tintoretto used colour:

> Why should Titian & the Venetians be Named in a discourse on Art? Such Idiots are not Artists.
>
> Venetian, all thy Colouring is no more
> Than Boulster'd Plasters on a Crooked Whore.
>
> Ibid.

The colouring skill of Rubens was also praised:

> To My Eye Rubens's Colouring is most Contemptible. His Shadows are of a Filthy Brown somewhat of the Colour of Excrement.
>
> Ibid.

A great many of Reynolds's assertions so infuriated Blake that his marginal notes consisted simply of contemptuous epithets:

> A Liar!
> A Mock!
> Villainy!
> A Sly Dog!
> Nonsense!
> O Poverty!
> A Fine Jumble!
> Infernal Falsehood!
> Abundance of Stupidity!
> Damned Fool! (etc. etc.)
>
> Ibid.

Blake, like Hogarth, came from an unprivileged background but, unlike Hogarth, he had difficulty making a living. Much of his poetry was an expression of his own violently anti-church brand of religion, written with a strange personal vocabulary of mystical symbols. He was a friend of Tom Paine and helped Paine escape to France when *The Rights of Man* proved too inflammatory for a jittery government to tolerate. He claimed that the technique of his most remarkable work – a book whose text and illustrations were engraved as one – was revealed to him in a dream by his dead brother, Robert. Blake was almost certainly a little mad.

249

The short burst of British creative genius which began with Hogarth ended with two artists, Constable and Turner, both of whom were landscape painters:

Landscape painting is the obvious recourse of misanthropy.
William Hazlitt (1778–1830)
Possibly true of Turner, who was secretive and crotchety, but untrue of Constable.

The traditional method of painting landscapes was to make sketches and take notes in the field but to compose and paint the picture in the studio. Trees were painted to represent trees in general, not any tree in particular. Foliage and grass were painted a kind of dun colour; a landscape was supposed to be 'brown as an old violin'. Constable was the first major painter to see that foliage and grass were full of water and they glinted and shone in the sunshine. So instead of painting greenery so that it looked like a bunch of dead seaweed he made it sparkle with highlights: 'Constable's snow'. The effect was so remarkable that the painter Fuseli said that Constable 'makes me call for my great coat and umbrella'.

Several of Constable's landscapes were bought by Frenchmen and exhibited in Paris, where they created much interest and influenced the French school of landscape painting; for which he was awarded two gold medals by the King of France. The English public simply did not understand what Constable was doing, and most critics viewed his faithful portraits of simple country scenes with considerable distaste:

Two landscape-painters of much reputation in England, and one of them in France also—David Cox and John Constable, represent a form of blunt and untrained faculty which in being very frank and simple, apparently powerful, and needing no thought, intelligence or trouble whatever to observe, and being wholly disorderly, slovenly and licentious, and therein meeting with instant sympathy from the disorderly public mind now resentful of every trammel and ignorant of every law—these two men, I say, represent in their intensity the qualities adverse to all accurate science or skill in landscape art; their work being the mere blundering of clever peasants.
John Ruskin (1819–1900)
Lectures on Landscape: 'Colour'

Turner was also, in a way, a 'clever peasant' as he was the son of a barber and became England's greatest landscape painter. But, unlike Constable, Turner was successful at an early age. His particular genius for painting the awesomeness of nature and the elements was very much to the Romantic taste of the time, but the later way in which he handled colour and the remarkable, luminous effects he achieved – years ahead of the Impressionists – was too much for some people to take.

One critic suggested that these particular atmospheric effects were produced:

> ...as if by throwing handfuls of white and blue and red at the canvas, and letting what would stick, stick.
>
> *Literary Gazette*, May 1842

Mark Twain later described *The Slave Ship* as resembling:

> A tortoise-shell cat having a fit in a platter of tomatoes.
>
> Mark Twain (1835–1910)

As Turner's genius matured his choice of subjects became more original, and his inventive treatment of them more implicit and Romantically dramatic.

This move away from classical teachings so saddened one distinguished Victorian critic that he burst briefly into verse:

> Turner had strength to bear that tempering
> That shatters weaker hearts and breaks their hope.
> He still pursued his journey step by step—
> First modestly attired in quiet grey,
> As well became sincere humility;
> Then with a plume of colour he adorned
> His simple raiment and so walked awhile;
> Until at last, like his beloved Sun,
> He set in forms of strangest phantasy,
> Coloured with gold and scarlet, and the lands
> Of his conception grew as dim and vague
> As shadows. So his mighty brain declined.
>
> Philip Gilbert Hamerton (1834–1894)
> *Turner*

The Royal Academy was doing its best to stem the tide of what many of its members considered to be vulgar, emotional, worthless paintings.

An annual banquet was instituted to which the leading figures in society were invited. Strangely, although it was the 'Royal' Academy, no reigning monarch ever attended an annual banquet. The Prince Regent, possibly the one member of a British royal family to be interested in British artists, was a frequent guest and, in 1812, presented the Academy with an enormous two-ton bronze lantern to hang in the Great Room of Somerset House. This was much admired until it fell down in the middle of the Annual Dinner of 1815, narrowly missing Sir Walter Scott.

An annual exhibition was inaugurated where the products of Academy teachings could be seen, admired, and bought:

> The Royal Academy ... is ... a mercantile body, like any other mercantile body ... who, with the jealousy natural to such bodies supported by authority from without and by cabal within, think them-

251

selves bound to crush all generous views and liberal principles of art, lest they should interfere with their monopoly and their privilege to be thought Artists and men of genius.

William Hazlitt (1778–1830)
On the Catalogue Raisonné of the British Institution, 1816

Hazlitt almost became a professional painter. He painted a few portraits; one of Wordsworth he tore up, but one of Charles Lamb is in the National Portrait Gallery.

But the Romantic movement was seeing art much more as a personal expression of the artist than as a kind of gifted working-to-rule:

Genius has sometimes done lovely things without knowledge and without discipline. But all the learning of the Academies has never yet drawn so much as one fair face, or ever set two pleasant colours side by side.

John Ruskin (1819–1900)
Lectures on Landscape

Many Academy-trained painters found it increasingly difficult to find a market for their paintings in the Grand Manner, their huge history pictures depicting biblical and battle scenes in the classical style. The eighteenth-century taste for European art was on the wane, and as the nineteenth century progressed and new tastes developed the Old Masters came under a more penetrating critical scrutiny:

Rembrandt is not to be compared in the painting of character with our extraordinarily gifted English artist, Mr Rippingille.

John Hunt (1775–1848)
The Examiner

Edward Rippingille was a popular painter of such gentle rural scenes as *A Country Post Office* and *Going to the Fair*.

The poet Shelley, on a visit to Naples, saw Marcello Venusti's copy of Michelangelo's fresco in the Sistine Chapel, the *Last Judgement*:

I cannot but think the genius of this artist highly overrated. He has not only no temperance, no modesty, no feeling for the just boundaries of art ... but he has no sense of beauty ... What a thing his 'Moses' is; how distorted from all that is natural and majestic, only less monstrous and detestable than its historical prototype.

Percy Bysshe Shelley (1792–1822)
Letters

It was perhaps typical of Shelley to get in a dig at Moses himself. The copy which Shelley saw was painted in 1549 and showed the *Last Judgement* as it looked in the Sistine Chapel before the big fuss. Certain austere minds of the Counter-Reformation objected to the nudity – Aretino, who was a public moralizer and a private pornographer, wrote 'such things may be suitable in a bathroom, but not in the holiest chapel' – and a painter, Daniele da Volterra, was ordered to paint over the nude parts of most of the figures. This earned him the nickname *il brachettone*, 'the breeches-maker'.

252

William Hazlitt was luckier than Shelley, he managed to see the real – but breeched – fresco on the wall of the Sistine Chapel:

> It is like an immense field of battle, or charnel house, strewed with carcases and naked bodies: or it is a shambles of art. You have huge limbs apparently torn from their bodies and stuck against the wall: anatomical dissections, backs, and diaphragms, tumbling 'with hideous ruin and combustion down', neither intelligible groups nor perspective nor colour, ... the whole is a scene of enormous, ghastly confusion, in which you can only make out quantity and number, and vast, uncouth masses of bone and muscle.
>
> William Hazlitt (1778–1830)
> *The Vatican*

The Greek notion of beauty left a Russian cold:

> I have seen the Venus of Medici, and I think that if she were dressed in modern clothes she would be hideous, especially about the waist.
>
> Anton Chekhov (1860–1904)
> Letter to his sister

> For centuries the Medici Venus was regarded as the epitome of classic beauty. Then in 1820 the Venus de Milo was dredged up and the Venus of Medici was utterly eclipsed.

As far as the Academical painters were concerned the wells were drying up. Young aristocrats of the eighteenth century, even if they knew or cared little about art, at least pretended that they did because it was expected of the *ton* and it was fashionable to be a patron of the arts. The story ·was rather different in the nineteenth century. It was no longer the done thing to be, or try to be, a connoisseur, a dilettante. Byron, who seemed to epitomize the Romantic movement to his contemporaries, particularly those on the Continent, wrote:

> You must recollect, however, that I know nothing of painting; and that I detest it, unless it reminds me of something I have seen, or think it possible to see, for which I spit upon and abhor all the Saints and subjects of one half the impostures I see in the churches and palaces; and when in Flanders, I never was so disgusted in my life as with Rubens and his eternal wives and infernal glare of colours, as they appeared to me; and in Spain I did not think much of Murillo and Velasquez. Depend upon it, of all the arts, it is the most artificial and unnatural, and that by which the nonsense of mankind is the most imposed upon.
>
> Lord Byron (1788–1824)
> Letter to John Murray, 14 April 1817

Those artists who were committed to turning out paintings of the old school made valiant attempts to measure up what they wanted to paint with what the public was prepared to spend money upon. They tried exhibiting their paintings by subscription: showing them in an exhibition hall and charging for admission. This began a brief era of enormous canvases – quantity rather than quality being more likely to attract the sauntering passer-by.

One such do-it-yourself entrepreneur was the history painter Robert Ker Porter. He hired the Lyceum theatre, which was going through a bad patch and changing daily from being a Roman Catholic chapel to a debating society hall to an exhibition hall, and exhibited three gigantic canvases, one of which, a battle-piece entitled *Storming of Seringapatam*, was 120 feet wide.

This kind of exploitation met with a certain amount of success, but its dependence on novelty-value meant that it carried with it the seeds of its own destruction, as Benjamin Haydon found out in 1846 when he exhibited his *Banishment of Aristides* and *Nero Playing the Lyre during the Burning of Rome* at the Egyptian Hall in Piccadilly. Downstairs in the Egyptian Hall there was a rival novelty on display, the American dwarf 'General' Tom Thumb:

> April 13. They rush by thousands to see Tom Thumb. They push, they fight, they scream, they faint, they cry help and murder! and oh! and ah! They see my bills, my boards, my caravans, and don't read them. Their eyes are open, but their sense is shut. It is an insanity, a *rabies*, a madness, a *furor*, a dream. I would not have believed it of the English people.
>
> B. R. Haydon (1786–1846)
> *Memoirs*

The exhibition closed with a loss to Haydon of £111-8s-10d. This was the last of a series of grievous disappointments and two months later he committed suicide. He was not a very good painter.

But a great many painters were prospering. Fortunes were made and knighthoods won by the emergence during the nineteenth century of a taste for what might be termed major minor painting: excellent technique applied to trivial, sentimental subjects. The children of the Industrial Revolution, if they survived and prospered, liked to cover their walls with pictures or prints which they could understand and which possessed qualities, like a high finish or photographic realism, which they were able to admire.

The Fancy pictures, inaugurated by Gainsborough, of idealized peasants standing about in charming poses, and the Anecdotal pictures, popularized by Sir David Wilkie, of simple scenes of village activity were added to with a whole new range of subjects and treatments. Queen Victoria's favourite English painter, Edwin Landseer, developed an extraordinarily successful technique of endowing animals with human characteristics. His paintings of coy, sad, comical, noble and bleeding animals were so popular that at the peak of his career he kept 126 engravers busy full time turning out copies of works such as *Dignity and Impudence*, *Fighting Dogs Getting Wind*, *The Stag at Bay*.

254

Landseer was knighted in 1850 and when he died in 1873 he left over £200,000.

Other favourite subjects: the last remnants of regiments bravely meeting their end, jolly cardinals quaffing wine in a panelled room, storms at sea, apple-cheeked farm labourers playing with ragged but healthy children, death-beds, and literary pictures depicting a moment of high domestic drama, or a pious renunciation of something evil, or young love blossoming, or, a very popular form, a dramatic scene which was left unexplained – the Problem picture:

> Good furniture pictures, unworthy of praise, and undeserving of blame.
>
> John Ruskin (1819–1900)
Modern Painters

The taste for Neo-Classical pictures and statues depicting historical or mythical figures was given impetus in the eighteenth century when Pompeii was excavated. This form of art, rendered in highly finished, naturalistic detail, was popular right through the nineteenth century, perhaps due to the fact that much of it was mildly but distinctly erotic. But even if wispily covered breasts and bare marble bottoms were socially acceptable in most Victorian homes, providing the work carried a title like *Innocence* or *Psyche at her Bath*, there was always the danger of offending a prudish guest:

> At breakfast, the first morning after their arrival, Mrs. Disraeli addressed the lady of the house in these words: 'I find that your house is full of indecent pictures.' Knowing well the character of their hostess, dismay might have been observed on the faces of the guests; undaunted, Mrs. Disraeli continued: 'There is a most horrible picture in our bedroom; Disraeli says it is "Venus and Adonis". I have been awake half the night trying to prevent his looking at it.'
>
> William Fraser (1859–1933)
Disraeli and his Day

The account does not specify the method Mrs. Disraeli adopted to divert her husband's attention from the vile painting.

Wordsworth had a nasty experience at the auction rooms:

> I was once walking with him in Pall Mall; we darted into Christie's. A copy of the 'Transfiguration' was at the head of the room, and in the corner a beautiful copy of the 'Cupid and Psyche' (statues) kissing. Cupid is taking her lovely chin, and turning her pouting mouth to meet his while he archly bends his own down, as if saying, 'Pretty dear!' You remember this exquisite group? ... Catching sight of the Cupid, as he and I were coming out, Wordsworth's face reddened, he showed his teeth, and then said in a loud voice, 'THE DEV-V-V-VILS!'
>
> B. R. Haydon (1786–1864)
Letter to Miss Mitford

In 1880 Mark Twain came across a shocker in the Uffizi gallery in Florence:

> There, against the wall, without obstructing rag or leaf, you may look your fill upon the foulest, the vilest, the obscenest picture the world possesses — Titian's Venus. It isn't that she is naked and stretched out on a bed — no, it is the attitude of one of her arms and hand. If I ventured to describe that attitude there would be a fine howl — but there the Venus lies, for anybody to gloat over that wants to — and there she has a right to lie, for she is a work of art, and art has its privileges. I saw a young girl stealing furtive glances at her; I saw young men gazing long and absorbedly at her; I saw aged, infirm men hang upon her charms with a pathetic interest ... There are pictures of nude women which suggest no impure thought — I am well aware of that. I am not railing at such. What I am trying to emphasize is the fact that Titian's Venus is very far from being one of that sort. Without any question it was painted for a bagnio and it was probably refused because it was a trifle too strong.
>
> Mark Twain (1835–1910)
> *A Tramp Abroad*

Mark Twain's reaction, clearly made after long and careful study of the picture, is probably a good example of the Victorian double-standard in operation. He often maintained that it was quite proper for an author to strike attitudes in his books which were at variance with the author's genuine opinions and that it was important for an author to maintain his public 'face'. Twain in private enjoyed a bit of smut and wrote at least one mild piece of pornography, but his public utterances tended to be sternly moralistic. Perhaps this was due to the control exercised by his wife, who censored him as well as his work.

By the middle of the nineteenth century there was a strong feeling among young artists that Academic teachings based on the Old Masters of the Italian Renaissance were no longer relevant. This point of view was put into print, in a famous passage, by John Ruskin, who went even further and blamed the Renaissance for debasing the whole development of European art:

> Instant degradation followed in every direction — a flood of folly and hypocrisy. Mythologies, ill-understood at first, then perverted into feeble sensualities, take the place of the representation of Christian subjects, which had become blasphemous under the treatment of men like the Caracci. Gods without power, satyrs without rusticity, nymphs without innocence, men without humanity, gather into idiot groups upon the polluted canvas, and scenic affectations encumber the streets with preposterous marble. Lower and lower declines the level of abused intellect; the base school of landscape gradually usurps the place of the historical painting, which had sunk into prurient pedantry, — the Alsatian sublimities of Salvator, the confectionery idealities of Claude, the dull manufacture of Gaspar and Canaletto, south of the Alps, and in the north the patient devotion of besotted lives to delineation of bricks and fogs, cattle and ditchwater.
>
> John Ruskin (1819–1900)
> *Stones of Venice*

An outcome of this restlessness with the state of things in the art world was the formation, in 1848, of what was probably the first group of British artists to band together, the Pre-Raphaelite Brotherhood. The original members were John Everett Millais, William Holman Hunt and Dante Gabriel Rossetti.

It was all a little muddled, very Romantic, literary and revolutionary. There was all the claptrap of a secret brotherhood: a magazine, a mysterious symbol, PRB, to be put onto their paintings, even a private jargon full of oddly hearty, jolly phrases.

One of their main objectives was to return to the unsophisticated, sincere style of painting which had existed in the Middle Ages before Raphael and other Renaissance painters put a gloss on. In fact, they knew hardly anything about medieval painting, but they succeeded in evolving a new style of painting very much at variance with current fashion. Wherever possible they used actual locations: Holman Hunt went to Palestine to paint sacred subjects, like *The Scapegoat*, against their real backgrounds. And real props: a later follower, Ford Madox Brown, had a trying time carting lambs from Clapham Common daily for his picture *The Pretty Baa Lambs*. They achieved a new kind of realism by the painstaking application of minute detail.

In 1850 Millais exhibited his *Christ in the House of his Parents*. In keeping with the Brotherhood's aims the picture, showing Christ as a boy being comforted by his mother in his father's workshop after cutting his hand, was painted realistically, from models, and represented the Holy Family as ordinary people:

> In the foreground of the carpenter's shop is a hideous, wry-necked, blubbering, red-haired boy in a nightgown, who appears to have received a poke playing in an adjacent gutter, and to be holding it up for the contemplation of a kneeling woman, so horrible in her ugliness that (supposing it were possible for any human creature to exist for a moment with that dislocated throat) she would stand out from the rest of the company as a monster in the vilest cabaret in France or the lowest gin-shop in England.
>
> Charles Dickens (1812–1870)
> *Household Words*

> This hostility, which Dickens regretted later when the work of the Brotherhood became widely admired, was shared by most critics at the time. *The Times* found the treatment of the theme 'revolting', and the carefully painted detail 'loathsome'.

Four years later Holman Hunt exhibited *The Light of the World*, a deeply religious picture showing Christ standing in a doorway with a lantern:

> The face of this wild fantasy, though earnest and religious, is not that of a Saviour. It expresses such a strange mingling of disgust, fear, and imbecility, that we turn from it to relieve the sight. The manipulation, though morbidly delicate and laboured, is not so mas-

sive as the mute passion displayed in the general feeling and detail demands. Altogether this picture is a failure.

Athenaeum, 6 May 1854

> The picture was not a failure with the public. So many reproductions of it were sold that it became the most popular religious painting ever painted in Britain. Perhaps the nearest thing the Church of England has had to an ikon.

Some of the painters associated with the Pre-Raphaelite Brotherhood were also poets, which was not surprising considering how much of Romantic art and music was based upon literary matter. But one painter-poet who worked with the Brotherhood briefly had a few more strings to his lyre; William Morris was not only a painter and a poet but he also designed books and type-faces, he founded the Arts and Crafts movement, he translated the Icelandic sagas, illuminated manuscripts, founded the Society for the Protection of Ancient Buildings, was a socialist orator, a dyer, and a designer of, amongst other things, church interiors, murals, furniture, jewellery, glass, wallpaper, carpets, tapestries, printed materials, and stained-glass windows:

> Of course we all know that Morris was a wonderful all-round man, but the act of walking round him has always tired me.
>
> Max Beerbohm (1872–1956)
> Quoted by S. N. Behrman: *Conversation with Max*

Art in England in the middle of the nineteenth century gently bogged down to a state where much of it was financially successful and most of it was commonplace and trivial. The attempt by the Pre-Raphaelites to break away from the influence of the Renaissance was by taking a step backwards in time and so was hardly an advance, more an interesting arabesque. As music and the theatre were also more or less in the same state it was clear that the political, social and economic influences on Victorian life were such that although minor art flourished, it was extremely unlikely that any major breakthrough in the arts could get under way, let alone be recognized and approved. If a new, modern vision of art was to arise and replace the traditional approach then it had to come from somewhere else.

If a single painting could be said to have been the hinge between traditional and modern art it is Édouard Manet's *Déjeuner sur l'herbe*. This was exhibited in Paris in 1863 at the Salon des Refusés, a 'fringe' salon instituted by the Emperor Napoleon III to exhibit the work of artists which had been rejected by the Paris Salon. The picture showed two young men enjoying a picnic in the Bois de Boulogne with two girls, but one of the girls was clad in a slip and the other was naked, and the picture was totally un-Academic in its lack of conventional finish, its drawing and its use of colour.

The public mostly laughed at the picture, but the critics were irate, almost to a man; some because of Manet's unconventional technique:

> Is this drawing? Is this painting? ... I see garments without feeling the anatomical structure that supports them and explains their movements. I see boneless fingers and heads without skulls. I see sidewhiskers made of two strips of black cloth that could have been glued to the cheeks. What else do I see? The artist's lack of conviction and sincerity.
>
> Jules Castagnary (1831–1870)
> *Salons*

Some because they resented Manet borrowing the design of his picture from two wholly respectable sources: Giorgione's *Concert champêtre* and Raphael's drawing, *Judgement of Paris*:

> Giorgione had conceived the happy idea of a *fête champêtre*, in which, although the gentlemen were dressed, the ladies were not ... now some wretched Frenchman has translated this into modern French realism, on a much larger scale, and with the horrible modern French costume instead of the graceful old Venetian one.
>
> Philip Gilbert Hamerton (1834–1894)
> *Fine Arts Quarterly Review*, Oct. 1863

> Much the same objection that Sir Joshua Reynolds brought to Benjamin West's *Death of Wolfe*.

Some critics were considerably alarmed by the thought that as they could not understand the picture it was probably a hoax:

> This is a young man's practical joke, a shameful open sore not worth exhibiting this way.
>
> Louis Étienne (nineteenth century)
> *Le Jury et les exposants*

But most of the critics just took a long and baneful look and decided that the picture was immoral and disgusting and common:

> The nude, when painted by vulgar men, is inevitably indecent.
>
> Philip Gilbert Hamerton (1834–1894)
> *Fine Arts Quarterly Review*, Oct. 1863

> Unfortunately, the nude hasn't a decent figure and one can't think of anything uglier than the man stretched out next to her, who hasn't even thought of taking off, out of doors, his horrid padded cap. It is the contrast of a creature so inappropriate in a pastoral scene with this undraped bather that is so shocking.
>
> Thoré (1807–1869)
> *L'Indépendance Belge*

> The French never did like the picture and only with difficulty was the nation persuaded to buy the picture when Manet died.

Over the next decade the modernist painters in Paris broke even further away from tradition; they began painting everyday objects and commonplace scenes; they used the new knowledge of the spectrum to experiment with putting spots or globs of primary colours side by side on the canvas instead of mixing them on the palette; and they were not so much concerned with painting the subject as painting the effect the subject had on their eye through the play of light in between.

The first exhibition of the Impressionist painters, as they came to be called, was held in the photographer Nadar's studios, 35 boulevard des Capucines, on 15 April 1874. It included pictures by Cézanne, Boudin, Degas, Monet, Pissarro, Renoir and Sisley.

As an American writer pointed out later:

> The vitality of a new movement in art or letters can be pretty accurately gauged by the fury it arouses.
>
> Logan Pearsall Smith (1865–1946)
> *Afterthoughts*

On those terms Impressionism was full of vitality:

> This school has abolished two things: line, without which it is impossible to reproduce the form of a living being or an object; and colour, which gives form the appearance of reality ... the practitioners fall into a senseless, mad, grotesque mess, fortunately without precedent in the history of art, for it is quite simply the negation of the most elementary rules of drawing and painting. A child's scrawls have a naïveté and a sincerity that make you smile, but the excesses of this school are nauseating or revolting.
>
> Émile Cardon (nineteenth century)
> *La Presse*

It was not the sort of painting likely to **appeal** to the Pre-Raphaelites:

> The new French School is simply putrescence and decomposition.
>
> Dante Gabriel Rossetti (1828–1882)
> Letter

Or to the Church of England:

> Degas is nothing but a peeping Tom, behind the coulisses, and among the dressing-rooms of the ballet-dancers, noting only travesties on fallen debased womanhood, most disgusting and offensive. It demands no unusual penetration to detect on these walls that satanic and infernal art whose inspirations are verily set on fires of Hell.
>
> (nineteenth century)
> *Churchman*

The unconventional way in which they handled colour was particularly baffling and exasperating:

> Just try to explain to Monsieur Renoir that the torso of a woman is not a mass of decomposing flesh, its green and violet spots indicating the state of complete putrefaction of a corpse.
>
> Albert Wolff (nineteenth century)
> *Le Figaro*

The painting which seemed to most critics to epitomize the dangers and delusions of Impressionism was Cézanne's *A Modern Olympia*. A lady critic (under a male pseudonym) wrote of it:

M. Cézanne gives the impression of being a sort of madman who paints in a fit of *delirium tremens* ... why look for a dirty joke or a scandalous theme in the Olympia? In reality it is only one of the weird shapes generated by hashish.

'Marc de Montifaud' (nineteenth century)
L'Artiste

Many people who were upset and worried by what *The Times* called 'the revolution that has taken place in the art of painting' hopefully put it down to hashish-smoking, drink or general moral turpitude among the artists who lived *la vie Bohème*.

Until Cézanne, painters had been looked upon as a fairly respectable segment of society; slightly strange, usually poor, but, when successful, open to admiration and friendship, though not to social equality:

Society is so constituted in England, that it is useless for celebrated artists to think of bringing their families into the highest circles, where themselves are admitted only on account of their genius. Their wives and daughters must be content to remain at home.

Samuel Rogers (1763–1865)
Table-Talk of Samuel Rogers

Rogers was talking about John Hoppner, a fashionable portrait painter of the late eighteenth century whose wife and daughter grumbled that they were never asked to dine with his Duchesses and Dukes; to which Hoppner had to admit, 'I might as well attempt to take the York waggon with me as you.'

There had been wretchedly poor painters, and beastly painters who left their wives and got drunk, but in the main painters behaved like everybody else socially. Those of them who managed to make their fortunes enjoyed their fine houses, servants, coach and civic honours. And painters dressed like everybody else. Cézanne's fellow Impressionists were well scrubbed, with neatly trimmed beards, clean boots and sober clothes; Fantin-Latour's picture of Manet and his group, *A Studio in the Batignolles Quarter*, which includes Renoir, Zola and Monet, has been described as resembling, amongst other things, Jesus painting among the disciples, doctors attending an anatomy lesson, and a meeting of up-and-coming naval architects.

Cézanne was different. He was the embodiment of the modern concept of the Artist as Genius, totally preoccupied with his talent and quite indifferent to considerations of social esteem, his own personal comfort or other people's feelings. He was unkempt, foul-mouthed and filthy; he once refused to shake hands with Manet on the grounds that he had not washed for eight days. He was a nervy, brooding figure, sometimes trundling his canvases to the Salon, where they were refused, in a cart. When somebody once asked him politely what was the subject of his new submission to the Salon, he replied 'a pot of shit':

The first wild man of modern art.
Roger Fry (1866–1934)
Cézanne: A Study of his Development

Meanwhile, back in Britain, the Royal Academy and painters of 'good furniture pictures' were going from strength to strength. Sir Edward Poynter and Sir Frederic – later Lord – Leighton led taste away from the Pre-Raphaelites and back to the marble and maidens of Victorian Neo-Classicism. In 1869 they were joined by a Dutchman, Lawrence Alma-Tadema (knighted in 1899), who specialized in rendering the surface texture of his marble columns, slave-girls and fur so realistically that the public had to be restrained from leaping forward and stroking them.

The first picture Alma-Tadema exhibited in England, *The Pyrrhic Dance*, was so enthusiastically received that he moved to England and became a British subject. Ruskin wrote of the picture:

The general effect was exactly like a microscopic view of a small detachment of black beetles, in search of a dead rat.
John Ruskin (1819–1900)
The Art of England: 'Classic and Gothic'

Ruskin continued to be implacably opposed to the pictures then being painted by Academicians:

I takes and paints,
Hears no complaints,
And sells before I'm dry;
Till savage Ruskin
He sticks his tusk in,
Then nobody will buy.
Shirley Brooks (1816–1874)
Punch, 1856

One rebel artist who was influenced by the new work being done in Paris was the American painter James McNeill Whistler, who had met a number of the leading French painters and whose picture *The White Girl* was the most praised exhibit in the Paris Salon des Refusés in 1863. He moved to London in 1859 and began to develop a style much inspired by Japanese art. In defiance of the Victorian convention that every picture should tell a story he painted atmospheric, moody scenes in soft, fuzzy colours, and, in keeping with his aesthetic approach, he called his pictures by musical terms such as 'nocturne', 'symphony' and 'harmony'.

One of these pictures, *Symphony in Grey and Green*, was exhibited at the Dudley Gallery in 1872:

I never saw anything so impudent on the walls of any exhibition, in any country, as last year in London. It was a daub professing to be a 'harmony in pink and white' (or some such nonsense); absolute rubbish, and which had taken about a quarter of an hour to scrawl or daub—it had no pretence to be called painting. The price asked for it was two hundred and fifty guineas.

John Ruskin (1819–1900)
Val d'Arno: Lecture III

To Ruskin, absorbed in a number of enlightened projects like warding off the soul-destroying effects of the Industrial Revolution, encouraging economic reform and setting up a social Utopia, almost all aspects of Whistler must have seemed loathsome: his dandyism; little breakfast parties in his house on the Embankment with each wall painted a different colour; his blue butter and tinted rice-pudding; his efforts, like those of the 'clever peasant' Constable, to find beauty where others saw only ugliness; his acceptance of the new heresy that the purpose of art was not to elevate or improve but just to be good art.

The old ethic was that art—a picture, a piece of sculpture, a garden—should be either Beautiful, filling the breast of the spectator with serenity and a love of goodness, or it should be Sublime, causing the spectator to start back in awe at the great mystery of nature and reflect for a moment on the insignificance of his own puny being. It was not the free, loose use of colour in Whistler's pictures that troubled Ruskin: Turner had been looser and freer fifty years previously. It was Whistler's whole approach to painting. Whereas Turner's paintings, even those consisting almost wholly of what Constable called 'tinted steam', were Sublime in intent, Whistler's decorative studies of bits of the Thames seemed merely ridiculous.

And so when Whistler exhibited *The Falling Rocket, or a Nocturne in Black and Gold* at the first exhibition of the new Grosvenor Gallery, Ruskin returned to the attack with a piece which expressed the exasperation which most pre-Impressionism critics and artists felt with the New Art. Whistler brought an action for libel which made Ruskin's words probably the best known in the whole history of art criticism:

I have seen, and heard, much of cockney impudence before now; but never expected to hear a coxcomb ask two hundred guineas for flinging a pot of paint in the public's face.

John Ruskin (1819–1900)
Fors Clavigera: Letters to the Workers and Labourers of Great Britain, No. 79

The whole episode abounded in small ironies, beginning with Ruskin addressing his art criticism to the workers and labourers of Great Britain, none of whom would have been allowed in to see the picture. Whistler won the case and was awarded a farthing damages. The costs bankrupted him. Ruskin, too old and unbalanced to give evidence, had given most of his fortune away and his costs had to be paid for him by friends. Whistler eventually sold the picture for eight hundred guineas.

The aesthetic cult of the late nineteenth century had roots which went as far back as 1835, when Théophile Gautier, in *Mademoiselle de Maupan*, wrote that everything beautiful was good and everything ugly was bad; that roses were preferable to potatoes and that pretty vases were better than useful ones. His friend Baudelaire wrote: 'To glorify the cult of images is my single great passion.' It was an attitude which was incomprehensible to old-guard Victorians:

> What right has the art of painting, or building, or making objects beautiful, to be called Art, *par excellence*, any more than the art of making shoes? A picture at best can only represent faithfully the scene or incident to which it refers, and anyone can judge of it who has a good eye and knows the story.
>
> *Spectator*, 1864

The aesthetic movement encouraged its adherents to cultivate taste and beauty in their style of life as well as in their art. The languid, droopy appearance which they affected in their clothes and manner gave rise to much mirth in solid, middle-class journals like *Punch*.

In 1881, Gilbert and Sullivan produced the comic opera *Patience* which mocked many of the aesthetes' affectations.

The hero Bunthorne, who reflected elements of Whistler and Oscar Wilde, described himself during a duet in the third act as:

> A most intense young man,
> A soulful-eyed young man,
> An ultra-poetical, super-aesthetical,
> Out-of-the-way young man!...
>
> A Japanese young man,
> A blue-and-white young man,
> Francesca da Rimini, miminy, piminy,
> *Je-ne-sais-quoi* young man! ...
>
> A pallid and thin young man,
> A haggard and lank young man,
> A greenery-yallery, Grosvenor Gallery,
> Foot-in-the-grave young man!
>
> W. S. Gilbert (1836–1911)
> *Patience*

The new directions in which art was moving brought it into the awareness of a new public. Passions were aroused between rival coteries, and devotees of one school would hotly defend it against the others. Women began to become involved:

> Enthusiasm about art is become a function of the average female being, which she performs with precision and a sort of haunting sprightliness.
>
> Robert Louis Stevenson (1850–1894)

Female admirers of art tended to hunt in packs:

> Mrs. Ballinger is one of the ladies who pursue Culture in bands, as
> though it were dangerous to meet it alone.
>
> Edith Wharton (1862–1937)

And take it very seriously:

> All loved art in a seemly way,
> With an earnest soul and a capital A.
>
> James Jeffrey Roche (1847–1908)
> *The V-A-S-E, and other Bric-à-Brac*

The capital 'A' was significant to those who believed in Art for Art's
sake; for Art, as distinct from art, came to be used as a kind of aesthetic
classification meaning, roughly, a search for pure beauty, an end in
itself:

> When the flush of a new-born sun fell first on Eden's green and gold,
> Our father Adam sat under the Tree and scratched with a stick in
> the mould;
> And the first rude sketch that the world had seen was joy to his
> mighty heart,
> Till the Devil whispered behind the leaves, 'It's pretty, but is it
> Art?'
> Wherefore he called to his wife, and fled to fashion his work anew—
> The first of his race who cared a fig for the first most dread review.
>
> Rudyard Kipling (1865–1936)
> *The Conundrum of the Workshops*

Reviews, both dread and favourable, had considerable influence in
a society which supported a great number of newspapers and journals,
even though the difficulty of putting a visual experience into words
dogged art criticism:

> It has been the fate of arts to be enveloped in mysterious and in-
> comprehensible language.
>
> Sir Joshua Reynolds (1723–1792)
> *Discourse VII*

> This tendency to degenerate into a mere mouthing of meaningless
> words seems to be peculiar to so-called art criticism. There has never
> been, so far as I know, a critic of painting who wrote about it
> simply and clearly, as Sainte-Beuve, say, wrote about books, or
> Schumann and Berlioz about music. Even the most orthodox of the
> brethren, when he finds himself before a canvas that genuinely
> moves him, takes refuge in esoteric winks and grimaces and mysteri-
> ous gurgles and belches.
>
> H. L. Mencken (1880–1956)
> *Selected Prejudices*

One Academy painter, in an attack on those critics who approved
of the new styles of painting, accused them of preferring to write about
difficult modern work because it gave them a chance to show off:

> ... Alas! for Art,
> When its disciples care not to impart
> Their meaning fully; but, like poor tide-waiters,
> Just leave it to the whim of the spectators.
> This suits the critics, for they must be bold;
> From a gold-digging nuggets of pure gold
> The veriest fool may reap; but to extract
> Gold from a dunghill is a godlike act.
>> Henry Nelson O'Neil, A.R.A. (1817–1880)
>> *The Age of Stucco*

Henry O'Neil, who dabbled in writing verse and playing the viola, exhibited stirring pictures like *The Lay of King Canute*, *Mozart's Last Moments* and *The Landing of H.R.H. the Princess Alexandra at Gravesend*.

A distinguished French poet blamed writers for the whole thing:

> This modern painting has been made by writers: if they would only keep quiet it would disappear in a year.
>> Paul Valéry (1871–1945)

They did not keep quiet. It was an art critic, Roger Fry, who gave England its first good long look at the work of the progressive French painters. In 1910 he mounted an exhibition at the Grafton Gallery of what he called the Post-Impressionists, mainly pictures by Cézanne, Van Gogh and Gauguin. These were a revelation to British artists and changed the course of painting in this country.

The exhibition created a tremendous amount of interest, even with the general public, and opinions were strongly expressed:

> Works of idleness and impotent stupidity, a pornographic show ... The drawing is on the level of that of an untaught child of seven or eight years old, the sense of colour that of a tea-tray painter, the method that of a schoolboy who wipes his fingers on a slate after spitting on them.
>> Wilfred Scawen Blunt (1840–1922)
>> *My Diaries*, II

The *Morning Post* recommended taking drastic action:

> If the movement is spreading it should be treated like the rat-plague in Suffolk. The source of the infection ought to be destroyed ... Van Gogh is the typical matoid and degenerate of the modern sociologist. *Jeune Fille au Bleuet* and *Cornfield with Blackbirds* are the visualized ravings of an adult maniac. If that is art it must be ostracised, as the poets were banished from Plato's republic.
>> Robert Ross (1869–1918)
>> *Morning Post*

Much of the adverse reaction came from the customary British suspicion of anything new and French, a fear that the strange pictures might be an elaborate hoax, and a distaste for the gregarious way in which the French painters lived *la vie Bohème*, all in a bunch, producing their art in waves. As a poet and art critic expressed it, in a rather splendid sentence:

We in England don't have movements if we can help it.

Laurence Binyon (1869–1943)
Saturday Review

Perhaps we didn't before 1910, but after 1910 Britain, and most other countries, experienced a whole stream of movements: Fauvism, Cubism, Expressionism, Futurism, Neo-Plasticism, Vorticism, Symbolism, Dadaism, Surrealism, Pop Art, etc.

Most of these movements were accompanied by a twentieth-century innovation, the art manifesto: literature intended to explain what the movement was trying to do:

Every time a new revolutionist gives a show he issues a manifesto explaining his aims and achievements, and in every such manifesto there is the same blowsy rodomontadizing that one finds in the texts of the critics.

H. L. Mencken (1880–1956)
Selected Prejudices

Modern Art had arrived in what seemed to those who didn't understand it, or didn't like it, or both, all its ugly nastiness:

A morbid and decadent youth
Says – 'Beauty is greater than Truth' –
And by Beauty I mean
The obscure, the obscene –
The diseased, the decayed, the uncouth.

Cecil J. Sibbert
The Outspan: Modern Art as I See It

Cecil Sibbert was Chairman of the South African National Gallery.

From all the slimy muck that is creeping into so-called art nowadays, Heaven help us!

Tom Walls (1883–1949)
Letter to Sir Alfred Munnings, President of the Royal Academy

The famous actor's interests were centred upon riding to hounds and training racehorses. His ashes were scattered over the Derby course at Epsom.

Many of the painters used a deceptively simple style:

Dufy is merely a childish scene-painter, a scribbler of all sorts of nursery nonsense.

Sir Lionel Lindsay (1874–1961)
Addled Art

A famous judge wrote:

Klee's pictures seem to me to resemble, not pictures, but a sample-book of patterns of linoleum.

The Hon. Sir Cyril Asquith (1890–1954)
Letter to Sir Alfred Munnings

One of the more controversial figures of modern art, always worth a giggle to the newspapers, was the sculptor Jacob Epstein. When his statue *Rima* was unveiled in Hyde Park it was greeted with the usual mixture of mirth, dismay and puzzlement.

An elderly novelist wrote:

> Since hearing from you I've seen the Epstein. My dear fellow! How can you use the word aesthetic in its connection? It's nothing but a piece of unrealized affectation. I confess it makes me feel physically a little sick. The wretched woman has two sets of breasts and a hip joint like a merry thought. No, really!
>
> John Galsworthy (1867–1933)
> Letter to Edward Garnett, 14 June 1925

The strangeness of Epstein's sculpture together with the oddness of Gertrude Stein's poetry and the seemingly inpenetrable mystery of Einstein's Theory of Relativity brought forth a limerick. Dr. Bergen Evans called it 'the Philistine's Favourite':

> There's a wonderful family called Stein,
> There's Gert and there's Epp and there's Ein;
> Gert's poems are bunk,
> Epp's statues are junk,
> And no one can understand Ein.
>
> Anon.

Gertrude Stein, a rich American experimental poet who lived and worked in Paris, was something of an influence on the young Picasso, if only because she bought some of his pictures. They were both, he in art and she in literature, attempting to break new ground:

> They are in my belief turning out the most Godalmighty rubbish that is to be found.
>
> Leo Stein (1872–1947)
>
> Gertrude Stein's brother Leo, an art critic and collector, did not share all his sister's tastes.

Miss Stein's interest in revolutionary movements in art caused her name to be connected, wrongly or rightly, with many of the wilder forays into new territory:

> Gertrude Stein is the mama of dada.
>
> Clifton Fadiman (b. 1904)
> *Appreciations*
>
> Dadaism was founded by expatriate Bohemian artists in Zurich in 1916. The word 'dada' was given to the movement by the Rumanian poet Tristan Tzara at 6 p.m. on 6th February, 1916, according to the leading dada artist Hans Arp, who claims that he was present at the time with his twelve children and a brioche struck up his left nostril.

Modern art was not only distrusted by many, perhaps most, of the general public; politicians, particularly those who believed that anything so mysterious and potentially inflammatory as art should be kept under strict state control, also became alarmed. Modern art seemed to them to contain the seeds of decadence, to be the tool of an international conspiracy aiming to plunge the world into anarchy. In 1937 Hitler put on an exhibition of what he called Decadent Art, mostly the cream of German Expressionism but including some of Picasso's work, and subjected the German nation to a steamy denunciation of it.

Much the same thing went on in the Soviet Union. It would seem that the anger aroused by modern art in totalitarian bosoms overcame political considerations; the work of Picasso, a fervent and notable Communist, was attacked as strongly by spokesmen of the Soviet Union as by Dr Goebbels:

> His work presents an unhealthy apology for the aesthetics of capitalism, provoking the resentment of ordinary people ... His sickness has created atrocities that are repellent. Every one of his paintings deforms man, his body and his face.
>
> V. Kemenov

In the U.S.A., too, leading figures thumped tables and raised their voices in anger, accusing modern painters of breaking down moral standards and being thoroughly un-American. In 1949 a U.S. Congressman, speaking through a red mist, used phrases remarkably similar to those used by Dr. Goebbels and the Soviet art critics when he warned his countrymen what modern art was aiming to do to the old homeland:

> So-called modern or contemporary art in our modern beloved country contains all the isms of depravity, decadence and destruction. Cubism aims to destroy by designed disorder. Futurism aims to destroy by a machine myth. Dadaism aims to destroy by ridicule. Expressionism aims to destroy by aping the primitive and insane. Klee, one of its three founders, went to the insane asylums for his inspiration. Abstractionism aims to destroy by the creation of brainstorms. Surrealism aims to destroy by the denial of reason. Salvador Dali ... Spanish surrealist, is now in the United States. He is reported to carry with him at all times a picture of Lenin. Abstractionism, or non-objectivity in so-called modern art, was spawned as a simon pure, Russian communist product ... Who has brought down this curse upon us; who has let into our homeland this horde of germ-carrying art vermin?
>
> Representative George A. Dondero, of Michigan
> Speech to Congress, 16 Aug. 1949

A fine example of what the Irish-American writer Ernest Boyd termed 'Ku-Klux-Kriticism'.

This kind of political pronouncement on changes of taste in art did not happen in Britain. The government traditionally did not involve itself in the art world, even when its help was needed, and until very recent years politicians held the view expressed by Lord Melbourne when he was asked to do something about setting up a system of schools to teach design:

God help the Minister who meddles with art.

William Lamb, second Viscount Melbourne (1779–1848)
Quoted by F. W. Haydon: *Memoirs of B. R. Haydon*

British politicians tended to leave problems of art to the Royal Academy to deal with.

Ever since its inception the Academy had come under fire from critics, who continually warned that it was not where the good painters were to be found:

The pride and self-respect which are the natural concomitants of genius will be more likely to keep a man out of the Academy than bring him into it.

The Times, 20 July 1830

The reputation of the Academy has got to a point where election would be positively distressing to a serious painter.

Evening Standard, 22 Feb. 1961

But when the modern art movements were gaining momentum at the beginning of the century the Academy was in a position of great power. The last quarter of the nineteenth century had been a golden era for those artists who could paint the sort of pictures which an enormous number of picture-buyers wanted. And a large section of this middle-class, rich public took its instructions as to what was currently tasteful from the Academy exhibitions.

Rebel painters attacked the Academy for its unwillingness to recognize any merit in modern art and its patronage of mediocre and superficial work. And it was an occasion for sadness and anger when, as frequently happened, a young painter lost interest in the *avant-garde* and was received into the bosom of the R.A. One of these was Sir Gerald Kelly, President 1949–1954. As a young man he had studied in Paris and it seemed likely that he would develop his work on progressive lines. But in 1922 he became an associate of the Academy:

He is described in the telephone book as an artist; and the statement might have passed unchallenged indefinitely had not the Royal Academy recently elected him as an associate. He is hardly to be blamed for this disgrace. He struggled manfully. Even at the last moment, when he felt the thunderclouds about to break over his head, he made a last desperate coup to persuade the world that he was an artist by marrying a model. But this device deceived nobody. The evidence of his pictures was too glaring ... It saddens me more than I can say to think of that young life which opened with such brilliant promise, gradually sinking into the slough of repectability. Of course,

it was not as if he had been able to paint; but to me the calamity
is almost as distressing as if that possibility had ever existed.

Aleister Crowley (1875–1947)
The Confessions of Aleister Crowley

The famous 'Great Beast', Crowley, was himself untainted by any suspicion of respectability. He was, oddly, Gerald Kelly's brother-in-law.

From its position of strength, which steadily declined as the twentieth century grew older, the Academy fought against the influence of modern art. It could scarcely have done otherwise; to have accepted modern art would have meant accepting that the principles and traditions of academic art, which had lasted for some six hundred years, were no longer valid.

Succeeding Presidents of the Academy made it clear that they saw little merit in the work of the Impressionists, Cézanne and Matisse, and they poured scorn on the more extreme movements like Cubism, Surrealism and Abstract art.

The arch villain of those to whom modern art was an enemy was Picasso. His range, fame and fertile genius were such that the mere mention of his name was enough to redden the necks of 'a tree should *look* like a tree' traditionalists. So when, in 1949, Sir Alfred Munnings gave his Presidential speech at the Royal Academy dinner, with a distinguished amateur painter as his guest of honour, his reference to Picasso showed plainly what he thought of the man who was then arguably the world's greatest living painter:

'On my left I have our newly-elected extraordinary member of the Academy, Mr. Winston Churchill. And I remember him saying to me, "Alfred, if you met Picasso coming down the street, would you join with me in kicking his ... something ... something!" [Laughter.] I said, "Yes, sir! I would!" [Prolonged laughter.]'

Sir Alfred Munnings (1878–1959)
Speech at the Royal Academy Dinner, Burlington House, 28 April 1949

This turned out to be virtually the last of that kind of laugh. The speech, which was broadcast by the B.B.C., was deeply resented by many members of the Academy and there were resignations.

Some later Presidents have tried to close the gap between Academic and modern art, but it is a considerable gap. The rapid social and economic reshuffling of the first fifty years of this century had resulted in the middle dropping out of the art market, leaving only extreme art at one end of the scale and the Academy at the other end. It was in that vanished middle area that the artist used to earn most of his living:

The nineteenth-century artist was lavishly paid for his work, 'art' being a valuable commodity. The last fifty years, however, has seen a steady decline in the value of a newly painted picture, and, since World War Two and the ensuing improverishment, and with the com-

271

ing of the welfare state, the virtual disappearance of the picture-buy-
ing rich-man, the collector of new pictures, the artist no longer has
the temptation to grow rich. At the start of his career, he knows that
what he paints has, as it were, no commercial value. There are various
semi-charitable institutions, and now there are institutes, from which
he can derive support if he pleases or impresses by his extremism.
But there is nothing to be gained by painting a pleasant, a recognizable or comprehensible picture (unless he be so inferior an artist,
and so unimaginative a man that the Royal Academy is, in fact, his
natural home).

Wyndham Lewis (1884–1957)
The Demon of Progress in the Arts

Wyndham Lewis was the founder of Vorticism, an 'advanced' art
movement. He drew a clear distinction between 'advanced' art, which
is what he believed art should be, and 'extreme' art, which he thought
was self-defeating.

Whether or not due to the increasing shortage of cash customers,
art movements certainly became more extreme as the twentieth century
progressed. Many movements turned inwards and became esoteric and
self-exploratory; some experimenting, to the delight of the popular
press, with dramatic techniques such as dragging a naked model, or
riding a bicycle, across wet paint, and cladding a stretch of the coastline
of New South Wales in plastic sheeting.

Once a movement alienated art from human experience it had the
effect of alienating humans from that particular kind of art:

Abstract art? A product of the untalented, sold by the unprincipled
to the utterly bewildered.

Al Capp (b. 1909)
Quoted in *National Observer*, 1 July 1963

Al Capp created the enormously successful American comic strip 'Li'l
Abner'.

Twentieth-century Economic Man put art way down in his list of
priorities:

Few have heard of Fra Luca Parioli, the inventor of double entry
book-keeping; but he has probably had more influence on human
life than has Dante or Michelangelo.

Herbert J. Muller (b. 1905)
The Uses of the Past

Except, sometimes, when looked upon not as a pleasure but as an
investment:

To my mind the old masters are not art; their value is in their
scarcity.

Thomas A. Edison (1847–1931)
Golden Book, 1931

The wonder, it might be argued, is not that Britain has produced
so few great artists but that it has managed to produce any good artists

at all, so little encouragement have they received through the centuries from their own countrymen.

With the doubtful exception of Charles I, who at least amassed a great art collection even if it was almost wholly foreign, and George IV, who was really more interested in the decorative arts, what was written about Queen Elizabeth I could be applied to most of our monarchs:

> There is no evidence that Elizabeth had much taste for painting; but she loved pictures of herself.
>
> Horace Walpole (1717–1797)
Anecdotes of Painting in England

> Walpole revealed in the Preface that he intended the work to be 'The Lives of the English Painters', but he found that the country had produced so few good painters that he was obliged to widen his scope and to change his title.

Stung by the loss to the nation of Sir Robert Walpole's great collection of paintings, which were bought by Catherine the Great of Russia, Wilkes the politician proposed that the government should form a national collection of good pictures. After being prodded by relays of artists for seventy-odd years the government finally laid out a little money and in the 1820s the National Gallery was opened, for all to enjoy:

> How often my Soul visits the National Gallery, and how seldom I go there myself!
>
> Logan Pearsall Smith (1865–1946)
Afterthoughts

Many visitors from other shores reported scathingly on the position of art in England:

> There is nothing on earth more terrible than English music, except English painting. They have no sense of sound, or eye for colour, and I sometimes wonder whether their sense of smell is not equally blunted and dulled: I should not be surprised if they cannot even distinguish between the smell of a ball of horse-dung and an orange.
>
> Heinrich Heine (1797–1856)
Lutezia

> English painting is entirely derivative: it is what study and imitation of the French have made it.
>
> G. J. Renier (twentieth century)
The English: Are they Human?

> Because they have no sun, the English can be neither philosophers nor artists: they have no spark of synthetic genius.
>
> J. P. Oliveira Martins (1845–1894)
A Ingletierra de Hoje

synthetic = constructive.

> Of all supposed English tastes, that of art was the most alluring and treacherous. Once drawn into it, one had small chance of escape, for it had no centre or circumference, no beginning, middle, or end, no object, and no conceivable result as education.
>
> Henry Adams (1838–1918)
> *The Education of Henry Adams*

Karel Čapek, the Czech writer, put it all down to the early loss of Church patronage:

> Art is what is deposited behind glass in galleries, museums and in the rooms of rich people; but it does not move about here in the streets, it does not twinkle from the handsome cornices of windows, it does not take up its stand at the street-corner like a statue, it does not greet you in a winsome and monumental speech. I do not know: perhaps it is only Protestantism which has drained this country dry in an artistic respect.
>
> Karel Čapek (1890–1938)
> *Letters from England*

Under the medieval Church English artists certainly did very good work, as good as any in Europe, in illuminating manuscripts, designing stained-glass windows and building Perpendicular cathedrals. Perhaps more remarkable were the contributions which British artists made in later centuries when, in the teeth of the fashion for continental culture, they established a lead in the fields of miniature painting, landscape gardening, and painting water-colours.

It could be said that the golden era for British artists arrived about the time of Hogarth and his prints, when the patron was replaced by the customer, and it finished after the First World War when the supply of customers dwindled.

It is highly unlikely that the need for a bit of visual stimulation from colours and shapes has declined. What is much more likely is that the need is now met by the ordinary impedimenta of living: methods of colour reproduction and standards of graphic design have improved rapidly since the First World War and a citizen is surrounded now by stimulating images on record sleeves, carrier-bags, posters and advertisements, clothes and furnishings, television and the cinema. If a picture is needed to brighten up a wall anybody can, and most young people do, cut what they want from the pages of a Sunday Colour Supplement. The role played by art and artists has, it seems, changed:

> Painting has become, all art has become, a game by which man distracts himself. And you may say that it has always been like that, but now it's entirely a game. What is fascinating is that it is getting more difficult for the artist. He must really deepen the game to be any good at all, so he can make life a bit more exciting.
>
> Francis Bacon (b. 1909)
> *Theories of Modern Art*

The Royal Academy still provides a continuity of tradition in its schools and exhibitions. The Summer Exhibition remains an important event in the London social season and débutantes, however much they would prefer to be galloping Blaze over the water-meadow, dutifully saunter the galleries making suitable noises. The Academy's series of special exhibitions has had some remarkable successes, producing queues of a length and orderliness rivalling those outside Lenin's tomb in Red Square.

In 1975 the Academy mounted a special exhibition to commemorate the two hundredth anniversary of the birth of Turner. In his will Turner left nearly three hundred paintings and nearly twenty thousand water-colours to the nation, together with a large sum of money, so that they could be on permanent exhibition. Legal problems arose and the government of the day managed to duck out of its responsibilities; Turner's charitable fund for artists was never formed and the great bulk of his work was stacked away in cellars, only the cream being exhibited. The 1975 Turner Exhibition brought a large and wide selection of his work to light and the public was able to see his pictures as he had intended them to in his will. The Exhibition was an outstanding success and Britain made up its mind that Turner was Britain's greatest painting genius.

Perhaps the best comment on it all came from Turner himself. He was once asked at a Royal Academy dinner to make a statement about art. His reply, in its entirety, was:

It's a rummy business.
J. M. W. Turner (1775–1851)

FOOD AND DRINK

Food and Drink

Food, like sex and the weather, is an ever-interesting topic of conversation and ever since man learnt to write he has expressed himself forcibly on the subject of those foods and drinks which he disliked. Which is hardly surprising. Nobody can be expected to affect academic detachment about something which he puts into his mouth and swallows.

Man has always been wary about unfamiliar forms of nourishment:

> A poor man begged food at the Hall lately. The cook gave him some vermicelli soup. He ladled it about some time with the spoon, and then returned it to her, saying, 'I am a poor man, it is true, and I am very hungry, but yet I cannot eat broth with maggots in it.'
>
> William Cowper (1731–1800)
> Letter to Lady Hesketh, 27 Nov. 1787

Each new addition to the range of edible matter might have been a giant stride ahead for mankind but it must have been a nervy step for the person making it:

> He was a very valiant man who first adventured on eating of oysters.
>
> Thomas Fuller (1608–1661)
> *The History of the Worthies of England*

> Many others are credited with this statement, or something like it, including James I. The valiant man was probably Chinese as China seems to have eaten oysters before any other nation. At the time of Thomas Fuller oysters were extremely cheap and were looked down upon as rather nasty things which the poor ate. A hundred years later Boswell recorded that Dr. Johnson slipped out to buy his cat some oysters rather than embarrass his negro servant who might then have taken it out on the cat. During the nineteenth century oysters began to become scarce and their price rose sufficiently high for them to become socially acceptable.

Such has been the importance of food to the human race both as a source of pleasure and as fuel that almost everything we eat or drink has at some time or other been denounced as illegal, immoral, irreligious, dangerous or nasty.

Even the humblest of vegetables:

> Abstain from beans.
>
> Pythagoras (sixth century B.C.)

279

Quite what the Philosopher of Samos meant by his famous maxim has been debated ever since. One school of thought holds that Pythagoras believed that all living matter, e.g. beans, held the souls of the dead and that Pythagoras lost his life because, being pursued, he would not escape across a field of beans. According to the writings of Diogenes Laertius, who was gossipy but inaccurate, Aristotle thought Pythagoras banished beans because they resembled the testicles. Others, like Plutarch, Cicero and St. Jerome, believed he was warning against beans because they were an aphrodisiac; St. Jerome went as far as to forbid nuns to eat the things because, he wrote, *in partibus genitalibus titillationes producunt*. Later writers like John Lyly and Thomas Fuller decided that as beans were used by the Greeks in voting for magistrates Pythagoras was warning his followers to stay away from politics. It might just have been a comradely warning, as nowadays a public-spirited man might pencil on the canteen menu 'Don't have the pie'. But majority opinion insists that Pythagoras was merely warning of the inescapable aftermath of bean-eating:

My bowels shall sound like an harp.

Isaiah xvi. 11

This was certainly Dean Swift's opinion, as he stated quite clearly in his advice on how to bed a newly married couple:

Keep them to wholesome food confin'd,
Nor let them taste what causes wind:
'Tis this the sage of Samos means,
Forbidding his disciples beans.

Jonathan Swift (1667–1745)

Cauliflower has been attacked for pretentiousness:

Cauliflower is nothing but cabbage with a college education.

Mark Twain (1835–1910)
Pudd'nhead Wilson's Calendar

And the taste of cabbage, when it has been boiled in traditional English style, has been adversely described:

Boiled cabbage *à l'Anglaise* is something compared with which steamed coarse newsprint bought from bankrupt Finnish salvage dealers and heated over smoky oil stoves is an exquisite delicacy. Boiled British cabbage is something lower than ex-Army blankets stolen by dispossessed Goanese doss-housekeepers who used them to cover busted-down hen houses in the slum district of Karachi, found them useless, threw them in anger into the Indus, where they were recovered by convicted beachcombers with grappling irons, who cut them in strips with shears and stewed them in sheep-dip before they were sold to dying beggars. Boiled cabbage!

Cassandra (William Connor) (1909–1967)
Daily Mirror, 30 June 1950

Perhaps the American equivalent of English boiled cabbage is, at any rate to children, the dreaded spinach:

MOTHER: It's broccoli, dear.
CHILD: I say it's spinach, and I say the hell with it.

Caption to cartoon by Carl Rose, 1935

280

Even the gentle lettuce was attacked as an enemy of love-making:

Lettyse doth extynct veneryous actes.

Andrew Boorde (1490?–1549)
A Dyetary of Helth

veneryous=sexual

Andrew Boorde's warnings on these pages as to the effects of various foods upon amatory encounters should not be lightly dismissed. He was no detached theorist. A great traveller, and doctor, he was the unfrocked suffragan bishop of Chichester and just before his death in his sixtieth year he was sent to prison for keeping three whores in his chambers at Winchester.

Perhaps it was Dr. Boorde's warning which was referred to by a later writer:

It is said that the effect of eating too much lettuce is 'soporific'.

Beatrix Potter (1866–1943)
The Tale of the Flopsy Bunnies

Dr. Boorde did not consider the onion to be suitable food for, say, a chaste and busy business executive:

Onyons doth promote a man to veneryous actes, and to sompnolence.

Andrew Boorde (1490?–1549)
A Dyetary of Helth

And those whose duties required them to remain in the public eye for hours at a time, e.g. judges, sentries and royalty, would have taken heed of Dr. Boorde's words about the herb thyme:

Tyme ... causeth a man to make water.

Andrew Boorde (1490?–1549)
A Dyetary of Helth

Another vegetable suspected of encouraging lechery was the artichoke:

Artichokes! Artichokes!
Heats the body and the spirit.
Heats the genitals.
Catherine de Medici was fond of artichokes.

Paris street-vendors' cry (early seventeenth century)
Quoted by H. E. Wedeck: *Dictionary of Aphrodisiacs*

The Jerusalem artichoke also came under attack, about the same time, on the grounds of its unpalatability:

These roots are dressed divers wayes, some boile them in water, and after stew them with sacke and butter, adding a little ginger. Others bake them in pies, putting Marrow, Dates, Ginger, Raisons of the sun, Sacke, etc. Others some other way as they are led by their skill in Cookerie. But in my judgement which way soever they be drest and eaten, they are a meat more fit for swine, then men.

John Gerard (1545–1612)
Herball

The Jerusalem artichoke is not an artichoke and has nothing to do with Jerusalem. It is the root of a species of sunflower. 'Jerusalem' is a corruption of its Italian name 'Girasole articiocco'.

Another vegetable which used to be looked upon with surprising distaste was the cucumber, which at one time was thought to be downright dangerous:

Raw cucumber makes the churchyards prosperous.

English country proverb, sixteenth century.

Dr. Johnson told me, that Gay's line in the *Beggar's Opera* 'As men should serve a cucumber' &c., has no waggish meaning, with reference to men flinging away cucumbers as too *cooling*, which some have thought; for it has been a common saying of physicians in England, that a cucumber should be well sliced, and dressed with pepper and vinegar, and then thrown out, as good for nothing.

James Boswell (1740–1795)
The Journal of a Tour to the Hebrides, with Samuel Johnson, LL.D.

Fruit caused some comment. Dr. Boorde was alarmed by the effect of figs on his own particular area of interest:

[Figs] ... doth stere a man to veneryous actes, for they doth urge and increase the sede of generacyon. And also they doth prouoke a man to sweate; wherfore they doth engender lyce.

Andrew Boorde (1490?–1549)
A Dyetary of Helth

A visitor from France was shocked at the way the English brazenly consumed rhubarb:

Sweets are strange; a very usual one is a sort of cake with ... the stewed stems of the rhubarb plant whose medicinal properties are well known; yet these prudish people openly advertise the defects of their most private internal economy by their shameless partiality for this amazing fare.

Francis Wey (1812–1882)
Les Anglais chez eux

Monsieur Wey, a writer and art-critic from Paris, found much to endure and little to admire when he paid a little visit to England in 1856. All he found really praiseworthy were our women, horses and trees. Happily, in that order.

An American writer who knew England well had none of our partiality for the medicinal plant:

RHUBARB, n. Vegetable essence of stomach ache.

Ambrose Bierce (1842–1914?)
The Enlarged Devil's Dictionary

Other growing things were detested not because they were dangerous, or had an improper effect, but simply because they tasted nasty
to the writer:

> The Abbé Voltaire, alias Arouet,
> Never denounced the seed of the caraway;
> Sufficient proof, if proof we need,
> That he never bit into a caraway seed.
>
> Ogden Nash (b. 1902)
> *The Caraway Seed*

And again:

> Parsley
> Is gharsley.
>
> Ogden Nash (b. 1902)
> *Further Reflections on Parsley*

Dr. Johnson did not approve of Scotland's national food:

> OATS. n.s. A grain, which in England is generally given to
> horses, but in Scotland supports the people.
>
> Samuel Johnson (1709–1784)
> *Dictionary*

Presumably Scotland has chosen to ignore an earlier, and grim,
warning from a distinguished herbalist:

> Otemeale is good for to make a faire and wel coloured maid to looke
> like a cake of tallow.
>
> John Gerard (1545–1612)
> *Herball*

The plant which has undoubtedly caused more distress and alarm
than any other is garlic.

Garlic was always looked upon with deep distrust. In India the
priestly caste, the Brahmins, were forbidden to eat it.

The prophet Mohammed waved it away, saying 'I am a man who
has close contact with others'. In China, in the first century A.D., Hsuan-
Ch'uang ruled that those who wanted to eat garlic could do so outside
the town.

The Romans were suspicious of it:

> If ever son a parent's aged throat
> With impious hand has strangled,
> His food be garlic ...
>
> Horace (65–8 B.C.)
> *Odes.* Trans. F. W. Newman 1875

In the Middle Ages the great medical school at Salerno in Italy gra-
ciously acknowledged the super-vegetable powers of garlic, admitting
that 'it hath a secret power against poisons', but also spoke of side-
effects:

> Since *garlic* then hath powers to save from death,
> Bear with it though it makes unsavoury breath.
>
> Salerno Regimen of Health (twelfth century)

The English bore with garlic, and used it for centuries both for eating purposes and to nail above the back door to keep demons away.

It was only in the nineteenth century that England made up its mind that garlic was really rather awful:

> There are *two* Italies ... The one is the most sublime and lovely contemplation that can be conceived by the imagination of man; the other is the most degraded, disgusting, and odious. What do you think? Young women of rank actually eat — you will never guess what — *garlick*!
>
> Percy Bysshe Shelley (1792–1822)
Letter, Naples, 22 Dec. 1818

A medical writer listed it among the horrors to be faced when travelling on the Continent:

> Another article of cuisine that offends the bowels of unused Britons is garlic. Not uncommonly in southern climes an egg with a shell on is the only procurable animal food without garlic in it. Flatulence and looseness are the frequent results.
>
> Dr. T. K. Chambers
A Manual of Diet in Health and Disease, 1875

Mrs. Beeton mentioned the existence of garlic with the correct, middle-class note of steely disapproval:

> The smell of this plant is generally considered offensive and it is the most acrimonious in its taste.
>
> Mrs. Beeton (1836–1865)
Cookery and Household Management

The biggest drawback to garlic, even to those who love it, is its powers of pervasion:

> There's no such thing as a little garlic.
>
> Arthur Baer (b. 1886)

Ambrose Bierce came out strongly against a great favourite of children and harassed housewives:

> CUSTARD, n. A detestable substance produced by a malevolent conspiracy of the hen, the cow and the cook.
>
> Ambrose Bierce (1842–1914?)
The Enlarged Devil's Dictionary

And another good filler for hungry children:

> MACARONI, n. An Italian food made in the form of a slender, hollow tube. It consists of two parts — the tubing and the hole, the latter being the part that digests.
>
> Ambrose Bierce (1842–1914?)
The Enlarged Devil's Dictionary

In these days when baked bread has given way to pre-packed, machine-sliced blocks of extruded plastic foam, many British citizens think longingly of the long, crusty loaves made every few hours on the continent of Europe.

Continental bread was not always one of the reasons for crossing the channel:

> On the Continent the household bread is usually unwholesome and nasty, and captain's biscuits are never to be obtained. It is prudent to carry a store of them to use when the staff of life is found especially abominable.
>
> Dr. T. K. Chambers
> *A Manual of Diet in Health and Disease*, 1875

And to some holidaymakers French bread is still unwholesome and nasty:

> We went to France for our holidays and took six large sliced loaves of bread with us. We still had one left after thirteen days. It was still good to eat. This is a tribute to a Leicester bakery.
>
> Letter to *Leicester Mercury*
> Quoted by Derek Cooper, *The Bad Food Guide*, 1967

The quality of contemporary British bread inevitably affects the quality of the British sandwich:

> Sandwiches were invented by an Englishman, John Montagu Sandwich. His other claim to fame is that during the period when he ran the British Navy its corruption and incapacity were outstanding. Sandwiches can be a good stop-gap if the bread is eatable. Most sandwiches are made from pre-sliced factory bread, a sort of chewy wadding.
>
> Derek Cooper (b. 1925)
> *The Bad Food Guide*, 1967

> The food consisting of a slice of something between two pieces of buttered bread was named after John Montagu, fourth Earl of Sandwich, when, in 1762, he remained at the gaming table for twenty-four hours with no other nourishment but sandwiches. But he did not originate the idea. Records show that three rather spectacular whores had anticipated him. In 1748 Horace Walpole wrote to George Montagu, 'She [Fanny Murray] was complaining of want of money; Sir Richard Atkins immediately gave her a twenty-pound note; she said, "Damn your twenty-pound note, what does that signify!" – clapped it between two pieces of bread-and-butter, and eat it.' Casanova records in his *Memoirs* that Kitty Fisher did the same (the banknote is variously reported as being £100 and £1000), and Mrs. Baddeley followed suit with a banknote thoughtfully provided by a near relation of George III. Perhaps we should really be talking about cheese-and-tomato murrays.

When bread is elderly or of dubious quality the answer is usually to toast it. Hot buttered toast has always seemed to be the most delightful and innocent of foods. And yet:

> He [Lord Castlereagh] was forbidden to eat hot buttered toast, to a healthy stomach indigestible, to a diseased one ruin. His servant

the last morning brought it to him ignorantly; Lord Castlereagh ate heartily of it; his brain filled with more blood, he became insane, and cut the carotid artery.

B. R. Haydon (1786–1846)
Correspondence and Table Talk

In fairness it must be remarked that reasons other than a hearty meal of hot buttered toast have been given for the statesman cutting his own throat; over-work, temporary unsoundness of mind, even blackmail. A few years later the painter Haydon also committed suicide.

The most eminently dreadful soup on record was the Black Broth which the Spartans ate to prove their toughness and disdain for creature comforts. The recipe: pork stock, vinegar, salt.

A citizen of Sybaris who made a stopover in Sparta and had the privilege of dining with the Spartans in their mess-hall commented:

It is natural enough for the Spartans to be the bravest of men; for any man in his senses would rather die ten thousand times over than live as miserably as this.

Quoted by Athenaeus (*fl. c.* A.D. 200)
The Deipnosophistai

In this book, *Connoisseurs in Dining*, Athenaeus collected a great number of anecdotes of ancient Greek feeding habits.

To a modern traveller the equivalent of Spartan Broth is probably that local form of fish soup, full of bits of ugly, alien fish, which is the speciality of Mediterranean seaports:

Take breath, gentle maiden; the while I explain to the patient reader the ingredients of the diabolical preparation known as 'zuppa di pesce'. The guarracino, for instance, is a pitch-black marine monstrosity, one or two *inches* long, a mere blot, with an Old Red Sandstone profile and insufferable manners whose sole recommendation is that its name is derived from korakimos (korax=a raven; but who can live on Greek roots?). As to the scorfano, its name is unquestionably onomatopoetic, to suggest the spitting-out of bones; the only difference, from a culinary point of view, between the scorfano and a toad being that the latter has twice as much meat on it. The aguglia, again, is thin as a lead pencil. Who would believe that for this miserable sea-worm with verdigris-tinted spine, which an ordinary person would thank you for not setting on his table, the inhabitants of Siren land fought like fiends; the blood of their noblest was shed in defence of privileges artfully wheedled out of Anjou and Aragonese kings defining the ius quoddam pescandi vulgariter dictum sopra le aguglie; that a certain tract of sea was known as the 'aguglie water' and owned up to the days of Murat, by a single family who defended it with guns and man-traps? And everybody knows the totero or squid, an animated ink-bag of perverse leanings, which swims backwards because all other creatures go forwards and whose indiarubber flesh might be useful for deluding hunger on desert islands, since, like American gum, you can chew it for months, but never get it down.

These, and such as they, float about in a lukewarm brew of rancid
oil and garlic, together with a few of last week's breadcrusts, decay-
ing sea-shells and onion-peels, to give it an air of consistency.
This is the stuff for which Neapolitans sell their female relatives.

Norman Douglas (1868–1952)
Siren Land

The French word 'soupe' originally meant anything that was cooked
in a liquid, hence the English word 'sop'. Later, 'soupe' came to mean
the liquid itself. England adopted that but kept the original as well, so
we now have 'sop' and 'soup' which originally meant the same thing.

Fish has formed a significant part of most nations' diet, being nourishing, an alternative to meat on fast days and, until recent years, cheap
and easy to harvest.

Dr. Johnson objected to fish, mildly, because his eyesight was so poor
that he had to eat it with his fingers in order to locate the bones.

But personal prejudices have been expressed against individual kinds
of fish:

Once for a maid of Wales I sighed,
My landlord's daughter at Portmadoc;
But she was soon disqualified
By showing appetite for haddock:
No wife of mine shall eat that fish,
Nor serve it for my breakfast dish.

Frank Sidgwick
The Not Impossible She

'Turbot, Sir,' said the waiter, placing before me two fishbones, two
eyeballs, and a bit of black mackintosh.

Thomas Earle Welby (1881–1933)
The Dinner Knell

An early attempt at imaginative treatment of fish for a dinner-party
proved fatal:

Sir Josslebury Putcher is dead! He had the Honour to be choaked
yesterday by a fishbone at the Duke of Ne——'s Table; His Grace's
Dinner it seems was in a Masquerade; no fish appeared in its proper
form or nakedness, and poor Sir Josslebury died by mistaking Prawns
fryed in butter (one of whose heads Armour the careless Cook had
neglected to take off) for plain English Skirits.

Charles Boyle, fourth Earl of Orrery (1676–1731)
Letter to Counsellor Kempe, 30 Jan. 1729

Birds were much prized by the Romans as a delicacy for the table,
particularly song-birds and those of beautiful plumage.

As usual there were warnings against eating certain species:

Wood-pigeons check and blunt the manly powers: let him not eat
this bird who wishes to be amorous.

Martial (*c.* A.D. 40–104)
Epigrams, Bk. XIII, Epig. 67

Non-airborne domestic fowl have been bred for the table since the beginning of civilized life. The most popular edible fowl has proved to be the hen, which provides not only eggs for the pot but also, ultimately, itself. There are more hens in the world than any other bird:

A hen is only an egg's way of making another egg.
Samuel Butler (1835–1902)
Life and Habit, VIII

Less popular than the hen, for practical reasons, has been the goose:

The goose is a silly bird — too much for one to eat, and not enough for two.
Charles H. Poole
Archaic Words

Turkey has held its place in the affections of eaters although, to the despair of turkey breeders, it is firmly associated in the public's mind with once-a-year celebrations like Thanksgiving and Christmas.

The most ludicrous thing about this exceptionally ungainly and odd-looking fowl is that no country seems to have got its name right:

England: 'Turkey'. The turkey had nothing to do with Turkey. It had been domesticated by the Aztec Indians in Mexico. Merchants from the Levant imported the birds into England from about 1540. As these importers were known as 'Turkey merchants' the birds came to be called 'Turkey birds', which soon became simply 'turkeys'.

France: Orig. *Coq d'Inde*, then *dindon*. As the bird first arrived in France, about 1520, from the Spanish possessions in America, which were known as the 'Spanish Indies', the French called it the 'Spanish Indies Cock'. Some regions of France decided that the bird had been introduced by a Jesuit priest so, for a time, the popular name for it was *jésuite*. It was not, in fact, introduced by a Jesuit but by one of Sebastian Cabot's officers.

Germany: *Calecutische Hahn*. Calico came from Calicut, a town in southern India, but turkeys did not.

Holland: *Kalkoen*. Another reference to calico and Calicut, neither of which had anything to do with turkeys.

India: *Peru*. In Peru, as distinct from Mexico, the turkey was unknown.

One faint connection that turkey might have had with calico, suggested one writer, was its flavour:

What a shocking fraud the turkey is. In life preposterous, insulting — that foolish noise they make to scare you away! In death — unpalatable. The turkey has practically no taste except a dry fibrous flavour reminiscent of a mixture of warmed-up plaster of paris and horsehair. The texture is like wet sawdust and the whole vast feathered swindle has the piquancy of a boiled mattress.
Cassandra (William Connor) (1909–1967)
Daily Mirror, 24 Dec. 1953

288

The taste of grouse, well hung, is a special pleasure for those who like it. For one who didn't it was something else:

> House-warming at Zola's ... very tasty dinner ... including some grouse whose scented flesh Daudet compared to an old courtesan's flesh marinaded in a bidet.
>
> Edmond de Goncourt (1822–1896)
> *Journal,* 3 April 1878

Because rabbits were rather good at reproducing themselves they were usually cheap and plentiful and they were a useful stand-by for families who could not afford much else:

> For rabbits young and rabbits old
> For rabbits hot and rabbits cold
> For rabbits tender, rabbits tough,
> We thank Thee, Lord: we've had enough.
>
> Anon. country verse

The main worry with meats was what was done to them:

> I shrink instinctively from one who professes to like minced veal.
>
> Charles Lamb (1775–1834)
> *Essays of Elia:* 'Grace Before Meat'

> CHOP, n. A piece of leather skillfully attached to a bone and administered to the patients at restaurants.
>
> Ambrose Bierce (1842–1914?)
> *The Enlarged Devil's Dictionary*

By no means all four-legged animals and winged things made good eating, as a keen experimenter discovered:

> Dr. Buckland used to say that he had eaten his way straight through the whole animal creation, and that the worst thing was a mole — that was utterly horrible ... Dr. Buckland afterwards told Lady Lyndhurst that there was one thing even worse than a mole, and that was a blue-bottle fly.
>
> Augustus J. C. Hare (1834–1903)
> *The Story of My Life,* 4 June 1882

> Dr. Buckland was a popular and respected visitor to the London Zoological Gardens, where his little hobby was well known. He lived near the zoo and would be observed hovering when a rare beast was taken ill. One day, when Dr. Buckland was away on holiday, a leopard died and was interred, as was then the custom, beneath a flower bed. On his return Dr. Buckland seized a spade, disinterred the corpse, and enjoyed a somewhat gamy leopard steak.

Vegetarianism, the total rejection of flesh-eating in any shape or form, began in the East as a discipline for the priestly caste. The first recorded teachings in the Mediterranean world came from Pythagoras, who preached 'abstain from meat' as well as 'abstain from beans'; part of his philosophy of returning to the Golden Age, the ascetic, happy life that once was lived.

289

Ovid, five hundred years later, put the case well:

Oh, how criminal it is for flesh to be stored away in flesh, for one greedy body to grow fat with food gained from another, for one live creature to go on living through the destruction of another living thing! And so in the midst of the wealth of food which Earth, the best of mothers, has produced, it is your pleasure to chew the piteous flesh of slaughtered animals!

Ovid (43 B.C.–A.D. 18)
Metamorphoses, Bk. XV, 1.88

Vegetarianism did not catch on much in England until the nineteenth century; meat-eating was much too popular. But there were a great number of citizens who, like Beau Brummell, could not be bothered to eat vegetables. Although Brummell, when asked at dinner if it was true that he never touched them, proved not to be a fanatic about it:

I once ate a pea.

George (Beau) Brummell (1778–1840)

Modern meat-eaters tend to view vegetarianism with tolerance:

Vegetarianism is harmless enough, though it is apt to fill a man with wind and self-righteousness.

Sir Robert Hutchison (1871–1960)
Ex-President of the Royal College of Physicians

Six of the medieval Seven Deadly Sins still bite home to varying extents on modern consciences; Pride, Wrath, Envy, Lust, Avarice and Sloth are all more or less familiar demons. The odd man out is Gluttony. Apart from the occasional compulsive eater, twentieth-century man is moderate in his intake of the various pre-frozen and processed delights offered by the food industry.

It was rather different in the Middle Ages, when there was either a great deal of food available or, more usually, hardly any at all. And, as the fast days heavily outnumbered the feast days, when an opportunity did occur for a peasant or a noble to indulge his potentially enormous appetite he did his best to eat himself into a stupor.

Chaucer's Pardoner deplored this practice:

O glotonye, ful of cursednesse!
O cause first of oure confusioun!
O original of oure dampnacioun,
Til Crist hadde boght us with his blood agayn!

Geoffrey Chaucer (c. 1340–1400)
The Canterbury Tales: 'The Pardoner's Tale'

It was straining the argument somewhat attributing the Fall of Man to Adam's failure to control his need for a bite of apple, but the Pardoner, with his fake relics, his pillow case 'which that he seyde was Oure Lady veyl' and his jar of old pig bones, was more of a licensed confidence-trickster than a theologian.

A few lines later he suggested that a glutton was hardly a social asset:

> O wombe! O bely! O stynkyng cod,
> Fulfilled of dong and of corrupcioun!
> At either ende of thee foul is the soun.
>> Geoffrey Chaucer (*c.* 1340–1400)
>> *The Canterbury Tales:* 'The Pardoner's Tale'

wombe = belly; bely = bellows; cod = gut; fulfilled = filled full; dong = dung; soun = sound.

Another, and rather good, argument against gluttony had been put by earlier writers, thoughtful though un-medical men like Juvenal and Theognis, who had observed that gluttons tended to die younger than more moderate eaters.

This observation became an English proverbial saying:

> They have digged their grave with their teeth.
>> Thomas Adams (1612–1653)
>> *Works*

An early Christian Father warned of the heating effect of too much meat:

> What then will become of you a young girl physically sound, dainty, stout, and ruddy, if you allow yourself free range among flesh dishes? ... If, as you lie on your couch after a meal you are excited by the alluring train of sensual desires; then seize the shield of faith.
>> St. Jerome (*c.* A.D. 340–420)

A hymn-writer believed that the pleasures of the table were among the first corruptions that youth must gird itself against:

> The appetite of taste is the first thing that gets the ascendant in our younger years, and a guard should be set upon it early.
>> Dr. Isaac Watts (1674–1748)

It narrowed the chances of achieving academic distinction:

> It is selde sean that they which ffyll their belys
> overmych be disposede to their bookys.
>> William Nelson (fifteenth century)

It impaired judgement:

> The greatest Drunkards are the worst Judges of Wine. The most Insatiable Leachers the most Ignorant Criticks in Women, and the Greediest Appetites, of the best Cookery of Meats—for those that Use *Excess* in any Thing never understand the Truth of it, which always lies in the *Mean*.
>> Samuel Butler (1612?–1680)

It could put a strain on married life:

> The Lord Chancellor [Lyndhurst] has been ill from childish over-eating. Not long since, after a hasty dinner, he ate heartily of plum-pudding. He wanted *'more'*. Lady Lyndhurst begged of him not to eat any more. He persisted, and she began to cry.
>
> B. R. Haydon (1786–1846)
> *Correspondence and Table-Talk*

> Colonel —— was at Byron's house in Piccadilly. Lady Byron in the room, and 'luncheon' was brought in —veal cutlets, etc. She began eating. Byron turned round in disgust and said, 'Gormandizing beast!' and taking up the tray, threw the whole luncheon into the hall.
>
> B. R. Haydon (1786–1846)
> Letter to Miss Mitford, 31 May 1824

It was unbecoming to a lady:

> How disenchanting in the female character is a manifestation of relish for the pleasures of the table!
>
> William Charles Macready (1793–1873)
> *Reminiscences*

It indicated that the lady was, perhaps, not entirely a lady:

> If once you find a woman gluttonous, expect from her very little virtue.
>
> Samuel Johnson (1709–1784)
> Letter, 26 July 1783

But, above all, gluttony invoked Supreme disapproval:

> A greedy man God hates.
> Old Scots proverb.

It is just possible that the oldest word in the world still used in more or less its original form is the word 'booze'.

Man's first drink was water, lapped up from rivers or collected as it fell from the skies. But just as he progressed from eating raw berries to preparing a more interesting and satisfying range of foods so he learnt that by mixing water with various other things a change took place for the better; it bubbled, took on a colour and was more fun to drink. It also produced pleasant side-effects.

Since that day when a happy alternative to water was discovered many poets and thinkers have looked in dismay at those who ignored the alternative and stuck to drinking water:

> The mere beverage of the beast.
> Hilaire Belloc (1870–1953)

It has been argued that unbrewed and unfermented water produced an inferior kind of human being:

> All the great villainies of history, from the murder of Abel onward, have been perpetrated by sober men, and chiefly by teetotallers. But all the charming and beautiful things, from the Song of Songs to

bouillabaisse, and from the nine Beethoven symphonies to the Martini cocktail, have been given to humanity by men who, when the hour came, turned from tap water to something with colour to it, and more in it than mere oxygen and hydrogen.

H. L. Mencken (1880–1956)
Selected Prejudices, Second Series

And that it did not stimulate the creative urge:

No poems can please nor live long which are written by water-drinkers.

Horace (65–8 B.C.)
Epistles, I, 19

Even the occasional doctor pointed out its deleterious effects:

Water ... doth very greatly deject the appetite, destroy the natural heat, and overthrow the strength of the stomach.

Tobias Venner (1577–1660)
Via Recta ad Vitam Longam

Hilaire Belloc mused on what sort of people they were who banded together in an attempt to persuade drinkers of alternative liquors that water was better:

What are these that from the outer murk
Of dense mephitic vapours creeping lurk
To breathe foul airs from that corrupted well
Which oozes slime along the floor of Hell?
These are the stricken palsied brood of sin
In whose vile veins, poor, poisonous and thin,
Decoctions of embittered hatreds crawl:
These are the Water-Drinkers, cursed all!

Hilaire Belloc (1870–1953)
Heroic Poem in Praise of Wine

There have been cases of people with a pathological antipathy towards water in any shape or form:

LADY AT DINNER PARTY: You mean to tell me that you never, ever let water touch your lips? Then what do you use to clean your teeth, pray?
RETIRED MAJOR: A light Sauterne, madam.

Anon.
Venerable joke

A contemporary of Belloc's was not that bigoted. He did not care what contact he had with water, with one exception:

I don't care where the water goes if it doesn't get into the wine.

G. K. Chesterton (1874–1936)
Wine and Water

The first home-made alternative drink to water was probably beer:

LADY CHURCHILL: I hate the taste of beer.
SIR WINSTON: So do many people—to begin with. It is, however, a prejudice that many have been able to overcome.

Sir Winston Churchill (1874–1965)

Early man made his primitive beer by banging some sort of seed, such as barley, with a stone and leaving it to ferment in a mixture of water and honey.

By about 2000 B.C. beer had become the national drink of the Egyptians. They made theirs by fermenting lightly baked barley dough in date-water. They sometimes used their beer as a medicine.

England's drink in the Middle Ages was ale; a dark, powerful brew of malt, yeast and water. The strength of the ale brewed and sold in ale-houses was strictly controlled by ale-conners: government inspectors in leather breeches. The legend is that the ale-conner poured a little ale on to an oak bench and sat on it. If, when he rose, the bench did not rise with him the ale was understrength.

As well-off households brewed their own beer it followed that common ale-houses catered for the lower end of the income-bracket. And ale-wives had no need to be over-fastidious either in their personal appearance or in their brewing methods.

Perhaps a typical example of a Tudor 'Tippler', or tavern keeper, was Elynour Rummyng:

Her face was 'Lyke a rost pygges eare,
Brystled wyth here'
and her nose, 'Neuer stoppynge,
But euer droppynge',
her head dress 'Wrythen in wonder wyse ...
With a whym wham,
Knit with a trym tram,
Upon her brayne pan',
And 'Her shone smered with talowe,
Gresed upon dyrt
That baudeth her skyrt.'

It seems unlikely that Elynour's ale was under-strength:

Than Elynour ...
   Skommeth it into a tray
Whereas the yeest is,
With her maungy fystis:
And somtyme she blennes
The donge of her hennes
And the ale together ...

John Skelton (1460?–1529)
The Tunnyng of Elynour Rummyng

Elynour Rummyng really existed. She brewed her ale in Leatherhead, Surrey, she was a contemporary of John Skelton's, and the circumstantial evidence clearly suggests that Skelton's poem was an eyewitness report. In the Surrey County Record Office there is a Court Book of Packenesham Manor, one of Leatherhead's manors, which states that on 'the 18th day of August in the Year of the Reign of King Henry VIII the 17th (1525), Robert a Dene ale taster there comes and being sworn presents that … Eleanor Romyng (fine 2d.) is a common Tippler of ale and sells at excessive prices by small measures at excessive price therefore she is in mercy'. It has been established that John Skelton enjoyed an occasional day's fishing at Leatherhead. The only known inn near Leatherhead's river, the Mole, was 'The Running Horse'. It seems very likely that Skelton visited the inn during his fishing trips and there met the unlovely Mrs. Romyng serving out her powerful but excessively priced ale. 'The Running Horse', a sixteenth-century building with parts even earlier, is still functioning in Leatherhead, close to the small bridge over the Mole, and beer can still be enjoyed there, though very, very much weaker than that of Mrs. Romyng, and even more expensive.

John Aubrey mentioned another natural substance which ale-wives blended in to give their ale a boost:

Under the Cathedral-church at Hereford is the greatest Charnel-house for bones, that ever I saw in England. In A.D. 1650 there lived amongst those bones a poor old woman that, to help out her fire, did use to mix the deadmen's bones: this was thrift and poverty: but cunning alewives putt the Ashes of these bones in their Ale to make it intoxicateing.

John Aubrey (1626–1697)
Brief Lives

At the end of the fourteenth century an innovation in brewing was imported from the Continent; the introduction of hops into the ale-brewing process. The new brew was called 'beer'.

The English reacted strongly against this heresy of introducing a bitter herb into their sweet, strong ale and ignored the stuff. Beer dropped so low in price that in 1418 Henry V was able to supply his troops at the siege of Rouen with London-brewed beer at half the price of ale.

By the reign of Henry VIII, beer had established a foothold:

About the 15th of Henry VIIIth divers things were newly brought into England, whereupon the Rythme was made:
    Greeke, Heresie, Turkey-cocks, and Beer,
    Came into England all in a yeare.

John Aubrey (1626–1697)
Brief Lives

This couplet was popular for centuries. The list of imports was varied from time to time, but beer seems to have remained in most versions; probably because it rhymed with 'year'.

Henry VIII tried to ban the brewing of beer, and medical writers spoke out stoutly of the dangers of making a habit of beer drinking:

> And nowe of late dayes it is much vsed in Englande to the detryment of many Englysshe men; specyally it kylleth them the which be troubled with the colycke, and the stone, & the strangulation; for the drynke is a colde drynke; yet it doth make a man fat, and doth inflate the bely.

> Andrew Boorde (1490?–1549)
> *A Dyetary of Helth*

But beer won. It kept better than ale and eventually people preferred the taste of it.

In the U.S.A. the authorities had always encouraged the brewing of ale and beer in the hope of discouraging the drinking of cheap spirits. The first brewery in Pennsylvania was built by William Penn and many eminent public men were concerned with brewing, including Thomas Jefferson, Patrick Henry and Israel Putnam. George Washington brewed his own at Mount Vernon.

In Germany, in the fifteenth century, a different process of fermentation was developed which required low temperature storage of the fermented liquor. The product was named after the German word for storage, 'lager'.

The German nation was so enthusiastic in its consumption of beer that in the nineteenth century a philosopher was moved to remark:

> This nation has arbitrarily stupefied itself for nearly a thousand years: nowhere have the two great European narcotics, alcohol and Christianity, been more wickedly misused ... How much moody heaviness, lameness, humidity, and dressing-gown mood, how much beer is in German intelligence!

> Friedrich Nietzsche (1844–1900)

The other alternative to water which man soon discovered was the juice of grapes, left to ferment. This produced a liquid which was not as thirst-quenching as beer but was more colourful, more subtle in taste and a little of it rapidly induced a curious, not unpleasant feeling:

> Wine turns a man inside outwards.
> Thomas Fuller (1608–1661)
> *Gnomologia*
>
> Thomas Fuller, divine, and author of the *Worthies*, was an amiable, witty man. He suggested for his own epitaph, 'Fuller's earth'.

Ancient Egypt had flourishing vineyards by 3000 B.C. The Greeks and the Romans enjoyed their wine, by all accounts a somewhat dark and acid fluid, which they wisely took diluted with water. And it was the Romans who first began to be connoisseurs, preferring, for instance, the wines of the Falernian region to others, thus giving the world a new snobbery, with its own language:

It's a naive domestic Burgundy without any breeding, but I think you'll be amused by its presumption.

James Thurber (1894–1961)
Caption for cartoon, *New Yorker*

Wine was mentioned in the Old Testament almost instantly; Genesis ix. 20, 'Noah began to be an husbandman, and he planted a vineyard.' It was the first thing he did after the flood. Unhappily, in verse 21, 'he drank of the wine and was drunken'. But then he had been through rather a trying time.

The prophet Mohammed had a nasty experience with wine when young, and when later he became a religious leader he pronounced wine to be an abomination and forbade Muslims, his followers, to drink any kind of alcohol. The prophet's early experience was described graphically, though not very clearly, by Leonardo da Vinci, who wrote of the incident from the wine's point of view:

Wine, the divine liquor of the grape, finding itself in a golden richly chased cup upon Mahomet's table, after being transported with pride at such an honour, was suddenly assailed by a contrary feeling, and said to itself: 'What am I doing? What is it that I am rejoicing at? Cannot I see that I am near to my death, in that I am about to leave my golden dwelling in this cup and enter into the foul and fetid caverns of the human body, to be there transformed from a sweet fragrant nectar to a foul and disgusting fluid?' It cried to heaven demanding vengeance for such injury and that an end might be put to such an insult, so that since that part of the country produced the most beautiful and finest grapes in the whole world these at least should not be turned into wine. Then Jove caused the wine which Mahomet drank to rise in spirit up to the brain, and to infect this to such a degree as to make him mad; and he committed so many follies that when he came to his senses he made a decree that no Asiatic should drink wine; and thus the wine and its fruits were left at liberty.

Leonardo da Vinci (1452–1519)

Wine had always played an important part in the Christian religion. The early communion suppers, the 'Love Feasts', adapted from the Jewish tradition of ritual meals, made a feature of drinking wine and it was monasteries, needing wine for their services, who kept the good vines going during the Dark Ages.

The Romans had hopefully planted vines wherever they went, regardless – indeed ignorant – of certain climatic features which vines needed to produce good wine, so there must have been a considerable quantity of really dreadful local wine produced from unsuitable soils; the region around Paris was notorious for its *vin de Suresnes*, which apparently tasted like light, mild vinegar. Vines had been planted in Glastonbury and other regions of England, but these eventually succumbed to the grey skies and frosts, although a sparkling Welsh wine was produced as late as the nineteenth century on the hills above Cardiff.

During the Middle Ages there were a number of strange wines for sale and in Chaucer we find the first known reference to the swift potency of mixed, perhaps fortified, wine:

> Keep clear of wine, I tell you, white or red,
> Especially Spanish wines which they provide
> And have on sale in Fish Street and Cheapside.
> That wine mysteriously finds its way
> To mix itself with others—shall we say
> Spontaneously?—that grow in neighbouring regions.
> So when a man has had a drink or two
> Though he may think he is at home with you
> In Cheapside, I assure you he's in Spain
> Where it was made, at Lepé I maintain,
> Not even at Bordeaux. He's soon elate
> And very near the 'samson-samson' state.

> > Geoffrey Chaucer (1340?–1400)
> > *The Canterbury Tales:* 'The Pardoner's Tale'
> > Trans. Nevill Coghill

'*samson-samson*' = Chaucer's onomatopoeic word for the sound made by a drunkard snorting through his nose.

Chaucer was the son of a vintner, so no doubt knew his wines.

Spanish wines were rather suspect, being full-bodied and sweet:

> All swete wine and grose wynes doth make a man fatte.

> > Andrew Boorde (1490?–1549)
> > *A Dyetary of Helth*

Robert Burton, discussing the causes of melancholia, included in his list dark, thick wines:

> All black wines, over-hot, compound, strong thick drinks, as Muscadine, Malmsey, Alicant, Rumney, Brownbastard, Metheglen, and the like, of which they have thirty several kinds of Muscovy, all such made drinks are hurtful in this case, to such as are hot, or of a sanguine choleric complexion, young or inclined to head-melancholy.

> > Robert Burton (1577–1640)
> > *The Anatomy of Melancholy*

Brownbastard = a dark, sweet Spanish wine made from the Muscadine grape. Was still on wine-merchants' lists until about 1939.

It would appear that heavy, sweet Spanish wine had a distinct bouquet:

> Sir Robert Walpole advised the King to take Lady Deloraine [as mistress] till Madame Walmoden could be brought over. His Majesty said she stank of Spanish wine so abominably of late that he could not bear her.

> > Lord Hervey (1696–1743)
> > *Memoirs of the Reign of George II*

298

Ordinary local Spanish wine, drunk in Spain, could come as a disappointment to a visitor unaccustomed to its particular charms:

> The Spanish wine, my God, it is foul, catpiss is champagne compared, this is the sulphurous urination of some aged horse.
>
> D. H. Lawrence (1885–1930)
> Letter from Palma to Rhys Davis, 25 April 1929

German wine production centred mainly along the banks of the Rhine and the Moselle. Vineyards dating back to the twelfth century produced white wine which was esteemed by many, but not all:

> The Germans are exceedingly fond of Rhine wines; they are put up in tall, slender bottles, and are considered a pleasant beverage. One tells them from vinegar by the label.
>
> Mark Twain (1835–1910)
> *A Tramp Abroad*

The consumption of wine throughout the world has increased so enormously since the last war that modern blending and marketing methods have been brought in to the wine trade to increase quantity, if not quality:

> The point about white Burgundies is that I hate them myself ... so closely resembling a blend of cold chalk soup and alum cordial with an additive or two to bring it to the colour of children's pee.
>
> Kingsley Amis (b. 1922)
> *The Green Man*

Some people, of course, just did not like any kind of white wine:

> 'White wine', he used to say dogmatically, 'is bad, it cuts the legs.'
>
> Edward Whymper (1840–1911)
> Quoting his guide, Jean-Antoine
> *Travels Amongst the Great Andes of the Equator*

The Bible sternly warned Catholics against the dangers of drinking white wine:

> Look not upon the wine when it is yellow, when the colour thereof shineth in the glass. It goeth in pleasantly: But in the end, it will bite like a snake, and will spread abroad poison like a basilisk.
>
> Proverbs xxiii. 31–32
> *The Douai Version, with Bishop Challoner's Notes*, 1914

Whilst, at the same time, warning Protestants against the other colour:

> Look not thou upon the wine when it is red, when it giveth his colour in the cup, when it moveth itself aright. At the last it biteth like a serpent, and stingeth like an adder.
>
> Proverbs xxiii. 31–32
> The Authorized Version, 1604

The Knox Translation of 1950 struck a happy medium and warned us not to look upon wine when it is tawny.

Lord Byron found that red wine had a lowering effect upon his spirits. He found stimulation instead by drinking what is probably the oddest substitute for claret the mind has yet boggled at:

> I think you told me, at Venice, that your spirits did not keep up without a little claret. I *can* drink, and bear a good deal of wine (as you may recollect in England): but it don't exhilarate — it makes me savage and suspicious. Laudanum has a similar effect; but I can take much of *it* without any effect at all. The thing that gives me the highest spirits (it seems absurd, but true) is a dose of *salts*.
>
> Lord Byron (1788–1824)
Letter to Thomas Moore, 1821

> This was not a pose; he noted in his diary (6 Jan. 1821), 'A dose of salts has the effect of a temporary inebriation, like light champagne, on me.'

A Puritan preacher was worried about a curious second effect which gaseous drinks produced:

> Those bottled windy drinks that laugh in a man's face and then cut his throat.
>
> Thomas Adams (*fl.* 1612–1653)
Works, Vol. III

The Rev. Thomas Adams could not have been referring to champagne, which was a still wine in his time; Dom Pérignon, the Benedictine monk, did not discover how to put the fizz into it until the latter part of the century.

He might have been referring to an English wine which Henry Fielding wrote about in his *Journal of a Voyage to Lisbon*, a tipple which had the virtue, it seems, of only disrupting the nation's affairs every seven years:

> This wind is a liquor of English manufacture, and its flavour is thought very delicious by the generality of the English, who drink it in great quantities. Every seventh year is thought to produce as much as the other six. It is then drank so plentifully, that the whole nation are in a manner intoxicated by it, and consequently very little business is carried on at that season.
>
> Henry Fielding (1707–1754)
The Journal of a Voyage to Lisbon

> What was this *wind*, which Fielding went on to say resembled the red wine of Portugal and was so popular in the metropolis that several taverns were set apart 'solely for its vendition'? A clue lies in the fact that owing to supplies of claret from France being disrupted by inconvenient wars and smuggled supplies being unreliable, a kind of home-made fruit wine became very popular at that time. There is internal evidence in the recipe of that substitute concoction to support a theory that it might have become popular under the name *wind*; one of its chief ingredients was parsnips.

In 1851 Mr. Thomas Cook invented the holiday tour industry by discovering that he could get reduced rates from the railway if he took his teetotal party from Leicester to Loughborough in one lump. From this he progressed to taking parties of teetotallers on guided tours of the Continent. The next step was taking non-teetotallers on guided tours of the Continent. It was on one of the latter tours, through Italy, that Mr. Cook, a zealous Baptist abstainer from drink, seeing his flock scrambling into the railway station buffet to buy cheap, local wine, cried out what must be the definitive comment on cheap, local wine:

> Gentlemen, do not invest your money in diarrhoea!
>> Thomas Cook (1808–1892)
>> *Temperance Jubilee Celebrations at Leicester and Market Harborough arranged and compiled by Thomas Cook*, 1886

The principle of distillation – that if you boil up a liquid, collect the steam and then condense this back into a liquid you end up with a much stronger solution than when you started – was well known to the ancient Greeks.

The Arabs seem to have been the first to use the process to produce alcohol, which they used for medicinal purposes. But in the thirteenth century the Italians learned the trick from the Arabs and brewed up *acqua di vite*. France followed, producing *eau de vie*, and sometime in the fifteenth century the Highland lairds set up pot stills and distilled *uisgebeatha*, a literal translation into Celtic of the Latin word *aquavitae*, 'water of life'. The word *uisgebeatha* eventually became anglicized into 'whisky'.

The French claim to have discovered Cognac by accident, when the peasants of the Charente district boiled down their poor-quality white wine to make it easier and cheaper to cart away. This idea of distilling wine rather than liquor made from grain, or other vegetable substances, spread to other countries where the powerful end-product became known as 'brandy', from the Dutch *brandewijn*, 'burnt wine'.

By the middle of the seventeenth century most countries were drinking some kind of brandy. And with the rough and ready methods of those days it must have been a fierce and fiery fluid:

> Yesterday I saw Mr. Rushworth, which was a great mortification. He hath quite lost his memory with drinking Brandy: remembred nothing of you, etc. His Landlady wiped his nose like a child. He was about 83, onwards to 84.
>> John Aubrey (1626–1697)
>> Letter to Anthony Wood, 1689

It continued to be a drink not to be trifled with:

> BRANDY, n. A cordial composed of one part thunder-and-lightning, one part remorse, two parts bloody murder, one part death-hell-and-the-grave, two parts clarified Satan and four parts holy Moses! Dose, a headful all the time. Brandy is said, by Emerson, I think, to be the drink of heroes. I certainly should not advise others to tackle it.
>> Ambrose Bierce (1842–1914?)
>> *The Enlarged Devil's Dictionary*

Dreadful though much professionally brewed brandy must have been before legislation controlled what went into the stills and what came out, the products of home-made stills must have been even more lethal.

Many areas of the world which produced a staple crop capable of being distilled into some sort of strong spirit produced a local *eau de vie*, e.g. in the Far East rice was distilled into saki, in Ireland potatoes were pounded down and then boiled up to make poteen. In many cases these moonshine liquors turned out to be *eaux de mort*.

Surplus apples were used in the U.S.A. to produce a kind of apple brandy:

> Essence of lockjaw.
> Local name for New England applejack

But the most popular form of do-it-yourself spirit in the U.S.A. was moonshine corn liquor:

> A sudden violent jolt of it has been known to stop the victim's watch, snap his suspenders and crack his glass eye right across.
> Irvin S. Cobb (1876–1944)

In the middle of the seventeenth century a Dutchman, Franciscus de la Boe, professor of medicine at the University of Leiden, distilled spirits in combination with the juice of juniper berries and happened upon a new alcoholic drink. The Dutch called the juniper berry *genever*, from the French word *genièvre*, but in England it soon became known simply as 'gin'.

Like so many newly discovered consumables – tea, potatoes, coffee, chocolate, butter, boiled cabbage (in Egypt), sugar – gin was first thought of as a medicine. The attitude presumably was that until a new food or drink had been proved harmless the safest thing to do was to rub a bit of it on, or pour a spoonful of it down, somebody who was ill anyway.

Gin did not remain a medicine for very long. By 1792 the Dutch were producing 14,000,000 gallons of it annually, 10,000,000 gallons of that for export:

> Gin, cursed Fiend, with Fury fraught,
> Makes human Race a Prey,
> It enters by a deadly Draught,
> And steals our Life away.
> Rev. James Townley (1714–1778)

The metre of the verse makes it sound suspiciously like a hymn; but it doesn't seem very likely.

302

The trouble with drinking alcoholic drinks was that though, as was universally acknowledged, a moderate consumption produced many beneficial effects, a few too many produced drunkenness:

> Drunk'ness, the darling favourite of Hell.
> Daniel Defoe (1661?–1731)
> *The True-Born Englishman*

Drinking too much has been roundly condemned for a variety of reasons by writers both ancient:

> Woe to you that are mighty to drink wine, and stout men at drunkenness.
> *Isaiah v. 22*

And modern:

> Drinking makes such fools of people, and people are such fools to begin with, that it's compounding a felony.
> Robert Benchley (1889–1945)

It was held that heavy drinking was rife amongst young people:

> [youth] ... is a state of continual inebriety for six or seven years at least, and frequently attended by fatal and permanent consequences, both to body and mind.
> Philip Stanhope, fourth Earl of Chesterfield (1694–1773)
> *Letters to his Son*

That people who drank heavily were unpredictable in their actions:

> A man who exposes himself when he is intoxicated, has not the art of getting drunk.
> Samuel Johnson (1709–1784)

> Better sleep with a sober cannibal than a drunken Christian.
> Herman Melville (1819–1891)

That alcohol was the enemy of love-making:

> Drink, sir, is a great provoker of three things ... Marry, sir, nose-painting, sleep, and urine. Lechery, sir, it provokes and unprovokes: it provokes the desire, but it takes away the performance.
> William Shakespeare (1564–1616)
> *Macbeth*, Act II, sc. iii

That drunkenness was abhorrent to those who were fastidious about the company they kept.

> One evening in October,
> When I was far from sober,
> And dragging home a load with manly pride,
> My feet began to stutter
> So I laid down in the gutter
> And a pig came up and parked right by my side.
> Then I warbled, 'It's fair weather
> When good fellows get together',

Till a lady passing by was heard to say:
'You can tell a man who boozes
By the company he chooses!'
Then the pig got up and slowly walked away.

This little verse, popular in America as a recitation, was attributed to Benjamin H. Burt by the actor DeWolf Hopper in his book *Once a Clown, Always a Clown*, but it has also been attributed to Aimor A. Dickson. The chances are that it began life in Ireland.

That a woman who enjoyed a drink was beyond redemption:

One who tips off the liquor with an appetite, and exclaims '*Good! Good!*' by a smack of her lips, is fit for nothing but a brothel.

William Cobbett (1762–1835)
Advice to Young Men

There was a strong feeling among Englishmen in the sixteenth century that the Dutch were to blame for most of their drink problems:

The *English*, who hitherto had, of all the northern nations, shewn themselves the least addicted to immoderate drinking, and been commended for their sobriety, first learn'd, in these *Netherland* wars, to swallow a large quantity of intoxicating liquor, and to destroy their own health, by drinking that of others.

William Camden (1551–1623)
Annals (under the year 1581)

The anti-puritan Thomas Nashe severely deplored the new, imported, attitude towards drunkenness:

Superfluitie in drink: a sinne, that euer since we haue mixt out selues with the Low-countries, is counted honourable: but before we knew their lingring warres, was held in ye highest defree of hatred that might be. Then, if wee had seene a man goe wallowing in the streetes, or line sleeping vnder the boord, we would have spet at him as a toade, and cald him foule drunken swine, and warnd all our friends out of his company: now, he is no body that cannot drinke *super nagulum*.

Thomas Nashe (1567–1601)
Pierce Pennilesse, his Supplication to the Divell

Super nagulum referred to one of those hearty drinking games which, like drinking toasts – a barbaric custom revived in Renaissance Italy – ended up with everybody being far drunker than they either intended or wanted to be. In drinking *super nagulum* the drinker up-ended his mug and let the last drop, or 'pearl', fall onto his thumb-nail. If it stayed there all was well, but if he had left too much drink in the mug and the drop rolled off he had to drink another whole mugful.

Thomas Nashe went on to describe eight different kinds of drunkenness:

The first is Ape drunke, and he leapes, and sings, and hollowes, and daunceth for the heauens:
the second is Lion drunke, and he flings the pots about the house, calls his Hostesse whore, breakes the glasse windowes with his dag-

ger, and is apt to quarrell with any man that speaks to him:
the third is Swine drunke; heauy, lumpish, and sleepie, and cries
for a little more drinke, and a fewe more cloathes:
the fourth is Sheepe drunke, wise in his own conceipt when he
cannot bring foorth a right word:
the fifth is Mawdlen drunke; when a fellow wil weepe for kindnes
in the midst of his Ale, and kisse you, saying, By God, Captaine,
I loue thee: go thy waies, thou dost not thinke so often of me as
I do of thee, I would (if it pleased God) I could not loue thee so
well as I doo: and then he puts his finger in his eie, and cries:
the sixt is Martin drunke, when a man is drunke, and drinkes himself sober ere he stirre:
the seuenth is Goate drunke, when, in his drunkennes, he hath no
minde but on Lecherie:
the eighth is Fox drunke, when he is craftie drunke, as manie of
the Dutchmen bee.

Thomas Nashe (1567–1601)
Pierce Pennilesse, his Supplication to the Divell

This piece might well have originated the phrase 'beastly drunk'.

Puritans strove hard to convince their weaker brethren that getting
drunk was a bad thing. Philip Stubbes, who came out with all guns
firing on matters like these, painted an awesome picture of what the
demon drink did to men:

How they stut and stammer, stagger and reel to and fro like madmen
... A man once drunk with wine or strong drink rather resembleth
a brute than a Christian man. For do not his eyes begin to stare and
to be red, fiery and bleared, blubbering forth seas of tears? Doth
he not foam and froth at the mouth like a boar? Doth not his tongue
falter and stammer in his mouth? Doth not his head seem as heavy
as a mill stone, he not being able to bear it up? Are not his wits
and spirits, as it were, drowned? Is not his understanding altogether
decayed? Do not his hands, and all his body vibrate, quaver and
shake, as it were, with a quotidian fever? Besides these, it casteth
him into a dropsy or pleurisy, nothing so soon; it enfeebleth the
sinews, it weakeneth the natural strength, it corrupteth the blood,
it dissolveth the whole man at the length, and finally maketh him
forgetful of himself altogether, so that what he doth being drunk,
he remembereth not being sober. The drunkard, in his drunkenness,
killeth his friend, revileth his lover, discloseth secrets, and regardeth
no man.

Philip Stubbes (*fl.* 1583–1591)
The Anatomie of Abuses

A scholarly friend of Milton's father wrote a long poem condemning
the prevailing vices of society in the reign of James I, 'a worke not
vnpleasant to be read'. It included a brief but emotional plea to
drunkards:

Would any heare the discommodities
That doe arise from our excesse of drinke?
It duls the braine, it hurts the memorie,
It blinds the sight, it makes men bleare-eyd blinke;

305

It kils the bodie, and it wounds the soule;
Leaue, therefore, leaue, O leaue this vice so foul!

John Lane (*fl.* 1620)
Tom Tel-Troths Message

A century later the satirist Samuel Butler described a drunkard. But this time there was a hint of compassion; a touch of the there-but-for-the-Grace-of-God-might-very-well-go-I. Which might well have happened; he certainly ended his days in poverty:

> A Sot has found out a Way to renew, not only his Youth, but his Childhood, by being stewed, like old Eason, in Liquor ... He has washed down his Soul and pist it out; and lives now only by the Spirit of Wine or Brandy ... He governs all his Actions by the Drink within him, as a Quaker does by the Light within him; has a different Humour for every Nick his Drink rises to, like the Degrees of the Weatherglass, and proceeds from Ribaldry and Bawdery to Politics, Religion, and Quarrelling, until it is at the Top, and then it is the Dog-Days with him, from whence he falls down again, until his liquor is at the Bottom, and then he lies quiet, and is frozen up.

Samuel Butler (1612–1680)
The Genuine Remains in Prose and Verse

As might be expected from a Restoration playwright, diplomat and rake, Sir George Etherege's objection to over-indulgence in the bottle was less on moral and humanitarian grounds than on its effect on love-making:

> To unbosom myself frankly and freely to your Grace, I always looked upon Drunkenness to be an unpardonable Crime in a young Fellow, who, without any of the foreign Helps, has Fire enough in his Veins to do Justice to *Coelia* whenever she demands a Tribute from him. In a middle-age Man, I consider the Bottle as only subservient to the nobler Pleasure of Love; and he that would suffer himself to be so far infatuated by it, as to neglect the Pursuit of a more agreeable Game, I think, deserves no Quarter from the Ladies.

Sir George Etherege (1635–1692)
Letter to the Duke of Buckingham, 12 Nov. 1688

A critic at the end of the seventeenth century managed to deplore drunkenness and stiffen his conscience towards another weakness at the same time:

> I always esteemed Drunkenness the most odious of Vices. There is something to be said for Whoring: Whoring is according to Nature.

John Dennis (1657–1734)
The Impartial Critic

Apart from some red-necked literary exchanges with Pope, Addison, Swift and Steele, Dennis is notable for having invented stage thunder. This was for one of his own plays, *Appius and Virginia*, produced at Drury Lane in 1709. The play failed and was taken off to make way for a production of *Macbeth*. Dennis went to the opening night and suddenly heard his thunder being used. With which he leapt to his feet and bellowed, 'That is my thunder, by God! The villains will play my thunder but not my plays!' This was the origin of the expression 'to steal one's thunder'.

During the eighteenth century steady and massive drinking was widespread throughout all ranks of society. Drunkenness had become socially acceptable in some spheres of polite society:

> Keeping bad company leads to all other bad things. I have got the headache today, by raking out so late with that gay libertine John-son.
>
> Hannah More (1745–1833)
> Letter to her family, 1776

This somewhat unusual description of a night out with Dr. Johnson must, alas, be put down to an attack of girlish flippancy overwhelming Miss More. Dr. Johnson was in his sixty-eighth year and had given up wine in favour of tea. Hannah More was then hovering about the more decorous fringes of the theatrical world, from which she was soon to rebound to the heights of the Evangelical movement. Her most popular work, *Coelebs in Search of a Wife* (1809), is now high on the list of the world's most unreadable books.

There was, however, another alternative to water on the market, and making steady progress. Or rather three alternatives, chocolate, coffee and tea, all of which arrived in England in the seventeenth century.

Cocoa beans had been used by the Aztecs both as money and as the raw material for a drink. Columbus brought some back to Spain, which managed to keep them a Spanish monopoly for a hundred years; they then leaked through to France and by 1700 most European countries had elegant chocolate houses, which sold the chocolate either as a lump to be taken home and scraped into the chocolate-pot and covered with hot water, or as a warming drink to be consumed on the premises.

About the beginning of the eighteenth century the English improved the flavour of chocolate by adding milk, but imported chocolate carried such a high import duty that it remained a rich household's pleasure until the nineteenth century.

The great era of chocolate drinking was the latter part of the seventeenth century. It was socially desirable, being so expensive, and was the favourite drink of French and Spanish courts, who attributed all sorts of medicinal qualities to it; for instance, it was believed that a cup of chocolate with a little amber dust dissolved in it was a fine restorative for a man who had 'drunk too deeply of the Cup of Pleasure'.

Aristocrats believed that there was little that the strange, bitter drink could not accomplish:

> The marquise de Coëtlogon took too much chocolate, being pregnant last year, that she was brought to bed of a little boy who was as black as the devil.
>
> Mme. de Sévigné (1626–1696)
> *Letters*

When new methods of milling cocoa beans were developed in the U.S.A. in 1827 a new drink, 'cocoa', was put on the market. The product of the bean was no longer a chic drink, a privilege of the *ton*:

> Cocoa is a cad and coward,
> Cocoa is a vulgar beast.
> G. K. Chesterton (1874–1936)
> *The Song of Right and Wrong*

Chocolate always had a slight and entirely unmerited reputation for briskening amatory fervour. When the popular night-time drink of cocoa also acquired a reputation for being a mild aphrodisiac the *New Statesman* magazine ran a competition for the best poem celebrating this myth:

> Half past nine – high time for supper;
> 'Cocoa, love?' 'Of course, my dear.'
> Helen thinks it quite delicious,
> John prefers it now to beer.
> Knocking back the sepia potion,
> Hubby winks, says, 'Who's for bed?'
> 'Shan't be long,' says Helen softly,
> Cheeks a faintly flushing red.
> For they've stumbled on the secret
> Of a love that never wanes,
> Rapt beneath the tumbled bedclothes,
> Cocoa coursing through their veins.
> Stanley J. Sharpless,
> 'Cupid's Nightcap'
> *New Statesman and Nation*, 7 Nov. 1953

The legend is that coffee – originally promoted as a medicine, of course, 'a certain remedy for eye troubles, roaring in the ears, and lung congestion' – was discovered by an Arabian goatherd named Kaldi about the year A.D. 850. Noticing that a strange restlessness and hilarity came over his flock whenever they munched the berries of a certain evergreen shrub he tried a handful himself and became exhilarated.

Muslims found that a heavy intake of coffee helped them through their very long religious ceremonies, so the priests decided that coffee must be a narcotic, or some kind of non-alcoholic alcohol, and banned it under the terms of the Koran. But it continued to be used by Arabs to sustain them; which it must have done very ably, being customarily taken in such a thick and concentrated form that it was not so much a drink as a tablespoonful of essence-of-caffeine.

The practice of coffee-drinking seeped into Europe during the sixteenth century, but ironically it was in England that it first became popular. About 1652 a certain Pasqua Rosée opened up the first public coffee-houses in St. Michael's Alley, London, where gentlemen could meet, relax, and sustain themselves on the new beverage which, Rosée claimed, 'quickens the spirits, and makes the heart lightsome' and at the same time 'is neither laxative nor restringent'.

Coffee-houses tapped a need and soon became part of the daily routine of merchants, politicians, lawyers, writers and wits; the convenient place where they met, read the news-sheets, drank the fashionable fluid, and gossiped. Many a marriage was connived, a reputation shredded, a career nipped in the bud, a poem conceived, a colleague's beggary plotted in coffee-houses such as Jonathan's, the Cocoa-Tree, Button's, Will's, and Lloyd's. Lloyd's Coffee-House in Tower Street, where the insurers of ship's cargoes were in the habit of meeting in order to do business, eventually developed into the great insurance exchange, Lloyd's of London.

Coffee-houses also prospered in other European cities but when, due to changing social conditions, their influence finally waned they were replaced by two quite different phenomena: on the continent arose the 'cafe', in England the 'gentleman's club'.

During the heyday of London coffee-houses they, and the coffee they served, came under brisk attack from Puritans, particularly lady Puritans. An anonymous pamphlet protested that coffee-drinking encouraged idling and talkativeness, and led men to:

> Trifle away their time, scald their chops, and spend their money, all for a little base, black, thick, nasty, bitter, stinking, nauseous puddle water.
>
> *The Women's Petition against Coffee*, 1674

The ladies of France were more concerned by other effects which coffee was reputed to have on men. In 1695 a report emerged from the École de Médecine in Paris that a regular intake of coffee deprived men of their generative power. It was as well to know this when entertaining the clergy:

> Coffee is not as necessary to ministers of the reformed faith as to Catholic priests. The latter are not allowed to marry, and coffee is said to induce chastity.
>
> Charlotte-Elisabeth, Duchesse d'Orléans (1652–1722)
> *Letters*
>
> The Duchesse was Louis XIV's sister-in-law.

The French nation continued its love-hate relationship with coffee until well into the nineteenth century.

M. Brillat-Savarin, the doyen of all writers about food and drink, issued a grave warning to parents:

It is the duty of all papas and mammas to forbid their children to drink coffee, unless they wish to have little dried-up machines, stunted and old at the age of twenty.

He went on to describe what befell a wretch who over-indulged:

I once saw a man in London, in Leicester Square, who had been crippled by immoderate indulgence in coffee; he was no longer in any pain, having grown accustomed to his condition, and had cut himself down to five or six cups a day.

Jean-Anthelme Brillat-Savarin (1755–1826)
La Physiologie du goût ou Méditations sur la Gastronomie Transcendante

M. Brillat-Savarin's great work was a collection of recipes, anecdotes, ideas and philosophical musings about food and drink, treating eating and drinking as an art: an unprecedented attitude. To the annoyance of professional writers on cookery matters he was neither a writer nor a cook but a provincial lawyer, a cousin of Mme. Récamier. During the French Revolution he prudently withdrew to New York where he earned a living playing the violin in a theatre pit-orchestra. His sister died in her hundredth year, after a huge dinner, calling loudly for dessert.

The ladies of Germany, unlike the ladies of England, took immediately to the new drink and by the eighteenth century the craze for it had reached such proportions that Johann Sebastian Bach composed a cantata mocking the coffee-mad ladies of Leipzig. The last line of the libretto stated:

The cat cannot stop chasing mice, the spinsters must remain coffee addicts.

Libretto: Christian Henrici
Music: Johann Sebastian Bach (1685–1750)
Kaffee-Kantate

Perhaps the trouble with English coffee was the coffee beans:

Coffee, as drunk in England, debilitates the stomach, and produces a slight nausea ... it is usually made from bad Coffee, served out tepid and muddy, and drowned in a deluge of water.

William Kitchiner, M.D. (1775–1827)
The Cook's Oracle

Dr. Kitchiner had many other enthusiasms besides cookery. His works included *Loyal, National, and Sea Songs of England; Of Telescopes*, and *The Pleasure of Making a Will*. The poet Tom Hood was so taken with the doctor's versatility that he wrote two odes in his honour, *Ode to Dr. Kitchiner* and *To W. Kitchiner M.D.* This last began:

Hail, multifarious man!
Thou wondrous, Admirable Kitchen Crichton
Born to enlighten
The Laws of Optics, Peptics, Music, Cooking,
Master of the piano – and the Pan ...

During the eighteenth and nineteenth centuries the English developed a technique for making coffee which won for it an international reputation which it has held ever since:

> The tea is always excellent in England, but nowhere do they drink worse coffee.
>
> B. Faujas de Saint-Fond
Voyage en Angleterre, 1797

> English coffee tastes like water that has been squeezed out of a wet sleeve.
>
> Fred Allen (1894–1956)
Treadmill to Oblivion

> Coffee in England is just toasted milk.
>
> Christopher Fry (b. 1907)
Quoted by *New York Post*, 29 Nov. 1962

During its long history coffee has not only been denounced by religious bodies, condemned for its deleterious effects on the human body and disliked for its taste, but its cultivation has also been regretted for humanitarian reasons:

> Whether coffee and sugar are really necessary to the happiness of Europe, is more than I can say, but I affirm — that these two vegetables have brought wretchedness and misery upon America and Africa. The former is depopulated, that Europeans may have a land to plant them in; and the latter, is stripped of its inhabitants, for hands to cultivate them.
>
> Bernardin de Saint-Pierre (1737–1814)
Voyage à l'Ile de France

The most enduring slogan in the English language plugging a product must surely be, after nearly two hundred years of constant use, the line, 'The cup that cheers but does not inebriate'; referring to a cup of tea.

As is the way with these things it is a slight misquotation. The original line was, 'The cups that cheer but not inebriate' and it came from William Cowper's poem *The Task*, published in 1785. But the line is even older than that. It is clearly an echo of a phrase used by Bishop Berkeley in his book *Siris*, published in 1744, when he wrote of a liquid 'of a nature so mild and benign ... as to warm without heating, to cheer but not inebriate'. The interesting thing is that this liquid was not tea but tar-water.

The idea of drinking an infusion of wood-tar in cold water was brought back from America by the philosopher George Berkeley, bishop of Cloyne, who enthused about the medicinal qualities of the drink in a number of books and pamphlets, e.g. 'It is good not only in fevers, diseases of the lungs, cancers, scrofula, throat diseases, apoplexies, chronic disorders of all kinds, but also as a general drink for infants' (*Further Thoughts on Tar-Water*, 1752), which reads a little like a testimonial for snake-oil. But Dr. Johnson spoke highly of tar-water, which was more than he did for the bishop's philosophical theory that matter did not exist, and Henry Fielding, dying of the dropsy on his way to Lisbon, wrote of tar-water helping to ease his suffering.

Despite all these testimonials tar-water had only a short, although brilliant, period of popularity. Perhaps its flavour still lingers in the faint but agreeable taste of creosote which lurks in the popular American bottled drinks based on the kola nut.

By the time Cowper wrote his lines on tea, tar-water was almost forgotten. Tea had become the national alternative to beer.

Tea – 'a certain remedy for paralysis, apoplexy, and consumption' – had been drunk by a rich few since it was first offered for sale over the counter at Garway's Coffee House, London, at about £4 a pound. It remained very expensive for about a hundred years, being a monopoly of the East India Company and heavily taxed, a circumstance which contributed via the Boston Tea Party to the American War of Independence.

But tea, unlike coffee, appealed strongly to women, even though its use was restricted to those who could afford its crippling price: it was non-alcoholic, but most of all it lent itself to ritual. There was the mystique of the infusion, the display of specially made silver and china paraphernalia, the ceremony of handing round, the sugar bowl with choice of pieces of sugar to nibble or soft sugar to stir in. It was the politest of drinks.

Daniel Defoe called attention to the feminine pressure behind the growing interest in tea when he wrote about Nottingham:

> The chief Manufacture carried on here is Framework-knitting of Stockens, the same as at Leicester, and some Glass and earthen Ware. The latter is much increased by the Consumption of Tea-pots, Cups, &c. since the Increase of Tea-drinking, as the Glass-houses, I think, are of late rather decreas'd. A Proof, one would think, that the Luxury of the Males is less predominant than that of the Females; or, rather as some would say, that the Men are brought over by the Ladies to join with them in the love of the Tea-table: and indeed the latter seems pretty much the case; whether it be owing to Gallantry and Complaisance, or to Effeminacy and Indolence, let those concerned in the Observation answer.
>
> Daniel Defoe (1661?–1731)
> *A Tour Thro' the Whole Island of Great Britain*

By the middle of the eighteenth century a potentially vast market existed for cheap tea and entrepreneurs managed to tap this, mainly by smuggling. Other European nations, such as Holland, which had trade with the East put a far lower duty on tea than did the East India Company, so supplies were run in to English ports from Emden, Dunkirk and Boulogne. This tea, although somewhat dusty and of inferior quality, sold for as little as two shillings a pound.

And so, to the fury of many, like the philanthropist and social reformer Jonas Hanway, tea became available to the lower orders:

> Your very chambermaids have lost their bloom; I suppose by drinking tea.
>
> Jonas Hanway (1712–1786)
> *An Essay on Tea*

Hanway's 'essay', which was a full-length book, annoyed Dr. Johnson, who by then was consuming a vast number of cups of tea per day (as no doubt Dr. Johnson bought un-smuggled tea it is not surprising that his tea-cups, which are preserved in the Lichfield museum, were tiny).

Jonas Hanway wanted the nation to eschew tea and take to drinking ground-ivy. He put up many arguments against tea:

> Since tea has been in fashion, even *suicide* has been more familiar amongst us than in times past.
>
> *Ibid.*

He also worked out that if there were 1,000,000 servants, mechanics and labourers working 280 days a year and each one took an hour off in every twelve to brew up, tea cost the nation £583,333 per annum in lost working hours. But what really agitated him was that if breeding-pairs really took to the effete habit of drinking tea England might run short of cannon-fodder:

> You may see *laborers* who are *mending the road* drinking their tea; it is even drunk in *cinder-carts*, and what is not less absurd, sold out in cups to *Haymakers*. He who should be able to drive *three Frenchmen* before him, or she who might be a breeder of such a race of men, are to be seen *sipping* their tea!
>
> Ibid.

> Hanway, a colourful figure of his time, applied a lifetime of zeal to such causes as succouring foundlings, finding seamen for the navy without recourse to kidnapping, preventing Jews from becoming naturalized, protecting young chimney-sweeps from dangerous exploitation, urging solitary confinement for convicts, etc. etc. For all or some of these activities he had a small street, and a 'place' off Oxford Street, named after him, and a monument in the north transept of Westminster Abbey. He adopted an ancient eastern ceremonial device used for protection against the sun and carried it as protection against the rain, thus becoming the first man in England to walk about the streets under an umbrella.

In spite of all the exhortations to ignore the oriental leaf it grew steadily more popular among all classes and dropped steadily in price.

One of the last rearguard actions was fought by William Cobbett:

I view the tea-drinking as a destroyer of health, an enfeebler of the frame, an engenderer of effeminacy and laziness, a debaucher of youth and a maker of misery for old age.

William Cobbett (1762–1835)
The Vice of Tea-Drinking

But there was no holding tea. Towards the middle of the nineteenth century a change was brought about in our feeding habits and 'tea' was transformed from a mere hot drink to a full ceremony and, in the north of England, a complete early-evening meal. At the beginning of the nineteenth century the custom was to have a huge breakfast and keep going on that until dinner, which was not until about eight o'clock in the evening. In 1840 Anna, wife of the seventh Duke of Bedford, bridged the gap by inventing Tea. That is to say, the tea-party: table-cloth, tiny sandwiches, a big cake, little cakes, anchovy toast, 'bite or stir' sugar, Indian or China tea, chat. A graceful, very feminine occasion summarized by an American writer as:

Giggle, gabble, gobble, git.

Oliver Wendell Holmes (1809–1894)

By the twentieth century Britain was drinking five times as much tea as coffee. It had become the national drink, ubiquitous and commonplace:

If I had known there was no Latin word for tea, I would have let the vulgar stuff alone.

Hilaire Belloc (1870–1953)

In ancient Rome the social implications of people eating and drinking together rather than in solitude were explored to the full. Rich Romans, many of whom were *nouveau riche*, used dinner-parties as a means of demonstrating their wealth and superiority. An invitation to dine could be bestowed as patronage or withheld as a snub.

The Romans thought eight to be the maximum number for a good dinner-party or orgy, but this number was usually filled out by a quantity of hangers-on, the 'parasites', aspiring poets and others who hopefully clung close to their patron, as well as a considerable quantity of slaves, carvers, boys, musicians and dancers milling about the eating area. In Rome it was considered a perfectly respectable aim in life for a rich man or woman to gratify, and extend, his or her sensual appetites, so foods became richer and rarer and hosts tried to outdo each other with displays of conspicuous wealth and waste.

A whole section of Roman society depended on being asked to dinner by someone important, perhaps because some kind of favour was needed, but often because it was the only chance of getting something decent to eat. Behind Rome's marble walls were rookeries of small tenements peopled by poor gentry with nothing to do all day but look forward to the evening when they could sally forth to the public baths in their one good set of finery and hope to wheedle an invitation to some influential man's dinner table.

Sometimes to be disappointed when they got there:

> Twice thirty were we, Mancinus, your invited guests, and nothing was served us last night but a boar. There were no grapes ... nor honey-apples ... nor pears ... nor pomegranates ... rural Sassina sent no cones of cheese; there came no olive from Picenian Jars. A boar, and nothing else! and this too a tiny one, and such as could be slaughtered by an unarmed dwarf.
>
> Martial (c. A.D. 40–104)
> *Epigrams:* Bk. I, epig. 43

The behaviour of some hungry guests caused comment:

> Whatever is served you sweep off from this or that part of the table: the teat of a sow's udder and a rib of pork, and a heathcock meant for two, half a mullet, and a bass whole, and the side of a lamprey, and the leg of a fowl, and a pigeon dripping with its white sauce. These dainties, when they have been hidden in your sodden napkin, are handed over to your boy to carry home: we recline at table, an idle crowd. If you have any decency, restore our dinner; I did not invite you, Caecilianus, to a meal tomorrow.
>
> Martial (c. A.D. 40–104)
> *Epigrams:* Bk. II, epig. 37

> No miserliness or gluttony is equal to Santra's. When he has been invited and has hurried off to the grand dinner which he has for so many nights and days fished for, he asks thrice for kernels of boar, four times for the loin, and for each leg of a hare ... And when his napkin is already bursting under his thousand thefts, he secretes in the reeking folds of his gown gnawed vertebrae, and a turtle-dove shorn of its head already gobbled up ... When that greedy fellow has carried these things home up two hundred stairs, and anxiously shut himself in his locked garret, the next day—he sells the lot.
>
> Martial (c. A.D. 40–104)
> *Epigrams:* Bk. VII, epig. 20

Athenaeus mentioned in his *Deipnosophistai* a celebrated Roman glutton who always turned up at table wearing gloves so that he could grab hold of the meat while it was too hot to handle and so get more than anybody else.

Less hygienic methods were also practised:

> A tart, repeatedly handed round at the second course, burnt the fingers cruelly with its excessive heat. But Sabidius' gluttony was more ardent still; straightway, therefore, three and four times he blew

315

upon it with his full cheeks. The tart, indeed, grew cooler, and seemed to allow the fingers; but not a man could touch it — 'twas filth!

Martial (*c.* A.D. 40–104)
Epigrams: Bk. III, epig. 17

Meals in the Middle Ages were frequently huge and protracted occasions and efforts were made to formulate rules of behaviour.

The key to the eating problem was that forks had not yet arrived as an implement to eat food with. Fingers were used.

Forks first came into polite use in Venice in the early sixteenth century. At the beginning of the seventeenth century a traveller from England noted the bizarre custom:

> I observed a custom in all those Italian cities and towns through which I passed that is not used in any other country that I saw in my travels, neither do I think that any other nation in Christendom doth use it, but only in Italy. The Italian and also most strangers that are commorant in Italy do always at their meals use a little fork when they cut their meat. For while with their knife which they hold in one hand, they cut the meat out of the dish, they fasten their fork which they hold in their other hand upon the same dish, so that whatsoever he be that sitting in the company of any others at meal, should unadvisedly touch the dish of meat with his fingers from which all at the table do cut, he will give occasion of offence unto the company, as having transgressed the laws of good manners, in so much that for his error he shall be at the least brow-beaten, if not reprehended in words.

Thomas Coryat (1577?–1617)
Crudities

Coryats Crudities, published in 1611, was the first book to be written about continental travel.

The fork was introduced into France in the sixteenth century by Henry III, who was rather effete and liked Italy, only to be sternly denounced by Louis XIV as a useless luxury.

England did not take to the fork until late in the seventeenth century. Into the reign of Queen Anne it was still acceptable to eat with the fingers plus a spoon and a pointed knife which was also used for trimming trees, digging out candle stumps, and removing obnoxious matter from horses' hooves.

In the Middle Ages the food was put onto the table in various dishes and the diner took what he wanted and dumped it onto his trencher. These trenchers were sometimes of wood but frequently a slice of stale or 'flat' bread about six inches by four inches. The advantage of the bread trencher was that all the juices and sauces soaked into it and when the meal was over any chinks could be filled up by eating the trencher. Traces of the bread trencher linger on in the slices of bread on which game and Tournedos steaks are still served in our more hair-raisingly expensive restaurants.

The dishes of food were in servings for two and each diner dipped into the bowl with his fingers and fished about for something solid, then let his neighbour have a go. It was therefore a matter of some concern what a neighbour did with his fingers between dips:

> Let thy fingers be clean.
> Thou must not put thy fingers into thine ears,
> Or thy hands on thy head.
> The man who is eating must not be cleaning
> By scraping with his finger at any foul part.
>
> Fra Bonvicino (thirteenth century)

Fleas were a problem. The floor was strewn with rushes, sometimes scented with herbs but rarely bug-free. And as the floor was the polite place to dump bones and unchewable lumps there was much activity below the board from the household dogs, also rarely bug-free:

> You must not scratch your throat whilst you eat, with the bare hand.
> But if it happens that you cannot help scratching, then courteously take a portion of your dress, and scratch with that.
>
> Tannhäuser (fourteenth century)

A small manuscript on vellum called the 'Boke of Curtasye' (MS. Sloane 1986. Re-printed Percy Society, Vol. 19, 1841) gave full instructions on how all manner of fourteenth-century uncouthness could be corrected. This manuscript was put into print in the late fifteenth century by Wynken de Worde, Caxton's apprentice and successor, and parts of it crop up in various other improving publications such as *The Booke of Demeanor* and *The Boke of Kervynge*.

Some of the behaviour which these courtesy books attacked was richly medieval:

> Let not thy privy members be lay'd open to be view'd, it is most shameful and abhorr'd, detestable and rude.

Many of the stern admonitions were directed at the ladies:

> If thou sit by a right goode manne,
> This lesson look thou think upon.
> Under his thigh thy knee not fit,
> Thou art full lewd, if thou does it.

A number of the table-manners taught were surprisingly genteel, like the rules laid down by a Victorian nanny: sit upright, lay your trencher straight in front of you, do not let your spoon stand in the dish but clean it carefully:

> Bite not on your bread and lay it down,
> That is no curtesy to use in town;
> But break as much as you will eat ...

But most of the behaviour frowned upon was robust enough:

> Beware of thy hinder parts from gun blasting.

317

This was at least a clear, positive instruction on a point of etiquette which the Emperor Claudius, some fifteen hundred years previously, had doubts about on humanitarian grounds:

> He is reported to have had some thoughts of making a decree that it might be lawful for any man to break wind at the table, being told of a person whose modest retention had like to have cost him his life.
>
> Suetonius (c. A.D. 70–c. 160)
> *De Vita Caesarum*

The writers of cookery-books and manuals of etiquette continued, through the centuries, their uphill struggle against gross behaviour at table:

> Fill not your mouth so full that your cheeks shall swell like a pair of *Scotch-bag-pipes*.
>
> Hannah Wolley (*fl.* 1670)

> It is not becoming a person of quality, when in the Company of Ladies, to handle them roughly: to put his hand in their necks or their bosoms; to kiss them by surprize ... you must forbear hawking or spitting as much as you can, and when you are not able to hold, if you observe it neat and kept cleanly, you must turn your back and rather spit in your Handkerchief than the Room ... If his Lordship be set by the fire, you must be careful how you spit into the Chimney.
>
> *Rules of Civility* (1685)

These teach-yourself-polite-manners books were designed, of course, for the rising middle class; the aristocracy had no need of them:

> My cold is so bad, that I could not go to church today, nor to court; but I was engaged to Lord Orkney's, with the Duke of Ormond, at dinner; and ventured, because I could cough and spit there as I pleased.
>
> Dean Swift (1667–1745)
> Letter to Mrs. Dingley, 28 Dec. 1712

The nobility, or some of it, clung to its coarseness to the last George, to the wonderment of Victorians:

> I have been told, by one who heard it from an eye-witness, that a great Whig duchess ... turning to the footman who was waiting on her at dinner, exclaimed, 'I wish to G—that you wouldn't keep rubbing your great greasy belly against the back of my chair.'
>
> G. W. E. Russell
> Quoted by Gillian Avery in *Victorian People*

The overthrow of the Roman Empire put an end to large-scale junketings and large-scale eating, ushering in some centuries of widespread warfare, famine, even cannibalism.

The Middle Ages, and the feudal system, brought law and a little order into ordinary life, and into eating and drinking. Countrymen fared better than those who had to live in towns, where fish and meat had to be brought in by painfully slow transport and was almost inevitably high or rancid. This was the era of spices – or, for poor people, herbs – which besides having a pleasant taste served to conceal the gaminess of the meat and fish. As there was no winter fodder, almost all cattle was killed off in the late autumn and salted down for eating during the winter. Spices were used to cheer up this otherwise unappetizing boiled meat. Fresh fruit was looked upon as dangerous and until the eighteenth century the English ate their fruit in dried form: figs, dates and 'raisins of the sun'. Salads were for rich people only. All this, combined with the fact that about the only vegetables eaten were cabbages and onions, meant that the medieval Englishman's diet was almost totally lacking in vitamin C and it is probable that the whole nation suffered, lightly or severely, from scurvy.

During the Middle Ages spices had as big an effect on the economy of European nations as does oil in the twentieth century. The supplies had to be brought overland from the East via Venice, which grew exceedingly rich not by holding 'the gorgeous East in fee', as Wordsworth suggested, but by holding the Western nations to ransom. It was to break this monopoly of the spice trade that Spain and Portugal sent their navigators out to find a sea route to the East.

Cooking with spice was international. When spices eventually went out of fashion national differences in eating became more apparent.

The Scots habit of eating oats was a constant source of mirth to Englishmen who, like the Romans, believed oats to be fit only for horses.

The big joke about Welshmen was their supposed passion for consuming toasted cheese:

> I find written among old jests how God made Saint Peter porter of heaven, and that God of His goodness, soon after His Passion, suffered many men to come to the kingdom of heaven with small deserving; at which time there was in heaven a great company of Welshmen which with their cracking and babbling troubled all the others. Wherefore God said to Saint Peter that He was weary of them and that He would fain have them out of heaven. To whom Saint Peter said, 'Good Lord, I warrant you, that shall be done.'
>
> Wherefore Saint Peter went out of heaven-gates and cried with a loud voice, 'Caws pob' – that is as much as to say 'roasted cheese' – which thing the Welshmen hearing, ran out of heaven a great pace. And when Saint Peter saw them all out, he suddenly went into heaven and locked the door, and so sparred all the Welshmen out.
>
> *Merry Tales, Wittie Questions and Quicke Answeres*, 1567

A stronger version of the story turned up over two hundred years later:

> WELCH RABBIT (i.e. a Welch rare bit). Bread and cheese toasted. See
> RABBIT. – The Welch are said to be so remarkably fond of cheese,

that in cases of difficulty their midwives apply a piece of toasted cheese to the *janua vitae*, to attract and entice the young Taffy, who on smelling it makes most vigorous efforts to come forth.

Francis Grose (1731?–1791)
A Classical Dictionary of the Vulgar Tongue

Whereas other European nations developed tastes for sauces, hams, various sausages and subtle soups, England settled for a simple diet of roast or boiled joints of meat and a range of meat puddings. To the rest of the Continent, England was a nation of beer-swilling beef-eaters:

Go back, you dissolute English,
Drink your beer and eat your pickled beef.
La Répentance des Anglais et des Espagnols, 1522

Flesh-eaters, and insatiable of animal food; sottish and unrestrained in their appetites; full of suspicion.

Nicander Nucius of Corcyra
Travels, 1545

The English, on their part, have always been deeply suspicious of foreign cooking and foods. During the eighteenth century, with France an enemy, Francophobia flourished and a tradition grew that 'Frenchified' cooking was to be looked down upon as messy, mysterious, dangerous and a waste of good, honest food:

As to the repast, it was made up of a parcel of kickshaws, contrived by a French cook, without one substantial article adapted to the satisfaction of an English appetite. The pottage was little better than bread soaked in dish washings, luke-warm. The ragouts looked as if they had been once eaten and half digested: the fricassees were involved in a nasty yellow poultice; and the rotis were scorched and stinking, for the honour of the fumet. The dessert consisted of faded fruit and iced froth, a good emblem of our landlady's character; the table-beer was sour, the water foul, and the wine vapid.

Tobias Smollett (1721–1771)
The Expedition of Humphry Clinker

This piece of ingratitude managed to name most of the French dishes which particularly horrified the English.

kickshaws = corruption of *quelque chose*. Small morsels of food, elegant but not very nourishing.
pottage = vegetables and meat boiled in water until soft.
ragout = from *ragoûter*, to revive the taste. Originally highly spiced sauce to cheer up dull meat but came to refer to pieces of meat and vegetables stewed in highly seasoned stock.
fricassees = stewed or fried meat in a sauce. Usually rabbit or birds.
roti = roast.
fumet = the smell of well-hung game.

The English continued to be wary of ragouts, perhaps because of the difficulty of identifying the contents:

'Hot, smoking hot, on the fire was a pot
Well replenish'd, but really I can't say with what;
For, famed as the French always are for ragouts,
No creature can tell what they put in their stews,
Whether bull-frogs, old gloves, or old wigs, or old shoes.
                                    R. H. Barham (1788–1845)
                        Ingoldsby Legends: 'The Bagman's Dog'

The prejudice against foreign food was not narrowly confined to France:

The Portuguese had need have the stomach of ostriches to digest the loads of greasy victuals with which they cram themselves. Their vegetables, their rice, their poultry are all stewed in the essence of ham, and so strongly seasoned with pepper and spices that a spoonful of pease or a quarter of an onion is sufficient to set one's mouth in a flame.
                                    William Beckford (1760–1844)
                        Italy; with Sketches of Spain and Portugal

Recipes were one thing, but what happened to the food before it was cooked was another. Food-handling was always a problem in towns, and hair-raising things were done to London's food supplies during the eighteenth century, both by accident and design:

The bread I eat in London, is a deleterious paste, mixed up with chalk, alum, and bone-ashes; insipid to the taste, and destructive to the constitution ...

The milk ... should not pass unanalysed, the produce of faded cabbage-leaves and sour draff, lowered with hot water, frothed with bruised snails, carried through the streets in open pails, exposed to foul rinsings discharged from doors and windows, spittle, snot, and tobacco-quids from foot-passengers, over-flowings from mud-carts, spatterings from coach-wheels, dirt and trash chucked into it by roguish boys for the joke's sake, the spewings of infants, who have slabbered in the tin-measure, which is thrown back in that condition among the milk, for the benefit of the next customer; and finally, the vermin that drops from the rags of the nasty drab that vends this precious mixture, under the respectable denomination of milk-maid.

I shall conclude this catalogue of London dainties, with that table-beer, guiltless of hops and malt, vapid and nauseous; much fitter to facilitate the operation of a vomit, than to quench thirst and promote digestion; the tallowy rancid mass called butter, manufactured with candle-grease and kitchen stuff; and their fresh eggs, imported from France and Scotland.
                                    Tobias Smollett (1721–1771)
                        The Expedition of Humphry Clinker

Xenophobia also extended to foreigners' eating habits and table-manners. Tobias Smollett, 'traduced by malice, persecuted by faction, abandoned by false patrons' as he put it, fled 'with eagerness' to make a tour of France and Italy, only to find that they ordered matters differently over there, and not at all to his liking:

> There is nothing so vile or repugnant to nature; but you may plead prescription for it, in the customs of some nation or other. A Parisian likes mortified flesh: a native of Legiboli will not taste his fish till it is quite putrefied: the civilized inhabitants of Kamschatka get drunk with the urine of their guests, whom they have already intoxicated: the Nova Zemblans make merry on train-oil: the Groenlanders eat in the same dish with their dogs: the Caffres, at the Cape of Good Hope, piss upon those whom they delight to honour, and feast upon a sheep's intestines with their contents, as the greatest dainty that can be presented. A true-bred Frenchman dips his fingers, imbrowned with snuff, into his plate filled with ragout: between every three mouthfuls, he produces his snuff-box, and takes a fresh pinch, with the most graceful gesticulations; then he displays his handkerchief, which may be termed the *flag of abomination*, and, in the use of both, scatters his favours among those who have the happiness to sit near him.
>
> Tobias Smollett (1721–1771)
> *Travels through France and Italy*

Dr. Johnson also disapproved of some practices he met with in Paris:

> ... 'The French are an indelicate people: they will spit upon any place. At Madame ——'s, a literary lady of rank, the footman took the sugar in his fingers, and threw it into my coffee. I was going to put it aside: but hearing it was made on purpose for me, I e'en tasted Tom's finger. The same lady would needs make tea *à l'Angloise*. The spout of the teapot did not pour freely; she bade the footman blow into it.'
>
> Samuel Johnson (1709–1784)
> Boswell's *Life*, 5 Nov. 1775

Smollett, ill, bad-tempered at the best of times, came up against another revolting custom on his continental tour:

> I know no custom more beastly than that of using water-glasses, in which polite company spirt, and squirt, and spue the filthy scourings of their gums, under the eyes of each other. I knew a lover cured of his passion, by seeing this nasty cascade discharged from the mouth of his mistress. I don't doubt but I shall live to see the day, when the hospitable custom of the ancient Aegyptians will be revived; then a conveniency will be placed behind every chair in company, with a proper provision of waste paper, that individuals may make themselves easy without parting company. I insist upon it, that this practice would not be more indelicate than that which is now in use.
>
> Tobias Smollett (1721–1771)
> *Travels through France and Italy*

A few years later a Frenchman complained about the nasty custom

322

of using a mouth-wash at the table, but he took it to be an English habit. The other custom which disturbed him was without doubt English:

There are some customs here not quite consistent with that scrupu-lous delicacy on which the English pique themselves. Towards the end of dinner, and before the ladies retire, bowls of coloured glass full of water are placed before each person. All (women as well as men) stoop over it, sucking up some of the water, and returning it, often more than once, and, with a spitting and washing sort of noise, quite charming, — the operation frequently assisted by a finger elegantly thrust into the mouth! This done, and the hands dipped also, the napkins, and sometimes the table-cloth, are used to wipe hand and mouth. This, however, is nothing to what I am going to relate. Drinking much and long leads to unavoidable consequences. Will it be credited, that, in a corner of the very dining-room, there is a certain convenient piece of furniture, to be used by anybody who wants it. The operation is performed very deliberately and undis-guisedly, as a matter of course, and occasions no interruption of the conversation.

Louis Simond
A Journal of a Tour in Great Britain, 5 March 1810

The twin horrors of mouth-scouring and chamber-potting seem to have been almost an obsession with fastidious Frenchmen. Fifty-five years after Smollett mentioned the matter the great Brillat-Savarin was still going on about it:

In houses where a point is made of following the latest fashions, serv-ants, at the end of dessert, distribute bowls of cold water among the guests, in each of which stands a goblet of hot water. Whereupon, in full view of one another, the guests plunge their fingers in the cold water, as if to wash them, fill their mouths with the hot, gargle noisily, and spit it out into the goblet or the bowl.
  I am not the only person to have spoken out against this useless, indecent, and disgusting innovation ...
  Ever since the official appearance of these new-fangled bowls I have been grieving night and day. A second Jeremiah, I deplore the vagaries of fashion; and all too well informed by my travels, I never now enter a dining-room without trembling at the thought that my eyes might fall upon the odious *chamber-pot.**

* It is common knowledge that there are, or were a few years ago, dining-rooms in England where it was possible for a man to answer the call of Nature without leaving the room: A curious facility.

Jean-Anthelme Brillat-Savarin (1755–1826)
La Physiologie du goût ou Méditations sur la gastronomie transcendante

The 'curious facility' had been enjoyed for a great number of years, not only by diners but also by gentlemen travelling in their coaches (silver or pewter), ship's captains (silver or pewter) and judges on the bench (pewter, or occasionally porcelain vases). Nowadays the facility is rarely

323

made use of, although still, on an English night, the moon shining over an estate will illume a crocodile of dinner-jacketed figures, wreathed in cigar-smoke, picking its way carefully towards the compost heap, or lined up like a firing-squad opposite the rose-bed.

From the late seventeenth century to the early part of the nineteenth century men of fashion prided themselves on the amount of drink they could consume before passing out – as distinct from the later pride in how much could be consumed without passing out – and aristocratic drunkenness was so commonplace that the expression 'drunk as a lord' was not so much a joke as a straightforward simile.

But from the early part of the eighteenth century onwards heavy drinking, particularly of gin, became widespread amongst poor people.

Queen Anne imposed a tax on gin imported from Holland in an effort to control the rising tide of drunkenness, but as the selling of gin was not controlled by licence, as was beer, the drink shops just made their own brew, using a daunting range of raw materials including lime-water, oil of turpentine and sulphuric acid. This they were able to sell very cheaply, hence the contemporary slogan 'drunk for a penny, dead drunk for twopence'.

As the nation became more industrialized and there was a growing drift away from the countryside and into over crowded towns drunkenness increased. Working hours were very long, living accommodation was cramped and unattractive, and often the only relaxation open to a worker with only a copper or two to spend was the brilliantly lit, warm, friendly drink shop:

> Ha! see where the wild-blazing Grog-Shop appears
> As the red waves of wretchedness swell,
> How it burns on the edge of tempestuous years
> The horrible Light-House of Hell!
>
> McDonald Clarke (1798–1842)
> *The Rum Hole*

Clarke was known to the New York admirers of his work as The Mad Poet.

Forces mustered to fight the good fight. Philanthropists and reformers got together to combat the demon drink, supported by powerful manufacturers who objected to drunkenness both on pious grounds – they tended to be nonconformists – and for the more practical reason that their labour force was rendering itself unfit for work.

And so the temperance movement arose, dedicated not as its name would suggest to urging moderation but, for the first time in the Western world, to the total abolition of alcoholic drinks. Some groups did try to allow beer, to begin with, but as their enthusiasm grew so their aim became more absolute.

The first temperance society was probably one formed in 1808 at

Saratoga in the U.S.A. Europe's first was formed in 1818 at – of all places – Skibbereen, Ireland, and by 1840 England had societies springing up all over the country; and a new word for a man who did not drink – 'teetotaller'.

> There should be asylums for such people. But they would probably relapse into teetotallism as soon as they came out.
>
> Samuel Butler (1835–1902)
Note-Books

Temperance workers were fervent creatures, and sometimes toilers in the same vineyard (if one might be permitted the expression) came to blows.

In 1858 Dr. Lees, who embraced the teachings of the Council of the United Kingdom for the Suppression of the Traffic in Intoxicating Drinks which stood for 'total and immediate prohibition by law', fell out with a Mr. J. Bartholomew Gough of the National Temperance League, which held that the law should be left as it was and sweet reason brought heavily to bear on the topers. Dr. Lees wrote allegedly libellous comments on Mr. Gough's bearing and behaviour:

> ... I mean that he is *often intoxicated* – not with alcohol, but other narcotics. I do not tell you of what I have heard, and which for long I struggled to *disbelieve*, but of what I KNOW. I have *seen* him clearly intoxicated with some drug, and seen it more than *once*. I know also that he used to consume *tobacco* by chewing; for he once consulted me on the matter, partly to throw me off the true scent. I know a score of persons who have *seen him* in the same condition – some who have seen him helplessly, almost *idiotically* intoxicated. I know others who have seen him *insensible* in the streets of London – '*nervous apoplexy*' called! Vomiting of matter with a *strong vegetable appleish odour* was among the symptoms; and I can, if necessary, tell you some shops where your informant *bought opium*. I do not care to tell you of his prevarication, of his mercenariness, his meanness, and his sponging; of his fondness for visiting styes [brothels] and low localities; for the *tastes of a lifetime* cannot be got rid of, or the marks of the Beast be easily eradicated ...
>
> Letter from Dr. Lees to Mr. W. Wilson
8 Jan. 1858

> The ensuing court action ended rather messily. The plaintiff, Mr. Gough, turned out to be a not entirely reformed drunkard and was awarded five guineas damages.

A good deal of temperance propaganda was in the form of tracts and leaflets. They told a sorry story:

> Drink has drained more blood,
> Hung more crepe,
> Sold more homes
> Plunged more people into bankruptcy,
> Armed more villains,
> Slain more children,

Snapped more wedding rings,
Defiled more innocents,
Blinded more eyes,
Twisted more limbs,
Dethroned more intellects,
Wrecked more manhood,
Dishonoured more womanhood,
Broken more hearts,
Blasted more lives,
Driven to more suicide, and
Dug more graves than any other poisoned
     scourge that ever swept its death-
     dealing waves across the world.

General Evangeline Booth (1865–1950)

Many temperance writings were anonymous. Possibly because of the author's modesty but more probably because the author did not embrace the cause but was merely earning himself a quick half-guinea. Sometimes the message was spelt out in clear, muscular couplets:

The Saloon Bar

A bar to Heaven, a door to Hell, —
Whoever named it, named it well!
A bar to manliness and wealth,
A door to want and broken health;
A bar to honour, pride and fame,
A door to sin and grief and shame;
A bar to hope, a bar to prayer,
A door to darkness and despair;
A bar to honoured, useful life,
A door to brawling, senseless strife;
A bar to all that's true and brave,
A door to every drunkard's grave;
A bar to joy that home imparts,
A door to tears and aching hearts;
A bar to Heaven, a door to Hell, —
Whoever named it, named it well!

Anon.

Sometimes the message was introduced more sneakily:

'Karl Marsh is sold into slavery!' said a man to me the other day.
'Sold into slavery!' I cried; 'is there anything like that now-a-days?'
'Indeed there is,' was the answer.
'Who bought him, pray?'
'Oh, it's a firm, and they own a good many slaves, and make shocking bad masters.'
'Can it be in these days? Who are they?' I asked.
'Well, they have agents everywhere, who tell a pretty good story, and so get hold of folk; but the names of the firm are Whisky and Wine.'
I had heard of them. It is a firm of bad reputation, and yet how

extensive are their dealings! What town has not felt their influence? Once in their clutches, it is about the hardest thing in the world to break away from them. You are sold, and that is the end of it; sold to ruin sooner or later. I have seen people try to escape from them. Some, it is true, do make their escape; but the greater part are caught and go back to their chains.

Chatterbox, 1878

Perhaps the most famous, certainly the most beguiling, of the temperance ballads was 'Lips that touch Liquor':

> You are coming to woo me, but not as of yore,
>   When I hastened to welcome your ring at the door;
> For I trusted that he who stood waiting me then,
>   Was the brightest, the truest, the noblest of men,
> Your lips, on my own, when they printed 'Farewell',
>   Had never been soiled by the 'beverage of hell;'
> But they come to me now with the bacchanal sign,
>   And the lips that touch liquor must never touch mine.

George M. Young (1846–1919)

This was much parodied in anonymous verses like:

> 'Lips that touch wine-jelly
> Must never touch mine, Nellie.'

Wags also made play with the ambiguity of the last line, 'must never touch mine'. My liquor? Nobody seems to have noticed that the lines were written by a man.

A tricky point, which many a temperance lecturer must have faced at question time, was the undeniable fact that wine flowed freely in the Bible and was regularly drunk by Christ without adverse comment from Him. An American teetotal poet grasped the nettle and had a go at an explanation:

> Taking our stand on the immovable rock of Christ's character we risk nothing in saying that the wine of miracle answered to the wine of nature, and was not intoxicating. No counter proof can equal the force of that drawn from His attributes. It is an indecency and a calumny to impute to Christ conduct which requires apology.

Abraham Coles (1813–1891)

It is odd that few temperance lecturers and writers seem to have pointed out that excessive drinking almost invariably brought its own punishment:

> The drunkard now supinely snores,
>   His load of ale sweats through his pores;
> Yet when he wakes, the swine shall find
>   A crapula remains behind.

Charles Cotton (1630–1687)

crapula = sickness or headache following upon excess.

327

In 1937 appeared a full, accurate, first-hand description of a crapula, or hangover. It made awesome reading:

A hangover is when your tongue tastes like a tram-driver's glove.

When your boots seem to be steaming and your eyes burn in their sockets like hot gooseberries.

Your stomach spins slowly on its axis and your head gently swells and contracts like a jelly in the tideway.

Voices sound far off and your hands tremble like those of a centenarian condemned to death.

Slight movements make you sweat, even as you shiver from the deadly cold that is within you.

Bright lights hurt the eyes, and jeering, gibbering people from the night before seem to whisper in your ears, and then fade with mocking horrible laughter into silence.

The finger-nails are brittle and your skin hangs on you like an old second-hand suit.

Your feet appear to be swollen, and walking is like wading through a swamp of lumpy, thick custard.

Your throat is cracked and parched like the bottom of an old saucepan that has boiled dry. The next moment the symptoms change, and your mouth is stuffed with warm cotton wool.

When you brush your hair you are certain that there is no top to your skull, and your brain stands naked and throbbing in the stabbing air.

Your back aches and feels as though someone is nailing a placard to your shoulder blades.

Knee joints have turned to dish water and eyelids are made of sheets of lead lined with sandpaper.

When you lean on a table it sways gently and you know for certain that you are at sea.

Should you step off a kerb you stumble, for it is a yard deep and the gutter yawns like a wide, quaking trench.

You have no sense of touch and your fingertips feel with all the acuteness of decayed firewood smeared with putty.

The nostrils pulsate and smell the evil air.

You believe that you are in a horrible dream but when you wake up you know that it will all be true.

Your teeth have been filed to stumps and are about to be unscrewed one by one from your aching jaw.

You want to sleep, but when you close your eyes you are dizzy, and you heel over like a waterlogged barrel crammed with old, sodden cabbage stalks in the Grand Junction Canal.

When you read your eyes follow each letter to try to spell the words, but in vain — no message reaches your empty, sullen brain.

Should you look at a simple thing like a tree, it will appear that the bark is gradually crawling upwards.

Lights flash and crackle before you and innumerable little brown dwarfs start tapping just below the base of your skull with tiny, dainty hammers made of compressed rubber ...

O Death, where is thy sting?

Cassandra (William Connor) (1909–1967)
Daily Mirror, 1937

Nobody put the argument *against* abolishing drink more clearly, and gently, than did a 'polite, jovial' Dean of Christ Church in an epigram:

> If all be true that I do think,
> There are five reasons we should drink:
> Good wine, a friend, or being dry,
> Or lest we should be, by and by,
> Or any other reason why.
>
> Dr. Henry Aldrich (1647–1710)

Entertaining, and being entertained, at dinner-parties was an important part of middle-class social life.

Being served a poor dinner could, if the food was really disgusting, provoke powerful feelings of hatred and contempt in the breast of the still-hungry guest, even stir up thoughts of Glencoe-like retaliation. The very least a poor dinner did was to disappoint the guest and leave him with a feeling of personal affront:

> This was a good dinner enough, to be sure; but it was not a dinner to *ask* a man to.
>
> Samuel Johnson (1709–1784)
> Boswell's *Life*, 5 Aug. 1763

You might have thought that dining with the compiler of a cookery book was as sure a way as any of getting a decent dinner. Not, it seems, necessarily. In 1805 Dr. Hunter of York, a scholar and compiler of recipes, invited to dinner a namesake, Dr. Alexander Gibson Hunter, a medical man.

Dr. Alexander Gibson Hunter's report lacked enthusiasm:

> In the centre a bad thin soup, poisoned with celery; at top a dish of threaded skate, bedevilled with carrots and turnips—this supposed in York to be both a Phoenix and a chef d'oeuvre; at bottom, roast beef, *so-so*; at side, ill-boiled beetroot, stewed with a greasy sauce, without vinegar; potatoes, veal cutlets, cold and not well-dressed; anchovy toast and tartlets. Second course: two partridges, ill-trussed and worse roasted; at bottom, an old hare, newly killed and poorly stuffed; at sides, celery and some other trash; in short, a very poor performance on the whole.
>
> Alexander Gibson Hunter (1729–1809)

> The above is interesting in that it provides a map showing where the various dishes would be deployed about the table for a rather shabby meal of the Jane Austen period. There would seem to have been a great deal to eat, but until the Regency a course consisted of a number of dishes not meant to be finished but just dipped into and left on the table. Dr. Alexander Gibson Hunter founded York Lunatic Asylum.

During the 1830s the continental technique of serving meals crept into England, where it was known as dinner *à la Russe*. This was more

329

or less the system still in use, where the courses are brought in, served, and then taken out. It came as a shock to the more conservative diners:

> The present system of dinner-giving I consider thoroughly tainted with barbarism and vulgarity ... As tables are now arranged, one is never in peace from an arm continually setting on or taking off a side dish, or reaching over to a wine cooler in the centre; then comes the more laborious changing of courses, with the leanings right and left, to admit a host of dishes, that are set out only to be taken off ... yet this is the fashion and not to be departed from.
>
> Thomas Walker (1784–1836)
> *The Original*

Nineteenth-century folk were fond of their food and they duly noted in their diaries and their journals those occasions when they were asked out to a dinner which fell short of expectation. For instance, when the hors d'œuvres were peculiar and the temperatures were all wrong:

> The company was numerous, the dinner endless. Besides, we had as hors d'oeuvres good old English dishes, liver and bacon, Irish stew, rump steaks, of each of which Sir F. Burdett partook largely. The plate was handsome but quite cold; the soup was frozen and the champagne hot.
>
> Henry Richard Fox, third Baron Holland (1773–1840)
> Diary, 9 Dec. 1829

Or when a lady from Yorkshire was given Frenchified food:

> The humour I am in is worse than words can describe. I have had a hideous dinner of some abominable spiced-up indescribable mess, and it has exasperated me against the world at large.
>
> Charlotte Brontë (1816–1855)
> Letter to Ellen Nussey, 17 Oct. 1841

Food did not have to be expensive and complicated to invite criticism. Simple fare prepared the old traditional way was also offered:

> Who hath not met with home-made bread,
> A heavy compound of putty and lead—
> And home-made wines that rack the head,
> And home-made liquors and waters?
> Home-made pop that will not foam,
> And home-made dishes that drive one from home—
> Home-made by the homely daughters.
>
> Thomas Hood (1799–1845)
> *Miss Kilmansegg*

At the other end of the scale from homely meals was the formal Victorian banquet, an invitation to which meant that the recipient had 'arrived' in his own particular calling, however bitter or brief his jour-

330

ney had been; an evening, in those days, of eating and drinking in great depth and at great length:

> A banquet is probably the most fatiguing thing in the world except ditch digging. It is the insanest of all recreations. The inventor of it overlooked no detail that could furnish weariness, distress, harassment, and acute and long-sustained misery of mind and body.
>
> Mark Twain (1835–1910)
Mark Twain in Eruption

The quality of the dinner a hostess served up to her guests depended heavily upon whether she had a skilful cook or one who was intractable and indifferent. An ambitious hostess's first concern was getting hold of one of the former. Her second problem was keeping her:

> The cook was a good cook, as cooks go: and as cooks go she went.
>
> Saki (H. H. Munro) (1870–1916)
Reginald

The manner in which one cook went involved violence, even though the master was a lover of flowers and gardens:

> [Walter Savage Landor] ... had one day, after an imperfect dinner, thrown the cook out of the window, and, while the man was writhing with a broken limb, ejaculated, 'Good God! I forgot the violets!'
>
> Richard Monckton Milnes, Lord Houghton (1809–1885)
Monographs

Nineteenth-century middle-class society was very conscious of table-manners, as it was of any form of social etiquette which helped to keep the swans separated from the geese, and deviations were frowned upon; sometimes on the grounds of health:

> The practice of eating a mutton chop, beef steak or drinking hot and strong tea or coffee while in the bath ... is a very bad practice.
>
> 'Professor' R. D. B. Wells (fl. 1885)
Water, and How to Apply it in Health and Disease

The dread of making a social gaffe at table must have haunted timid Victorians:

> When I sat next the Duchess at tea,
> It was just as I knew it would be,
> Her rumblings abdominal
> Were something phenomenal –
> And everyone thought it was me.
>
> Anon.

To assist the parvenu pick his, or her, way through the elaborate web of rules designed to keep him, or her, out there were a great number of helpful publications, like *Manners and Rules of Good Society*, 1880, which went through thirteen editions in seven years, an indication of the brisk demand. The author is given as A Member of the Aristocracy, which does not seem very likely as a classic gaffe is made in assuring the reader that 'Fish is eaten with a silver fish-knife and fork', which would have made a genuine member of the aristocracy wince in anguish. Special fish knives and forks made of silver – supposedly because steel knives spoilt the taste of fish – were a Victorian middle-class invention. Before that era fish was eaten with a fork and a crust of bread, so putting out silver fish-knives was a clear sign that the hostess had no old family silver.

Rules were laid down governing all aspects of the process of eating; which implements were to be used for what – 'soup should be eaten (not drunk) with a table-spoon and not with a dessert-spoon'; 'the points should be cut off asparagus and then eaten with a knife and fork'; 'jellies, blancmanges, iced puddings, &c., should be eaten with a fork'. There seemed to have been a conspiracy to make things difficult for the polite diner. Peas had to be balanced on the curved back of the fork. Salt was not to be sprinkled over the food but poured in a little heap at the side of the plate, where it over-salted everything next to it.

But woe betide those who were ignorant of, or forgot, the rules:

> The man who bites his bread, or eats peas with a knife, I look upon as a lost creature.
>
> W. S. Gilbert (1836–1911)
> *Ruddigore*

> Rose Maybud (a Village Maiden) had learnt about life from an etiquette book 'composed, if I may believe the title-page, by no less an authority than the wife of a Lord Mayor'.

The new United States of America, vigorous and rapidly expanding, can perhaps be forgiven for not having had much time to develop genteel, artificial niceties in the way it ate. Some of its feeding habits seemed uncouth to visiting middle-class English writers:

> One nasty custom ... I must notice. Eggs, instead of being eaten from the shell, are poured into a wine-glass, and after being duly and disgustingly churned up with butter and condiment, the mixture, according to its degree of fluidity, is forthwith either spooned into the mouth, or drunk off like a liquid. The advantage gained by this unpleasant process, I do not profess to be qualified to appreciate, but I can speak from experience, to its sedative effect on the appetite of an unpractised beholder.
>
> Thomas Hamilton (1789–1842)
> *Men and Manners in America*

A lady writer had a trying time and rather regretted that the North was about to win the Civil War:

> The total want of all the usual courtesies of the table, the voracious rapidity with which the viands were seized and devoured, the strange uncouth phrases and pronunciation; the loathsome spitting, from the

contamination of which it was absolutely impossible to protect our dresses; the frightful manner of feeding with their knives, till the whole blade seemed to enter into the mouth; and the still more frightful manner of cleaning the teeth afterwards with a pocket knife, soon forced us to feel that we were not surrounded by the generals, colonels, and majors of the old world; and that the dinner hour was to be any thing rather than an hour of enjoyment.

Frances Trollope (1780–1863)
Domestic Manners of the Americans

Mrs. Trollope, mother of the novelist Anthony Trollope, sailed for America in 1829 hoping to recoup the family fortunes by opening a dry-goods store in Cincinnati. The store failed, but a book which Mrs. Trollope subsequently wrote strongly criticizing Americans was hugely successful. It was loathed in the U.S.A.

The habit some Americans had of eating with their knife seemed peculiarly repulsive to sensitive Englishmen. The novelist Thackeray kept being pained by glimpses of the practice:

The European continent swarms with your people. They are not all as polished as Chesterfield. I wish some of them spoke French a little better. I saw five of them at supper at Basle the other night with their knives down their throats. It was awful.

W. M. Thackeray (1811–1863)
Letter to an American friend, 21 July 1853

What a company, bon Dieu! I was drawing a picture for the girls of the opposite side of the table in the Alabama Steamer with every man with his knife down his throat—Yesterday on this boat (the Thomas Small) every woman had her knife down her's too. I vow every one.

W. M. Thackeray (1811–1863)
Letter headed 'On the Mississippi', Easter Saturday and Sunday, 1856

Thackeray was on a lecture tour of the U.S.A. His theme was 'The Four Georges': he disapproved of them too.

One of the earliest lessons which well-brought-up children were taught was not to bolt their food. But Victorian nannies might well have pondered the thought that had a Swede visiting Britain not guzzled his dinner when he thought nobody was looking the world would have been deprived of the Swedenborg Society and the entire New Jerusalem Church:

Swedenborg ... went into a little inn in Bishopsgate Street, and was eating his dinner very fast, when he thought he saw in the corner of the room a vision of Jesus Christ, who said to him, 'Eat slower'. This was the beginning of all his visions and mysterious communications.

Caroline Fox (1819–1871)
Journals and Letters of Caroline Fox, 7 April 1847

Bolting the food led to indigestion, and an upset stomach, according to one Victorian, led to all manner of ill-considered actions including, he hinted, John Henry Newman becoming a Roman Catholic:

> How many serious family quarrels, marriages out of spite, alterations of wills, and secessions to the Church of Rome, might have been prevented by a gentle dose of blue pill?
>
> Charles Kingsley (1819–1875)
>
> It was as a result of an article by Kingsley which appeared in *Macmillan's Magazine* attacking Newman's Catholic writings, and the subsequent controversy, that Newman wrote his *Apologia pro Vita sua*.

In 1817 Dr. Kitchiner wrote, with characteristic charm and inaccuracy, 'unless the stomach be in good humour every part of the machinery of life must vibrate with languor' (Introduction to *The Cook's Oracle*).

More frequently it is the good-humoured, replete stomach which induces languor. The stomach which is out of sorts tends to send the machinery of life whirring into action, usually of a misanthropic nature:

> My friend sups late; he eats some strong soup, then a lobster, then some tart, and he dilutes these esculent varieties with wine. The next day I call on him. He is going to sell his house in London and retire into the country. He is alarmed for his eldest daughter's health. His expenses are hourly increasing, and nothing but a timely retreat can save him from ruin. All this is the lobster; and when over-excited nature has had time to manage this testaceous encumbrance, the daughter recovers, the finances are in good order, and every rural idea effectually excluded. In the same manner old friendships are destroyed by toasted cheese, and hard salted meat has led to suicide.
>
> Rev. Sydney Smith (1771–1845)
>
> Sydney Smith enjoyed superb digestion. Carlyle suffered from chronic indigestion. If Smith and Carlyle had been born with each other's digestive systems it is possible that we might never have heard of either of them.

Nothing was more hateful to those men who loved their food than to find that a delicacy they particularly enjoyed did not agree with them. 'I like it but it doesn't like me.'

History records that one such sufferer, a fancier of buttered muffins, found the perfect way out:

> Mr.——, who loved buttered muffins, but durst not eat them because they disagreed with his stomach, resolved to shoot himself; and then he ate three buttered muffins for breakfast, before shooting himself, knowing that he should not be troubled with indigestion.
>
> Topham Beauclerk (1739–1780)
> Quoted in Boswell's *Life*, 16 April 1779
>
> Charles Dickens lifted this story, changed muffins to crumpets, and it appeared as one of Sam Weller's anecdotes – 'next mornin' he gets up, has a fire lit, orders in three shillin's wurth o' crumpets, toasts 'em all,

eats 'em all, and blows his brains out'. The muffin-addict, whose name was tactfully suppressed by Boswell, was a Mr. Delmis. Mr. Delmis, clearly a man who planned things carefully, ate his buttered muffins and then loaded and primed a brace of pistols. The second pistol proved to be surplus to his requirements.

Heavy eating had become so much a part of the social scene by the end of the century that a visiting celebrity could end up, after a round of banquets and dinners, entertained within an inch of his life. As a friend discovered when he kindly invited Mark Twain to dinner:

Dear Lee—I can't. I am in a family way with three weeks undigested dinners in my system, and shall just roost here and diet and purge till I am delivered. Shall I name it after you? Yr. friend, Sam'l L. Clemens.

Mark Twain (Samuel L. Clemens) (1835–1910)
Ms. in New York City Public Library

During most of the nineteenth century, as in previous centuries, a family ate and entertained at home. Food was cheap, if not always what it seemed to be:

Little drops of water,
Little grains of sand,
Make the milkman wealthy,
And the grocer grand.

Anon. (nineteenth century)

Cooks, of varying degrees of skill, cost only a few pounds a year. There was no point in eating out and, indeed, nowhere to go. A gentleman might have his club, but lesser men had only a various assortment of fairly unsavoury chop-houses and women had nowhere at all.

Eating out was originally a lowly practice, born of necessity. During the Middle Ages, before the advent of chimneys and fireplaces made cooking possible in ·humble homes, a poor countryman fortunate enough to have a piece of meat would take it along to the village oven to have it cooked. The townsman would take his piece to his local cook-shop. This establishment would have joints of meat turning on spits, and fires to roast meat and poultry brought in by customers, who had the choice of sitting down and eating in the shop or taking their cooked meat home. Cook-shop prices were strictly controlled by the authorities.

Travellers on the road could usually eat in their inn. Inns, and taverns, usually provided an 'ordinary', a set meal at a set price, which the traveller could sit down to alongside a mixed group of cut-purses, poets, whores and fellow-travellers, or order something better to be served in his room. Travellers' diaries tended to be full of peevish comments about vile meals endured whilst *en route*.

From the sixteenth century on most towns had coffee-houses and

335

chop-houses where men could smoke a pipe, read the gazettes, and eat a slab of meat or a pudding, and drink a bottle or two of wine. Chop-houses were usually patronized by clerks, traders, craftsmen, who could afford to buy themselves a hot meal but not a very good one:

> Now for a chop house or coffee-room dinner! Oh, the 'orrible smell that greets you at the door! Compound of cabbage, pickled salmon, boiled beef, saw-dust, and anchovy sarce. 'Wot will you take, sir?' inquires the frowsy waiter, smoothin' the filthy cloth, 'soles, macrel, vitin's — werry good, boiled beef — nice cut, cabbage, weal and 'am, cold lamb and sallard.' — *Bah* the den's 'ot to suffocation — the kitchen's below — a trap door vomits up dinners in return for bellows down the pipe to the cook. Flies settle on your face — swarm on your head; a wasp travels round; everything tastes flat, stale, and unprofit-able. As a climax he gets the third of a bottle of warm port as a pint.
>
> Robert Smith Surtees (1803–1864)
> *Handley Cross*

In 1765 M. Boulanger, who sold very good soup in his Dining Room in Paris, put up a board outside which said *Venite ad me; vos qui stomacho laboratis et ego restaurabo vos* (Come to me, those with laboured stomachs and I will restore you). M. Boulanger's soup became known as a *restaurant* (restorative) and the word came to be applied to the establishment itself and finally to any Dining Room which provided high-quality food.

More noblemen's chefs retained their heads during the French Revolution than did noblemen and when times became more stable these surplus master-cooks began opening their own restaurants, usually concentrating on their own speciality. By the beginning of the nineteenth century there were over five hundred of these restaurants in Paris, and when Napoleon had fallen the English flocked across the Channel to wine and dine.

By 1880 the French-style restaurant, that is to say an elegant establishment serving very good food and wine, had come to London.

They were not cheap:

> Wine and roast; yes, yes!
> Count the bill; woe, woe!
> *Turkish Proverbs*
> Printed in Venice, 1844

The first of the new-style restaurants were built as part of the huge Grand Hotels which were then being put up, often at railway termini like Euston and Charing Cross, and a splendid restaurant with an enormous French menu soon became as much a part of a great hotel's style as its marble halls, its Palm Court and its orchestras.

It was the great hotels of the 1880s which at last persuaded the English middle and upper classes that eating out was not only enjoyable

336

but less bother and it provided a chance to give the servants a night off without losing creature comforts.

By the nineties it had become, for the first time, socially acceptable to entertain guests in a public place.

And a new ordeal had arisen to test the ability of young men to cope with adulthood; protesting to the waiter about the bill:

Tell me not in figures wavy
    That my bill is twelve-and-nine,
When I had but soup of gravy
    Steak, potatoes, cheese, and wine.

I'm a poet, I'm a rhymer,
    Hardly versed in trader's tricks,
But a pint of *Laubenheimer*
    Ought not to be four-and-six.

Though I'm not at all unwilling
    To assist you to success,
I must say I think a shilling
    Far too much for watercress.

Bills are long, and cash is fleeting,
    And I wish to make it clear
That the bill you are receipting
    Is the last I settle here.

When you've fleeced your guests and fined them,
    I may venture to explain,
They will shake the dust behind them,
    And they won't come back again.

So I leave you, poorer, sadder,
    Lest you make me poorer still;
Sharper than the biting adder
    Is the adder of the bill.

Adrian Ross (1859–1933)

Perhaps the most humiliating ordeal for a young man playing the host was failing to attract the attention of a lazy, dozing waiter. To just such a waiter came a fitting end:

By and by
God caught his eye.

David McCord (b. 1897)
Epitaphs: 'The Waiter'

Up to the end of the Second World War luxury hotels had a good run for their money, but the supply of rich patrons steadily diminished through the years and now there are few left in the world with menus and service up to the early standards of magnificence.

Country hotels and old coaching inns also changed their style. The privately owned premises were steadily bought up by large catering conglomerates who installed managers and rationalized the menus:

337

A meal which we had in a delightful Georgian coaching inn, 'somewhere in Wessex', is perhaps typical of how very often what should be a pleasant occasion is turned into a numbing agony.

The food, once you contrived to get it, was the usual 11s 6d chain hotel lunch. The dining room was presided over by a headwaiter in his early seventies in flapping tails, and everything had got totally out of his hands long before we arrived. There were fifteen tables with about 45 to 50 people. To serve them was the old man who, in fact, was permanently *hors de combat* wrestling with bottles of light ale which seemed to erupt all over everything by the time he'd finished shaking them up. There was a village lad and a village lass, red in the face with confusion, and the situation was only saved by an imperturbable body from Inverness who had the whole room to run. We waited twenty minutes, which is a long time with two hungry children twisting in their seats to watch other people eat. The order had been taken within the first five minutes by the old man who had then stuck it on his spike on his sideboard. We found out later that as he always muddled the orders, to avoid confusion nobody took any notice of them. After twenty minutes the Scots body arrived with a flurry, removed dishes, flicked crumbs, fetched paper napkins, (carefully cut in half to remind us of wartime shortages), and took the order quickly, kindly, and comfortingly. Ten minutes later the packet soup came and, after a fairly lengthy interval for digestion, up steamed our waitress: 'There's the curry for the wee girlie. The steak pie was off, so I've brought you the boiled ham, sir, and the veg will be here directly.' My ten-year-old daughter got a great plate of English-style curry (stewed steak and diced tinned carrots with curry powder added) that would have floored a navvy. I got a child's portion of boiled ham. There was a small problem with the water as they had only one jug in the hotel. ('I've asked them time and time again, but they won't do a thing,' the waitress whispered. 'And the money they're making too!')

We all had tinned fruit salad. The alternative, the 'cheese board', held a crumble of Cheddar. In the hall the manager's wife, in twinset and pearls, hoped we'd had a nice meal:

'We're proud of our name for good food in these parts. Come and visit us again.'   Derek Cooper (b. 1925)
The Bad Food Guide, 1967

Rapid changes swept through the restaurant business during the post-war years. Foreign restaurants became popular and soon even smallish towns had a Chinese restaurant. Other ethnic waves followed; Italian, Indian, Greek, Armenian, even Japanese restaurants opened and kept open. There was also a blossoming of chic, fanciful little restaurants, rather like food boutiques, with odd names, imaginative décor and casual, sexy waiters and waitresses. Most of these places managed to enjoy a brief, gay life before withering.

The latest invasion has come from establishments selling 'Take-Away' food. Ironically, these High Street shops selling hot food over the counter have brought the wheel full-circle back to the original medieval cook-shops.

As far as the home is concerned, the biggest change in what P. G. Wodehouse called 'browsing and sluicing' is probably not the decline in huge, formal meals, or shorter menus, but the odd form our food is in nowadays when we buy it. Coffee comes as a powder. Fish arrives as a frozen rectangular block. Soup, stiff with preservatives, comes in a tin or as a powder. Potatoes no longer wear their jackets but arrive pale and naked in an impenetrable plastic bag. Embryonic mashed potato comes in little dry lumps, like cattle-feed pellets. Bread, untouched by human baker, arrives wrapped and sliced in a soft lump, the 'crust' seemingly sprayed on. Beer, urged upwards by gas, emerges from a steel dustbin.

Even the sausage, the fine old British banger, knobbly and individual, is being displaced by a product of automation; a computerized, portion-controlled, geometrically accurate disc. As T. S. Eliot might well have written, 'this is the way the world ends, not with a banger but a Wimpy'.

When an occasional voice is raised in protest at what is being done to our nourishment the manufacturers point out that we are not forced by them at pistol point to accept their 'convenience' foods and their weak, gassy near-beer; if people refused to buy the stuff they wouldn't try to sell it.

If this be true and twentieth-century society has forgone, or forgotten, the pure unpunished pleasure of enjoying real food and drink, however simple and cheap, then, according to the old gourmet Brillat-Savarin, we are indeed a sorry lot:

> Those ... to whom nature had denied an aptitude for the enjoyments of taste, are long-faced, long-nosed, and long-eyed: whatever their stature, they have something lanky about them. They have dark, lanky hair, and are never in good condition. It was one of them who invented trousers.
>
> Jean-Anthelme Brillat-Savarin (1755–1826)
> *La Physiologie du goût ou Méditations sur la gastronomie transcendante*

Index of Authors and Sources

341

Eldon, Lord, on Oxford degree
examination, 78; on hanging literate
mutineers, 81
Elford, Sir William, letter from Mary
Russell Mitford, 154
Elyot, Sir Thomas, on ignorant tutors,
63
Emerson, Ralph Waldo, on musical
appreciation, 6; on students, 56; on
Swinburne, 161; letter from Swinburne,
162; on libraries, 167; on brandy,
301
Ephorus, on music, 1
Era, on Ibsen, 224
Erasmus, on schoolmasters, 64
Erskine, Thomas, 1st Baron, on Scott,
145
Etherege, Sir George, on drunkenness,
306
Étienne, Louis, on Manet, 259
Evans, Abel, epitaph for Vanbrugh, 147
Evans, Bergen, on philistinism, 268
Eve, Mr. Justice, on music, 1
Evelyn, John, on pub organs, 22; on
production of *Hamlet*, 202; on
actresses, 203
Evening Standard, on Royal Academy,
270

Fadiman, Clifton, on Gertrude Stein,
268
Faujas de Saint-Fond, B., on English
coffee, 311
Faulkner, William, on writers, 104; on
Henry James, 172
Felltham, Owen, on music, 1; on
audiences, 196; on truth on stage, 200
Fer, Jambe de *see* Jambe de Fer
Ferdinand, Archduke, letter from
Maria Theresa, 32
Field and Stream, reviews *Lady Chatterley's
Lover*, 175
Field, Eugene, on Creston Clarke's
acting, 229
Fielding, Henry, on tar-water, 34; on
public schools, 74; on acting styles,
210; on 'wind' (drink), 300
Fitzgerald, Edward, on Mendelssohn
and 'Champage Charlie', 35, 46; on
E. B. Browning's death, 160
Flaubert, Gustave, on criticism, 107; on
writing for money, 129; on George
Sand, 155; on Eugène Sue, 156

Ford, Ford Madox, on Fielding, 137
Ford, Henry, on history, 85
Forde, Thomas, parodied, 66
Foster, Stephen Collins, on piano as
banjo substitute, 31
Fox, Caroline, on Swedenborg's eating,
333
Fox, Henry Richard *see* Holland, H. R.
Fox, 3rd Baron
Franklin, Benjamin, on education, 78
Fraser, William, on the Disraelis, 255
Frederick II (the Great) of Prussia, on
German singers, 26
Fry, Christopher, on English coffee,
311
Fry, Roger, on J. S. Sargent, 241; on
Cézanne, 263
Fuller, Thomas, on oysters, 279; on
beans, 280; on wine, 296; suggested
epitaph, 296

Galen, on music, 1
Galli-Curci, Amelita, on opera singing,
39
Galsworthy, John, on Epstein, 268
Galt, John, on anachronistic painting,
248
Gardner, Ed, on opera, 19
Garnett, Edward, letter from D. H.
Lawrence, 175; letter from
Galsworthy, 268
Gauguin, Paul, on revolution in
painting, 248
Gay, John, on school beatings, 73; on
authorial rivalry, 105; on cucumbers,
282
Gentlewoman, on Ibsen, 224
George II of England, hatred of artists,
235
George III of England, on Shakespeare,
214
Gerard, John, on Jerusalem artichokes,
281; on oatmeal, 283
Gibbon, Edward, on Oxford University,
79–80; on Gordian, 110
Gilbert, W. S., on classical music, 46;
on Tree's *Hamlet*, 223; on aesthetic
movement, 264; on table manners,
332
Gissing, George, on writers and readers,
168
Glass, Montague, on singers, 9
Globe, on Ibsen, 225

General Index

Abbott, Edwin, 86
Abelard, Peter, 62
Abstract art, 269, 272
acting, style, 140, 142, 207, 210; as low
  art, 179; women and, 180, 196, 199,
  202–203; historical origins, 181;
  critics on, 229–230; standard of, 231
actors, disreputability, 180, 185; and
  fame, 181; as hypocrites, 182;
  ethics, 182; excommunication of,
  185; child, 194, 229; puritans on,
  197; actresses in England, 199, 202–
  204, 211; male actors, 202; payment,
  204; rehearsals, 210; strolling, 211;
  sensitivity, 211–212; and stock
  companies, 212; talents of, 212–213;
  actor-managers, 221, 223, 227; and
  directors, 227; and audience, 231;
  abnormality of, 237; see also theatre
Addison, Joseph, opera by, 25; and
  Dennis, 306
aestheticism, 264
agents, literary, 170–171
alcohol, in Germany, 296; cause of
  impotence, 303; and temperance,
  324; see also drink
Aldershot, ballet in, 3
ale, 294–296
Alexandria, library in, 110
Alfred the Great, 61
Algonquin Hotel, New York, 229
Alleyn, Edward, 210
Alma-Tadema, Sir Lawrence, 262
amber, 307
American War of Independence, 142, 312
Angelico, Fra, 239
animals, eating of, 289; see also meat;
  vegetarianism
Anne, Queen of England, eating habits,
  316; gin tax, 324
Anne of Cleves, portrait, 242
aphrodisiacs see lechery
applause, 180

applejack, 302
Arabs, and spirituous drinks, 301; and
  coffee, 302
Arbuthnot, Dr. John, 6, 122
Archimedes, death, 59
architecture, religious, 240
aristocracy, and writing, 129; manners,
  318, 332; drunkenness, 324; see also
  nobility
Aristotle, and music, 3–4; and
  education, 59, 68; book collector,
  110; on Pythagoras' testicular beans,
  280
arithmetic, 86, 90
Armour (the cook), 287
Arnold, Matthew, 169
Arnold, Thomas, educational principles,
  83, 90, 96
Arp, Hans, and 'dada', 268
art, **235–275**; importance exaggerated,
  226; patronage, 235, 239, 240, 242,
  253; subject for rape, 238; and
  madness, 238; religious, 239–240;
  collecting, 242–244; academies of,
  245, 247, 270; fashionable, 253; in
  nineteenth century, 254;
  suggestiveness, 255–256; function and
  purpose, 263–264, 274; women and,
  264–265; reviews of 265–266; modern
  movements, 267–272; official
  disapproval, 269–270; market for,
  270–272; see also painting; also names
  of individual artists and movements
artichokes, 281
artists, overpaid, 235; and individual
  genius, 237–238, 252, 261; position
  of, 237–239, 261; versatility, 238–239,
  242; moral dissoluteness, 261, 266
Arundel, Thomas Howard, 2nd Earl of,
  242–243
asparagus, 332
Athenaeus, 286, 315
'at-homes', 33

355

Peel, Sir Robert, 158
Peele, George, 192
Pegler, Westbrook, 10
Pembroke College, Cambridge, 75–76
Penn, William, and brewing, 296
Pepusch, John Christopher, 22
Peri, Jacopo, 19
Perignon, Dom, 300
Peter Pan (Barrie), 229
Peterhouse College, Cambridge, 75
Petty, Rev. William, 243
philistinism, 268
pianos, 23, 30–31; and popular music, 47
Picasso, Pablo, 268–269, 271
Pinero, Arthur Wing, 222
Pirandello, Luigi, 228
Pissaro, Lucien, 260
Pixérécourt, Guilbert de, 217
plague, and theatre, 189
Plato, and music, 3, 4; and education, 59; character, 105; and acting, 179
Plautus, 183
playwrights, abnormality of, 237
Plutarch, 280
poetry, brevity of, 101; audience for, 103; beginnings, 107–108; defined, 107–108; rhyme in, 110; and superstition, 119; writing of, 129; Romantic Revival, 142–143, 147–148; decadent, 166; experimental, 174; unpopularity of, 176
poets, self-esteem, 103; characteristics, 103; abnormality of, 103–104, 237; unreliability of, 148; Georgian, 173; and publishers, 176; royal disapproval, 235
Poets Laureate: Cibber, 123; Davenant, 199; Dryden, 196; Duck (near-miss), 328; Shadwell, 118; Southey, 144, 146; Wordsworth, 144
political economy, 91
Pompadour, Mme., 14
poor, and education, 14, 71, 78, 94
pop culture, 50–51
Pope, Alexander, 119–123, 138; ignorance of poverty, 71; love-making, 123–124; literary earnings, 124, 129, 131; poisons Curll, 128; and Dennis, 306
pornography, 127–128
porridge, 283
port wine, 302

Porter, Cole, 49
Porter, Sir Robert Ker, 254
portraits (paintings), 241–242, 245–246
Portugal, and spice trade, 319; food in, 321
Post-Impressionist Exhibition (1910), 266
potatoes, distilled, 302; as medicine, 302; packaged, 339
poteen, 302
pottage, 320
poultry *see* hens
Poynter, Sir Edward, 262
prawns, 287
Pre-Raphaelite Brotherhood, 146, 257–258, 260
printing, 112, 114, 125; *see also* books; publishers
prisons, preferable to schools, 95
producers (theatrical), 227
Prokofiev, S., 36
prose, 109–110; experimental, 174
prostitution, and theatre, 197–198, 204; art as, 236
Protestants, and art, 240, 274; and red wine, 299; *see also* puritans
public houses, music in, 22
public schools *see under* schools
publishers, and music, 32; relationship to authors, 105–106, 118, 171–172; origins, 114; rewards, 118; and copyright, 125; subscription publishing, 130–131; position, 170; function, 170; and poetry, 176
Punch, 264
Purcell, Henry, 18
puritans, and music, 3–4, 21; hymn-singing, 4; whimsies, 66; and education, 70; and stage, 188–190, 193, 195, 197; destroy religious art, 240–241; on drunkenness, 305; on coffee, 309
Putcher, Sir Josslebury, 287
Putnam, Israel, 296
Pythagoras, invents clavichord, 17

Quarterly Review, 150–152
Queen's Theatre, London, 220
Queensberry, Catherine Douglas, Duchess of, 23
Quin, James, 207, 210

rabbits, as food, 289, 320

371